AUTHENTICALLY
JEWISH

AUTHENTICALLY JEWISH

Identity, Culture, and the Struggle for Recognition

STUART Z. CHARMÉ

RUTGERS UNIVERSITY PRESS
New Brunswick, Camden, and Newark, New Jersey, and London

Library of Congress Cataloging-in-Publication Data

Names: Charmé, Stuart Z., author.
Title: Authentically Jewish: identity, culture, and the struggle for recognition / Stuart Z. Charmé.
Description: New Brunswick: Rutgers University Press, [2022] | Includes bibliographical references and index.
Identifiers: LCCN 2021046807 | ISBN 9781978827592 (paperback) | ISBN 9781978827608 (hardback) | ISBN 9781978827615 (epub) | ISBN 9781978827622 (pdf)
Subjects: LCSH: Jews—Identity. | Jews—Social conditions—21st century. | Judaism—History—21st century. | Social perception—History—21st century. | Sartre, Jean-Paul, 1905–1980.
Classification: LCC DS143. C44 2022 | DDC 305.892/4—dc23/eng/20211012
LC record available at https://lccn.loc.gov/2021046807

A British Cataloging-in-Publication record for this book is available from the British Library.

Copyright © 2022 by Stuart Z. Charmé
All rights reserved
No part of this book may be reproduced or utilized in any form or by any means, electronic or mechanical, or by any information storage and retrieval system, without written permission from the publisher. Please contact Rutgers University Press, 106 Somerset Street, New Brunswick, NJ 08901. The only exception to this prohibition is "fair use" as defined by U.S. copyright law.

References to internet websites (URLs) were accurate at the time of writing. Neither the author nor Rutgers University Press is responsible for URLs that may have expired or changed since the manuscript was prepared.

∞ The paper used in this publication meets the requirements of the American National Standard for Information Sciences—Permanence of Paper for Printed Library Materials, ANSI Z39.48-1992.

www.rutgersuniversitypress.org

Manufactured in the United States of America

To my partner, Nancie, and to our children, Sara and Tal, in memory of their grandparents, Sam and Miriam Charmé, and Dan and Val Zane.

Inside every Jew is a mob of Jews. The good Jew, the bad Jew. The new Jew, the old Jew. The lover of Jews, the hater of Jews. The friend of the goy, the enemy of the goy. The arrogant Jew, the wounded Jew. The pious Jew, the rascal Jew. The coarse Jew, the gentle Jew. The defiant Jew, the appeasing Jew. The Jewish Jew, the de-Jewed Jew. Shall I go on?

—Philip Roth, Operation Shylock

The authentic Jew makes himself a Jew, in the face of all and against all. . . . At one stroke, the Jew, like any authentic man, escapes description. . . . He is what he makes himself, that is all that can be said.

—Jean-Paul Sartre, Antisemite and Jew

Contents

Introduction — 1

Part I Theoretical Perspectives on Jewish Authenticity

1. The Changing Faces of Jewish Authenticity — 11
2. Recognition and Authenticity: From Sartre to Multiculturalism — 22

Part II Authentically Jewish Religion

3. Orthodoxy and the Authentic Jew — 43
4. Reforming Jewish Tradition and the Spiritual Quest — 58
5. The Experiential Authenticity of Jewish Meditation, Jewish Yoga, and Kabbalah — 72
6. The Messianic Heresy and the Struggle for Authenticity — 86

Part III Authentic Jewish Peoplehood

7. Creating a National Jewish Culture in Israel — 105
8. Shtetl Authenticity: From *Fiddler on the Roof* to the Revival of Klezmer — 124
9. Becoming Jewish: Intermarriage and Conversion — 137
10. Authentically Jewish Genes — 149

Part IV Struggles over Authentication and Recognition

11 Lost Jewish Tribes in Ethiopia — 161

12 Recognizing Black Jews in the United States — 174

13 Authenticating Crypto-Jewish Identity — 188

14 Newly Found Jews and the Regimes of Recognition — 203

Conclusion — 225

Notes — 233
Bibliography — 271
Index — 293

Introduction

Several years ago, I spit into a small glass tube, sealed it in an envelope, and dropped it in a mailbox. Six weeks later, I logged onto the Ancestry.com website to get my DNA results. The report said that my ethnic background was "100 percent European Jewish," particularly from "Jews in Central and Eastern Europe." While I was not surprised by the results, I did wonder about what significance, if any, they had for either my own sense of Jewishness or how I might be seen by others. Does the apparent genetic purity of my ethnic roots make me more authentically Jewish than people with more complicated genetic histories, despite the fact that I am not a religiously observant Jew? Or maybe those who keep kosher and maintain a way of life more consistent with Jewish religious law represent something more authentically Jewish than the tiny strands of my DNA can claim for me.

As I reflected on the various experiences that composed the mosaic of my life as a Jew, I mused about my other Jewish "credentials" and the ways in which different people and groups might regard them. I was born to a Jewish mother and was circumcised soon after, though I do not know whether the cutting was done with ritual flair by a *mohel* or just by a doctor in the hospital. I had all sorts of Jewish education and participation, from the Workmen's Circle Yiddish program where I learned the Hebrew aleph-bet and a handful of Yiddish words as a kindergartner to the Orthodox Talmud Torah where I wore *tzitzit*, learned to hyphenate the word *G-d*, and practiced reading daily prayers with a stopwatch (the faster the better). I was bar mitzvahed and confirmed at a Reform synagogue, but I gravitated to a Reconstructionist one by the time I was married and had a family. We lived in Israel for a year in the early 1990s around the time of the Oslo Accords. There have been some Jewish traditions—religious, cultural, musical, culinary—that we observe in our home and many more that we do not. My sense of Jewishness is progressive, feminist, and decidedly nontheistic. Is it "100 percent Jewish," like my DNA? Does that question even make sense?

The multiplicity of backgrounds of people who identify as Jewish as well as the diversity of their beliefs, rituals, and traditions have generated inescapable debates about who and what can or should be considered "authentically Jewish." The answers to such questions are predictably divisive, since the assertion that someone or something is authentically Jewish usually implies that certain other people and things should not be considered as either authentic or Jewish. Although many Jews may think of Judaism as a single shared religion, Jewish people as a unified collective identity, and various kinds of food, literature, music, and dance as expressions of a single shared Jewish culture, there are also competing understandings of Judaism, Jewish peoplehood, Jewish culture, and Jewish identity that give rise to conflicting views of authenticity.

This book focuses on how questions of authenticity are negotiated among different Jewish individuals, groups, and communities who offer competing claims about which groups, personal experiences, religious practices, and cultural traditions they recognize as "authentically Jewish." My goal is not to make any final determinations of who and what are authentically Jewish, for I do not believe that there are any fixed or final answers to these questions. Rather, my aim is to understand the assumptions and reasons that continue to produce conflicting understandings and struggles in the process of recognizing and authenticating such claims. Of course, this does not mean that all approaches to Jewish authenticity are equally plausible or persuasive. The ones that are fixed and rigid tend to be less useful than the ones that are more tentative and self-reflexive.

Authenticity is a complex concept that touches on philosophical, anthropological, political, psychological, and religious issues. *Culture and Authenticity*, Charles Lindholm's comprehensive guidebook to different manifestations of authenticity, distinguishes between "personal authenticity" and "collective authenticity."[1] The realm of what is authentically Jewish includes elements of both of these kinds of authenticity. In some cases, they are woven together in a complex whole, but in other cases, the different types of authenticity represent forces pulling in opposite directions.

Collective and Personal Authenticity

Collective authenticity is an issue of the utmost importance to any group that thinks of itself as a single tribe, people, or nation. It is the glue that holds the group together, establishes relationships between them, and differentiates them from other groups. Collective authenticity is generally understood in terms of shared ancestry and history, common language, and cultural traditions that include everything from special foods and festivals, folk songs and dances, and inside jokes to religious beliefs and practices, all of which are passed down from one generation to the next.

In 1969, seven years before the publication of his enormously popular book *World of Our Fathers: The Journey of the East European Jews to America and the Life They Found and Made*, Irving Howe observed that "it seems unlikely that anyone can choose a tradition, let alone simply decide to discard the one in which he has grown up. . . . A tradition signifies precisely those enveloping forces that shape us before we can even think of choices."[2] Yet the question of how much individual choice and selectivity operate in the transmission of Jewish tradition is at the heart of discussions of what is authentically Jewish. By 1983, when Howe was asked to address a graduating class of Reconstructionist rabbis, he suggested that many assimilated American Jews had already lost a sense of what an authentically Jewish life was. He told these new rabbis that they would need to help such Jews to regain the collective authenticity that comes from "the experience of living in a rich and coherent culture, one that possessed its own manners, styles, values."[3]

The maintenance of a "coherent culture" and the collective authenticity it expresses requires groups to pay particular attention to the boundaries that separate their group and culture from others. This means determining if and when outsiders will be allowed to join the group, how the cultural and social influences of the broader environment within which Jews live will be managed, and who has the authority to make these decisions. For this reason, collective authenticity is produced in a social process that includes discussion, disagreement, struggle, and often conflict about the parameters of what things the people within the group are willing to recognize as legitimate and authentic and what things must be rejected as unwelcome contamination from alien religious, cultural, or social influences.

The question of what is authentically Jewish has been at the heart of most of the disputes and tensions that have fragmented Jewish communities in the modern world. The original fissures that produced the different denominations of modern Judaism reveal fundamental differences about models of authority and authenticity. More recent challenges posed by feminist, secular, Messianic, New Age, and unaffiliated Jews have continually tested the boundaries of what will be recognized as authentically Jewish by various segments of the Jewish community. I hope to show that these boundaries are dynamic and continually being renegotiated.

In its simplest formulation, *personal authenticity* is a product of the modern rise of individualism and the notion that a person's "real self" can be found only by looking within themselves. Personal authenticity is usually described less as a simple quality that a person may possess and more often as the goal or outcome of an ongoing process—a search or quest for authenticity within the realm of personal experience. Unlike collective authenticity, which assumes individual acceptance of the authority and meaning of tradition as something distinct from individual choice, personal authenticity represents the elevation of the individual as the supreme authority and the director of the quest for authenticity, on which the emergence of the individual's true self depends.

Jewish Consumers and the Market for Jewish Identity

The cultural shift in recent decades from an emphasis on collective authenticity grounded in conformity with traditional authorities and norms to a focus on the quest for personal authenticity has been accompanied and reinforced by a major development in the global economic system in the period since the 1960s. Marketers in the emerging consumer culture have realized that the packaging and branding of goods and services need to address consumers' growing desire for self-expression and self-realization. As Francois Gauthier describes, "For the consumer, brands are means of production of meaning, identity, and subjectivity, and they are active in mediating belonging and community. Consumption and identity are thus intricately knit together today as every choice, however routine, has potentially profound existential consequences. This is why the 'market for identities is the biggest market of all.'"[4]

Gauthier's observation also applies to the market for Jewish identity, community, and authenticity. As ties to institutional religion and traditional cultural attachments have weakened and the desire for exploring new cultural and spiritual experiences has grown, many Jews have begun to participate in an expansive cultural and spiritual marketplace where they can choose from an eclectic assortment of cultural and religious traditions. They can seek products, activities, and experiences that reflect their individual identities and their sense of what can serve as authentic expressions of their Jewish identities in particular. The combination of an unprecedented degree of individual autonomy and an all-encompassing consumer culture has created the possibility of building, expressing, and performing one's identity out of an almost unlimited range of possibilities. As a result of the new consumer approach to matters of religious, ethnic, and cultural belonging and identification, Thomas Luckmann observes, "The individual is more likely to confront the culture and the sacred cosmos as a 'buyer.'"[5]

On the simplest level, the new consumer-oriented Jewish culture includes basic things like "synagogue-shopping" or "shul-shopping," where people visit different synagogues in search of one that feels the most comfortable or has the best rabbis or the friendliest congregation.[6] The marketing of Jewishness follows the same principles as that of all other goods and services in which "brand authenticity" has become an important factor.[7] The executive director of "The Kitchen, a nondenominational 'startup synagogue' in San Francisco" proudly described its brand as "edgy and contemporary" with a "bold energy."[8]

Traditional marketing firms now offer assistance in branding not only synagogues but also Jewish day schools, community centers, camps, museums, and higher educational institutions in order to promote the specific experiences they offer. Opportunities for Jewish yoga, Jewish meditation, and Jewish mysticism are plentiful and offer a full range of spiritual practices outside of normal Jewish worship. Jewish vacations can include heritage tourism to sites in Eastern Europe or Israel where Jewishness is carefully packaged for maximum experiential impact. Klezmer music ensures the Jewish flavor of weddings and *b'nai mitzvot*. Jewish films, documentaries, and series thrive at Jewish film festivals and on streaming platforms like Netflix. Inexpensive DNA tests now offer scientific "proof" of Jewish roots. One thing that links all of these examples is the fact that each of them offers an opportunity to experience something that promotes itself as authentically Jewish and contributes to the formation and maintenance of an authentic Jewish identity.

Since the beginning of the current century, more and more of the elements out of which people build their senses of self—their personal experiences, cultural background, ethnicity, and religion—have been enveloped by the global economy of advanced capitalism and subjected to branding. Sarah Banet-Weiser explains that the ingredients out of which people build identities are "increasingly formed as branded spaces, undergirded by brand logic and articulated through the language of branding."[9] Jeremy Carrette and Richard King describe "a silent takeover of 'the religious' by contemporary capitalist ideologies by means of the increasingly popular discourse of 'spirituality.'" Key to this branding process is the preservation of "an 'aura' of authenticity."[10] In fact, according to Banet-Weiser, "Authenticity *itself* is a brand."[11] As authenticity has become not only a brand but also a lifestyle and a personal aesthetic, some critics complain about the inauthenticity of authenticity. Andrew Potter calls authenticity a "hoax" in which "we get lost finding ourselves."[12] Yet marketers emphasize that people think of authenticity as a valuable goal in their lives without knowing precisely what it is. Whatever it is, they want to be recognized by others as authentic, to at least have the appearance of authenticity in the ways they have constructed their lives.[13]

Today's cultural and spiritual marketplace offers multiple ways in which to express and consume Jewishness. The chapters that follow will demonstrate a variety of ways in which the question of Jewish authenticity has been challenged and renegotiated in cultural contexts where traditional boundaries between religious traditions have blurred, and religious identities have been assembled out of disparate pieces from different sources and traditions.[14] The topics discussed will demonstrate how the rhetoric of authenticity has influenced discussions of Jewish religion, culture, and identity.

The Plan of the Book

The book is organized into four sections. The first section provides a theoretical overview of different approaches to authenticity and how they apply to Jewish history, religion, and culture. I begin chapter 1 by introducing the major tension in concepts of authenticity that will be explored in the book, the opposition between essentialist and nonessentialist approaches. The essentialist approaches assume that there is a core of relatively fixed and stable characteristics that define the Jewish people, their culture, and religion; mark their boundaries; and are enforced by their religious authorities. While essentialist forms of authenticity have often supplied a degree of certainty, security, and comfort for their proponents, especially at times when norms and traditions are being challenged, they fail to capture the dynamic qualities of a living culture and religion or the demographic diversity of the people who want to participate in it.

The nonessentialist approach is presented from the perspective of anthropologists, historians, cultural studies theorists, and most particularly the existentialist philosophy of Jean-Paul Sartre. This perspective highlights the importance of change, innovation, rupture, and reconstruction as natural parts of Judaism and Jewish cultural life from its onset, but even more so in the modern world, where individualism and personal choice have a bigger role in questions of religion, culture, and identity than ever before.

While the popularity of Sartrean existentialism has faded, it still offers a useful starting point, since Sartre was the first person to use the concepts of authenticity and inauthenticity to describe particular ways of being Jewish. In chapter 2, I trace Sartre's influence on discussions of Jewish authenticity. As the existentialist focus on authenticity gained cultural resonance in the latter half of the twentieth century, many Jewish thinkers extended and expanded Sartre's ideas on Jewish authenticity. I track some of this development through a discussion of the debate over Jewish pride versus self-hatred, as well as looking at the ways that figures like Albert Memmi and Alain Finkielkraut added new dimensions to Sartre's original ideas about Jewish authenticity. In their own way, Orthodox Jews were equally invested in defending the authenticity of their approach to Judaism and Jewishness in contrast to other alternatives that were emerging.

One of the most important elements in Sartre's analysis of Jewish authenticity was its attention to the role of "recognition" by others in revealing certain aspects of a person's identity. Sartre focused only on the antisemites' negative and hostile form of recognition of Jews, which he insisted was nonetheless something that authentic Jews needed to confront. But recognition has far broader implications in the construction of Jewish identity and authenticity, so I have expanded my consideration of the role of recognition in a variety of new directions, particularly struggles over recognition among groups of Jews and their role in authenticating Jewish traditions and identities. I present this in the context of more recent discussions of the politics of recognition by philosophers like Charles Taylor and Will Kymlicka and its connection to the principles of multiculturalism.

The second section of the book explores how the debates about authenticity and recognition have been intertwined with various manifestations of Jewish religion in the last half-century. Chapter 3 deals with the long-standing tension between Orthodox and liberal forms of Judaism and the struggle of non-Orthodox Jewish individuals and groups to have their religious practices and traditions recognized as authentically Jewish by Orthodox Jews. This section begins with a discussion of the various ways that essentialist models of Jewish authenticity have been used to justify the singular legitimacy of Orthodox Judaism, rejecting the possibility of liberal Judaism as an authentic form of Judaism yet still recognizing non-Orthodox Jews as Jews. I approach Orthodoxy itself as a particularly modern construction or "invention" of Jewish tradition that produced its own internal debates over recognition and authenticity that have become more contentious as the Orthodox world has become more polarized.

Chapter 4 turns to the liberal Jewish efforts to define Jewish authenticity in more individualistic and spiritual terms reflecting different ways of being religious and criticizing the Orthodox standards of authenticity as inflexible and outdated. I present Erich Fromm and Mordecai Kaplan as examples of a more individualistic and spiritual turn in recent approaches to religion, with a greater focus on religion as a quest for authentic experience and self-realization.

In chapter 5, I examine the quest for spiritual experience that led many Jews to explore Asian religious practices such as meditation and yoga. I show how these practices were able to be refashioned and rebranded as authentically Jewish by inventing new origin stories to connect them to classic Jewish narratives, repackaged with Jewish terms, and otherwise infused with Jewish spirituality. In contrast, the marketing of Jewish mysticism by the Kabbalah Centre for consumption by non-Jews as well as Jews created questions about its Jewish authenticity, which Orthodox experts in Kabbalah refused to recognize.

Chapter 6 is the last chapter of this section, and it considers the religious issue of heresy and the resistance from most of the mainstream Jewish world to recognize Messianic Jews as having any Jewish authenticity. The future status of Messianic Jews remains uncertain, in spite of the overwhelming opposition to granting them recognition. Some Messianic Jews have launched major efforts at rebranding their movement and are hopeful about the possibility of eventually being included in the broader Jewish communal world. I consider their arguments for the inclusion of Messianic Judaism as a nonnormative perspective that nonetheless can be included as part of a religiously diverse Jewish world.

The third part of the book looks at four different examples that illustrate aspects of the issue of Jewish peoplehood: Zionism and Israel (chapter 7), the culture of Eastern Europe and klezmer (chapter 8), intermarriage and conversion (chapter 9), and Jewish genetics (chapter 10). Inspired by the essentialist models of European nationalism, classical Zionist thinkers developed a sense of Jewish authenticity in which land, language, and folk traditions provided the glue holding the Jewish people together. Three examples that illustrate the major ingredients of authentically Jewish life in Israel that were being reconstructed were the idealization of the Sabra and Mizrahi Jew as indigenous folk archetypes, the renewal of Hebrew to establish a linguistic link to the life of ancient Israel, and the twentieth-century invention of Israeli folk dance. Of course, this Zionist project changed dramatically over time as individualism and global cultures transformed Israeli expressions of Jewishness in recent decades.

In addition to turning to Israel as an anchor for modern Jewish authenticity, many American Jews have sought to reclaim their cultural roots in the premodern Eastern European Jewish life that was destroyed during the Holocaust. In chapter 8, I discuss the idealized reinvention of Ashkenazi Jewish cultural roots with two examples illustrating the commodification of Jewish authenticity in the latter part of the twentieth century. The enormous success of the Broadway show *Fiddler on the Roof* and the revival of klezmer music each have provided vicarious experiences of shtetl authenticity that offer a more natural and spontaneous expression of Jewish ethnicity that has been reimagined for the present day.

A very different search for Jewish authenticity has confronted those who lack a genealogical connection to premodern Jewish life, since their own family history is non-Jewish. The issue of Jewish authenticity for intermarried families and converts to Judaism raises questions about whether religious conversion is the best vehicle for being incorporated into the Jewish people and the tensions involved in recognizing converts as authentically Jewish.

The final topic in this section deals with the issues raised by the mass commodification of genetic testing and its implications for scientifically uncovering Jewish authenticity in DNA results. I argue that turning to genetic essentialism as a guarantor of Jewish authenticity ultimately leaves us with highly limited and problematic ideas of kinship and peoplehood that are little more reliable than pseudoscientific racial theories of Jewishness.

The last section of the book explores four examples of groups who claim to be descendants of groups who became separated from the main population of the Jewish people centuries ago. In some cases, the claimed connection is to specific tribes of ancient Israel that disappeared nearly three millennia ago. These include Ethiopian Jews (also known as Beta Israel or Falasha), Black Jews in the United States, and various groups in Africa and South Asia who claim to be descendants of lost tribes of ancient Israel. In other cases, such as the Crypto-Jews in the United States, the supposed link to the Jewish people is through Sephardi Jews who were forced to convert to Christianity more than six hundred years ago. The claims of these "lost branches" of the Jewish people and their efforts to be recognized as

Jews in Israel or in the United States have raised complicated issues about the role of colonialism and Christian influence in the origins of their groups, the impact of race on assumptions about Jewishness, and the different processes of recognition and nonrecognition that have been extended by segments of the mainstream Jewish community.

What I call "normative recognition" has been commonly offered to prospective Jews whose goal is to immigrate to Israel. It is recognition that is accompanied by socialization into the norms of mainstream, usually Orthodox, Judaism. Another approach is "multicultural recognition," where new Jews are embraced as they are, and their idiosyncratic forms of Jewish practice are recognized as part of a growing multicultural diversity of the Jewish people. I conclude that even though supporting historical evidence for these groups' claims is thin, they are constructing new forms of Jewish identity that may still be recognized as authentically Jewish.

PART I
THEORETICAL PERSPECTIVES ON JEWISH AUTHENTICITY

1 The Changing Faces of Jewish Authenticity

Long before anyone attached the word *authentic* to someone or something Jewish, members of the Jewish people would doubtless wonder or disagree about what doctrines, laws, and traditions could be trusted to be genuine and authoritative. Then as now, one of the most common ways of answering such questions was to refer to the story of where a tradition came from and who were the first Jewish leaders or authorities to mention it. Such stories, sometimes labeled "etiological" or "origin" stories, are a valuable source of stability and reassurance not only for early tribal cultures but for modern ones as well, since they explain why certain traditions exist and why they are important.

Today, the most basic approach to determining the authenticity of a particular Jewish tradition is to focus on its roots and origins. Generally, this means establishing a narrative link between the tradition and a moment in the past, when group identities and cultural traditions were anchored in the shared rhythms and taken-for-granted fabric of daily life. This effort to uncover the authority of the past endows previous generations with a sacred aura of importance. The idealized ancestors who are the sources of traditions may be associated with fairly recent generations—perhaps those of one's grandparents or great-grandparents. More likely, the sense of who one really is will be linked to a lineage and heritage stretching back from the present day to ancestors who lived centuries, or even millennia, earlier. Whether recent or distant, the lives of one's ancestors embody the timeless essence that defines the unique way of life that every cultural, religious, ethnic, and national group tries to preserve.

Cultural and religious traditions or rituals are considered authentic, in this view, when they are determined to be as old and uncorrupted as the members of a group claim them to be, having been faithfully passed down from generation to generation. In other words, authenticity is treated as a straightforward matter that can be verified by objective analysis of narrative records and surviving relics that reveal the original source of meaning and value. For example, the authenticity of a Jewish custom or ritual, like circumcising male babies, or celebrating holidays such as Passover or Sukkot, assumes that the roots of these practices can be found in the beliefs, traditions, and way of life of those ancestors whose lives and experiences are recounted in the origin stories that are sacred to Jews. Thus the collective authenticity of both Jewish traditions and Jewish people can be measured by the reliability of their lineages or pedigrees. This form of authenticity has been variously labeled "historical," "genealogical,"[1] "objective,"[2] and "nominal"[3] by various philosophers and anthropologists.

Expressive Authenticity and the Jewish Dilemma

In the modern world, historical authenticity has often had to compete with a personal form of authenticity known as *expressive authenticity*. This is the idea that individuals and groups are authentic when the beliefs they affirm, the actions they perform, and the things they create all reflect or express something about their unique, innermost selves, who they "really are," rather than their conformity to some set of inherited social roles, traditions, and rituals.

Many philosophers and historians trace the emergence of expressive authenticity as a new moral virtue to both the Enlightenment's establishment of the innate sacred rights of every individual along with Romantic reaction in the eighteenth century to disorienting transitions in the modern world that had disrupted the secure sense of meaning and place found in premodern life. As the old hierarchical social, economic, political, and religious order crumbled, Romantic writers and philosophers idealized their inner, natural feelings. In addition, they romanticized the simplicity of rural, pastoral life as the embodiment of the sense of meaning and connection to the natural world that had been lost in their newly desacralized world.[4]

The French philosopher Jean-Jacques Rousseau was central to this shift in focus to the interior life of the individual. He offered a detailed portrait of his private inner self, where he found refuge from what he considered the increasingly artificial and alienating experience of life in modern society.[5] According to philosopher Charles Taylor, Rousseau's turn inward was only possible because a new modern concept of the self had emerged, one that replaced external authorities with the authority of one's own inner voice and feelings as the guide toward self-fulfillment and self-realization.[6] In effect, observes anthropologist Charles Lindholm, Rousseau became the inventor of expressive authenticity.[7]

Rousseau saw examples of uncorrupted authenticity in the natural, spontaneous feelings of children, rural peasants, and "primitive" tribes. Although he commented on Judaism in the ancient world as excessively legalistic and ceremonial, Rousseau said nothing about the Jews of his own time and place, and there is little evidence that he had much personal contact with Jews or considered their unique position in the emerging modern world.[8] His comments about civilization's corrupting influence and the natural self that lies beneath people's civilized facades failed to acknowledge the awkward situation that would exist for European Jews.

The Enlightenment's celebration of the sacredness of every individual provided the justification for the emancipation of Jews as individual citizens, but the expected price for equality was their assimilation to the proper roles and etiquette of civilized society. Their inner Jewish selves lacked the natural purity and goodness of the child, peasant, or primitive. Rather, premodern Jewishness was regarded as a coarse, vulgar, uncivilized dimension that needed to be eliminated, or at least hidden. Emancipation for the Jews was therefore not an invitation for the free expression of their true inner reality as Jews.[9] Ultimately, it was the refusal to recognize the particularity of Jewish experience that eventually produced Zionism. One of the primary benefits that Zionist thinkers associated with a homeland for Jews was to have a place where the full expressive authenticity of the Jewish people could be nurtured and celebrated.

The paradoxical cost of emancipation for the expressive authenticity of the Jews was still an issue nearly two centuries later when Sartre wrote about the bind that French Jews were in. For Sartre, whose contempt for the corrupting influence of social conventions and civility was every bit equal to Rousseau's, the exclusion of the Jews from bourgeois society because of antisemitism had inadvertently enabled Jews to maintain some degree of an inner natural authenticity. Sartre wrote, "What I particularly appreciate in my Jewish friends is a gentleness and subtlety that is certainly an outcome of antisemitism."[10] He noted that Jewish feelings had a "disarming freshness and uncultivated spontaneity" and that "there is a sincerity, a youth, a warmth in the manifestation of friendship of a Jew that one will rarely find in a Christian, hardened as the latter is by tradition and ceremony."[11] We will return to Sartre's approach to Jewish authenticity in the next chapter.

The new emphasis on expressive authenticity that Rousseau discussed also had an impact on emerging understandings of national or ethnic identity. Ideally, when people are true to themselves and true to their heritage, it is immediately expressed in the way they live their lives.[12] Romantic philosophers like Johann Gottfried Herder described what it meant to belong to a people, or "folk," a group that constitutes a particular nationality or ethnic group. Herder argued that a people is not just an artificial collection of rational individuals who come together for some political purpose but rather an *organic* whole, held together by its own authentic and distinctive spirit, values, and ideas, all of which are reproduced and expressed in each member of that group. This spirit of a people, or its *volksgeist*, is the product of their collective history, which binds them together by means of their shared language, their roots in a particular land or territory, their kinship ties, and their inherited cultural, religious, and folk traditions. These are the elements that tell people who they really are and how they are different from other peoples. In other words, people are authentically themselves only when they understand themselves as individual expressions of a particular people, its traditions, and the *volksgeist* that flows through them. Each people's *volksgeist* is that group's unique way of being in the world.[13]

Essentialism, Tradition, and Change

The idea that members of a people, nation, or ethnic group—such as the Jewish people—represent an organic whole raises the question of whether the culture and traditions associated with such a group are best understood as a naturalistic object with fixed qualities and an essence that preexist any one individual in the group. If so, two different forms of authenticity are implied. On the one hand, if culture and tradition are treated as though they are archeological treasures from the past, whose nature and meaning were established by their original creators, then the focus is placed on "historical authenticity" and the degree to which each member of the group reproduces its traditions faithfully. On the other hand, if a people or nation is compared to a living organism, endowed with its own collective will, soul, spirit, or destiny, then the focus is shifted to "expressive authenticity," and the authenticity of individual members of the group is directly linked to their being microcosmic expressions of the group's collective self.

Each of these approaches understands a people and its tradition as a naturalistic object with clearly defined boundaries and characteristics that exist prior to, and independent of, whatever shifting interpretations may have occurred over time.[14] As anthropologists Richard Handler and Jocelyn Linnekin point out, "To imagine the collectivity as a species eliminates the problem of fuzzy boundaries: people can claim that any individual is or is not a member of the nation. . . . There are no ambiguous or divided affiliations, and the nation, as a collection of individuals, is as definitively bounded as a natural species."[15] In other words, to consider the characteristics of one's ethnic, cultural, or religious group as natural and organic reinforces models of authenticity that ignore or suppress any suggestion that the group's norms might actually be more fluid and therefore subject to the methods of interpretation employed in the present.

In their own ways, both historical and expressive authenticity are examples of essentialist approaches to authenticity. Both assume some underlying core or solid foundation, whether in the traditions of the past, the collective spirit of one's people, or within the depths of one's own self. Essentialist approaches to group authenticity provide a major conceptual structure for understanding the differences between religious, national, and even racial groups. In each case, collective identity is reinforced by what Anthony Smith calls the "cult of authenticity," the goal of which is to preserve the biological and cultural purity of a people from the corruption or contamination that is associated with strangers and outsiders. This concern with preserving the authenticity of the group comes with a sense of specialness and destiny. Individuals discover who they really are and the ultimate meaning of their lives by embracing the feeling of being one of the "chosen people."[16] This feeling is celebrated in stories of shared traditions and kinship bonds that bind the group together, define its boundaries, and justify its members' beliefs, values, and way of life.

It is generally agreed that concerns about both historical and expressive authenticity only emerged in response to the modern world, which created cracks in the previously seamless integration of Jewish beliefs and traditions into everyday life.[17] Still, it is worth considering that the unstable and contested nature of tradition in general, and Jewish tradition in particular, is nothing new.[18] Throughout the history of civilization, all groups have developed strategies for establishing communal solidarity, enforcing conformity, and dealing with deviance, heresy, or other unauthorized innovations.

It is true that Jews have consistently understood themselves as a single people united by a common historical experience, culture, and religious commitment, all of which is embodied in their sacred origin narratives. Yet at the same time, Jewish communities around the world have developed in many different directions as a result of local and historical circumstances, religious syncretism, and cultural mixing. The result has been not only the progressive historical development of different forms of Judaism over time but also the simultaneous coexistence of conflicting Judaisms, diverse Jewish cultures, and heterogeneous Jewish populations at various moments in history.

Even in classical antiquity, argues Shaye D. Cohen, "there was no single or simple definition of *Jew*. . . . Jewishness was a subjective identity, constructed by the individual him/herself, other Jews, other gentiles, and the state." There were no specific qualities or criteria—that is, no "essence"—that would enable one "to determine who was 'really' a Jew and who was not."[19] Boundaries between Jews and non-Jews—as well as the relative weight of ethnicity, nationality, and religion to determinations of Jewishness—were shifting at that time, just as they are in different ways today, reflecting changing social and political factors.

The question of Judaism's essence, or "authentic Judaism," has regularly arisen in periods when communal consensus has fractured and borders between acceptable and unacceptable practices have become unbearably fuzzy, notes Efraim Shmueli. Rather than a single, uniform system, the history of Jewish culture is a series of cultures, no single one of which alone can be said to be the essence of Judaism, whether the prophetic ethical vision of liberal Judaism or the halakhic system of Orthodox Judaism. Authenticity assumes different shapes and qualities in response to specific times, places, groups, models of authority, concepts of self, and attitudes toward change.

Although certain concepts like God, Torah, and Israel are found throughout Jewish history and give the impression of continuity and permanence, Shmueli denies that any of them constitute an essence. He writes, "While the concepts have endured, their meanings have changed, the inevitable result of the changes occurring in the ontologies underlying these concepts and experiences."[20] In any given period of time, moreover, the reigning, or hegemonic, perspective of what is authentically Jewish reflects the views of those who have successfully gained power and authority and the suppression of alternative views as heretical or lacking Jewish authenticity. So the success of the rabbinic perspectives of the Pharisees, for example, meant that other sects like the Essenes, or Gnostics, or Jewish followers of Jesus received little attention in subsequent Jewish texts that were taken as normative.[21] As Jonathan Webber notes, "It is not just the notion of 'authentic Judaism' that can be seen as a construct in response to circumstances; Jewish identities in general are largely to be understood as constructs in response to the circumstances."[22] The result is that "there are multiple *authentic* Judaisms."[23] Some Jewish ideas, values, or traditions may gain widespread acceptance while others are abandoned or rejected. Yet such consensus is never permanent, and over time, the Jewish ideas and traditions that are considered acceptable may shift dramatically.

The inevitable changes that occurred in the history of Jews and Judaism have always been couched in terms of a return to what is authentic and essential and a repudiation of alternative views as inauthentic. Although cultural, ethnic, and religious identities continually recreate and redefine themselves, when change occurs, it is usually accompanied by the claim that innovators are merely rediscovering or returning to the true tradition.[24] On the other hand, cultural and religious innovations may be rejected as inauthentic by traditionalists at the moment of their introduction, but later generations will reclaim what had been seen as new and heretical as now representing the "authentic" tradition.[25] The inevitable reality of cultural change means that people are not merely passive recipients of a fully formed culture but rather active agents who express their culture in ways that contribute to the future development of those cultures and identities.

Abandoning the idea that there is a single, constant, essential formulation of Judaism or Jewishness over time does not deny the fact that a majority of Jews at a particular moment in history may reach a consensus about whether certain ideas, texts, experiences, or traditions are authentically Jewish or not. The point is to realize that such judgments reflect a snapshot in a changing historical and cultural landscape where rupture, changes, and innovations are always just around the corner, and where elements that have been excluded as deviant, inauthentic, or illegitimate continue to lurk in the shadows of the tradition.[26] Even as provisional definitions in particular communities at particular historical moments establish what is recognized as authentically Jewish for some Jews, certain other practices, ideas, interpretations, and people that have been suppressed may eventually resurface and find expression.

The paradox of authenticity is that in the name of preserving the connection to the past and to the world of their ancestors, people engage in their own reconstructions and revisions of tradition that include selectivity, innovation, reinvention, and transformation—sometimes slow and imperceptible and sometimes abrupt and extensive. The paradox is that traditions are embraced as a portal to the past, but their real function is to shape the meaning and understanding of the past in ways that are responsive to the needs of the present.[27]

Crises of confidence in tradition have occurred regularly in Jewish history, observes Neil Gillman, whether in response to the destruction of the ancient Temples or the expulsion of Jews from Spain, when "the tradition had to be looked at afresh and defended in a new and compelling way, or stretched to accommodate a new reality and reestablish the Jewish community."[28] Struggles over questions of authenticity arise when there is profound disagreement over "how much stretching the tradition can take and still remain recognizably Jewish."[29] Modernity and its aftermath have arguably stretched Jewishness in ways that would likely have been unrecognizable to many premodern Jewish communities. Premodern Jewish life unfolded under an all-embracing "sacred canopy" where broad consensus existed about gender roles, social practices, religious traditions, and the rabbinic authorities who monitored them. As a "pariah people," most Jews lived in insular communities to a large degree segregated physically, economically, and socially from the surrounding non-Jewish world.

The combination of the new ideas of the Enlightenment and the political emancipation of large swaths of European Jews radically disrupted their organic sense of community, their economic and social relations with the outside world, and the unquestioned authority of their religious leaders. A widening tension between allegiance to tradition and the new freedom of individuals to make their own choices about different aspects of Jewish tradition made it increasingly difficult to reach an agreement on what was authentically Jewish as well as the best path for Jewish survival.

A broad range of Jewish responses to the new opportunities to participate in the broader non-Jewish world reflected their efforts to recalibrate an understanding of what was authentically Jewish. Steven Cohen describes the repositioning of different factions within the Jewish community as a sorting process in which everyone was engaged in separating the "kernel" of Judaism, which represented the authentic essence that needed to be preserved, from the outdated "husk" of primitive beliefs and superstitions that had no relevance for the modern world.[30] New Jewish denominations emerged, some wanting to keep their distance from the modern world and preserve a large kernel of Jewish religious life, others emphasizing a smaller kernel that focused on the progressive social values of the biblical prophets. Meanwhile, Zionists considered all Jewish life in diaspora as an unnecessary and inauthentic husk, while the essential kernel to be reclaimed was a Jewish national language and homeland.[31] Each group defended its own position as the most authentically Jewish and warned against the dangers posed by competing perspectives they considered not only illegitimate and inauthentic but also insufficient to sustain modern Jewish life.

Existential Authenticity and the Critique of Essentialism

In the twentieth century, a new approach to authenticity appeared that took as its starting point the rejection of the essentialism on which most earlier models of authenticity had been based. Of foremost interest to existentialist philosophers was the danger of *inauthentic* ways of understanding the foundations of the various identities embraced by human beings. The importance of this existentialist critique of essentialist approaches to authenticity and its anticipation of newer theories of authenticity will be given special attention in this book.

The word *existential*, like the word *authentic*, is used in lots of different, sometimes contradictory, ways. For some people, "existential authenticity" describes the intensity of an experience that resonates with deep personal meaning and feels connected to one's innermost sense of self.[32] Defined in this way, existential authenticity becomes a form of *expressive* authenticity and the striving for self-fulfillment. While this kind of experiential authenticity will come up later in this book, our philosophical starting point for understanding existential authenticity will take a different tack, based on the work of the existentialist philosopher most associated with Jewish authenticity, Jean-Paul Sartre. Expanding his concepts and supplementing them with more recent analyses of authenticity offered by cultural studies theorists and anthropologists can help build a convincing case for preserving a non-essentialist model that avoids some of the problematic and even toxic aspects of traditional historical and expressive authenticity.

The idea that authentic life rests on some inherent essence that is the common possession of all true members of a nation, ethnic group, or religion through whom that essence is expressed is certainly a perspective that persists to this day.

All too often, however, this approach has provided a foundation for racism, ethnocentrism, and religious chauvinism. Far from being the foundation for an authentic life, essentialism is often based on questionable presuppositions, self-deception, and inevitable bad faith.

The central point of existentialists like Sartre was that the experience of meaning and authenticity is not an inherent quality of reality but rather something that human beings create, imagine, construct, and perform. It is not something that is either buried in the past or hidden deep within, predetermined by genes or human nature, revealed on mountaintops or in sacred scriptures, or existing in any other form that is independent of the free exercise of human interpretation and imagination. The existentialist critique of traditional theories of human nature as well as social categories and identities that presuppose some preexisting core was all summarized in Sartre's dictum, "Existence precedes essence."[33] That is the starting point, regardless of other factors that may influence, limit, or distort one's experience in the world.

This is not to deny that cultural or religious rules, boundaries, and traditions exist, or that a whole variety of historical, economic, social, political, and physical factors impinge on who a person is and can be. Rather, it is to emphasize that these elements will be reconfigured and reimagined in response to each individual person's own input and their relationships with other people in their social worlds.[34]

In the decades since Sartre delivered his famous lecture on this idea in 1945,[35] the critique of essentialism has been expanded and deepened by anthropologists, psychologists, sociologists, gender theorists, philosophers, and others. Almost all of these figures challenged in one form or another the central categories on which the authenticity of group memberships have always been judged. As a result, we have come to recognize the ways in which concepts of race, gender, ethnicity, culture, religion, and nationality are not simply descriptions of empirical facts about the world. Rather, they are ways of imposing human values and interpretations on human social existence that can be, and often have been, abused by creating hierarchies of power that separate the chosen groups and ways of being from the rest. Theorists have worked hard to deconstruct these categories and to demonstrate ways in which they are far more heterogeneous and impermanent than had been generally acknowledged.

The critiques of the essentialist premises behind certain models of authenticity have led some people to question the usefulness of continuing to label particular groups or traditions as "authentic."[36] Indeed, the safest way to talk about who and what is authentically or "really" Jewish is to enclose these terms in quotation marks as a way of signaling the difficulty and tenuousness in making such judgments, or to suggest that these are claims that others are likely to contest. Increasingly, anthropologists, historians, and others have pulled back the curtain surrounding the origin stories and cultural traditions of different groups, where authenticity claims are often revealed to be invented or imaginative (re)constructions. Folklorist Regina Bendix has observed, "The sheer mentioning of the word authenticity is likely to propel an immediate response to unmask it as yet another 'invention,' 'false consciousness,' 'ideological construct,' or 'historical formation.'"[37]

At the same time, Bendix acknowledged that despite the academic critique of authenticity's essentialist roots and the shaky foundations on which they rest, the search for authenticity continues to "live on in the popular imagination, informing notions of self and social life." Indeed, many people's sense of well-being and fulfillment requires what Bendix called "an authentically felt grounding to the social and cultural constructions that make up their lives."[38]

Members of a community may understandably find it offensive to hear outsiders call their sacred traditions "invented," "imagined," or "constructed," which very much sounds like their legitimacy or authenticity is being called into question. Jonathan Boyarin has expressed concern about trendy postmodern understandings of Jewish authenticity that may be popular among academic and intellectual Jews but that also seem unnecessarily dismissive of the perspectives of masses of ordinary Jews who "don't agonize over their own Jewishness too much but tend instead to 'just do it'" in a "taken for granted, unreflective, or essentialized" kind of way.[39] Boyarin is undoubtedly correct that most Jews are content with a fairly simple essentialist view of what is authentically Jewish and are none the worse for it. That is, until they are faced with painful conflicts with other Jews over issues of authenticity. At that point, it becomes much more useful to be able to see authenticity not just as based on fixed and timeless models but as a transformative process that establishes an understanding of the past that is relevant to contemporary goals and needs.[40]

Rather than abandon the concept of authenticity entirely, what Sartre tried to do in calling out the bad faith of essentialist views of authenticity was to clear the way for understanding the production of authenticity as dynamic, dialectical, and self-reflexive. Although he never filled out this alternative model in much detail, it would have been one that incorporated many of the postmodern perspectives on authenticity that subsequent interpreters have made.[41]

For Sartre, existential authenticity begins with lucidity about the lack of essence or permanent foundation of all individual and collective identities and vigilance against the idea that it can be discovered or established. Authenticity is not a fixed quality but rather a process or "project" of positioning oneself within a specific personal, family, cultural, and historical narrative. The resulting origin narratives selectively choose, condense, distort, and erase aspects of one's own particular past and present situation.[42] Authenticity requires neither finding nor expressing one's "true self" or the "real tradition" but simply maintaining an honest view of the process by which identities and traditions are constructed.

Paradoxically, one can only declare what is authentically Jewish if one simultaneously affirms its own potential and eventual inauthenticity—that is, that its truth and value exist in time and are therefore subject to change and that they can appear as permanently fixed or settled only through the lens of bad faith. Like junk food, essentialist forms of authenticity taste good and are filling, but ultimately, they leave one weighed down with a weak and unhealthy identity resting on shaky foundations. Existential authenticity is more like yoga. It requires finding identity positions of temporary stability but also realizing that they are not meant to be held indefinitely. On the contrary, hopefully they lead to greater flexibility, stretching, and expanding the range of one's possible positions in the future.

In an article on secular Jewishness, Paul Mendes-Flohr contrasts rigid, insular forms of Jewish cultural memory with others that possess what he calls a "critical awareness of the culture's presuppositions, prejudices, and blind spots, as it were; most significantly this... mode of cultural memory acknowledges the polyphonic character of its own evolution. By assuming a tolerant attitude toward the plural voices within their own tradition, the guardians of cultural memory are implicitly aware that no culture is utterly insular and untouched by other, 'alien' cultures."[43] Mendes-Flohr reminds us that authenticity does not constitute an impermeable boundary that preserves pure Jewishness and protects it from "contamination." There is a chorus of different Jewish voices that express particular approaches to Jewishness and Jewish authenticity. These different ways of being authentically Jewish are continually colliding with others and often being reconstructed in response to changing circumstances and interpretations that unfold in the course of history.

This "critical awareness" of how new layers of meaning develop within each generation is what makes modern Jews' position potentially different from those of earlier periods. What was previously unspoken about the revitalizing power of midrash on tradition is part of contemporary Jewish self-awareness. Neil Gillman turns to new midrash, or reinterpretations, as "a temporary consolidation, a plateau, the outcome of a struggle to rethink a tradition that has become, at least to some Jews, irrelevant. It is then inherently transitory, itself easily becoming anachronistic, lingering until we are shocked out of our complacency when our children tell us that we no longer 'speak' to them"[44] Gillman's understanding of the dynamic power of midrash to achieve "temporary consolidations" is a good way of understanding existential authenticity as the process of taking a position in relation to received tradition. It is similar to cultural theorist Stuart Hall's notion that group narratives (whether based on nationality, ethnicity, religion, race, or sexuality) need to create moments of "arbitrary closure" by which groups define themselves and their boundaries. Each temporary and arbitrary point of closure, each narrative definition of a community, is "a kind of stake, a kind of wager.... It is not forever, not totally universally true. It is not underpinned by any infinite guarantees. But just now, this is what I mean; this is who I am. At a certain point, in a certain discourse, we call these unfinished closures, 'the self,' 'society,' 'politics,' etc."[45]

What I am calling "existential authenticity" is a self-reflexive approach to the provisional and constructive creation of Jewish meaning that challenges the calm self-assurance with which many Jews still present the essentialist authenticity of their beliefs and practices. The existentialist insistence that all forms of cultural and religious meaning remain subject to the individual's power to reinterpret and reimagine can be a cause for concern for those who fear it can only produce a collapse of any genuine communal agreement on how to be Jewish. If ways of being Jewish become a free-for-all in which anyone can decide for themselves what it means to be Jewish, picking and choosing whatever ingredients feel right or meaningful and discarding those that don't, without regard to any external authorities, does "authentically Jewish" become "an empty concept"?[46]

Critics have often seen the existentialist celebration of the freedom to choose the meaning of one's own life as an open door to self-absorption and narcissistic pursuits, unmoored from any moral foundation outside the expression of the self. In the next chapter, I will suggest a more complex understanding of existential authenticity that addresses this concern. It will understand every Jew as firmly situated in a particular historical and cultural situation out of which meaning must be carved, but not in a solitary, solipsistic way. What is authentically Jewish is produced intersubjectively, in processes where struggles over recognition unfold in ways that include both conflict and solidarity, exclusion and inclusion.

2

Recognition and Authenticity

FROM SARTRE TO MULTICULTURALISM

Sartre was one of the earliest and most important figures to attempt a theoretical analysis of what it meant to be authentically, and inauthentically, Jewish in the face of the antisemitic fever that had spread over Europe during the Nazi era. When he wrote *Antisemite and Jew (Réflexions sur la Question Juive)* in Vichy France in 1944, Sartre wanted to deconstruct the claims of antisemites to a particular kind of cultural authenticity. He offered his own analysis of the antisemites' worldview in order to call attention to the potential *toxicity* of essentialist authenticity, which too often has been a source of nationalist, racial, and cultural exclusivity.[1]

Much as Herder had described in his analysis of national *volksgeists*, the French antisemites understood the essence of their identities as an irrevocable entitlement, transferred to them at birth from their parents, nurtured by the traditions of the place where they lived, and inherently expressed in everything they did. Their essentialist authenticity was part of the natural order of things, an exclusive possession that could not be earned or learned by those who were not born with it (such as Jews and other "aliens"), no matter how long they had lived in France or how well they spoke French.[2]

Understood in this essentialist way, nationalist, cultural, and tribal identities provide assurance to the members of a group that their place in the world rests on a solid, unshakeable foundation that they share with all the other members of their group. The appeal of essentialist identities, Sartre suggested, rests on an underlying anxiety and fear of facing the inescapably *unstable* nature of both individual and group identities. Rather than accepting the inevitable impact of social, economic, cultural, and demographic interactions with other less familiar groups of people, the antisemites pursued an illusory identity based on essentialist assumptions about their own mystical connection to the land, language, and religious and ethnic traditions of their country. They retreated into a nostalgic image of the past, a time when, they believed, there still existed a primordial connection linking all "true" members of the French people.

To the antisemites, the world outside the conventional social world of respectable French society included two different kinds of Other: the semicivilized yet inferior people of France's colonial empire and another alien and inferior population within their own borders, the Jews. Whatever the misguided intentions of those who had extended political rights to the Jews, the Jews could never truly belong in France. They would always be seen as "the stranger, the intruder, the unassimilated at the very heart of our society," wrote Sartre.[3]

At the same time, Sartre also insisted that Jews would need to confront the perceptions that non-Jews had of them, hostile though they were, if they were to deal honestly and authentically with their own identities. He considered the antisemites' "recognition" of Jews as a form of "bad faith" because it was a frozen form of recognition, distorted by preexisting prejudices that ignored the characteristics of the Jews' own experience of themselves as Jews. This kind of misrecognition could be profoundly damaging, especially when the targets of the distorted recognition internalized it as self-hatred or engaged in various strategies of evading or denying their own Jewishness.

"Realizing" Jewish Authenticity

Sartre understandably wanted to address the question of how oppressed groups such as the Jews might respond to their difficult situation. In the face of this hostile reality, he encouraged resistance rather than efforts to disguise, deny, or otherwise flee from the inescapable fact of being Jewish, a fact defined, at least in part, by antisemites. Sartre introduced the language of choice and authenticity to Jewish identity at a time when Jews had little political freedom to determine or define their social identities. His point was that even when little other freedom was available to them, Jews still retained some agency to determine the meaning of their Jewish identities, if only for themselves and no one else. Over the years, Sartre's analysis has been both hailed as courageous and incisive but also criticized as flawed, dated, and even somewhat essentialist in its portrayal of the Jews in France in the first half of the twentieth century.[4] That said, there remain useful insights in his analysis that remain suggestive and valuable for developing a model of Jewish authenticity.

Sartre wrote that "Jewish authenticity consists in choosing oneself as a Jew,—that is, in realizing one's Jewish condition," even if that choice was forced upon a person by others who labeled them as Jews. The challenge for Jews, or anyone else for that matter, is how to realize—that is, "make real"—a cultural, ethnic, or religious identity without succumbing to rigid or essentialist conclusions. Sartre's description of the process of developing an authentic Jewish identity includes a variety of terms such as "true and lucid consciousness of the situation" of being a Jew, and "assuming," "accepting," "realizing," "making," and "choosing" oneself *as a Jew*.[5] Jews are not limited only to the negative identity offered by the antisemite, insisted Sartre, but neither can they ignore or deny the fact that part of their identity as Jews has been established by the way they are recognized, accurately or not, by non-Jews.[6]

Since Sartre's Jewish acquaintances were mostly assimilated secular Jews, he said little about Jewish culture or religion in his essay. His diagnosis of Jewish *inauthenticity* applied primarily to Jewish intellectual circles in Paris, not the average French Jew. That inauthenticity could be seen in those Jews who tried to pass themselves off as non-Jews, to conceal their Jewishness, and to otherwise seek to avoid the stigmatized identity of being Jewish. Sartre insisted that being seen as a Jew establishes an aspect of who one is, though certainly not in Herder's romantic sense of a people's collective essence. Indeed, he expressed suspicion that the less assimilated Jewish immigrants from Eastern and Central Europe who remained more attached to Jewish tradition and Yiddish culture were trying to claim a solid foundation for their identities in the same problematic way that the French antisemites were attached to their inherited sense of Frenchness.[7]

By the 1960s, however, Sartre began to include the meaning received from Jewish culture and tradition as another authentically Jewish possibility. His exhortation to Jews to realize themselves as Jews can be seen as also involving the need to "recognize" and to "make real" certain Jewish realities that are absorbed and internalized in the process of growing up in a Jewish family or community.[8] Central to this process was dealing with the different forms of *recognition given by others*, those who are friendly and those who are hostile, members of one's family and community as well as the community of one's oppressors, those who claim authority and those who have been excluded from authority.

Whatever the particular context or situation within which people construct their life projects and senses of self, their actions contribute to the overall character of their own group identity, as well as the character of humanity as a whole in that period of history. In his essay, "Existentialism Is a Humanism," Sartre emphasized the ripples that flow out of every decision and action a person makes and the responsibility that it creates. He wrote, "I am therefore responsible for myself and for everyone else, and I am fashioning a certain image of man as I choose him to be. In choosing myself, I choose man."[9]

If there is no predetermined essence of what it means to be a Jew, any more than there is an essential human nature, then Jews need to accept the responsibility for creating the reality of Jewishness through their choices and actions. Accordingly, Sartre insisted, "To be a Jew is to be responsible in and through one's own person for the destiny and the very nature of the Jewish people."[10] Whether one chooses to be religious or not, to be kosher or not, to marry another Jew or not, to be institutionally affiliated or not, one's choices contribute to the collective character of the Jewish people. There is no essence of Judaism or the Jewish people apart from the open-ended project that emerges out of the collective actions of all individual Jews and the ways they give meaning to their collective history and traditions. This is the point Jay Michaelson makes when he insists that "real Jews" are not a particular strictly observant subset of Jews but rather all Jews who "take Jewishness seriously, in one form or another. . . . Real Jews are the ones who make Judaism real for themselves."[11]

While some people embrace the sense of security and certainty that comes from thinking of a cultural, religious, or social status quo as permanent and eternal, existential authenticity is a reminder of the permanent instability of the status quo, the freedom to uproot oneself from it, to contest or renew its assumptions and foundations and thereby contribute to the direction of its movement into the future. As people bring into reality new meaning for their religious, cultural, and ethnic history, their choices ripple throughout each group of which they are a part.

Existentialist philosophy is often assumed to encourage solitary choices based on an exaggerated sense of individual freedom and choice, yet a fuller reading of

Sartre can uncover his attention to the cultural, historical, political, economic, and physical limits that circumscribe human freedom. Although he never really elaborated a robust theory of authenticity, much less Jewish authenticity, it is possible to extract the outline of a dynamic model of Jewish authenticity based on the central philosophical categories laid out not only in *Antisemite and Jew* but also in Sartre's major philosophical work, *Being and Nothingness*. The model that follows is therefore inspired by Sartrean ideas, even if he never explicitly expanded his analysis of Jewish authenticity in this exact way.

A Tripartite Existentialist Model of Jewish Authenticity

A Sartrean approach to Jewish existentialist authenticity includes three major components. First, every individual or group is defined to some degree by factors over which they have no control. These factors represent the background context or stage on which people's lives unfold and are lived. This is their "existential situation" in the world, which includes all of the empirical facts about a person into which they are born and raised—their history or lineage, economic and political status, language, geographical location, physical or racial characteristics, exposure to various cultural traditions and beliefs, experiences of persecution and oppression, and so on. People are born into specific families, cultures, and religions, all with their own histories and origin myths to help them understand who they really are. For some people, these factors seem to represent deterministic forces, inescapable destinies, compulsory traditions, or other manifestations of an inherent essence. However, the full impact of a person's existential situation is modified by the second component in our model.

The second element in considering what is authentically Jewish approaches the factors that compose a person's existential situation not as a package that is passively accepted and passed on but rather as the field on which human agency, cultural development, and social change operate. It is based on the central existentialist premise that *the meaning* of each element of a person's historical, cultural, and personal situation remains open to revision, modification, and even rejection. Individuals and groups always retain their ability to transcend and transform any situation in which they are born or find themselves by constructing new meanings and incorporating new perspectives. They will decide what elements of their heritage to remember and preserve, as well as what kinds of changes or innovations may be necessary to create a meaningful way of living. Old traditions may be revitalized with new content, and origin myths may be revised and expanded to accommodate new ideas and concepts.

The existentialist focus on the power of every person to modify the meaning attached to any of the specific details of their life is not an invitation to self-absorption but rather a way of appropriating those details into a coherent sense of self. The resulting identity does not arise ex nihilo in a burst of self-creation. The construction of a person's sense of self is a complex dynamic process. Every person, wrote Sartre, "forms a synthetic whole with his situation—biological, economic, political, cultural, etc. He cannot be distinguished from his situation, for it forms him and decides his possibilities; but inversely, it is he who gives it meaning by making his choices within it and by it. To be in a situation, as we see it, is to choose oneself in a situation, and men differ from one another in their situations and also in the choices they themselves make of themselves."[12]

This process of developing one's identity as a member of a culture or people, says cultural theorist Stuart Hall, "is always constructed through memory, fantasy, narrative and myth. . . . Not an essence but a *positioning*."[13] Philosopher Charles Taylor makes a related point in emphasizing that the decisions, actions, and "positionings" that help produce an authentic identity occur against a "background of intelligibility" or a "pre-existing horizon of significance."[14] Whatever individual choices people may make or goals they pursue, Will Kymlicka concurs, their choices occur within the "intelligible contexts of choice" and "a secure sense of identity and belonging" provided by their cultural group memberships.[15]

Finally, what is authentically Jewish also involves consideration of a third element in addition to the weight of individual pasts and group histories or the continual reappropriation and reinvention of their meaning in the present and in projects aimed toward the future. This third element from Sartre's philosophy is crucial in regulating the balance between the inertia of static adherence and acceptance of all aspects of the situation into which one is born and the revolutionary potential to overturn and completely transcend one's situation in new directions. This component of identity is what Sartre called "being-for-others," or the way that authenticity is intertwined with the dynamics of the "recognition" provided by others when they accept or reject the particular way a person or group interprets their situation and traditions. Do they consider the choices that a person or group makes to be a legitimate, or authentic, embodiment of the group or tradition they claim to be part of?

To be sure, Sartre's early analysis of "the look of the Other" and the forms of recognition embedded within it characterized relations with other people as a reciprocal struggle for power, where people try to control the recognition they receive from others. During the course of his life, Sartre regularly revisited the question of relations with other people and the impact of the recognition they provide on the development of a person's sense of self. By the end of his life, Sartre revealed a greater appreciation of the importance of recognition from others within the family and wider society in the formulation of one's self. Indeed, in one of his later works he describes the presence of these elements of recognition at work even before the emergence of an individual sense of self within consciousness.[16]

Recognition of an individual or a group, and their approach to Jewish traditions and narratives, does not mean that there is any particular set of authorities or gatekeepers whose recognition is the final verdict on what is authentically Jewish. But it does mean that the positions and interpretations people express in relation to Jewish culture and tradition do not occur on a deserted island. Their authenticity emerges from an implicit negotiation with other people, Jews and non-Jews, and the degrees of recognition they offer.[17]

But debates about who and what is authentically Jewish inevitably involve disputes over recognition. Sometimes the innovations, changes, or reforms of some

Jews are rejected as unacceptable by others who claim to be defending their view of the right, or orthodox, approach against changes that are considered heretical. There will always be multiple juries making different decisions about recognition.

Michael Satlow suggests that there is "a range of different and yet all 'authentically' Jewish responses to Jewish history and traditions."[18] He notes that these different responses are authentically Jewish not because they share any common essential Jewish features, but because they all share certain "family resemblances."[19] Of course, this notion of family resemblances is a judgment that depends on two distinct forms of recognition. The first form of recognition is the discovery of some resemblance to another way of being Jewish. There is an aura about a person, ritual, tune, or story that feels Jewishly "familiar" enough. The second form of recognition involves a decision to accept what feels familiar in this way as a legitimate part of the Jewish "family" and its people, culture, and history.

As the examples in later chapters will show, the struggle for recognition will be an important element in the discussion of how what is authentically Jewish is negotiated among different Jewish groups. Granting or withholding recognition can be a way of policing acceptable boundaries of Jewishness and punishing those who deviate in ways that seem "unrecognizable," and it equally can be a means of empowering marginal and nonnormative forms of Jewishness that may someday be widely recognized as part of the Jewish family.

The suggestion in Sartre's model is that authenticity lies in maintaining the dialectical tension between these three dimensions, and inauthenticity is the result of an imbalance that privileges one at the expense of the others. For example, Sartre's portrait of the antisemite depicts a person who treats the contingent factors of his or her life as a fixed and permanent foundation rooted in a particular land and language and national traditions. Other people act as though their freedom is absolute and that they can float above any of the facts of their situation. Both of these attitudes are distortions. Yet even the person who realizes their own freedom to both transcend and determine the meaning of their situation, culture, and tradition, must also understand the power of others to contest, support, or influence various forms of recognition. Identifying what is authentically Jewish is thus a dynamic and dialogical process, involving the interactions and intersections between these three dimensions. Authenticity is permanently caught in this tension between allegiance to tradition and the inevitability of change and innovation, between continuity and rupture, and finally between different degrees of recognizability and recognition.

Although Sartre became infamously tied to his idea that the hostile recognition of Jews by antisemites is a major determinant of their identities, near the end of *Antisemite and Jew*, Sartre insisted that the concrete positive content of Jewishness ought to be recognized as much as other important dimensions of people's identities such as gender, race, and ethnicity are recognized in other people. Long before debates on multiculturalism and identity politics, Sartre advocated the importance of recognizing the particularities of race, religion, and ethnicity and the need to challenge the hegemony of the dominant groups in society. Ever since their political emancipation throughout Europe, Jews had struggled with the choice between the recognition of their civil rights and the recognition of their right to be different. Sartre challenged the universalist liberalism that erased particularistic social identities and proposed his own "concrete liberalism."[20] He insisted that only "total and sincere" acceptance of a Jew's "character, ... customs, ... tastes, ... religion if he has one, ... name, and ... physical traits"[21] would enable a Jew to live authentically.

Jewish Self-Hatred and Positive Jewishness

Sartre's existentialist model contrasted "authentic Jews" who heroically embraced their Jewishness, even in the face of hostility and opposition, with "inauthentic Jews" who denied or fled from their Jewish identity. Whatever the complex conditions of the situation in which Jews found themselves at different moments of history, they had to make choices that would reflect different understandings of authenticity.

The situation of Jews in America in the postwar period differed considerably from that of the French Jews under Nazi occupation that Sartre had written about. For American Jews, the tremendous loss suffered by the Jewish people during the Holocaust heightened their own anxiety over Jewish survival. In the United States, it was Jewish assimilation, not extermination, that seemed to threaten Jewish survival the most. According to historian Susan Glenn, tensions grew between "advocates of Jewish particularism and nationalism and defenders of liberal universalism and cosmopolitanism," with each side raising questions about the Jewish authenticity of the other side.[22] Those who were convinced that Jewish survival required unquestioned loyalty to the Jewish community and Jewish nationalism (Zionism) focused on the need for "positive Jewishness" to resist social and cultural assimilation. Those who deviated from their vision of a proud, positive assertion of Jewishness were accused of a slavish quest for acceptance by the non-Jewish world at the expense of loyalty to their own people.

At first glance, the accusation against assimilated American Jews sounded more or less like the same problem that Sartre had identified as the inauthenticity of many French Jews. Kurt Lewin, one of the early pioneers of social psychology, introduced the popular and eventually overused concept of "Jewish self-hatred" to explain the resistance of certain elite cultural and intellectual circles of the postwar American Jewish community to the agenda of positive Jewishness. In their defense, these Jewish intellectuals insisted that they were not fleeing or denying Jewishness as much as just offering a more flexible notion of Jewish identity. They questioned any lockstep assumptions of the Jewish community about Judaism or Israel, saw their Jewishness as only a part of a more universal and cosmopolitan identity, and even insisted on the *greater authenticity* of their identities compared to those of the defenders of positive Jewishness. At stake in the Jewish identity war was the question of who could claim the mantle of Sartrean authenticity.

In a 1949 essay titled "The Existence of Jews and Existentialism," Lionel Abel observed that Jewish chauvinism was hardly a guarantee of authenticity: "I think that there are many Jews whom Sartre would have to call authentic, since they insist upon their Jewishness, and are anything but unaware of their situation as Jews; but if the French philosopher observed them as carefully as he has their opposite numbers, the term 'authentic' would not come spontaneously to mind."[23] An article by prominent art critic Clement Greenberg was published in *Commentary* a year later with the title "Self-Hatred and Jewish Chauvinism: Some Reflections on 'Positive Jewishness.'" In it, Greenberg argued that "positive" Jewish identity was potentially just as dangerous and inauthentic as that of so-called self-hating Jews. Greenberg argued that the uncritically chauvinistic Jewish identity regarded by certain Jews as the only form of authentic Jewish identity was in reality quite the opposite. It was a simplistic Jewish identity that was intolerant of the actual diversity and pluralism among Jewish identities, and it paraded the same kind of ethnocentric arrogance that had been displayed by the Nazi persecutors of the Jews just a few years earlier. Greenberg wrote,

> The Jewishness of so many of these "positive" Jews is . . . very sensitive to criticism; . . . it is also aggressive and uncharitable; . . . it . . . has too little patience with conceptions of Jewishness other than its own. . . . Is not Jewish identity, as a mere fact, being made a primary virtue, as the Germans made their Germanness one? Is not a "Jewishness" defined almost entirely in terms of group loyalty and group conformity, and whose only content is its function as differentiation, being elevated as the supreme criterion by which every Jew is to be judged?[24]

Like Sartre, Greenberg rejected essentialist cultural identities and argued for the complexity of identity and its intersecting components. In ways reminiscent of more recent complaints about the blurring of the boundary between Jewish and non-Jewish identity, Greenberg questioned the idea that Jewish identity should crowd out all other aspects of identity. It is clear that his position on the coexistence within individuals of multiple identities and fluid boundaries was more compatible with the Sartrean priority of existence over essence and a model of identity that avoids the assumption of a stable, coherent core to be found within.

In the years after Sartre wrote his essay on authentic and inauthentic Jews, dramatic changes had occurred within worldwide Jewry, in the United States as well as in France, that necessitated a reevaluation of Sartre's original position. In France, some of the most obvious changes included the creation of the state of Israel, with the resultant elevation of Israel as a secular substitute for religion and foundation for Jewish ethnicity; the immigration to France of tens of thousands of Sephardi Jews from North Africa in the late 1950s and 1960s (most with a strong sense of a particular form of Jewish ethnicity); the politicization of French Jewry in the aftermath of the Six-Day War in 1967; and the rise of minority nationalism in France in the period following the upheavals of May 1968.

Judith Friedlander has described how the young Jewish leftists in France who were part of the generation of '68, most of whom had little attachment to Jewish tradition or history, began to reexamine their relationship to their Jewishness.[25] As other ethnic groups within France began to demand recognition of their unique languages and traditions, these Jews began to search for more substantial forms of Jewishness. They rejected the monocultural model of enlightenment democracy that prevailed at the time Sartre had written *Antisemite and Jew* for a more multicultural model that treated the state as an umbrella under which different peoples and languages could flourish.[26] Unlike those who expected the emancipation of the Jews to produce a totally assimilated group, the new generations of Jews gravitated toward a social model that did not require ethnic groups to sacrifice their cultural autonomy as the entrance price to political participation.

The positive recognition of ethnic, racial, linguistic, and religious minorities represented a shift away from a focus on the hostile attitudes of non-Jews that Sartre had described as a central determinant of Jewish identity. The process of recognition now involved not just the external judgment of others but also an internal judgment in which Jews themselves struggle with the Jewishness of other Jews as well as their own. Even when people see themselves and feel themselves to be Jews, that identity will be impacted by the degree to which it is recognized not just by non-Jews but also by other Jews. Where Sartre focused on the power of the antisemite to define the identities of Jews, the debates of Jewish authenticity in the postwar generation and since remind us of the internal struggle for recognition that occurs within and among Jews. In other words, being authentically Jewish may mean choosing the meaning of one's Jewish situation, but this choice will also be influenced by the degree to which particular groups of other Jews recognize that form of Jewishness as legitimate.

In fact, many Jews in the generation after the Holocaust did discover a new comfort in asserting their Jewishness in public, demanding recognition from others, and claiming full political rights. This new situation represented a dramatic change from the strategy that had been recommended by members of the Jewish *haskalah* more than a century earlier who advised Jews to display their authentic Jewish selves only in the privacy of their homes while being more cosmopolitan in public.[27] Of course, as Sartre argued, pretending to be like non-Jews in the public realm could never succeed in an antisemitic world, where Jews were identified as such, regardless of how cosmopolitan they appeared.

Jewish Responses to Sartre:
Albert Memmi, Alain Finkielkraut, and Jacques Derrida

Albert Memmi, a French Tunisian Jew, took Sartre's view of the authentic Jew in a different direction in his 1962 book *Portrait of a Jew*.[28] Memmi agreed with Sartre that it was paramount for Jews to begin with an acknowledgment of their difference, of the challenge of being non-Christians in a Christian world, of always being "outside of the religious world, the culture and the society to which I otherwise belong."[29] Yet Memmi also believed that it was necessary to supplement Sartre's portrait of Jewish victimization with an appreciation of the important positive content of Jewish culture, traditions, and the "reality of Jewish existence."[30] He understood Jewishness as more than just traditional religion. Jewishness, he wrote, "is first of all a collection of facts, conduct, customs, which I find in myself, but especially outside myself, throughout my entire life."[31] It is "a sum total of ways of living, of mental attitudes, of confused riches ... that constitutes a collective way of being."[32] This position was, of course, not so different from what Sartre had said about the range of elements that compose the existential situation within which every person lives their life, but the reality of antisemitism in the 1940s had focused Sartre's attention almost exclusively on the impact of that one factor on the Jews' sense of who they were.

In a sequel, *The Liberation of the Jew*, published four years later, Memmi returned to the problem of living an authentic life as a Jew while always remaining an outsider living among non-Jews. He now argued that the ultimate liberation of Jews and their only chance at authenticity depended on changing their situation as perpetual outsiders. This would only happen when they became the architects of their own national destiny by embracing the Zionist ideal.[33] He wrote, "Only Israel can infuse us with life and restore our full dimensions."[34] Here Memmi suggested that Jewish religious and cultural traditions, ideas, and patterns of thought had become mutilated and "defective" as a result of centuries of oppression and persecution. In addition, he agreed with Sartre that persecution as outsiders in every land where they lived had left the Jewish people searching for something else to hold on to. In response, he said they "held tightly to the myths of their origin which hardened in their clutching hands."[35] That is, their own desperate concept of Jewishness had become constricted and distorted.

In order to restore its "full dimension"—that is, its authenticity—Memmi argued, the Jewish people need to address not only the external oppression imposed on them by others but also their own internalized oppression. Memmi felt that Jewish culture had retreated into a defensive mode that had stifled the kind of experimentation and innovation that was essential for a "living and lively Jewish culture."[36] As a result, he insisted that not only did the Jewish people need to be liberated from external oppressors but Jewish culture needed to be liberated from a moribund tradition. He warned, "The weight of tradition and religion in the life of this collectivity is excessive and harmful. I am convinced that everything is paralyzed, fettered and inhibited by it."[37] Like Sartre, Memmi thought of religious tradition as an understandable compensatory strategy for people who lacked a sense of political, social, and cultural freedom. Only when that freedom was reclaimed would this people be able to resume creative work on their lives and culture.

It was in Zionism's goal of a Jewish homeland that Memmi felt the Jewish people would reclaim authentic life. Only with the normalization of life in their own land could Jews escape from both the external political oppression they experienced in diasporic life and also the internal burden of their own obsolete religious tradition. The new political and cultural freedom of a Jewish homeland would result in a flowering of Jewish creativity and produce new forms of "Jewish collective consciousness" expressed in art, philosophy, literature, sciences, ethics, and politics.[38] Taken all together, these factors would bring about a renaissance of authentically Jewish life.

Alain Finkielkraut, a French Jewish philosopher born in 1949, had grown up in the shadow of Sartre's call for Jews in France to remain authentic in the public affirmation of their Jewishness. His book *The Imaginary Jew* was published nearly forty years after Sartre's *Antisemite and Jew*. In this work, Finkielkraut reflected on the radical shift that had occurred in the expression of Jewish authenticity in his generation. While Sartre had condemned the bad faith of inauthentic Jews who denied or disguised their Jewishness and Memmi found other forms of inauthenticity in Jews who clung to a congealed form of Jewish culture that had been mutilated in response to persecution, Finkielkraut offered a quite different analysis of the dilemma of the Jews.

Finkielkraut confessed to having at one time been seduced by the idea that his Jewishness was some kind of inner defining force, the classic essentialist way of understanding authenticity in peoples, tribes, and nations that had been celebrated by philosophers like Herder. He recalled, "Jewishness coursed through my veins, was my inner truth, my flesh and blood. . . . I was one of the earth's living repositories of the *Jewish spirit* . . . imbued with the sensibility of my people, an authentic part of a larger process, a link in the uninterrupted chain of being, . . . I could therefore do without memory, for Jewishness thought and spoke through me."[39] It seemed so natural and effortless to be authentically Jewish, if only it were true.

The imaginary Jews described by Finkielkraut were quite comfortable being assertively "out" as Jews in public. But he noticed that something else had changed about their Jewishness. For many of them, their Jewishness had become primarily a public identity or role, almost like a kind of masquerade to be paraded and displayed to others. In the privacy of their homes, however, these Jews were just like other people who were not Jewish. Inverting the *haskalah* model, Finkielkraut described the imaginary Jew as someone who is a Jew in public and a cosmopolitan at home. Like the "positive Jews" condemned as inauthentic by Greenberg, the imaginary Jews' insistent affirmation of their Jewishness had become a kind of inauthentic role to play in public rather than a badge of authenticity. The dilemma of these imaginary Jews was not that they, like the assimilated Jews in Sartre's day, were victims of antisemitism who dreamed about what it would be like to be non-Jews. On the contrary, it was that, in many respects, Jews had become culturally indistinguishable from non-Jews. In the privacy of their homes, Jews enjoyed exactly the same consumer goods and tastes as non-Jews. They were making an effort to signal their Jewishness in public in order to help them preserve the appearance of difference and a pedigree of Sartrean authenticity. Yet their Jewishness, observed Finkielkraut, lacked real substance; it was "imaginary."[40]

The Jews of Finkielkraut's generation knew the new frustration of *not being labeled* by antisemites. Turning Sartre on his head, Finkielkraut pointed out that when the Other is indifferent to Jews, Jewishness as difference is annihilated. In this situation, the Jew must strike poses as a Jew to capture the attention and recognition from other people in order to justify their sense of being different. Imaginary Jewishness was neither a religious ideology nor a way of life for Finkielkraut's generation but merely "the repetitive, pretentious and vain proclamation of our alterity,"[41] a feeble attempt to distinguish oneself from the masses.

All of the metaphors that Finkielkraut used to explain this Jewishness conceive it as a contrived, hollow, and inauthentic performance. Jewishness was a masquerade, a hallucination, an ostentation, an imposture, and so on, the function of which was to somehow bridge the gap between "baby-boom comforts and the momentous, terrifying events of the recent past. Through such acts of fictive intensity, we exorcized the vapidity of our lives."[42] Jewishness of this sort is the epitome of Sartrean inauthenticity, Finkielkraut insisted, despite its invocation of Sartre's call for Jewish authenticity.

Echoing Sartre's analysis of human consciousness in *Being and Nothingness*, Finkielkraut describes Jewishness as both memory of the past and simultaneous rupture from it. Paradoxically, post-Holocaust memory connects Jews to a Jewish past, but it also confronts them with images of what they are not, what they can no longer be, and what they must move beyond.[43] Like Sartre, he rejected the possibility of finding what was authentically Jewish in essentialist categories that Jews have identified with. This is because Jewishness cannot be "arrested or frozen into nationality or religion."[44] Returning to a kind of Sartrean existentialism—in which human existence precedes any essential qualities of human nature, Finkielkraut notes with some satisfaction that "the Jewish people don't know what they are, only that they exist."[45]

If Sartre's indictment of assimilated French Jews of the 1940s was a snapshot of a particularly dark moment in French history, Finkielkraut's indictment of the hollowness of the Jewish posturing of postwar French Jews demonstrates a dramatic generational shift in the existential situation of this group of Jews during a period of postwar prosperity. His description of the Jews of his generation is surely limited, since not all of them had lost a sense of connection to Yiddishkeit and Jewish tradition and replaced it with a hollow quest for recognition of their Jewish difference. Yet there is no denying that Finkielkraut experienced something different from the Jews Sartre had observed. Jews no longer stood against a monolithic, dominant culture bent on either absorbing or destroying them. Instead, the division between "us" and "them" became harder to draw since the defining characteristics of "us" and of "them" had begun to blur. The heterogeneity of both "us" and "them" makes alterity an intergroup as well as intragroup phenomenon.

Finkielkraut's analysis is ultimately less a critique of Sartre's approach to Jewish authenticity than it is an account of how the axes of authenticity from one period can shift, congeal, and produce the opposite of their intended effect in another period. But this does not mean that the goal of authenticity is now untenable. Indeed, Sartre would likewise have been disappointed at the way in which his exhortation to authenticity had been transformed into its opposite.

Despite his critique of Shoah-centric Jewish identity as a parody of Sartrean authenticity, Finkielkraut nonetheless reinscribed a Sartrean model of authenticity when he talked about his own Jewishness as "the acute consciousness of a lack, of a continuous absence: my exile from a civilization which, 'for my own good,' my parents didn't wish me to keep in trust."[46] At some level, the cultural identity of pre-Holocaust Jews was no longer tenable, not just because it had been destroyed by the Nazis, but because of the essentialist temptations it presented. It was not simply a matter of his parents failing to teach him about Jewish culture. It was the impossibility of any authentic adhesion to a cultural identity. Authentic Jewishness for Finkielkraut was an existential enigma, an unfinished work that refused to be "encompassed by a stable and recognized concept."[47] He rejected the idea that an authentic Jewish identity could be built around either the lost culture of Europe's slaughtered Jews or a preoccupation with that loss. Like Sartre, Finkielkraut refused to give Jewishness any "unequivocal and precise content"[48] or to advocate a return to religious or nationalistic forms of identity. Finkielkraut wrote,

> To nationalize Judaism, or better yet, to make it a church, is to arrest it, in the sense of freezing a changing process or interrogating a smuggler who makes cross-border runs. It is thus to make Judaism subject, under the pretext of bringing our life and discourse into harmony, to the police state and its regime. Restrict the word *Jew* to a single truth and there we are: suddenly capable of judging, categorizing, classifying and finally diminishing those who don't conform to our idea of our common bond. . . . There are no phony Jews: there are only authentic inquisitors.[49]

Like the advocates of positive Jewishness, those who claimed to be authentic Jews had too often taken an oppressive role toward other Jews who may define their Jewishness in different ways. For Finkielkraut, it was a sure sign of inauthentic Jewishness and authentic injustice when some Jews claimed the authority to police the Jewishness of others and to declare who are the "real Jews" and who are the "phony Jews." Of course, in his own way, he was doing precisely the same thing.

Unfortunately, claims about authenticity regarding members of religious, ethnic, or national groups inevitably come down to establishing borders and boundaries that determine who is in and who is out. Finkielkraut suggests that Judaism needs its "smugglers" to maintain its vitality and creativity. Boundaries are places where questions of deviance, hybridity, change, and innovation are continually negotiated and redefined and where the provisional canons of authenticity expand and contract in response to the historical circumstances of the moment. Often, it is the smugglers who represent the vanguard of emergent understandings of authenticity.

Like Sartre, Finkielkraut wanted to avoid the dangers of any essentialist definitions of Jewish culture, religion, or peoplehood that foreclose the continuous process of change. He struggled with the fundamental paradox in the nature of cultural tradition. As anthropologists Richard Handler and Jocelyn Linnekin note, "Traditions are neither genuine nor spurious, for if genuine tradition refers to the pristine and immutable heritage of the past, then all genuine traditions are spurious. But if . . . tradition is always defined in the present, then all spurious traditions are genuine."[50] It is not that all claims of authenticity are necessarily suspect, just that one must conceptualize authenticity in a particular way that will recognize the dynamic instability of identities and cultures. Finkielkraut ultimately returned to a Sartrean perspective when he concluded, "Judaism's very lack of definition is precious: it shows that political categories of class or of nation have only a relative truth, and stands as a sign of their inability to encompass the world in its totality. The Jewish people don't know who they are, only that they exist, and that their disconcerting existence blurs the boundary, inaugurated by modern reason, between the public and the private."[51] In his rejection of essentialist authenticity, Finkielkraut reclaims an existential form of Jewishness based on the paradoxical situation that he both *is* a Jew and *is not* a Jew: "The word *Jew* is no longer a mirror in which I seek my self-portrait, but where I look for everything I'm not, everything I'll never be able to glimpse by taking myself as a point of reference."[52] Finkielkraut found himself in the postmodern situation in which it was impossible to "be Jewish" in a simple way. Jewishness transcended and exceeded who he was, but he likewise transcended and exceeded it. His sense of Jewishness could be neither fixed nor stable. It remained indeterminate and to some degree undefined. As Sartre had suggested, cultural identities must remain open and fluid to protect against the dangerous tendency to absolutize or essentialize them.

The question Finkielkraut raised was what authenticity would look like in a world not of antisemitism but of assimilation and acceptance, a world where Jews participate in the wider culture, blurring the boundaries between what is distinctively Jewish and what is not.[53] People in modern society, including Jews, are increasingly consumers rather than preservers of their cultural traditions. They live in a condition that includes both continuity and discontinuity with the past. It is for this reason that Sartre emphasized the philosophical puzzle that identity is never really "identical" with itself: Every human life is defined by that "which is what it is not, and which is not what it is."[54]

By this, Sartre meant to call attention to the idea that any statement about identity was merely tentative and already outdated, since we are always moving beyond that statement about what we are, transcending who we were a moment earlier. Because we are always more than what we have been up until this moment, it can be said that we *are not* what we *are*. This power of uprooting ourselves from the given moment as we reinterpret it and reintegrate it in new ways also means that we are always in a process of becoming—that is, who we *are* is really what we *are not* (yet). For Finkielkraut, as for Sartre, this means that the politics of identity need to be careful of reifying cultures and ethnicities into tightly bounded entities that can become imprisoning.

Like Sartre's own analysis of Jewish inauthenticity in the 1940s, Finkielkraut's critique of the inauthenticity of "imaginary" Jewishness among French Jews in the 1970s was a snapshot of a particular cohort of Jews during a certain period of history. He framed this snapshot against a postmodern understanding of Jewish authenticity highlighting the indeterminacy, absence, and rupture at the core of his Jewishness that left him adrift from his parents' personal experience of both Jewish tradition and the trauma of the Holocaust.

In 1980, the same year that Finkielkraut published *The Imaginary Jew*, a terrorist bomb set off at the Rue Copérnic Synagogue in Paris marked a new dramatic shift underway in the attitudes of French Jews and their approach to Jewishness. Antisemitic violence was now a clear and present danger, not a hazy memory from the previous generation. Unlike the assimilated Ashkenazi French Jews described by Finkielkraut, about half of all the Jews in France were immigrants from former French colonies in North Africa, and an overall majority of French Jews were

Sephardi.[55] These Jews tended to be more religious and traditional than other French Jews, and they therefore helped fuel a revitalization of Jewish culture that was neither imaginary nor empty, combined with a more muscular assertion of their political power as Jews, and a passionate support for Israel that had been incubated during their time living in Arab countries. These factors combined to produce a return to the kind of essentialist view of both Jewish religious tradition and ethnicity that Finkielkraut had pronounced dead.[56]

Finally, it is worth mentioning the reaction of Jacques Derrida to Sartre's analysis of Jewish authenticity and inauthenticity. Derrida was one of the most important French philosophers in the latter part of the twentieth century, rising in importance at the same time that the impact of Sartre and existentialism was waning. Although Derrida was born nearly twenty years before Finkielkraut, it was not until twenty years after Finkielkraut's *Imaginary Jew* was published, and half a century after Sartre wrote *Antisemite and Jew*, that Derrida directly responded to Sartre's description of different forms of Jewish identity in relation to his own sense of what it meant to be Jewish.

In a conference presentation in 2000 titled "Abraham, the Other," Derrida expressed both muted appreciation for Sartre's work on the situation of French Jews in the 1940s as well as serious misgivings.[57] On the one hand, he recalled his childhood in Algeria, where his earliest experiences of being Jewish were filtered through the lens of antisemitism. His first association of the term *Jew* as a name applied to him was as "an insult, a wound, and an injustice, a denial of right rather than the right to belong to a legitimate group."[58] It was a label imposed on him by others before he had any idea what it meant, just as Sartre had identified the antisemites' power to define Jews as Jews.

As Derrida shifted to his present sense of being Jewish, however, he strongly distanced himself from what he understood to be Sartre's position on inauthentic and authentic Jews. Although he complained that Sartre had reduced Jews to a fixed essence and established an unmanageable binary of authentic and inauthentic Jews, his description of his own Jewishness nonetheless traced some of the outlines of Sartre's fiercely antiessentialist suggestions about Jewishness. Using a dizzying display of the wordplay, paradoxes, and contradictions for which he is famous, Derrida emphasized a form of Jewishness that kept traditional religious, ethnic, or nationalist forms of identity at arm's length. His goal was to express a way of being Jewish without being Jewish, to affirm his Jewishness without affirming any stable form, without claiming either authenticity or inauthenticity, without determining any borders between what is authentic and what is inauthentic. It remains permanently destabilized by the perspectives of others who are beyond control and by the uncertainty of what is not yet and always unforeseeable. Derrida concluded with a nonconclusion: "I insist on presenting myself as a Jew, on saying and on declaring myself [*à dire et à me dire*] 'I am jew,' neither authentic nor inauthentic nor quasi-authentic, given that I do not know what I mean, that I could criticize, disavow, 'deconstruct' everything that I might mean, and that I suspect so many Jews more authorized than I am of not knowing any better than I do?"[59] Yet paradoxically, this act of simply declaring himself a Jew while rejecting any simple explanations of what that might mean is itself a kind of authentically Jewish position. As Sartre explains at the end of *Antisemite and Jew*, "Jewish authenticity consists in choosing oneself *as Jew* . . . the authentic Jew *makes himself a Jew*."[60] Crucially, Sartre says that in this moment of self-declaration "the Jew, like any authentic man, escapes description."[61]

The abandonment of essentialist views of Jewishness and Jewish authenticity has opened up a new situation in which a person's identity can be considered "authentically Jewish" when it recognizes the shifting and unstable foundation on which it rests. Philosopher Joseph Margolis described his own dislocated Jewish identity in a way that embodies the inner contradictions in being "authentically Jewish." Reminiscent of Sartre, Finkielkraut, and Derrida's perspectives on being Jewish, Margolis observed, "I am pleased to be a Jew because I am not one; and I am not one because I really am one."[62] In this cryptic sentence, Margolis suggests that one can be a Jew only by realizing that one cannot *be* a Jew in an *essentialist* sense. He sees himself as authentically ("really") Jewish because he is not willing to accept such assumptions that may lie behind traditional views of Jewishness. Similarly, cultural critic Maria Damon offers a similar description of her own sense of being authentically Jewish as intertwined with the process of deconstructing that Jewishness. She writes, "The kind of Jew I am is the kind who isn't sure what kind of Jew she is. . . . This doesn't mean dwelling in permanent inadequacy, performance anxiety, and self-erasure, though these can be useful if uncomfortable temporary positions. Rather, by looking for the clues, the words, I move, not toward a whole picture, but further into the complexities of 'becoming Jewish.'"[63]

Recognition, Multiculturalism, and Authenticity

Although Sartre's idea of "concrete liberalism" was only crudely sketched in his analysis of the Jewish situation in France in the 1940s, he established an important link between authenticity and recognition at a time when little attention was being paid to oppressed groups in society. He laid the foundation for understanding not only the discriminatory and oppressive power of recognition rooted in racist, religious, and nationalist chauvinism of people like the antisemites in France but also the redemptive power of reciprocal recognition.

Half a century later, the issue of recognition became a central concern of philosophers in their discussions of the increasing cultural, ethnic, racial, and even gender diversity within contemporary societies. Rather than encouraging and supporting a single homogeneous standard for everyone, usually based on the cultural ideas and values of historically dominant or hegemonic groups, supporters of multiculturalism emphasized the importance of both recognition and celebration of the diversity of ethnic, cultural, and linguistic identities within society as not only a valuable social resource but also a right to which members of various groups are entitled.

Like Sartre, contemporary philosophers such as Charles Taylor, Will Kymlicka, and others argued that liberal ideals about the universal rights of individual citizens have often failed to protect groups who have been marginalized in society because of differences in their language, ethnicity, religion, or race. In order to reverse previous patterns of discrimination and exclusion based on cultural, ethnic, and racial differences, they advocated that such differences be recognized within the political system with an attitude of appreciation, legitimization, and support for who people "really are."[64] Taylor's goal, like Sartre's, aims at protecting the nondominant groups that contribute to the cultural diversity of every society. For each of these groups, the possibility of appreciative recognition is a crucial part of identity, which emerges only in relationship to others. As Taylor writes, "We define our identity always in dialogue with, sometimes in struggle against, the things our significant others want to see in us"[65] When one's cultural identity as a member of a group is recognized, one enjoys the integration of one's own sense of identity with the respect of others. Alternatively, the failure to recognize the values and traditions of cultural, ethnic, or religious groups is a violation of the integrity of the group and its right to be who it really is.

The call for recognition of the particularities of who people "really are" represents an important stage in the development of identity. Psychologist Erik Erikson, one of the foremost theorists of identity, observed that the foundation of a secure sense of identity rests on experiences of mutual recognition in which a person "can *recognize* himself and feel *recognized*" not only as an individual but also as a member of his or her ethnic, national, and cultural groups.[66] This experience of recognition occurs in relationship to outsiders, who offer recognition to those who are different from themselves, and also in relationship to other members of the same group, whose recognition signifies shared membership in the group.

While the Jewish people sees itself as a single community on some levels, it is also a group with considerable racial, ethnic, cultural, linguistic, and religious diversity. Questions about recognizing what is authentically Jewish in relationship to any of these dimensions have often come up, and there is disagreement about the content or boundaries of Jewish culture, religion, tradition, or peoplehood. This results in the impossibility of establishing any set of specific characteristics or standards that represent the sine qua non of Jewishness. Any declaration of what is authentically Jewish assumes not only the power and authority to authenticate or recognize qualities and degrees of Jewishness but also the power to contest or reject others who claim such authority. As a result, the process of recognition necessarily remains unsettled and subject to ongoing negotiation and redefinition.

Critics of multiculturalism have often warned that recognition of different ethnic, linguistic, religious, or racial groups runs the risk of exaggerating the degree of homogeneity in a group's expression of its culture and of justifying "repressive demands for communal conformity."[67] A particular group may see itself as the true owners and guardians of a preexisting package of cultural traditions, practices, and values that individuals receive from their ancestors, care for during their lives, and pass on to the next generation. Such an approach places the focus on authenticity squarely in the past. According to Brenda Lyshaug, "It encourages individuals to live as if by the permission of their ancestors—or of leaders who claim to speak for their ancestors."[68] It means that different factions will work to achieve allegiance and obedience to their particular worldview and version of tradition and values, and to stigmatize unauthorized change or innovations as evidence of disloyalty, apostasy, or treason.

There are two different kinds of recognition that unfold among the many internal factions, sects, and subcultures within the Jewish people. On the one hand, recognition is an affirmation that certain people or groups who claim to be Jews are accepted by other groups of Jews as belonging within the boundaries of "us." We are all fellow Jews. On the other hand, recognition can also represent a judgment about the particular form of Jewish cultural or religious difference found in a certain Jew or group of Jews. In this case, recognition is about whether certain differences are considered acceptable, legitimate, and authentic.

Relations between various Jewish sects or denominations have always been fraught with controversies about who and what is recognized as authentically Jewish in the second sense. Orthodox Jews have often walked a narrow line between the first-level recognition of non-Orthodox Jews as Jews and a refusal of the second level of recognition—that is, acknowledging another form of Jewishness as legitimate. Thus in many cases, Orthodox Jews will recognize the abstract Jewish status of non-Orthodox Jews but not the concrete form of Jewishness they embody or embrace. Disputes between Orthodox and liberal Jews are paradigmatic of the conflict between the defenders of tradition and the advocates of reform that are likely to be found in any culture. If it is not possible, except by arbitrary declaration, to define the essence of Jewish culture, then we can expect changes to arise in response to various new social, political, and historical conditions that result in multiple ways of living a "culturally authentic life."[69] These changes will often reclaim strands of tradition "that have been marginalized, suppressed, or misconstrued by the dominant interpretation of their tradition."[70]

Sartre's aphorism that "in choosing myself, I choose man" was earlier cited as a template for a nonessentialist view of the Jewish cultural identity that says, "In choosing myself as a Jew, I choose the Jewish people." The purpose of this formulation is to shift the understanding of authenticity from a kind of reproduction of the past in the present within a group identity that is fixed or stable and shared uniformly by all Jews. Rather, authenticity is understood here as continually generated and renewed when the past is reclaimed through the agency and performance of individual Jewish people in the present. This understanding of authenticity as a dynamic process in the present must also include the fluid and changing nature of recognition as well.

Jewish cultural, religious, and ethnic identity emerges as a result of the actions and attitudes that people take in relation to their personal and group history, the shifting recognitions they are offered by others both outside and within their group, and the retrospective narratives they tell and are told that orient them to the world and people around them. Just as people's own relationship to the past is subject to revision and change, the recognition of their created identities is also an open-ended, unstable, and inconclusive process, since, as Patchen Markell describes, "all exchanges of recognition will tend to become obsolete as our identities shift over time and this would seem to deny the possibility of a *finally* satisfactory regime of recognition."[71] In other words, Markell argues, recognition is not simply a rubber stamp of approval placed on fully formed cultures and identities that were already there.[72] Rather it serves as a partner, along with individuals' own meaning-making process, which helps constitute the very identities on which it is focused. Authenticity therefore lies not in excavating and displaying some inner core of a person or group but in grasping the actively creative aspects of reciprocal recognition. A person's identity, says Markell, is the result of "ongoing and risky interactions through which we become who we are (or, more precisely, who we will turn out to have been)."[73]

In many situations, recognition occurs within a hierarchical relationship in which the more powerful party offers recognition to the weaker one, leaving the recognizer's identity intact and unchallenged. But recognition can have more radical implications. Drawing on the work of Nancy Fraser, Markell describes how some forms of recognition can be transformative for both the recognized and the recognizer. This happens when recognition of a different way of expressing Jewishness has an effect that destabilizes both parties' identities; highlights the reality of "multiple, debinarized, fluid, ever-shifting differences"; and allows for new conceptualizations and structures for identity.[74]

As much as people may seek to build their identities on what they understand to be authentically Jewish, any final imprimatur of authenticity remains out of reach, subject to the shifting parameters of recognition. Markell describes recognition as a dynamic and changing process: "If we cannot do without the bonds of recognition, we also cannot do without the dark space between recognitions, which is the space of movement, of actions, and of life."[75] Erich Fromm warned that the temptation to seek the comfortable security of full identification with a tribe, nation, race, religion, or ideology is an unconscious effort to recreate the familiarity and safety offered to children by their families. Yet he sees what is most authentically Jewish in the need to leave the "familiar" and to break the "ties of blood and soil."[76] Accepting the permanence of changes in customs and beliefs includes cycles of always embracing what David Hansen calls "leaving *and* remaining at home," balancing a sense of tradition and roots with an acceptance of the inevitability of change and a desire to absorb new traditions.[77]

The determination of what is authentically Jewish is always provisional, found at the intersection of the three factors that have been discussed, no one of which is sufficient. First, the situation of being a Jew, including its histories and traditions; second, the "making real" of that situation; and third, the dance of reciprocal recognition between Jews and other Jews as well as between Jews and non-Jews.

PART II
AUTHENTICALLY JEWISH RELIGION

3 Orthodoxy and the Authentic Jew

The echoes of Sartre's focus on Jewish authenticity that had inspired a postwar generation of Jews in France continued to reverberate among Jewish audiences in the United States and elsewhere, and the language of authenticity permeated discussions between different Jewish religious and political factions. In 1948, *Commentary Magazine* published a three-part series of translated excerpts from Sartre's analysis of Jews and antisemites. As existentialism's popularity grew, Sartre's categories of authenticity and inauthenticity in regard to Jewish identity became more familiar and common. While the "search for authenticity" would come to be a guiding principle for new innovative, countercultural approaches to Jewish tradition and observance in the 1960s and 1970s, such as the Jewish renewal movement, others had also turned to the language of authenticity and declared the search for it was over. Or rather, a search had never really been necessary since, for anyone who took the time to look, authentically Jewish life was available where it always had been, in the beliefs and practices of traditional Orthodox Judaism.

In 1961, an Orthodox rabbi from Chicago named Leonard Gewirth published *The Authentic Jew and His Judaism*.[1] Without mentioning Sartre's name, Gewirth borrowed Sartre's portrait of a Jew who denies, disguises, or apologizes for his Jewishness. Gewirth described the fear and anxiety some Jews felt about being identified as Jews. Their inability to accept who they really were and their attempts to flee from the embarrassment of being Jewish by assimilating had earned them the label "self-hating."

In addition to these inauthentic Jews, Gewirth also mentioned Jews who wanted to pray in English, without a hat or *talis*; who did not observe the rules for kosher food; and who abandoned anything that seemed nationalistic, parochial, or foreign.[2] These liberal Jews, Gewirth warned, were "tainted Jews" who appealed to "the universal spirit of Judaism" and modern rationality as excuses for shedding any distinctive Jewish customs.[3] For Gewirth, their practice of a corrupted and inauthentic form of Judaism made them little better than the inauthentic Jews who ran away from their Jewishness in all forms.

Gewirth's model of authenticity was hierarchical. The lowest form of authenticity was biological and only required acceptance of the fact that one had been born Jewish. Next came sociological authenticity, which referred to whether a person embraced a sense of Jewish ethnic belonging with other Jews. But the highest form of authenticity was religious. Here Gewirth's focus shifted from the attitudes and behavior of Jews to their actual conception of Judaism. Authenticity as a Jew, he insisted, required more than just openly accepting the fact of one's Jewish birth, expressing a sense of Jewish belonging, or practicing a "tainted" form of Judaism.

What makes someone an authentic Jew is the fact that he or she observes "authentic Judaism," the kind that accepts the rabbinical authorities and texts of Orthodox Judaism, especially the divinely ordained religious commandments enshrined in Jewish religious law, known as halakha. By rejecting this authority or trying to adapt Judaism to contemporary culture, Reform Jews, no matter how committed or sincere they might be, would never escape from inauthenticity. In its simplest form, Gewirth's presentation effectively made the term *Orthodox* synonymous with "authentic." It was clear that Orthodox Judaism alone was authentic Judaism and that the only authentic Jews were Orthodox Jews.

Fackenheim's 614th Commandment

Appealing to the popularity of existentialism and its focus on authenticity, Jewish philosopher and theologian Emil Fackenheim suggested in a 1967 essay titled "The 614th Commandment" that the search for Jewish authenticity needed to come to terms with the reality of living in a world that had recently witnessed the Nazis' genocidal attack on European Jewry. To be an "authentic Jew," he wrote, required "authentic understanding" of the Jewish situation and "authentic responses" to a world that had placed Jewish survival in jeopardy.[4] Echoing Sartre's description of Jewish authenticity, Fackenheim insisted that people who were authentically Jewish, regardless of whether they were religious or secular Jews, would adopt "a stubborn persistence" in their Jewishness and reject any attempt "to abandon it or escape from it."[5] For Fackenheim, Jewish authenticity rested on an obligation shared by all Jews, believer or agnostic, which he called the "614th commandment"—that is, a new commandment beyond the 613 of traditional Judaism.

Since Hitler had aimed at the annihilation of all Jews, Fackenheim argued, any Jews who willingly abandoned their Jewishness were contributing to Hitler's "posthumous victory" and dishonoring the memory of his victims. Thus the paramount form of resistance to Hitler's posthumous success had to include two elements: "First, a commitment to Jewish survival; and second, a commitment to Jewish unity."[6] Fackenheim suggested that such a commitment to Jewish group survival, even in the absence of traditional religious commitment, could still serve as a "profound, albeit as yet fragmentary, act of faith" that rejected any tendency toward despair about the future of the Jewish people or any desire to flee from Jewishness and association with the Jewish people.[7]

The arc of Fackenheim's appeal for Jewish authenticity ultimately bent toward a reaffirmation of God and Jewish tradition. Fackenheim acknowledged that religious Jews could not find authenticity by hiding in the world of a premodern ghetto, pretending that traditional Judaism could continue with business as usual while ignoring the radically transformative events that had shattered that premodern world. Nonetheless, it was secular, nonreligious Jews who, Fackenheim hoped, would both hear and respond to the 614th commandment in a way that engaged with "the religious resources of the Jewish past."

Fackenheim invoked the Sartrean emphasis on Jewish authenticity as a form of self-affirmation, but he transformed it by mixing in traditional Jewish religious rhetoric about binding new "commandments" that ultimately originate in the "commanding voice" of God. The agnostic who "hears" the 614th commandment to survive as a Jew but does not discern its divine source has not heard the fullness of the command.[8] True authenticity for Fackenheim required the defeat of Hitler's goal of Jewish annihilation by not only reaffirming membership in the Jewish people but also recommitting to Judaism's vision of a divinely ordered world that resists the ethical void represented by Auschwitz.

Although Fackenheim appreciated the importance of the freedom people can exercise in giving meaning to the particular historical situation into which each of them is born, he also was convinced that the instability and insecurity of the meaning of history was nonetheless an opportunity for encountering the timeless and absolute reality of God. Ultimately, his model of authentic Jewish life was an appeal to secular Jews to reach across the gulf created by the Holocaust to encounter a divine source of meaning.

In an essay published in *Commentary* in 1960, Fackenheim argued that liberal Judaism could not make claims to authenticity without recognizing the authority and authenticity of Jewish tradition. He insisted that the sense of personal authenticity that is expressed in individual determinations of Jewish meaning must yield to the higher authenticity of tradition. Fackenheim backed away from existentialist freedom and criticized liberal Jews' insistence on their freedom to "arbitrarily pick and choose from the Jewish past." By doing so, their religious practice reflected the trends of the present moment, but not necessarily the "spirit of Judaism."[9] For Fackenheim, any possible authenticity that might be associated with the religion of liberal Jews required that they grant ultimate authority to "the Jewish past." And if the past is to have authority to which one must conform, it must be more than a human invention; it must be an expression of "the authority of God."[10]

Fackenheim tried to offer an alternative to the choices of either passive submission to the authority of the past (which he associated with Orthodoxy) or the subordination of past religious and moral values to present-day standards (which was the approach of liberal Jews).[11] He hoped that there might be an authentic path that involved what he called a "genuine encounter" with the past, in which the past is judged and interpreted through the lens of the present and the present is simultaneously interpreted through the perspectives of the past. Despite Fackenheim's effort to respect a desire for expressive or existential authenticity, his approach to liberal Jews retained an insistence on traditional Jewish norms and traditions, and he stopped short of recognizing the kinds of pluralistic approaches to Judaism that many liberal Jews might be seeking. Though he himself was a Reform rabbi, Fackenheim thought the authenticity expressed by the 614th commandment might be a meeting ground between Orthodox and liberal Jews.

Orthodox Rejection of Non-Orthodox Jewish Authenticity

Major Orthodox religious leaders have shared Fackenheim's focus on the urgency of Jewish survival, but their overwhelming attention always returned to their insistence on Orthodox Judaism as the only feasible path to Jewish authenticity. One particularly prolific spokesperson on behalf of Orthodox Judaism has been Rabbi Jonathan Sacks, who served as the chief rabbi in the United Kingdom from 1991 to 2013. Like Rabbi Gewirth and many others, he described Jewish authenticity as multidimensional, related to the hybrid nature of Jewishness as both a set of religious beliefs and practices and also a biological or ethnic sense of peoplehood based on shared kinship.[12] For a fully authentic Jew, both elements were ideally intertwined, and the fact of having been born a Jew automatically triggered a binding obligation to accept certain fundamental principles about divine authority and revelation, Jewish halakha, and the traditions of rabbinic interpretation.[13]

In Sack's view, neither membership in the Jewish people nor the obligation to follow Jewish law are matters of individual choice or personal interpretation. The major purpose of Jewish halakha is to establish boundaries between what is acceptable for Jews and what is not, what is authentically Jewish and what is not. These boundaries predate and transcend any individual preferences. Sacks wrote, "Not everything can count as a legitimate interpretation of faith or practice. Were it otherwise, Judaism would have no substantive content as the religion of a people."[14] The only real choice confronting a Jew is whether or not "to understand tradition *in the traditional way*, as objective truth and external authority,"[15] which establishes the roles, duties, and responsibilities that come with being born as a member of the Jewish people.[16] Thus Sacks's understanding of authenticity rests on the acceptance of a normative and authoritative tradition that preexists one's birth, that is dutifully expressed and preserved in the lives of those who are authentically Jewish, and that thereby is passed down from one generation to another. It is very much an essentialist model of authenticity, focused on conformity with the relatively unchanging practices of previous generations as mediated by a select group of religious authorities.

The Orthodox commitment to the authority of Jewish law as enshrined in the teachings of the rabbis of the Talmud and present-day Orthodox authorities rules out any admission of legitimacy for non-Orthodox denominations as different forms of Judaism alongside Orthodox Judaism. Sacks wrote, "There is no validity to any Judaism that denies halakhic authority and fundamental beliefs. There are no denominations. Orthodoxy is not just 'one version of Judaism among others.'"[17] In rejecting the possibility of religious pluralism or diversity outside of Orthodoxy, the idea of nonhalakhic Judaism is simply excluded as an oxymoronic impossibility, lacking in any truth, authority, or authenticity.[18]

The tension between Orthodox and liberal Jews, for Sacks, is a result of their conflicting models of the self. He notes that Orthodox Judaism is still governed by the premodern view that the individual self is composed of a set of specific duties, roles, and responsibilities. If Judaism is a predetermined set of obligations, based on revealed laws, into which one is born, then individual choice is irrelevant. Authenticity is judged by factors that are external and prior to the self.

The enemy of Jewish authenticity for Sacks is the importance that modernity has placed on individual autonomy and personal meaning-making in the world, the "sovereign self" that Steven Cohen and Arnold Eisen described as the final creator and judge of authenticity for many contemporary American Jews. This has resulted in non-Orthodox interpretations of Jewish tradition that treat authenticity as a quality of the self rather than a characteristic emanating from divine revelations from the past.[19] This shift has blurred the boundaries between what is and what is not agreed upon as authentically Jewish. In Sacks's view, the autonomous self and its elevation of the individual commitment to being true to oneself makes it not only incompatible with but also hostile to Jewish authenticity. It represents "the archetypal biblical vice." Indeed, by defining expressive or existential authenticity only in terms of the authority of one's own inner self, any authority Orthodox tradition might have to demand obedience is completely nullified. It is no wonder that forms of Judaism that do not recognize the Orthodox model of halakhic Judaism are rejected by Sacks as both objectively and normatively inauthentic. Sacks explains, "From the perspective of the autonomous self, then, halakhic existence is inauthentic because it flees from making personal choice the center of its universe. From the perspective of tradition, much of contemporary ethics is inauthentic precisely *because* it makes personal choice the measure of all things."[20] To be sure, liberal Judaism, like modern individualism in general, may provide opportunities for the expression of personal authenticity, Sacks suggests. It just is not authentically Jewish.

While Orthodox Jewish leaders refuse to recognize the religious beliefs and practices of non-Orthodox Jews as an authentic form of Judaism, they do recognize the possible authenticity of non-Orthodox Jews *as Jews*. This description of non-Orthodox Jews as authentically Jewish people who practice a religion that is not Judaism is the result of differences in the halakhic requirements for ascribing Jewish status to an individual person, in contrast to the rules which determine what is necessary for religious beliefs and practices to be considered authentically Jewish. The birth of a non-Orthodox Jew to a Jewish mother meets the halakhic requirement for the recognition of Jewish status, even when the actual religious practice of the family can be dismissed as invalid—that is, not authentically Jewish—if it does not follow halakhic standards. Of course, this determination assumes that the lineage of the Jewish mother goes back unbroken to a time when earlier ancestors observed Orthodox halakha. Any non-Orthodox conversions in the maternal line would theoretically throw the Jewish authenticity of all subsequent generations into doubt. On a practical level, this splitting of the Jewish authenticity of a person from the authenticity of their religion enables Orthodoxy to uphold the idea of a single Jewish *people* without acknowledging any legitimacy to non-Orthodox views of Judaism.

While such a position might seem like a reasonable compromise from an Orthodox perspective, Sacks does acknowledge that non-Orthodox Jews can be expected to resent an Orthodox approach that seems both condescending and offensive in its delegitimizing of their religious beliefs and practices: "It is a strategy of which the non-Orthodox Jews might understandably not wish to avail themselves. Explicitly or implicitly, they will feel that it assaults their authenticity."[21] Indeed, liberal Jews may feel less than appreciative when an Orthodox rabbi describes Reform and

Conservative Judaism as "diluted, halakha-less, mitzvah-less movements" lacking in "genuine Torah and authentic yahadut" but reassures them that "None of this is meant to deny that those who call themselves Conservative or Reform are anything less than our brother Jews."[22] A simpler, though somewhat tautological, solution would be to say that the non-Orthodox approach to Judaism is not *Orthodox* Judaism rather than insisting that it is not Judaism at all. Of course, such a solution is impossible if non-Orthodox Judaism is regarded as an offense to the essence of true Judaism.

There are a variety of ways offered by Orthodox leaders to soften their refusal to recognize non-Orthodox forms of Judaism as legitimate or authentic. For example, Rabbi Sacks makes the distinction that even though non-Orthodox beliefs are heretical, the liberal and secular Jews who hold them are not heretics: "The beliefs remain heretical; but those who believe them are not heretics, for they do not ultimately or culpably believe them. Liberal and secular Jews remain Jews, even though neither liberal nor secular Judaism is Judaism."[23] He offers to include non-Orthodox Jews as members of the Jewish people without granting any recognition of their form of religion as authentic Judaism by taking advantage of a halakhic technicality to explain why non-Orthodox Jews "do not ultimately or culpably believe" in their particular form of "heretical" Judaism.

Rabbinic literature describes a variety of kinds of Jewish heresies, as well as serious consequences for those holding them. But it is possible to exonerate non-Orthodox Jews, despite their heretical religion, if they are considered to be lacking a deliberate and knowing rejection of Orthodox ideas and beliefs. How can that be, one might ask, considering that it is precisely the freedom claimed by modern Jews to decide the form and meaning of their religious practice, without regard to halakha, that Sacks described as "the archetypal Biblical vice"?[24] Yet Sacks and other Orthodox figures have enlisted an exculpatory fiction that implies that the non-Orthodox are simply ignorant of the truth, and they therefore cannot be held responsible for their mistaken ideas.

The legal analogy often used is one that considers Reform and Conservative Jews according to the principle of "children taken captive by heathens" and raised in a heathen religion. In such cases, the children involved remain Jews, even though the religion they have been taught is not Judaism. If non-Orthodox Jews have grown up in environments that taught them wrong ideas, then, like kidnapped children, they are still Jews who should not be held responsible for their heretical ideas. But comparing non-Orthodox Jews to children kidnapped by heathens hardly seems like an improvement over simply calling them heretics directly. For it implies that the parents and teachers who taught them heretical forms of Judaism are essentially heathens who have spiritually kidnapped innocent children. This framework is offensive for different reasons, not the least being that it refuses to take seriously the personal decision non-Orthodox Jews have made to create a different form of Jewish practice.

The essentialist model of Jewish tradition upheld by Orthodox Jews like Rabbi Sacks makes it impossible to conceive of the Jewish people as a multicultural group in which there is broad acceptance and recognition of diverse forms of Jewish life as legitimate expressions of the cultural and religious identities of the various Jews who hold them. This is because the differences between Orthodox and non-Orthodox perspectives on Jewish tradition are not just cultural or historical but also theological. If the fundamental beliefs and laws on which Orthodox tradition rests are taken to be true in an eternal, supernatural way, it becomes impossible to tolerate, much less legitimate, other Jewish religious perspectives that do not recognize the authority of Jewish law as understood by Orthodox Judaism.

Seventy Faces of Torah

Another way of softening the rejection of the authenticity of liberal Judaism has been offered by Norman Lamm, former chancellor of Yeshiva University. First, Lamm denied that Judaism is either dogmatic or monolithic, citing a robust tradition of debate and diversity of opinion in rabbinic Judaism. This sense of diversity is expressed in the idea that the Torah has seventy faces or facets. Nonetheless, the diversity within Judaism that Orthodoxy recognizes among the "seventy faces" is a far cry from interdenominational pluralism. There may be seventy faces of Torah, but all of them share certain Orthodox assumptions about Torah and halakha. What is not acceptable is an unlimited number of legitimate faces of Judaism. Lamm wrote, "If 'Torah' has an infinite number of faces, then it is faceless and without value or significance."[25]

Rather than suggesting outright rejection of everything that is non-Orthodox, however, Lamm allowed that there are different levels of recognition of the non-Orthodox world that remain possible. For example, insofar as non-Orthodox Jews have organized synagogues, led by rabbis whom they accept, their religious leaders and activities have "functional validity" for them. This is Lamm's polite way of saying that non-Orthodox Judaism may be valid *for them*, even if it is unacceptable to Orthodox Jews. Second, Lamm acknowledges that non-Orthodox Jews may be genuinely religious people who are sincere in their faith in God and their commitment to being Jewish. He recognizes their "spiritual dignity," the quality of their faith apart from its specific content. But the most important level of authenticity remains "Jewish legitimacy," which can only be judged against the divine standard of halakha. At this final level, Orthodox Jews have no choice but to reject the legitimacy of non-Orthodox Judaism: "Under no circumstances can an Orthodox Jew consider as Jewishly authentic a view of Judaism that excludes faith in God—such as humanistic Judaism—or one that condones the marriage of Jew with non-Jew; or one that rejects the halakhic structure of Sabbath observance or the laws of divorce or the institution of kashrut."[26] Orthodox rabbinical authorities perceive a bright line separating the Jewish authenticity of halakha and what they can only understand as the mistaken individualistic values on which various alternatives are based.

Authenticity and Jewish Survival

A different standard of Orthodox authenticity has been introduced by those who focus on the demographic factor of Jewish continuity rather than religious criteria about halakha. If success in passing on Judaism from one generation to the next is an indication of the most authentic way to be Jewish, as Elliot Abrams proposed in *Faith or Fear: How Jews Can Survive in a Christian America*, then Orthodoxy is the clear winner. The path of Jewish authenticity, according to Abrams, is a hybrid of religious observance and cultural separatism, with the former as a means to the latter. He argues, "The good Jew is ritually observant and resists assimilation, in some sense living apart, never fitting comfortably into American or any other society."[27] If the non-Orthodox part of the Jewish community declines the opportunity to embrace Orthodoxy, "doesn't it merit the contempt in which it believes the traditionally observant hold it?" Amazingly, at the same time that Abrams says the non-Orthodox are worthy of contempt for declining the Orthodox path, he suggests that the non-Orthodox at least must *"offer respect, admiration, and support* to those Jews who do make that choice."[28] After all, only traditional Judaism can thrive in America, while the "counterfeit faith" of non-Orthodox Jews is a "dead-end" that will die out in a generation or two.

This same survivalist standard of authenticity motivates the underlying questions of Jonathan Sacks's book *Will We Have Jewish Grandchildren?* Offering the book's title as the "single most burning question in today's diaspora,"[29] Rabbi Sacks shifts the focus from the preservation of Jewish tradition and halakha to the Jewish people's struggle for survival. Sacks's focus on Jewish intergenerational continuity echoes the urgency of Fackenheim's "614th commandment." Jewish authenticity will be measured by the future and the degree of success in passing Judaism on to the next generation. In this competition for Jewish survival among different forms of Jewish identity, only the "fittest Jews," those who are "proud, knowledgeable, and committed"[30] will be recognized as authentic Jews. Jews who are illiterate, indifferent or skeptical about Jewish tradition, open to intermarriage, or more concerned with their intellectual autonomy than protecting tradition lack this authenticity to survive as Jews.

For Menachem Kellner, the condition of Judaism in future generations is likewise a primary concern. He presents a less emotionally loaded question than Sacks's concern about "whether our grandchildren will be Jewish." It focuses on what kinds of Jews they will be, "how many different sorts of mutually exclusive and mutually intolerant Judaisms our grandchildren will face." The problem he envisions is one that is already substantially in place—that is, how will members of the Jewish people navigate conflicting and incompatible models of legitimacy and authenticity? Although Kellner agrees with the premise that Orthodox Judaism is the only true version of Judaism, he understands that either calling non-Orthodox Jews heretics or excusing them because they are like captive children brainwashed by heathens is patronizing and unhelpful.[31] But that means he must find a different solution to the intractable Orthodox dilemma. Is it possible to maintain "tolerant respect for non-Orthodox Jews and Judaisms without being forced to adopt a position of relativistic approval of them"?[32]

Kellner's solution to the authenticity problem starts by avoiding a separation of Jews into those who follow authentic Judaism and those who do not. Instead, he suggests a mitzvah metric that considers which of the halakhically prescribed mitzvot are being followed by different Jewish groups and individuals, regardless of their denominational self-definition.[33] This approach quantifies authenticity with the highest award going to those who follow the most mitzvot. A more colorful version of the same idea can be found in Charles Liebman's claim that Orthodox Judaism offers fuller access to Jewish tradition than other options, "the broadest assortment of wares": "If Judaism is a cafeteria, why patronize an establishment with a limited assortment?"[34] Whether comparing Judaism to a cafeteria is the most useful analogy is open to debate, but given that premise, the answer that Orthodoxy offers the most choices is a peculiar position for a group that emphasizes the absence of choice when it comes to Jewish religious observance. Perhaps there is a lot to "eat" in the Orthodox cafeteria, but the menu is fixed and unchanging, and there are no options for substitutions or personal favorites. And it is a place where women eat separately from men and are not allowed to be chefs.

Of course, counting mitzvot or items in the Orthodox cafeteria can hardly solve the problem of the authenticity of non-Orthodox Judaism, for it still operates within Orthodox definitions of Jewish mitzvot. Kellner still dismisses the Conservative/Reform approach as a diluted, nostalgic approach to Jewishness, "a sentimental attachment to half-remembered myths about what 'true' Jewish life used to be like."[35] In so doing, he offers no possibility for an approach to mitzvot among non-Orthodox Jews based on different priorities and values. As long as Orthodox Jews remain the mitzvah scorekeepers, the problem remains unresolved.

Ultimately, the tension between Orthodox and non-Orthodox Jews cannot be reduced to a split between one group who are the guardians of an ancient tradition in its pristine form and another group that has run away from that tradition. Rabbi Sacks's polarity between the authenticity of tradition and the authenticity of the autonomous self represents an exaggeration, if not a distortion, for it is clear that all forms of modern Judaism, including Orthodoxy, establish authenticity through a more complex process that includes present choices about the meaning of particular aspects of the past. Authenticity is a concept that is always in flux and continually renegotiated. Ultimately, the dichotomy cannot be reduced to the option of "tradition with no freedom of choice" versus "freedom of choice with no tradition." Tradition and choice always remain in a dynamic relationship.

The Invention of Orthodox Authenticity

The idea that Orthodox Jews represent a glimpse into the Jewish traditions and folkways of earlier generations of Jews living in the premodern shtetls of Eastern Europe is a compelling fantasy for many non-Orthodox Jews. For Lis Harris, a secular Jew and author of an ethnographic portrait of the Hasidic community in New York, observing the Hasidic world up close felt like finding a living snapshot of her own past, "some antique version of myself."[36] Certainly, Orthodox religious leaders do nothing to discourage this impression of Orthodox Jewish life as a simple continuation of the way Judaism has always been. The historical authenticity they claim rests on the presumption that they alone are the preservers of tradition in its original purity, in contrast to liberal "deviationists" who have decided to change, revise, or even abandon aspects of Jewish tradition in response to the ideas and values of the modern world. This perspective has also fueled not only what Jay Michaelson calls the myth of shtetl authenticity but also a widespread "anxiety of inauthenticity" among many American Jews "that someone, somewhere, is the real Jew, but I'm not it." This anxiety often prevents liberal Jews from affirming their own forms of Jewish authenticity.[37]

Traditionalist forms of religion like Orthodox Judaism typically arise in response to shifting trends in how other people are responding to their shared tradition. Yet in reaction to such changes, observe historians Martin Marty and Scott Appleby, groups claiming to protect the essence or fundamentals of a religious tradition inevitably assume a position that is itself "selective, partial, highly polemical and creative, and thus not truly traditional at all. Fundamentalists create something new out of the raw material of the past, the opportunities of the present, and the possibilities of the future."[38] The dilemma confronting self-proclaimed defenders of the faith is that in articulating precisely which beliefs and practices constitute the authentic essence of their tradition, they must single out just a small number of many different options for appropriating what they consider the essential elements of the past.[39] This is the reason that authenticity cannot be defined as something that resides in the past, nor can tradition be defined as a simple reproduction of that past in the present. For the question will always remain about which of all the possible parts of the past we choose to preserve and revitalize in the present and which parts are ignored, forgotten, or excluded.[40]

Orthodox Judaism employs several strategies to reconstruct the Jewish past in a way that balances strict religious observance with participation in the modern world. They are based, according to Samuel Heilman, on the epigram of Rav Avraham Kook, the first chief rabbi of Israel, which stated, "The old must be made new, and the new must be made holy."[41] This idea links authenticity with ongoing exchanges between the traditions of the past and the needs of the present. "New" ideas or practices could be accepted only if they were first "rediscovered" somewhere in the past, and practices from the past could retain their vitality and relevance only after they were reinterpreted to give them new meanings.

The interpretive reconstruction of the past in light of the present and the present in light of the past is accomplished through the processes of what Heilman calls "contemporization" and "traditioning." "Contemporization" involves applying Torah principles and laws to new situations. Modern applications can be "read out" of even obscure and archaic elements in the traditions and texts of the past. "Traditioning" works by "reading in" new modern meaning and relevance to older traditions, for example, reinterpreting menstrual taboos in terms of contemporary ideas of psychological and physical regeneration rather than female impurity. These processes are necessary to allow authenticity to be both grounded in the stable traditions of the past yet also flexible and interpretable in new situations. Those parts of the past that do not lend themselves to either contemporizing or traditioning may simply be ignored and forgotten rather than actively rejected.[42]

Jewish historians frequently refer to the "creation," "beginning," "construction," and/or "invention" of Orthodoxy as a particular modern development that emerged in response to innovations and reforms that were occurring elsewhere within the Jewish community.[43] Less obvious was the fact that Orthodoxy, too, had participated in dramatic innovations in the definition and practice of Judaism. Orthodox Judaism, like various forms of liberal Judaism, emerged out of the need to adapt Jewish religious life to new situations confronting Jews in the modern world. Where liberal Judaism found its authenticity in presenting changes as necessary and useful progress beyond the limitations in earlier forms of Jewish belief and practice, Orthodox Judaism defined its authenticity in terms of its role as the guardian of Jewish traditions and the bulwark against change. Its ideal of authenticity found expression in a romanticized image of the organic wholeness of Judaism and the Jewish people and an appreciation for its ancient laws and rituals.[44] Jacob Katz noted that "Orthodoxy was a method of confronting deviant trends, and of responding to the very same stimuli which produced these trends, albeit with a conscious effort to deny such extrinsic motivations."[45] Although the term *Orthodox* gradually became standardized, there were other terms as well—*Jewish Jews, Torah Jews, traditional,* or *observant.* Such terms were important branding tools for these Jews to differentiate themselves from other Jews who welcomed changes to Jewish observance and tradition that the Orthodox saw as illegitimate and disruptive.[46]

For many of the traditionally observant Jews who constituted an Orthodox Jewish community in the United States in the first part of the twentieth century, Orthodoxy was what Jenna Joselit calls an informal "invented culture" that was not particularly dependent on rabbinic authority.[47] Yet over time, other Jews came to America who reconstructed Orthodoxy in new ways. Far from being a static, unchanging tradition, those claiming the Orthodox mantle have continually been involved in redefining what authentic Orthodox Judaism is. In *Authentically Orthodox: A Tradition-Bound Faith in American Life*, Zev Eleff closely analyzes competing understandings of Jewish authenticity by Orthodox Jews in America, initially ignited by the collision between an indigenously American form of Orthodox Judaism and the massive influx of Eastern European Jews into the United States in the decades after 1880. He demonstrates that the "quest for authenticity," however that concept was understood, energized Orthodox Judaism and the ways that it engaged with, and disengaged from, American cultural norms and values such as pluralism, egalitarianism, and consumerism.[48] Just as Finkielkraut emphasized a recalibration of Jewish authenticity in postwar Paris, Eleff reveals how differently debates over authenticity played out against the American cultural landscape, sometimes driven by halakhic debates among religious leaders and sometimes merely reflecting folk traditions from different places of origin.

The postwar period in the United States stretched what was authentically Jewish in new directions. Economic success and general acculturation led Jews to the suburbs at a time of expanding consumerist culture in which marketers increasingly saw Orthodox Jews as a new group of potential customers to reach. Orthodox Jewish consumerism enabled Jews to enjoy the pleasures of a suburban lifestyle without sacrificing their authenticity. All that was necessary was an official certification that a meal at a fancy restaurant or a vacation at a luxury resort was "kosher." Kosher certification signaled not only adherence to Jewish dietary laws but reassurance that these new experiences were still authentically Jewish.[49] Etan Diamond notes that suburban consumer culture did not present an irresistible temptation that drew Orthodox Jews away from Jewish observance. On the contrary, "the expansion of a consumerist culture, far from being even loosely incompatible with Orthodox Judaism, actually made it easier to maintain traditional Jewish practice."[50] More aspects of traditional Orthodox life were gradually incorporated into the world of religious consumerism. For some Orthodox young men, for example, the yarmulke did not need to be just a simple head covering. It could also be a fashion statement reflecting a range of elements from the broader popular culture.[51]

Ultra-Orthodoxy and the Intensification of "Authentic" Judaism

At the same time that consumerism was shaping what was authentically Jewish in some Orthodox quarters, Orthodoxy was also undergoing a gradual rightward shift fueled by more conservative Jews who came to the United States from Europe after the Second World War. The Orthodox Jews who had come to the United States in earlier decades, notes Jenna Joselit, "would have been dismayed to learn that their own brand of Orthodoxy would not, in later years, pass muster as sufficiently authentic Orthodox behavior."[52] For half a century, New York's Orthodox Jews saw themselves as simply and unquestionably Orthodox, "the authentic and sole practitioners of traditional Judaism in New York." After World War II, they found themselves being told that their practice was lacking, "a subdivision or possibly even a dissident sect of traditional Jews but certainly not the denomination's authentic standard-bearers. . . . The authentic Orthodox, the true believers, it seemed, were to be found elsewhere."[53]

Ironically, the Orthodox Jews who had seen themselves as the protectors of authentic Judaism would find themselves displaced by even stricter Jews who now claimed that they alone followed an authentically Jewish way of life. The religious standards and lifestyle that had been just "Orthodox" were now referred to as "modern Orthodox," while a new more conservative movement of "ultra-Orthodox" or "Haredi" Jews took root and placed an intensified focus on halakha as the standard for judging everything.[54] What had been the existing consensus of authentic Jewish observance fractured into new criteria for recognizing what was authentically Jewish.

With the destruction of the traditional world of Eastern European Jewry in the Holocaust, the informal transmission of "living traditions" and lived experiences between generations collapsed. No longer was there a balance between community customs and halakha, nor were traditions rooted in generations of community custom.[55] In addition, the loss of much of the rabbinic leadership in Europe left a vacuum of religious authority. As some members of the Orthodox community turned to new sources of authority and authenticity, the ultra-Orthodox Jews elevated the scope and authority of Jewish halakha to new levels. They turned to rabbinic experts, whose mastery of Torah was treated as infallible and whose heightened scrupulosity about religious observance became authoritative for everyone.[56] The views of these halakhic masters were now recognized as "the authentic Torah viewpoint on the issue in question, thus implicitly—and at times, explicitly—branding all other positions as inauthentic and illegitimate."[57]

Haym Soloveitchik suggests that increased religious strictness was also a way of responding to a decline in Jewish ethnic difference. A stricter Orthodoxy would more effectively separate authentic ultra-Orthodox Jews from non-Jews, non-religious Jews, and even modern Orthodox Jews. It offered a new conception of authentic Judaism based on a narrow text-based approach, mediated by the establishment of new hierarchies of authority that maintained a clear separation from an impure and threatening environment.[58]

The ultra-Orthodox community understood its position in relation to mainstream Orthodox Jews in very much the same way as mainstream Orthodox Jews had felt the need to respond to developments and changes introduced by Jewish reformers. The sharp turn to a more conservative form of Orthodoxy aimed at revitalizing Jewish tradition once again by reinterpreting the Jewish past, and particularly by applying halakha in increasingly more expansive and strict ways. There was a familiar contradiction at the heart of the ultra-Orthodox move toward a more uncompromising approach to tradition and halakha. The tolerance of a diversity of interpretations of halakha that had been typical of rabbinic Judaism in the past was replaced with a notion of halakha as a fully codified set of rules that are all equally binding. Rulings that pushed observance beyond just the letter of the law and expanded what could be considered the stricter spirit of the law meant that halakha was expanding into new areas that had not been explicitly required in the past.[59] The norms of traditional Judaism and mainstream Orthodoxy gave way to the discovery of new meaning in old texts. Out of the many volumes of laws, legends, and different interpretations found in Talmudic, midrashic, and other Jewish texts, only the strictest interpretations were emphasized, and more moderate ones were ignored. New obligations were discovered, and existing ones were highlighted in new ways.[60] In the name of preserving tradition, they began to once again reconstruct tradition through a creative process of selective retrieval, suppression, emphasis, and de-emphasis.

Yet the ultra-Orthodox leaders were adamant that their new attention to the authority of Jewish legal texts and strict observance of Jewish law were nothing new at all. Indeed, they idealized the past as a time when people also were focused on fulfilling precisely these details of the law. Haym Soloveitchik writes, "The past is cast in the model of the present, and the current text-society emerges not as a product of the twin ruptures of migration and acculturation, but as simply an ongoing reflection of the unchanging essence of Jewish history."[61] Of course, this is precisely the myth constructed by most modern fundamentalist religious movements, that they alone represent the last pure remnants of the premodern leaders of their religion, that their version of tradition is the only true one, despite the obvious modern context for their views.

Flanked on one side by a new stricter form of Orthodoxy and on the other side by the various non-Orthodox forms of Judaism, mainstream Orthodox Jewish leaders have struggled with issues of authenticity and recognition in relationship to both sides. On the one hand, modern Orthodox Jews have long rejected any notion of Jewish pluralism that would recognize the authenticity of liberal Judaism, while simultaneously still recognizing non-Orthodox Jews as Jews. On the other hand, they also celebrate the tradition of pluralistic tolerance *within* rabbinic Judaism as a basis for reciprocal recognition among any groups on the Orthodox spectrum. Ironically, modern Orthodox Jews now find themselves the target of the same uncompromising, nonpluralistic position that they have taken toward non-Orthodox Jews. The authenticity of their own Orthodox approach to Judaism has been challenged by ultra-Orthodox Jews who reject pluralism even within Orthodoxy and recognize only their own Jewish observance as truly authentic.

In a symposium published in 1982 in the modern Orthodox journal *Tradition*, contributors were asked to address both of these questions, among others. First, they addressed the triumphalist attitudes of some mainstream Orthodox Jews regarding the future viability of non-Orthodox movements. But then they were also asked whether they themselves might share the same fate as the non-Orthodox movements and be supplanted by right-wing Orthodoxy. Some participants in the symposium lamented that the more intensive religious standards of ultra-Orthodox piety have made some modern Orthodox Jews feel inferior. In the words of David Berger, "The syndrome which identifies 'more extreme' with 'more authentic' is the key challenge for modern Orthodoxy with respect to the turn to the right among American Orthodox Jews."[62] At the same time, there were proclamations reaffirming that modern Orthodoxy is "the most legitimate expression of authentic Judaism"[63] and complaints that their own halakhic practices were mocked as "treif, outside the pale" by ultra-Orthodox Jews who valued stringency over mutual tolerance and respect.[64]

Although any kind of moderation or adaptation to the modern world in Jewish religious observance proposed by non-Orthodox Jews has been routinely condemned as weak and illegitimate by Orthodox leaders, many of their own arguments defending modern Orthodoxy from ultra-Orthodox criticism resemble the arguments made by non-Orthodox Jews. Modern Orthodoxy's "attempt to relate the truth of Torah to the social and intellectual milieu of a more general culture" is itself a traditional strategy that has characterized the development of Judaism and the perspectives of its greatest religious thinkers throughout its history, in contrast to ultra-Orthodox separatism.[65] The tricky part for modern Orthodox Jews is to defend a form of pluralism broad enough to justify themselves as authentically Jewish but not broad enough to grant liberal Judaism any such recognition.

The modern Orthodox need to defend some kind of religious pluralism in order to assert their own legitimacy represents a cautious acceptance of the dynamic quality of Jewish culture and religion, not as an eternal essence, but rather as something that formed in response to what Efraim Shmueli described as "a complex struggle of historical situations."[66] The inevitable changes that occurred in the history of Jews and Judaism have always been couched in terms of a return to what is authentic and essential and a repudiation of other models as inauthentic. Although cultural, ethnic, and religious identities continually recreate and redefine themselves, change usually occurs accompanied by the claim that innovators are merely rediscovering or returning to the original true tradition.[67]

The resistance of Orthodox Judaism to recognizing the constructed and reconstructed nature of Jewish tradition and the Jewish past is sometimes regarded as a sign of Orthodoxy's own *inauthenticity*. By reifying Jewishness into a rigid, monolithic structure, Orthodoxy has become "misguided and inauthentic," according to Reconstructionist rabbi Jacob Staub.[68] For non-Orthodox Jews, the lack of consensus about what exactly constitutes Jewishness is not an embarrassment, as Rabbi Gewirth suggested, but an honest recognition of the complexity and diversity of Jewish identities in the world. Indeed, the very premise of a stable and unchanging model of Orthodoxy rests on what might be considered an inauthentic foundation.

4 Reforming Jewish Tradition and the Spiritual Quest

Decades of sociological and demographic research have reinforced a common perception that the most important differences between the major Jewish denominations can be measured in terms of quantity of knowledge, intensity of belief and practice, and resistance to assimilation. In other words, many people would say that the difference between an Orthodox Jew and a Reform Jew is that an Orthodox Jew knows more about Judaism, has stronger beliefs about God, observes Jewish rituals and holidays with greater fervor, and maintains stronger boundaries in relation to non-Jewish culture than a Reform Jew does. When this kind of quantification of Jewishness is made, it is not unreasonable to conclude that Orthodox Jews are more authentically Jewish than Conservative or Reconstructionist Jews, who are more authentically Jewish than Reform Jews, who are more authentically Jewish than Humanistic Jews, and so on. This, of course, was the implication of Menachem Kellner's proposal to measure Jewishness according to the number of Jewish laws, or mitzvot, an individual Jew observes.

This hierarchical understanding of Jewishness has been reflected in a variety of jokes about different kinds of Jews. One joke from the 1950s, when concern about assimilation was growing, told the story of a Jewish grandmother who wanted to find an acceptable way to get a Christmas tree for her grandchildren. She called a rabbi from each of the three main denominations to ask if there was a "broche" (blessing) available to make the Christmas tree more Jewish. The Orthodox rabbi said it was not possible, and then he asked her, "But what exactly is Christmas?" The Conservative rabbi also said there were no *brochot* available for this purpose, and then he asked her, "But what exactly is a Christmas tree?" Finally, she talked to the Reform rabbi, who immediately agreed to help with the Christmas tree problem, and then he asked her, "But what exactly is a *broche*?"[1] Here, Jewish literacy and authenticity are linked with cultural separatism in the Orthodox rabbi. He preserves tradition as he believes it has always been and safeguards it from threats of dilution, corruption, and assimilationist syncretism that blur the boundary between Jews and non-Jews.

Authenticity in Reform Judaism

While Orthodox Jews will acknowledge the authenticity of most non-Orthodox Jews (as long as they were born to Jewish mothers), they simultaneously tend to portray non-Orthodox Jews as "deviationists" who have strayed from the original authentic form of Judaism. Not surprisingly, leaders of Reform Judaism have been insistent, from its very beginning, on presenting Reform Judaism, not Orthodox Judaism, as the most authentic form of Judaism for the present age. The theological architects of Reform Judaism did not see it as an alternative to, or modification of, a more authentic form of Judaism. As Jacob Neusner described, "Reform Judaism did not present itself as Brand X, and it did not concede it was a lesser version of a good thing that was authentically realized elsewhere, in Orthodox Judaism, for instance.... Reform Judaism thought of itself as Judaism pure and simple: the Judaism that everyone should practice, all Jews and Gentiles as well."[2] On one level, these religious leaders believed that Reform Judaism was not just one kind of Judaism but Judaism in its most real, true, and authentic form. The claims they were making about the core principles of Judaism also suggested that they considered their mission to include a need to correct the mistaken approaches of other forms of Judaism. Thus Reform Judaism understood itself as "the natural, right, authoritative, true Judaism" in contrast to other forms of Judaism that were "wrong, inauthentic, and untrue."[3]

Less concerned with rabbinic Judaism and the development of traditions of Jewish halakha than Orthodox Judaism is, classic Reform Judaism looked back to an earlier period of the Jewish prophets and the priority they gave to social justice over religious ritual, and also to more recent ideas from the nineteenth century reflecting confidence in human progress through science and reason. Reform leaders understood Judaism as an evolving organism that from its outset has undergone change and transformation, which were necessary for its survival. Such changes are not arbitrary or haphazard, and the authenticity claims of Reform Judaism rest on the assumption that certain core Jewish values remain valid beneath the accumulation of outdated rituals and practices. Thus, far from being a rupture with the past, Reform Judaism sees itself in continuity with specific Jewish precedents that are merely being restored and renewed for the present age.[4]

This model suggests that changes or innovations in Judaism are not deviations or dilutions but rather natural parts of its growth and improvement in response to the changing political and social situation of the Jewish people. Indeed, if Jewish tradition has been marked by continual transformation in response to changing times and environments, then it is those who want to cling rigidly to traditions of the past who are actually betraying the reality of a more dynamic tradition. Transformation does not mean a wholesale rejection of the Judaism of previous eras but rather a balance between preserving continuity with tradition and adapting to new ideas and situations in the present.

Transformations of any tightly held traditions seldom occur without resistance and warnings of impending disaster by the defenders of the status quo. For example, in 1983, the Reform Jewish movement in the United States decided that children would be recognized as Jewish as long as they had at least one Jewish parent, father or mother, and were raised as Jews. What became known as "patrilineal descent" meant that the halakhic requirement that only the children of a Jewish mother can be recognized as Jewish by birth would not be observed, nor would conversion to Judaism be required for children of non-Jewish mothers who were raised as Jews. Not that conversion to Judaism by Reform rabbis would have solved the problem, since Orthodox Jews consider Reform conversion to likewise be lacking in halakhic validity. The importance of the Reform movement's policy change was not actually about descent per se, whether from a Jewish mother or a Jewish father, but a more radical notion that what makes children *recognizable* as Jews by others, as well as to themselves, is a process of socialization and the experiences that come with being raised as a Jew.

In an article titled "Judaism without Limits,"[5] (1997) Jewish historian Jack Wertheimer cautioned that the growing lack of consensus among Jewish denominations regarding the criteria for recognizing someone as a Jew, the validity of conversions, and the understanding of authentically Jewish religion posed serious challenges to the Jewish community. For decades, Orthodox Jews had been telling non-Orthodox Jews that even if the religion they were practicing was not really Judaism, they at least remained Jews in the eyes of the Orthodox simply because of the biological fact of having a Jewish mother. Now, it seemed, even that partial recognition had been thrown in doubt. Wertheimer worried that even if patrilineal Jewish children grew up to become Reform rabbis, they would still not be recognized as Jews by either Orthodox or Conservative Jews, both of whom reject the validity of patrilineal descent. From a Conservative Jewish perspective, such hypothetical "rabbis with non-Jewish mothers" represent the peculiar phenomenon of "non-Jewish" rabbis. And from an Orthodox perspective, since Reform Judaism is not real Judaism and Reform rabbis are not real rabbis, they would be seen as "non-Jewish non-rabbis."

Wertheimer cautioned that new questions about Jewish status, along with increasing amounts of religious syncretism that have allowed the introduction of such things as Eastern meditation practices and yoga, pagan and Native American rituals and ideas, and various "New Age" forms of spirituality, threatened Judaism with "religious dilution," "anarchy and self-extinction," and "the breakdown of once-clear boundaries between what is Jewish and what is not."[6] Judaism cannot survive "without limits," he warned, and the freedom Reform Judaism allows in determining both its members and its practices cannot be tolerated without dire consequences.

Two years later, another Jewish traditionalist, Charles Liebman, worried that liberal Judaism had become too personalized and nonjudgmental and that it had placed individual self-realization ahead of communal and ethnic solidarity and Jewish peoplehood.[7] He dismissed the modern pursuit of expressive authenticity that focused on "individual meaning, journeys of discovery, spirituality and the search for fulfillment" as though none of these were authentically Jewish concerns. Furthermore, by focusing on "episodic and exceptional experiences" rather than "disciplined regularity or patterned coherence" and more on "moments of meaning and growth" than on "the binding duties," "obligations," "commitments," and "responsibilities" toward the Jewish people, personalized Judaism was ill-equipped, said Liebman, to maintain the strong ethnic boundaries and distinctive cultural traditions necessary for group survival.[8]

Of course, Reform Judaism does not consider respect for the autonomy of the individual to be a corrosive force on Judaism nor a biblical vice, as Jonathan Sacks also insisted. Rather, its classical formulation articulated in the 1885 Pittsburgh

Platform offered an early example of what in the latter part of the twentieth century became the idea of being "spiritual but not religious." In explaining why it was necessary to eliminate traditional Jewish religious laws about diet and purity, those early Reform leaders argued that such antiquated ideas were alien to "our present mental and spiritual state. . . . Their observance in our days is apt rather to obstruct than to further modern spiritual elevation."[9] In other words, they interfered with the spiritual authenticity of modern Jews, which could be better expressed through the ethical ideals of the Jewish prophets.

When Benjamin Netanyahu first took office as prime minister of Israel in June 1996, Orthodox Jews in Israel and elsewhere intensified their lobbying efforts to impose Orthodox standards for answering the "Who is a Jew?" question. To that end, they rejected the validity of conversions conducted by non-Orthodox rabbis, and they dismissed the religion of Reform and Conservative Jews as something other than Judaism. It was a frontal attack on the authenticity of non-Orthodox Jews. This was not a new position, per se, but a more aggressive reaffirmation of a long-standing rejection of non-Orthodox Judaism by the more conservative parts of Orthodoxy. Not surprisingly, the leaders of liberal Judaism reacted strongly to the delegitimization of non-Orthodox Judaism by Orthodox leaders. They quickly responded with articles not only defending liberal Judaism but also returning fire by questioning the authenticity of Orthodox Judaism itself.

Rabbi Simeon Maslin, then-president of Reform Judaism's rabbinical organization, the Central Conference of American Rabbis, published an article the same month entitled "Who Are the Authentic Jews?" and Reform leader Balfour Brickner offered a piece the following spring titled "Orthodox Have No Lock on Authenticity."[10] Resenting Orthodox Judaism's uncompromising stance on halakha, non-Orthodox writers insisted that it was the Orthodox who were ignoring Jewish tradition by seeking to freeze Judaism just when it needed to develop in new ways. After all, they suggested, it had been the prophets' refocusing attention on social justice rather than needless sacrifices, or the Pharisees' liberalizing and loosening of the written law rather than the Sadducees' rigid attachment to the Temple cult, that represented the path of what became a new understanding of authentic Judaism. In fact, throughout history, those Jews who refused to embrace needed changes inevitably became marginalized and separated from mainstream Judaism. Balfour Brickner responded directly to Orthodox rejection of non-Orthodox conversions and practices by arguing that halakha was only one possible source of Jewish authenticity, reflecting mainly the ideas and perspectives of Ashkenazi rabbis. Rejecting the monopoly on authenticity claimed by Orthodox leaders and their desire to impose their view of halakha on the entire Jewish population, he asked, "What arrogant bit of sophistry makes anyone think that Ashkenazi rabbis can legitimately impose their man-made rabbinic interpretations of Biblical law either on an entire diaspora or on Israel, the majority of whose citizens now ignore most of that law and desperately wish to be free of its odious tyranny?"[11]

Brickner challenged the idea that standards of authenticity exist separately from the beliefs and values of the majority of the Jewish population who are not Orthodox or that Orthodox Jews have the right to impose their standards of authenticity on Jews who have rejected halakha as the defining standard of Jewish authenticity.

Simeon Maslin acknowledged the nostalgia many Jews feel about immigrant ancestors from premodern pre-Holocaust Europe. But he then challenged the assumption that by holding themselves apart from modernity, dressing as they imagine nineteenth-century shtetl Jews did, and maintaining all sorts of problematic attitudes and practices in regard to a whole range of issues, Orthodox Jews represent the gold standard of authenticity: "Can one be a truly authentic Jew while rejecting, questioning, or modifying these commonly cited criteria of Jewishness? My answer is an emphatic yes."[12] Maslin's critique was aimed directly at what he saw as the Orthodox view of authenticity as something locked in the values and lifestyle of Jews from an earlier era. Such a model of authenticity risked becoming frozen in outdated approaches that were incapable of responding to religious and ethical realities in the modern world.

Jewish authenticity for Maslin depended on the ethical and spiritual dimension of various issues, which often diverged from Orthodox preoccupation with an unchanging tradition. For example, Jews who turn to new methods of "humane" slaughter that are less painful than kosher slaughter, or who are concerned about equal rights for women in all aspects of Jewish practice and liturgy, or who dismiss ultra-Orthodox dreams of rebuilding the temple in Jerusalem and reestablishing animal sacrifice as misguided are all more authentically Jewish than Jews who show little concern for social justice or understanding of the historical social contexts of Jewish texts and practices. Today's Orthodox, wrote Maslin, were ill-equipped to guide Jewish life in the twenty-first century. Far from being authentically Jewish, their approach is distorted by "their tribal exclusivism, their obsession with the punctilities of ritual, their contempt for k'lal Yisrael, their manner of dress, their romanticization of the past, and yes, their fanaticism."[13]

The model of authenticity that emerged from Reform Judaism was based on the necessity of making Judaism relevant and accessible for modern Jews. One of the important developments in liberal Jewish leaders' defense of their Jewish authenticity is the linkage of authenticity not with an inflexible preservation of the laws, rituals, and customs of the past but with a vetting of such expressions of Judaism in light of their contemporary relevance and contribution to the development of self-fulfillment and ethical sensitivity. *Inauthenticity* was now associated with the rigid attachment to the past and inadequate, or lack of, attention to these other factors. Where Orthodoxy defined authenticity in terms of loyalty to the notion of an unbroken chain going back to biblical ancestors, Reform Judaism insisted on a more dynamic approach that focused on the need to infuse meaning into rituals and traditions that had become meaningless and mechanical. What this means in practice is that final declarations of what is authentic based on the past are not possible, since some ideas and practices that were taken for granted for generations may eventually be seen as obsolete or ineffective while new ideas that at first had seemed radical or heretical may over time become recognized as normative and authentic.[14]

Ways of Being Religious, Ways of Being Jewish

The tension between approaching Jewish authenticity in relationship to "how Jewish" a person is, in contrast to "how they are Jewish," points to deeper questions about how the function of religion in general is to be understood.[15] Efforts to analyze religion as something that is expressed and experienced in a wide variety of ways—not just in terms of the depth of religious knowledge, fervor of belief, or intensity of observance—means that authenticity can be uncoupled and redefined apart from the quantitative measurement of these factors.

For psychologists of religion, analyzing the "how" of religious life rather than the "how much" question has been a topic of research and discussion since the mid-twentieth century, and a number of models have been proposed to describe different ways people have of being religious. Researchers have understood that religiosity is not simply a switch that is either in the "on-or-off" or "high-or-low" position, or something that might be fully understood by simple checklists of beliefs and ritual practices. Rather, they often described certain *ways of being religious* as psychologically more or less mature, more or less socially beneficial, and more or less tolerant of religious and other differences. Psychologists were particularly interested in understanding why devoutly religious people were often found to exhibit high amounts of prejudice and discrimination and to score higher than others on scales of dogmatism and authoritarianism.[16]

Psychologist Gordon Allport was one of the most influential figures in this new way of understanding different modes of being religious and some of their consequences. He suggested that more mature forms of religion showed greater tolerance of differences, religious and otherwise, while immature forms of religion were more narcissistic, more inclined to see their position as the exclusive truth, more likely to regard all other religions as wrong, and more likely to view the world as a struggle of us versus them. Allport became best known for his distinction between two different orientations toward religion, which he labeled "intrinsic" and "extrinsic." By "intrinsic" religiosity, Allport intended to describe people whose commitment is to the beliefs and values of their religion itself and who genuinely live those beliefs and values in their daily lives. He considered this form of religion superior to that of people who approached religion "extrinsically," which means their religion is motivated by certain instrumental or utilitarian goals. They participate in religion for the sake of various secondary benefits, such as the social status and affiliation provided by religion, a sense of belonging to a particular group or community, a sense of security, and so on. People with the highest extrinsic scores also tended to exhibit more suspicion and prejudice toward those who were different from them. Allport did not think of his intrinsic/extrinsic scale as a simple binary one, and he allowed that people may exhibit varying mixtures and combinations of both of these dimensions. Although he did not use the terms *authentic* or *inauthentic* to describe different forms of religion, it is easy to see parallels between the extrinsic orientation and what Sartre flagged as the inauthenticity of the antisemite or the genuine commitment of the intrinsic orientation with some characteristics of authenticity.

Although Allport's model has had tremendous impact for the study of religious behavior, it has been less useful for talking about ways of being Jewish. Allport had grown up as a Protestant Christian and the subjects on which his analysis was based were overwhelmingly American Protestant Christians. His view of intrinsic religion was skewed toward individual expressions of faith and failed to appreciate some of the reasons that a minority religious group like the Jews would feel so protective about their group's boundaries and derive meaning from their group identity and ethnic cohesion.[17] Other psychologists, including some who were Jewish, similarly approached the function of religion in terms of dichotomous "ways of being religious." Underlying many of their models was an implicit sense that different ways of being religious were expressive of different approaches to questions of authenticity.

Erich Fromm's Humanistic versus Authoritarian Religion

Erich Fromm, a Jewish psychoanalyst and social psychologist, fled from Germany to the United States in 1934 and spent many years trying to understand the moral collapse and conformist obedience that blossomed under Nazi authoritarianism. This included exploring the role of religion in responding to people's urgent needs for meaning and belonging. Fromm had been raised as an Orthodox Jew, and he retained a deep appreciation of the potential wisdom to be found in Judaism as well as in other religions, although he was not religiously observant or theistic in any traditional sense. Fromm distanced himself from Freud's dismissive and condescending attitude toward religion by suggesting that religion could be either very helpful or very harmful depending on how it functioned in a person's life and whether it offered an authentic expression of oneself.

Unlike Freud, who regarded religion as an infantile relic of humanity's past, Fromm understood the root of religion as the universal need of all people to develop a framework of orientation, a foundation for their values, and a compelling symbolic expression or collective narrative embodying their religious conclusions. He considered the metaphysical or supernatural truth of religion to be neither resolvable nor relevant. The only question that mattered was whether one chooses a kind of religion that succeeds in "furthering man's development, the unfolding of his specifically human powers, or one paralyzing them."[18]

In 1950, with the memory of the destruction wrought by European fascism still fresh, Fromm published a book entitled *Psychoanalysis and Religion* that presented an understanding of religious authenticity and spirituality based on psychological growth and humanistic values. Throughout his work, Fromm had analyzed the sense of powerlessness and insignificance from which many people in modern industrial society suffered. He thought that some of them found relief from those feelings by sacrificing their freedom to authoritarian leaders as well as authoritarian cultural and political institutions.[19] They suppressed their own spontaneity and creativity in the name of conformity to socially desirable feelings and attitudes rather than transparency and integration of their emotional and intellectual potentialities.[20]

Although Fromm did not use the term *authenticity*, it is clear that he associated authenticity with the perfection of human beings as individuals and as a species through the pursuit of justice, love, reason, happiness, and meaning. Focus on these goals could only be found in what he called the "humanistic" dimension of religion. Humanistic religion celebrates human choice, reason, experience, and power. Focused squarely on the social and psychological consequences of religion, Fromm emphasized God not as a supernatural ruler but rather as "the image of man's higher self, a symbol of what man potentially is or ought to become."[21]

Religion can also offer a serious obstacle to human perfection, however, and can lead people to abandon their sense of agency, reason, and power, resulting in an inauthentic life. This happens when religion is structured in an authoritarian way that requires submission to a power or authority outside of oneself. Whether this authority is God, divinely ordained laws, or religious leaders, the central focus is always on obedience and conformity. The result is a sense of *vicarious* meaning and power that comes from identifying with the source of authority, but it is at the cost, said Fromm, of self-alienation, since people have access to truth and goodness only indirectly, through God, on whom they are now utterly dependent.

Fromm acknowledged that authoritarian and humanistic elements can be found in all religions. By uncovering and rescuing the implicit humanistic side of religious traditions, he hoped to counter the common misconception that the authoritarian form of any religion is the whole religion, or at least the only authentic form of the religion.

In a creative expansion of the psychoanalytic idea of the Oedipal complex, Fromm proposed that the excessive identification people feel with their own group, tribe, nation, or religion was a form of "incestuous attachment." This attachment to the comfort and familiarity of one's own group makes it hard to achieve the necessary critical perspective on the group and its relations with other groups. Fromm suggested that the most important Jewish leaders in the Bible had to break this attachment in order to accomplish their purposes. It was for this reason, Fromm proposed, that Abraham needed to wander far from the place of his birth, and Moses learned who he was only by growing up in an unfamiliar environment, separated from his family and people.[22] Fromm would doubtless have considered the platform of "positive Jewishness" being promoted during the same period that he wrote his book on humanistic and authoritarian religion as an obvious example of an incestuous orientation that needed to be critically analyzed. He feared the ease with which people easily succumbed to authoritarian, ethnocentric, and xenophobic elements that can be found in both religious and secular political movements, all of which had contributed to the rise of fascism, racism, and totalitarianism in the twentieth century.

Fromm's rereading of Jewish tradition through the lens of its humanistic and authoritarian tendencies certainly demonstrates how traditions, texts, and stories can be read through different lenses that reflect the values and perspectives of a particular age. Ironically, both Fromm and Jonathan Sacks cite the same well-known Talmudic story as evidence of their conflicting ideas about what the authentically Jewish message is in the text. In the story, Rabbi Eliezer is trying to resolve a dispute with other rabbis about the application of Jewish law to an issue of purity and impurity. In his frustration that the other rabbis do not accept his authority, he implores God to give them a sign that he is indeed right. God obliges, and several of these supernatural signs occur—rivers reverse direction, trees uproot themselves and move hundreds of feet, and walls start to fall. Finally, a voice from heaven declares that Rabbi Eliezer is right. Yet the other rabbis remain unpersuaded either by these signs or even by God's own declaration in favor of Rabbi Eliezer. They respond by quoting Deuteronomy 30:12, stating that the meaning of laws and traditions is not based on supernatural signs and voices from heaven but rather on the conclusions determined by a majority of the rabbis.

For Fromm, the message of the story is clear. It emphasizes "the autonomy of man's reason with which even supernatural voices from heaven cannot interfere. God smiles, man has done what God wanted him to do, he has become his own master, capable and resolved to make his decisions by himself according to rational, democratic methods."[23] Indeed, the story can be seen as an explicit liberation from the symbols of authority—Rabbi Eliezer, supernatural revelation, God—all of which have been overturned. According to the story's epilogue, in which God is asked his reaction to the rabbis claiming their own power to overrule the authority of God, God acknowledges with pleasure the rabbis' act of self-empowerment and says, "My children have defeated me."

For Sacks, whose perspective rests on the continuing authority of Orthodox rabbis to interpret the Torah, the message is quite different. What the story teaches is nothing about the autonomy of human reason and freedom to construct new meanings or other innovations. On the contrary, the story is an affirmation of Orthodox rabbinical authority to interpret and apply the eternally valid revelation of Torah. The interpretation of Jewish law and tradition is *not* a democratic exercise. Only the community of sages is authorized to do this.[24] The fact that the other rabbis reject God's support for Rabbi Eliezer's position is not a demonstration of support for a creative new interpretation. On the contrary, the story reaffirms the authority of the rabbis and sages over all others and dismisses any other kinds of evidence that other people might provide for contrary points of view.[25]

Obviously, Fromm was selective in his use of elements from Jewish tradition that supported his message of human self-improvement and self-fulfillment. Like the figures of classical Reform Judaism, Fromm highlighted the Hebrew prophets not only as defenders of truth, love, and justice but also as people who dared to challenge the established authority of kings and priests. They embodied the critical perspective that he believed was necessary for people to look at the problems of their own group honestly, to reject the group's expressions of self-righteousness and suspiciousness of outsiders.[26] Only by transcending the incestuousness of one's own group, said Fromm, could one approach authentic religious experience, the sense of connection "not only in oneself, not only with one's fellow men, but with all life and, beyond that, with the universe."[27] This religious attitude toward the world is not possible when religion is reduced to obedience to rules and laws or passive acceptance of divine authority.[28]

The important distinction for Fromm was not between Jews who accept Jewish halakha and those who do not but rather between those who accept a destructive authoritarianism that feeds intolerance of those who are religiously different and those who pursue a humanistic path. This humanistic approach to Judaism sees God not as an all-powerful creator, redeemer, or law-giver but as "a symbol of all that is in man and yet which man is not, a symbol of a spiritual reality which we can strive to realize in ourselves and yet can never describe or define."[29] It is important to note that the shift from an authoritarian orientation to a humanistic one does not signal a victory for unbridled individualism or narcissistic self-indulgence, an outcome feared by the defenders of traditional authority. On the contrary, Fromm describes a level of psychological self-awareness that is experienced as a dynamic moment of awakening that is "simultaneously the fullest experience of individuality and of its opposite; it is not so much a blending of the two as a polarity from whose tension religious experience springs."[30]

Reconstructionist Authenticity

Mordecai Kaplan, the founder of the smallest and newest Jewish denomination, known as Reconstructionism, reached many of the same conclusions as Fromm while still holding onto a concept of Jewish peoplehood that Fromm seemed ready to discard as outdated tribalism. From his early book, *Judaism as a Civilization*, Kaplan had insisted on seeing Judaism as more than just a religion. Like Herder's notion of culture as the totality of forms of expression of a particular people or "volk," Kaplan proposed that Judaism be understood as "the nexus of a history, literature, language, social organization, folk sanctions, standards of conduct, social and spiritual ideals, esthetic values, which in their totality form a civilization."[31] He offered this as an alternative to traditionalist views of rabbinic Judaism that are based on supernatural premises about the Torah as permanently binding for all time, "a complete, finished, and perfect system of beliefs and practices, inherently relevant to all conditions of human life."[32]

As a civilization rather than a supernaturally revealed religion, argued Kaplan, Judaism has continually developed in response to changing historical contexts. The process of "reconstructing" its ideas, values, and traditions can be traced in the momentous changes that occurred when the nomadic Israelite tribes became an agricultural nation with its own land, when the alliance of the tribes introduced a monarchy and priestly religion of sacrifice, and when both monarchy and priesthood were replaced by the rabbinical approach. In modern times, Jewish civilization continued to evolve in response to its encounters with modern nationalism and modern science.

When Kaplan published one of his last books, *The Religion of Ethical Nationhood*, at the end of the 1960s, his discussion of Jewish peoplehood was infused with the language of spirituality, self-realization, and authenticity. Like Fromm, he sought to reframe Jewish religion in non-supernaturalistic terms that would make sense to a modern scientifically educated person. The focus was on the contribution Jewish religion could make to living a "creative life." He defined Judaism not so much as a system of beliefs and practices but as "the sum of all those manifestations of the Jewish people's will to live creatively."[33] Kaplan offered a view of salvation very much like the qualities Fromm saw in the ideal of humanistic religion. He wrote, "A religion should foster man's integrity, responsibility, loyalty, love, courage, and creativity. *The achievement of those traits on a personal and social scale constitutes man's fulfillment or salvation.*"[34] Just as Fromm described God as a symbol of human self-realization, Kaplan described an "authentic conception God" as "the eternally creative process" within people.[35]

Kaplan linked authenticity with wisdom, and wisdom with humanistic values. He notes, "Mature wisdom or authentic religion *depends upon faith in man*."[36] Just as Fromm calls God a symbolic horizon of human ideals that always recedes as humanity approaches it, Kaplan understood mature wisdom as something evolving along with humanity. As a result, it is impossible for authentic Jewish wisdom to present any final authoritative positions. When religion becomes authoritarian, when it locates the divine outside of the natural world, or when it sees God as the external source of power and creativity, it offers nothing more than "immature wisdom."[37] Kaplan and Fromm both warned against what they consider inauthentic or immature religion based on "blind acceptance of religious dogmas and habit-propelled rituals," anti-intellectualism and irrationalism, all of which inhibit human growth and reason.[38] They shared a desire for people to "replace faith in tradition and blind obedience to authority with an awareness of life's authentic values" and to see religion "as a means of rendering man creative and responsible."[39] To Kaplan, this was the "experience of salvation," the goal of an authentically Jewish life.

Forms of Spirituality and Authentic Experience

In their own ways, both Fromm and Kaplan anticipated broader cultural shifts in the function of religion within American society in the 1960s and following that were happening within the American Jewish community as well. In *After Heaven: Spirituality in America since the 1950s*, sociologist Robert Wuthnow explains that a shift in the ways that many Americans relate to their religious traditions has emerged in contemporary American culture. In the past, most Americans defined their religious practice as members of organized Jewish and Christian institutions where they attended services and conformed to common rituals, roles, and beliefs. Their sense of ethnic belonging and loyalty was reinforced by participation in organized religion. Authenticity was expressed in the stability and continuity of communal traditions from one generation to the next. This "spirituality of dwelling" reflected a secure connection to communities of origin and the traditions inherited from them, as well as a clear sense of boundaries between members of one's community and outsiders. This is the kind of "collective authenticity" implicit in Irving Howe's idea of tradition as a communal force that envelops and molds individuals from birth onward and provides the essential roles and values for living an authentically Jewish life.

Wuthnow found that in the last half-century or so, Americans have increasingly been abandoning the dwelling place that had been provided by the traditions and communal norms of institutional religions. Increasingly, they have begun to embrace a new orientation toward religion that Wuthnow describes as a "spirituality of seeking."[40] This approach emphasizes the search or quest for "personal authenticity," achieved through the exploration of the depths of one's own experiences, especially powerful and transformative ones. Social psychologist Daniel Batson tried to capture this new orientation by adding a new category to Allport's original concepts of intrinsic and extrinsic religiosity. Batson described "religion as quest," as a commitment to "honestly facing existential questions in all their complexity, while at the same time resisting, clear-cut pat answers."[41] Religion as quest rejects the mechanical repetition of childhood religious doctrines or practices or conformity to the consensus of their religious community. There is a heightened awareness of the tentativeness and incompleteness of religious answers.

The "spirituality of seeking" and "religion as quest" were very much the kind of postmodern Jewishness that Steven Cohen and Arnold Eisen heard about from moderately affiliated American Jews in the 1990s. These Jews experienced their Jewishness as "a journey of ongoing questioning and development" in which they choose which elements of Jewish practice or culture have meaning for them without regard to religious leaders or any other authorities.[42]

Indeed, mainstream synagogues and traditional sources of authority were being abandoned as empty and inauthentic, while the authenticity of the "Jew within" was expressed in meditation, mysticism, social activism, feminism, vegetarianism, and environmentalism. Cohen and Eisen observed, "Rabbis and communal institutions can and do continue to offer guidance for behavior and belief. But they are no longer viewed as custodians of authority or as gatekeepers to personal authenticity. For that one looks inward, to the experience of the self."[43] What Cohen and Eisen dubbed "the Jew within" comprises these fluid and changing experiences unfolding in the lives of individual Jews.

Having abandoned traditional religious authorities and supernaturalism, the quest orientation turns toward personal and collective *experiences* of Jewishness. The concept of experience can be understood in different ways that produce very different results in determining what is authentically Jewish. For the ancient Greeks, experience referred to practical knowledge, knowledge that comes from doing. In this sense, experience represents a kind of knowledge and expertise based on accumulated experiences. Within traditional Judaism, experience is best understood as the accumulation of certain traditional skills acquired through study and practice, as a result of which one could be considered knowledgeable and competent—that is, an "experienced Jew" or maybe a "Jewish expert." In this sense, experience refers to familiarity based on past acquaintance or performance. For Orthodox Jews, authenticity comes with this kind of experience and expertise. Those who lack such experience, in the form of knowledge, training, and exposure, cannot claim the same degree of authentically Jewish life. The more observant and educated Jews, from this point of view, might be considered more experienced, competent, and probably more authentic.

The modern focus on the authenticity of experience generally refers to something quite different from the model of experience as expertise. Experience can also be a great leveler among people with different levels of expertise or knowledge. It serves as the ultimate democratic ideal, something to which every person has access and about which they are the ultimate authorities. Moreover, experience is self-validating. It contains within itself its own personal truth and authenticity. No one can legitimately question my experience or dispute its significance to me. It is what is most uniquely mine, and therefore an authentic expression of myself, something against which all potential beliefs must be measured. Among classic psychologists of religion, from William James to Abraham Maslow, religious experiences, mystical experiences, and peak experiences have been seen as more primordial and authentic than religious beliefs or rituals, which are more routinized and commodified.[44]

Jewish Women's Experience

The focus on personal experience as a way to challenge traditional Jewish narratives, beliefs, and rituals is a central ingredient of existential authenticity. Perhaps the most powerful example of the power of experience to reconfigure Judaism has occurred in the work of Jewish feminists who insisted on placing experience at the starting point of religion. If Jewish beliefs, rituals, and dogmas rest on the experiences of earlier generations, then it is important to consider whose experiences in those generations were reflected in the tradition. Identifying whose experiences may have been left out has provided an important democratizing corrective to the tradition and its authenticity.

The feminist demand for the inclusion of women's "voices" in Jewish tradition was really a demand for recognition of Jewish women's experiences as an influence on Jewish religion, ritual, and theology. In their groundbreaking anthology *Womanspirit Rising*, coeditors Judith Plaskow and Carol Christ insisted on "experience" as a central feminist norm for the reconstruction and re-creation of religious tradition. Feminist Jews have attempted to create/discover a nonsexist form of Jewish life that demands contesting elements of received tradition. The result has been further battles over authenticity and the place of tradition: "For some, the vision of transcendence within tradition is seen as an authentic core of revelation pointing toward freedom from oppression, a freedom that they believe is articulated more clearly and consistently within tradition than without. Others believe that the prebiblical past or modern experience provide more authentic sources for feminist theology and vision."[45] Here the word *authentic* refers to both an essence and an ethical vision. In the latter sense, sexist traditions might include historically authentic parts of Jewish history, but they cannot be an authentic source of feminist Judaism.

In the introduction to her book *Standing Again at Sinai*, Judith Plaskow begins by addressing the potential conflict between feminism and Judaism—that is, are feminist revisions of Judaism still authentically Jewish? Plaskow argues that feminism and Judaism stand in opposition only when Judaism is seen as a monolithic tradition that was permanently fixed in the past rather than "a complex and pluralistic tradition involved in a continual process of adaptation and change"[46] Not only was rabbinic Judaism itself a dramatic break from the preceding system of priestly sacrifices performed in the Temple in Jerusalem, but it also suppressed other parts of Jewish culture and tradition. It is therefore necessary to "question rabbinic authority as the sole arbiter of authentic Judaism."[47] For Plaskow, the authenticity of feminist revisions is no different from any other developments within Jewish history, and can only be determined in retrospect: "Some feminist changes will endure because they are appropriate, because they speak to felt needs within the community and ring true to the Jewish imagination. Others will fall by the wayside as eccentric, mechanical, or false. To try to decide in advance which will be authentic is to confine our creativity and resources; it is to divert energy needed to shape the kind of Jewish community in which we want to live."[48] The implication, moreover, is that certain traditional practices that had been seen as authentic in the past may later be abandoned as inauthentic. This process may apply to halakha as much as anything else, and its status may change in different periods of time.

Normative practices reflect who has been in power and in a position to define norms. But if the privilege enshrined in tradition has resulted in the oppression of women, its authenticity is thrown into question. When alternative sources of authority (such as women's experience, traditions, etc.) are retrieved, the parameters of authenticity shift and Judaism becomes "a complex and pluralistic tradition involved in a continual process of adaptation and change—a process to which I and other feminists could contribute."[49] Today, Jewish laws and practices that do not acknowledge the full equality of women and the importance of their experience may become inauthentic expressions of Jewish values while feminist Judaism becomes the only really authentic Judaism. It is not that feminist Judaism claims to represent the true past but rather the fact that authenticity is a product of a living and ever-changing tradition.

5   The Experiential Authenticity of Jewish Meditation, Jewish Yoga, and Kabbalah

The cultural ferment of the 1960s and 1970s offered religious seekers new methods for exploring authentic experiences available within the spiritual traditions of Asian religions, which had gained enormous popularity in American culture. In his book *Turning East: The Promise and Peril of the New Orientalism*, Harvey Cox analyzed this new interest among Americans in Asian religions, a phenomenon in which Jews have been significantly overrepresented from the beginning. By some counts, nearly a third of American Buddhists are also Jewish, at least in background. Jewish spirituality blossomed as part of a general American turn to new paths and methods for exploring interior life and existential questions. Options included the Jewish Renewal Movement and New Age Judaism, Jewish yoga, Jewish meditation, and Jewish mysticism.[1] In each case, questions arose about whether these new forms of Jewish spiritual life were indeed "authentically Jewish."

Harvey Cox had observed that Jews who became involved in practices like yoga and meditation sometimes felt inauthentic, like squatters in someone else's spiritual territory. To be sure, some Jews "went native" and took on Hindu or Buddhist practices as their adopted spiritual traditions while perhaps retaining Jewishness solely as their ethnicity. Others approached yoga and meditation as purely psychological techniques that could be practiced apart from any particular religious belief systems. But Cox recommended a different option, which consisted of domesticating foreign traditions like yoga and meditation by looking at them not "as an exotic import, but as something with roots in [one's] own tradition."[2] In other words, he thought they needed to be reimagined and rebranded as "authentically Jewish." The goal would be to create a "kosher" brand of spiritual practices that combines Jewish authenticity with the personal authenticity of the experience.[3] The combination of these elements was at the heart of the emerging New Age Judaism, which sought to "construct a Jewish identity that is rooted in the past and yet creative and individualistic" and to "be authentically Jewish and yet be nourished by many non-Jewish intellectual and theological streams."[4]

Reclaiming Judaism's Lost Tradition of Meditation

Harvey Cox had issued an invitation to do what Jews have always done in response to a variety of philosophical, cultural, and religious ideas that they have encountered during their history. They reconceived what was new and strange as something not so new or strange at all. What seemed at first to be culturally alien ideas and practices could be reframed as elements that had merely been "forgotten" or doctrines that had been confined to a small group of initiates who passed down their secrets as an oral tradition. One way or another, the important point was that seemingly new ideas were already implicit in some part of Jewish tradition.

If the roots of meditation and yoga, or their equivalents, can be identified as forgotten parts of Jewish tradition, then it becomes possible to recognize them as authentically Jewish practices, not concessions to alien spiritual traditions from the East. Cox suggested that one might start by thinking about meditation as a "miniature Sabbath," since both practices involve learning the benefits of doing *nothing* as a path to higher awareness or mindfulness that accepts the world without a need to judge or control it.[5] Still, if meditation is such an important and authentic part of Jewish religious tradition, then why had so few Jews heard about it? The challenge for boosters of *Jewish* meditation was to explain how something that was allegedly so central to Jewish practice in earlier periods was so completely unknown to Jewish seekers in the last generation that they had to look outside of Judaism to find it. Gradually, an explanation for the "lost" Jewish meditation tradition began to emerge. It began by saying that the Judaism with which most people are familiar was developed for use by ordinary people while the practices of meditation represented a special wisdom confined to an elite group of sages.[6] Thus meditation was not something new for Jews but rather "an integral part of Jewish spiritual practice for at least three millennia."[7]

One of the most successful proponents of this strategy for "rediscovering" the Jewish origins of Eastern spiritual practices was Aryeh Kaplan, an Orthodox rabbi and author of a series of books in the 1970s intended to demonstrate the centrality of meditation in all aspects of Judaism (*Meditation and the Bible, Meditation and Kabbalah, Jewish Meditation*). Kaplan demonstrated that if Jews were interested in meditation, they had to look no further than their own backyard—in the ordinary Jewish activities of prayer, study, and ritual. They could also find role models for meditation in important biblical figures such as Abraham, Moses, David, the prophets, and others, all of whom were said to have used meditation to pursue higher states of consciousness as part of their relationship to God. Indeed, during the biblical period, Kaplan claimed, "a large proportion of the Israelite people" ("over a million," he says, according to certain midrash) practiced meditative techniques and were involved in schools of meditation led by "master prophets."[8]

Of course, such broad usage of the term *meditation* offers little for someone interested in learning specific techniques of meditation, for the conclusion is simply that all the great Jewish figures "meditated" in some form or another. Kaplan's reconstruction of this particular tradition of Jewish meditation does emphasize a strict demand for self-discipline and obedience to the commandments of Torah. Apparently, strict halakhic observance was necessary for meditation, even before the rabbinic system of halakha existed. Kaplan emphasized this point in order to contrast the intense discipline demanded by Jewish meditational schools with what he called "idolatrous schools of mysticism and meditation."[9] The latter were open to anyone, without any commitment to Torah and Judaism. Not surprisingly, this rediscovered history of Jewish meditation has contemporary relevance for Jews who have been dabbling in Buddhist or Hindu forms of meditation. For Kaplan, the techniques of these Asian traditions are no different from the "idolatrous schools" of the past, which offer spiritual cheap thrills but no real authenticity.

The effort to repackage meditation as authentically Jewish has taken two forms. First, there is the renaming of certain Jewish practices as potential sources of meditative exercises. For example, the concentration that Buddhists call mindfulness could be cultivated in relationship to traditional activities like prayer, performing mitzvot, or communicating with God. In other words, if one wanted the benefits of meditation, one could get them while observing the traditional Jewish religious lifestyle. Second, what seem to be customary Eastern meditation techniques can be reframed with Jewish terms. For example, a description of Jewish meditation might look indistinguishable from the typical process used in Zen meditation based on the counting of one's breaths, except that in Jewish meditation, one is instructed to visualize or vocalize the Hebrew letter *yud* while breathing in and the letter *heh* when breathing out. By replacing the sounds or images utilized in Hindu or Buddhist meditation with one of the Hebrew names for God ("Yah"), Eastern meditation is transformed into *Jewish* meditation.

Finally, there are certain Orthodox authorities who have proposed that the attraction some Jews may feel to Eastern practices of yoga and meditation may stem from the fact that these techniques were originally Jewish and were later borrowed by Hinduism and Buddhism. In other words, Jews already knew about yoga and meditation before the Hindus and Buddhists did. Apparently, Hindu yogis and Buddhist monks had appropriated Jewish spiritual practices, not the reverse, so it is only natural for Jews today to want to reclaim what is already theirs. Rabbi Daveed el Harar teaches that "yoga is a tradition that was actually passed down from Abraham, together with different techniques of meditation and so on and came to India through the children of Abraham."[10] Of course, most historians would probably find this claim of Jewish origins for Indian yoga rather implausible, if not silly, but the appeal of such theories for Jews cannot be denied. It allowed Jews who were attracted to meditational practices to rebrand them as their own hidden Jewish traditions.

Kaplan's history of Jewish meditation emphasized that meditation is a long and difficult process to master, which can only be done with the guidance of knowledgeable teachers. Only a select few masters have retained access to the advanced forms of meditation during the dispersion of the Jews around the world.[11] Nonetheless, he explained, diluted frameworks for meditation were left behind for average Jews to use. For example, the daily standing prayer known as the Amidah, according to Kaplan, has served the same function as a long mantra, one that is repeated three times every day.[12] More complicated meditational texts were written in ways that would keep the meditational practice hidden and secret: "Techniques were alluded to, but always in veiled hints, as if this teaching was bound to remain an oral tradition, never be put in writing."[13] At the same time, Orthodox proponents of Jewish meditation emphasize it as a deeper dimension of already living a completely

Orthodox life, something that can enhance the experience of traditional Jewish observance of study, prayer, and ritual celebration.

The intention of Kaplan's theory of the hidden tradition of Jewish meditation is to normalize meditation as something that "has been part and parcel of Judaism throughout the ages" and is referred to in all major Jewish texts yet has gone unnoticed by most Jews until recently. Jewish meditation has been hiding in plain sight, ready to be rediscovered if one knows where to look and how to uncover the secret meanings within them. In an article titled "Restoring the Meditative Side of Judaism," Zvi Zavidowsky, of the Nefesh Haya school of Jewish yoga and meditation in Jerusalem, describes techniques that he says were "'underground' or neglected until recently," "traditional but timeless," "authentic Jewish techniques . . . which for hundreds of years were passed on by oral tradition alone."[14] Jewish spiritual seekers who turn to Eastern practices need to know that neither Hinduism nor Buddhism has anything to offer that Judaism does not already have, only better.

For Kaplan, the process of reclaiming Jewish meditative tradition requires a kind of "verbal archeology" to find the "true meaning" of certain words.[15] This approach allows one to see precedents and examples of meditation among well-known biblical figures. When Isaac goes out into the field at sunset (Genesis 24:63), the Hebrew verb that is usually translated as "going for a walk" could also be understood as Isaac going to meditate. Or the description that "Jacob was left alone" as he awaited his meeting with Esau (Genesis 32:24) could also be understood as a moment of meditation.[16] Even prophetic experiences in the Bible are recast as products of meditation or meditative states. It certainly is not impossible to read these stories this way, though there is little in the texts themselves or their contexts to suggest that this is the real esoteric or hidden meaning within them.

As an explosion of books on Jewish meditation appeared in the years after Kaplan's books were published, it was common to find an opening section or chapter on the hidden tradition of Jewish meditation. Beginning in this way has helped assure Jewish readers that the terms and techniques related to meditation that many people associate with Eastern religions are in fact authentic Jewish practices as well, developed by Jewish teachers over the last two millennia.

Jewish Meditation and Experiential Authenticity

While Orthodox authorities generally focus on the alleged *historical authenticity* of meditation—that is, its connection to the most important figures in Jewish history and its implicit presence in classic Jewish texts, non-Orthodox rabbis tend to emphasize its *experiential authenticity*. The power of meditation is its appeal for disillusioned or alienated Jews who struggled to find something powerful in Jewish tradition to truly grab them. Rabbi Goldie Milgram has suggested that meditation transforms Judaism "from the purely intellectual process most of us grew up with into a spiritual practice that links us to Judaism in the most profound way. Meditation gets under our intellectual defenses and helps us to feel at one with creation and to experience an expanded life rich in conscious awe and joy."[17] These are the same characteristics that Erich Fromm identified as the essence of "humanistic religious experience."[18]

In Jeff Roth's *Jewish Meditation Practices for Everyday Life*, the stated goal of meditation is the "experience of awakening," the result of which is the ability to "see clearly our own lives and the world around us."[19] This kind of Jewish experiential authenticity is an alternative to the emptiness he finds in traditional Jewish prayer in liberal Judaism. The solution is not a return to Orthodoxy or an agenda of ethnic survival but using Jewish spiritual wisdom to confront universal truths about the nature and purpose of human experience. Often this will include a direct experience of God, "a path to God," "a medium for encountering God," or "a bridge that enables us to approach the Ultimate."[20] What exactly is the nature of God or the Ultimate in these experiences remains unspecified.

For many Jewish Buddhists, however, the purpose of meditation is a deeper experience of their own consciousness, and like Buddhism as a whole, this experience does not necessarily require a belief in God nor contribute to such belief. For Jews who have encountered more psychological or theologically neutral approaches to meditation from Eastern sources, the effort to link meditation with Jewish religious observance may be less important than reframing the essence of Judaism in more experiential terms.

Rodger Kamenetz's book *The Jew in the Lotus* offered an early description of the encounter between committed Jews and Buddhism, especially those Jewish Buddhists, or "Jubus," for whom Jewishness and Buddhistness were intermingled as a personal reality. Far from compromising the authenticity of their Jewishness, Jubus often reported that Buddhism had deepened and enhanced it. They saw no contradiction in practicing Buddhism and maintaining a strong Jewish identity. For some, there was a genuine sense of integration between the two. They described their Buddhist values not as a rejection of Judaism but rather as an expansion of Jewish values, which they found consistent with Buddhist insights into suffering, change, attachment, and desire. This is the point that Brenda Shoshana made in her book *Jewish Dharma: A Guide to the Practice of Judaism and Zen*, where she insisted that Zen and Judaism are essential to each other. She says they "illuminate, challenge, and enrich each other": "Zen practice deepens Jewish experience, and helps one understand what authentic Jewish spiritual practice is; Jewish practice provides the warmth and humanity that can get lost in the Zen way."[21] In fact, Shoshana suggested that the process of integrating Buddhism into a Jewish identity forces one to confront both traditions at a deeper level than those who merely "take on a ready-made identity as a Jew or a Zen student."[22]

For many Jubus, the experience of meditation offers access to a mystical side of religion that they feel has been abandoned by liberal Judaism's rationalist approach and Orthodoxy's legalistic approach. That is what makes the experience authentic for them. By the end of *The Jew in the Lotus*, Kamenetz wonders about a new syncretistic blend of Judaism and Buddhism that may be emerging. One Jubu who was asked by his son whether he was Jewish or Buddhist replied, "I've got Jewish roots and Buddhist wings."[23] As Zen seders marking both the exodus from Egypt and Buddha's liberation from suffering appeared and Buddhist-style meditation became a part of synagogue services and Jewish day school curricula, the boundaries of what is authentically Jewish began to shift in order to accommodate new forms of hybrid spirituality.[24] Meditation is no longer seen as an alien practice from another religion. It is as kosher as matzo.[25]

Authentically Jewish Yoga

The same process by which contemporary interest in Eastern practices of meditation have been domesticated and reinvented as ancient Jewish traditions or used to introject a new experiential dimension into Judaism has also been the case with Jewish attraction to yoga. Over the last thirty years or so, yoga has moved from being a spiritual practice firmly rooted in Hindu tradition to one increasingly included in the Jewish educational programming of a broad selection of mainstream American synagogues. Not only has yoga's origin in an alien non-Jewish culture and religion been effectively neutralized; the practice of yoga is now claimed as a valuable tool that can infuse Jewish education with an experiential depth and authenticity that offers a new level of Jewish engagement for many people.

The link between yoga and Jewish ideas or values most likely originated in yoga classes and centers, where a disproportionate number of the United States' estimated seventy thousand yoga teachers and millions of students turned out to be Jews, especially Jewish women. Many of them were interested in reconnecting or connecting more deeply with their Jewish backgrounds. The process of integrating yoga with Jewish religious practices and spiritual ideas continued in Jewish renewal retreats and workshops and in websites and books.

Over time, Hindu schools of Yoga were transformed into Jewish yoga through efforts to rediscover or reinvent ancient connections to hidden or neglected Jewish traditions. Creative ways of looking at yoga established additional ties to Jewish religious ideas and values to the point where yoga became quite at home in Jewish settings. Matthew Gindin pursued this line of thought when he described great women of the Bible like Sarah and Miriam as "yoginis"—that is, yoga masters.[26] He concluded, "In fact, mystical, devotional, and transformational meditation practices have been a part of the Jewish faith since Biblical times."[27] In short, meditation and yoga are potentially as Jewish as anything else Moses said or did. And in this sense, Jewish yoga demands to be recognized as part of a hidden or neglected Jewish tradition, an obscure corner of the Oral Torah. If the spiritual foundation of yoga can be found to be not only consonant with Jewish ideas and values but also a rediscovered tradition, then yoga becomes a Jewish activity and Jewish *yoga teachers* are transformed into *Jewish-yoga* teachers. At this point, yoga enters the domain of Jewish education for Jews affiliated with everything from the Jewish renewal movement to Orthodoxy.[28]

Jewish Yoga, Women, and the Body

The 2016 survey on "Yoga in America" estimates that nearly three-fourths of the thirty-six million Americans who practice yoga are women.[29] Although exact figures are hard to find, it is safe to assume that the vast majority of Jews who practice yoga are likewise women. In some ways, the efforts of some of them to combine yoga with their Jewish explorations and spirituality have parallels to Jewish women's early encounters with feminism. The creation of Jewish yoga, like the development of Jewish feminism, resulted from the difficult process of trying to harmonize disparate and seemingly incompatible parts of people's identities. As the women's movement transformed the consciousness of Jewish women of an earlier generation, they were faced with the options of abandoning Judaism as hopelessly sexist or rejecting feminism as anti-Jewish. For those who were unwilling to let go of either feminism or Judaism, other possibilities opened up for bringing feminist insights and analysis back to Judaism. The result has been a vibrant feminist Judaism that has produced dramatic changes in Jewish education and practice.

In the same way, Jews who felt that their experiences in the practice of yoga were profound and spiritually significant often looked for ways to connect those experiences with the Jewish parts of their lives. For some, yoga has offered a way to enrich their experience of Judaism and to ground it in their bodies in ways that are no less powerful and transformative than the feminist revolution in Judaism.[30]

Jewish yoga tends to present a more feminized model of authority and a valorization of the body as a source of knowledge that has special appeal to Jewish women. Some Jewish yoga teachers emphasize that it presents an alternative to traditional Jewish gender roles for men, what Jody Falk describes as "an egalitarian concrete connection to Judaism that bypasses those more male-dominated approaches."[31] Women are also attracted to the intertwining of Jewish yoga's physicality, its location of sacredness within the body, and its connection of the body to Jewishness.[32] It also opens theological possibilities for exploring how the body influences experiences of the sacred and conceptions of the divine. It appeals to those who are attracted to individual experience and personal spirituality over more traditional academic text study and religious ritual observance. Jody Falk writes, "I always felt like even my own spirituality was through my body, that somehow I felt a kind of God presence while focused on expanding, stretching, and playing with my own body's boundaries. . . . It seemed natural to want to merge that way of learning with understanding Jewish concepts, beliefs, and prayers. It has been fascinating to uncover the rich history of movement within the tradition. . . . Doing Jewish yoga is a way of reclaiming the body in connecting to God or your own personal version of Divinity."[33] This focus on the body creates a whole new approach to the interpretation of the meaning of Jewish texts and prayers. It incorporates the body as a vehicle of midrashic innovation. Take, for example, the idea that the central Jewish prayer, known as the Shema, a proclamation of the oneness of God, is really an invitation to "listen" to one's body. According to Falk, "The Shema in the body is a wondrous practice. . . . When do you actually listen to your body? What are the results when you do, and when you don't? At this point in the yoga class, we are standing, and we begin to listen. What does my body need now? Right now? And now? The repeated question is always answered if you let the body speak, and release from your mind making the choice."[34]

For many people, the marriage of yoga and Judaism offers a synthesis of body and spirit that is missing or underdeveloped in traditional Jewish learning.[35] Diane

Bloomfield, an Orthodox Jew and author of *Torah Yoga: Experiencing Jewish Wisdom through Classic Postures* (2004), describes its focus as the use of ancient yoga techniques of breath and movement coupled with the study of traditional and mystical Jewish texts. She developed it to allow Jewish practitioners to enjoy yoga without the distraction or discomfort of Hindu doctrines and Sanskrit prayers that normally accompany traditional yoga. Bloomfield describes Torah Yoga as a form of self-discovery that combines different sources of wisdom that function together symbiotically. Her goal as a Jewish yoga teacher is to show both how the experience of yoga is transformed when viewed through "Torah-centered eyes" and also how new depths of meaning come from the Torah when it is experienced with a "yoga-centered body." She writes, "With yoga, I discovered that the wisdom of Torah was also inside of me. I experienced Torah teachings as a reality that I could know and feel within myself, within my body. Because Torah was within me, practicing yoga was a new way to study Torah. Every yoga posture was a gateway to greater Torah consciousness."[36] The notion of "Torah study" in this context is obviously quite different from traditional forms of text analysis. It is neither a mastery of the interpretations of past sages and rabbis nor a creative application of sacred texts to contemporary issues. Rather, it is a personal realization mediated through bodily experiences. "Torah consciousness" is less a matter of accumulated knowledge or mastery of texts than a matter of personal self-realization.

Individualism and Universalism in Jewish Yoga

It is perhaps not surprising that as Jewish ethnic and communal ties have weakened in the American Jewish community, Jewish yoga has emerged as both *individualist* and *universalist*. It is individualist in the sense that Jewish yoga is part of individual Jews' experience of themselves, their bodies, and their personal relationships to some spiritual meaning or transcendent reality. Although it may be practiced in a group, the focus of attention appears to be more on inner life, self-awareness, and bodily experience than on membership in a congregation or religious/ethnic community.

In such cases, authenticity is understood as a category that precedes or transcends Jewish particularity. Indeed, the whole effort to establish a Jewish meditational lineage to make meditation more "kosher" misses the point, according to some liberal rabbis who are open to spiritual traditions from around the world. Reform rabbi Rami Shapiro recommends a more universalist perspective that transcends ethnicity, since "before we are Jews or Buddhists, we are humans. As humans, we are heirs to the genius of our kind. Krishna, Lao-Tzu, Confucius, Buddha, Jesus, Mohammed, St. Frances, Aurobindo, and Krishnamurti are no less my cousins than Moses, Micah, Hillel and the Baal Shem Tov. We can learn from all of them, but some will speak more powerfully to us than others."[37] From this perspective, Jewish meditation and yoga are part of a larger body of spiritual wisdom that is linked to other traditions and that offers insights and value regardless of practitioners' own religious identifications. When meditation and yoga are presented as tools to provide a deeper universal level of meaning through bodily exercises, they become unlinked from specific religious or cultural roots, and their authenticity shifts from a collective to an individual level. Thus the deeper experience of Torah that is accessible through Torah Yoga practice is not presented as a uniquely Jewish opportunity. Bloomfield explains, "I have taught Jews, Christians, and people of other religions, with varying levels of commitment to their faith, as well as people with little or no connection to any formal religion. Men and women of all ages participate in Torah Yoga classes. People enjoy Torah Yoga for many reasons. Those of different religions, as well as those who have no connection to any formal religion, are inspired by the universal Jewish teachings."[38] The book *Yoga and Judaism: Explorations of a Jewish Yogi*,[39] as well as the related website "Torah-Veda," moves in the same direction, defining its mission as one of blending Jewish mystical traditions with Eastern yoga traditions. They are committed to "awakening, nurturance and expression of spirituality, with a focus on the mystical traditions of Yoga/Vedanta and Judaism/Kabala. We seek the common threads that exist between these and various other spiritual and mystical traditions, exploring the possibilities for a new synthesis relevant to the spiritual needs of today."[40] This blending of religious or spiritual traditions is common in contemporary American culture and reflects not only a domestication of yoga but also a normalization of Jewish traditions as part of a larger postmodern spiritual ferment. The focus on Jewish spirituality and timeless Jewish wisdom in Jewish yoga means that traditional rootedness in Jewish history and culture along with concerns about Jewish identity formation, commitment to Israel, and traditional ritual observance are likely to be downplayed or absent. The result may be a kind of generic spiritual authenticity, but the boundaries necessary to consider something authentically Jewish have been mostly removed.

Kabbalistic Authenticity

It is no accident that the path leading from traditional yoga to the variety of forms of Jewish yoga quite often passes through Kabbalah along the way. Like yoga, Kabbalah appeals to the spiritually inclined, especially those looking for a more privatized, experiential form of Jewish connection. In the 1990s, Kabbalah became popular for those who found traditional synagogue Judaism too dry, repetitive, or otherwise alienating, as an alternative form of spiritual engagement with Jewish tradition that offers "an aura of Jewish traditionalism while de-emphasizing, or even rejecting outright, the authority of halakha."[41] At the same time, Kabbalah enables people to appropriate some of the satisfactions of popular Eastern practices like Zen Buddhism, Transcendental Meditation, or yoga "without leaving home"—in a cultural sense. When yoga is infused with Kabbalah, for example, practitioners combine the Kabbalistic idea of hidden powers and meaning in Hebrew letters with their physical embodiment in particular yoga poses and movements. The desired result is a heightened experience "that helps practitioners tap into their personal energies, fusing body movement with spiritual reflection and united by the teachings of kabbalah."[42]

Of course, Kabbalah, the Jewish mystical tradition, has not been a central part of mainstream Judaism throughout its history, and its revival reflects specific issues of the contemporary Jewish world as much as it does of earlier periods of Kabbalistic history. Kabbalah offered Jews who had abandoned traditional Jewish rituals and observances an alternative form of Jewish connection. For Ron Feldman, the author of *Fundamentals of Jewish Mysticism and Kabbalah*, contemporary Kabbalah is an answer to a whole new situation within the Jewish world. No longer is Kabbalah the exclusive domain of an elite group of rabbinic sages or charismatic rebbes who alone vouch for the meaning and authenticity of its doctrines. The patriarchal and hierarchical system of authority that spawned Kabbalah has been abandoned by many Jews, who are rediscovering and reinventing Jewish traditions that are more democratic and egalitarian. Drawing on the teachings of Rabbi Zalman Schacter-Shalomi, Feldman insists that a new Kabbalah is necessary, one in which "we learn to be Rebbes to each other, finding the 'rebbe spark' within each of us."[43]

Once again, we find evidence of the shift in Jewish religious behavior in the United States since the 1960s from more traditional, institutional forms of observance to more "hands-on" forms of Jewish spirituality based on *experiential authenticity*. The teachings and techniques of Kabbalah—prayer, meditation, chanting, breathing, fasting—all aim at the goal of "a personal *experience* of *devekut*—adherence (closeness to God), a peak *experience* that allows the seeker to glimpse the oneness of all creation and *experience* eternity. . . . Kabbalists are not satisfied with remembering and interpreting the reports of spiritual encounters by biblical figures; they want to have those *experiences* themselves."[44] It is the difference between just reciting the Shema's affirmation of the oneness of God and actually experiencing the oneness of all reality.[45]

The Marketing of Kabbalah

Much of the recent revival of Kabbalah became intertwined with a controversial school for Kabbalah founded by Rabbi Philip Berg, an Orthodox-trained rabbi who claims descent from a long line of rabbis and instruction from prominent twentieth-century Kabbalists in Israel. At first, Rabbi Berg sought Kabbalah students among disaffected and secular Israeli Jews. When he returned to the United States in the 1980s, he still saw Kabbalah as a form of Judaism intended for Jews. By the mid-1990s, however, Berg had begun to attract larger numbers of non-Jewish followers, eventually including celebrities like Madonna, who have invested time, money, and commitment to learning about this aspect of Jewish tradition. Berg reconceived the message of Kabbalah as one available to anyone regardless of their religious background, age, or ethnicity. He rejected the position that the study of Kabbalah is for Jews alone or that there are Jewish prerequisites to understanding Kabbalah.[46]

In this way, the California-based Kabbalah Centre and its worldwide network of Kabbalah schools in the United States, Israel, and elsewhere in the world have tried to do for Kabbalah what the Maharishi Mahesh Yogi did for Transcendental Meditation: to package and market Kabbalah creatively enough to attract new audiences who lacked the customary cultural or ethnic connection to those traditions. For Rabbi Berg, this may have seemed like the logical next step to move Kabbalah beyond an insular world of experts, much as his mentors had done in bringing Kabbalah to secular Israelis who lacked any familiarity or experience with it. In place of a strong Jewish identity and commitment to the Jewish community, the Kabbalah Centre's approach was based on a more generic "spirituality" rooted in Kabbalah.

Despite the fact that its founder is a rabbi, the Kabbalah Centre nowhere identifies itself as a specifically Jewish organization. In fact, the Kabbalah Centre's website specifically addresses the issue of Kabbalah's Jewishness. It presents the history of Kabbalah in a way that departicularizes its Jewish roots and universalizes its teachings. This is the opposite strategy from that undertaken by the proponents of Jewish yoga, who deliberately wanted to particularize yoga as something intrinsically Jewish. According to the Kabbalah Centre,

> It is quite understandable that Kabbalah could be confused with Judaism. Throughout history, many scholars of Kabbalah have been Jewish. But there have also been many non-Jewish scholars of this wisdom. The startling truth is that Kabbalah was never meant for a specific sect. Rather, it was intended to be used by all humanity to unify the world. . . . The second reason why so many people of different faiths become connected to Kabbalah is that it is a way of life that can enhance any religious practice. Christians, Hindus, Buddhists, Muslims, and Jews use Kabbalah to improve their spiritual experience. . . . The Kabbalah Centre steadfastly continues to make this wisdom available to all—regardless of gender, religion or age.[47]

The claim seems to be that Kabbalistic wisdom is related to a more foundational form of authenticity than the parochial issue of its connection to Judaism. It is universally authentic.

At the same time that Berg was claiming a higher form of spiritual authenticity that transcended Judaism, reaction to the Kabbalah Centre from the mainstream Jewish community, and in particular from Orthodox Jews, was swift and overwhelmingly negative. As Boaz Huss has documented in detail, hostile criticism of the Kabbalah Centre took a variety of forms, but all of them involved contesting any possible authenticity in its doctrines, practices, or leadership.[48] The Orthodox critique of the Kabbalah Centre's *Jewish* authenticity essentially consisted of a restatement of the singular authenticity of Orthodox Judaism as the only legitimate guardian and interpreter of all aspects of Judaism.

The critics began from an elitist and proprietary position that "real" Kabbalah can only be pursued by specialists who are also already committed as Orthodox Jews. Any Kabbalah study outside of the Orthodox community is ipso facto suspect. Accordingly, the Kabbalah Centre's egalitarian and universalist policy of offering instruction to both men and women, observant and nonobservant, and Jews and non-Jews was rejected as unacceptable, especially since none of them were required to observe Orthodox halakha.[49] The Orthodox insistence that Kabbalah should only be studied by middle-aged (over forty) Jewish men with covered heads who have spent decades first mastering Talmud and living according to halakha represents a quaintly anachronistic idea. Its main function is to restrict recognition of authentic Kabbalah to the Orthodox faithful.

One Chabad website compares Kabbalah to a beautiful flower "grounded in the fertile soil of the Jewish tradition and observance." When it is picked and removed from the roots that nourish it, it quickly begins to wither, rot, and stink.[50] It is no accident that a metaphor like this links Kabbalah to roots and soil. The clear implication is that only those who themselves are rooted in the same soil can create an authentic connection to Kabbalah. This is the response of the guardians of the boundaries, telling non-Jews and nonobservant Jews to keep out of the Jewish garden. They are trespassers who know nothing about the care and cultivation of the delicate Kabbalistic flowers that grow there, and their presence can only cause damage.

There is a great irony in the fact that what Orthodox authorities recognize as true and authentic Kabbalah is also one that has been totally domesticated, pruned, and appropriated by mainstream Jewish religious authorities. Non-Orthodox Jews and non-Jews who have embraced other versions of Kabbalah found in the wild are dismissed as fake and inauthentic because of their nonhalakhic lifestyles, as though strictly following the laws of Torah was the main concern of the original Kabbalists in the past. Also overlooked is the fact that Kabbalah itself was probably questioned or rejected by the religious establishment at the time of its beginnings, or that the Jewish mystical traditions of Kabbalah developed more in tension with traditional rabbinic Judaism than as an aspect of it. Only later was something that initially had been considered heretical appropriated as a part of the Orthodox canon of sacred texts, to be protected by Orthodox interpretations. Missing from today's Orthodox critics of the Kabbalah Centre is any recognition of the subversive antinomian challenge originally posed by Kabbalah to the religious hegemony of rabbinic authorities.

In the contemporary Orthodox world, however, Kabbalah has been normalized as part of the tradition in the same way that meditation and yoga were. It has been given an origin story that gives it the same pedigree as the Talmud itself. Along with the Oral Law, which is claimed to have been passed down from Moses to Joshua and down through the generations, the secret tradition of Kabbalah is said to have been received by Moses from God on Sinai and transmitted secretly from generation to generation, master to disciple. Later Kabbalists were simply rediscovering the same secret knowledge from God that they believed had been possessed by the kings of ancient Israel, prophets, and sages.

Huss concludes that it is the peculiar postmodern characteristics of the Kabbalah Centre that manage to antagonize Orthodox and liberal Jews alike, as well as academics and the media. While Orthodox leaders object to the Kabbalah Centre's disregard for Orthodox norms, gender roles, and exclusivity as prerequisites for Kabbalah study, media and anti-cult activists turned to some of the charges that have been commonly used against New Religious Movements for decades to delegitimize them as authentic religions. Accordingly, the Kabbalah Centre's leader was likened to a charismatic cult leader who brainwashed his followers and exploited them for financial gain. Many were put off by the unapologetic commercialization and commodification of the movement in an official line of products or its overinvolvement with celebrity pop culture. Some liberal rabbis objected to the Kabbalah Centre's encouraging of inappropriate superstitious ideas and magical practices to access sacred power, as well as a syncretic mixture of New Age ideas and techniques for spiritual transformation and physical healing.[51]

Huss points out that while Orthodox Jews found the Kabbalah Centre too modern in its disrespect for traditional norms, and liberal Jews and scholars found it not modern enough, neither really could understand or accept the new spiritual groups that have emerged to address the urgent quest for authenticity in a postmodern society. Huss writes, "The charge of inauthenticity is, to a large degree, a response to the postmodern nature of the KC, which transgresses the fundamental binary oppositions of modern Western discourse, such as the distinction between the modern and the non-modern, the secular and the religious, the authentic and the fake."[52] Indeed, it is no surprise to find a range of disputes over recognizing the Jewish authenticity of a spiritual movement that has challenged assumptions of the existing canons of authenticity at this moment in history. This is not an issue for which there can be a clear or firm verdict, for the impact of the Kabbalah Centre and other New Age Jewish groups will be felt over time in more mainstream Jewish groups.

It is certainly true that the revival of Kabbalah was driven both by a desire to connect to Jewish roots by some people but also by an effort to untether Kabbalah from its Orthodox Jewish roots to make it accessible to both Jewish and non-Jewish spiritual seekers. In the case of the Kabbalah Centre, a clear effort to departicularize Kabbalah and separate it from any specific Jewish context began with offering an alternative origin myth for Kabbalah. In this understanding, Kabbalah is treated as a form of universal wisdom that predates specific organized religions. Of course, the Kabbalah Centre acknowledges that Kabbalah was first transmitted to humans through Jewish religious figures, and it looks to primordial Jewish ancestors like Abraham and Moses as the original spiritual guardians of Kabbalah. At the same time, the Kabbalah Centre considers Kabbalah to be the source of all organized religions, though in most cases the essential message has become distorted and corrupted and empty dogmatism has replaced spiritual authenticity.[53] This attitude also extends to Judaism, which the Kabbalah Centre likewise regards as a corruption of Kabbalah, albeit one that is closest to Kabbalah's original spiritual message.

While Jewish ethnicity per se is abandoned, Jewish particularity is preserved in a spiritualized form in the idea that Jewish souls are different and more spiritually adept than non-Jewish souls. But Jewish souls are not limited to those who are born as Jews, and over time some of them became incarnated in people outside the Jewish community. According to some in the Kabbalah Centre, the attraction of certain non-Jews to Kabbalah and their skill in mastering it offers evidence of a Jewish soul.[54] This idea preserves a kind of privileged access to Kabbalistic wisdom for Jewish souls without closing the door to non-Jews who are lucky enough to have Jewish souls.

Jewish meditation, yoga, and popular forms of Kabbalah all demonstrate important ways in which Jewish tradition has been reinvented and reconstructed in response to changing religious trends in the larger American society. As Eastern religious practices took root in American culture as a whole in the last half-century, they also were appropriated in specifically Jewish ways. There are inevitable tensions between those who question the Jewish authenticity of new forms of Jewish knowing and learning and others who are convinced that new ways of engaging with Jewish ideas and values, like yoga, are essential to meet the needs and desires of a changing Jewish population. Jewish yoga may prove to be a harbinger of generational shifts among American Jews in the reduced salience of Jewish ethnic identity among some Jews and the growing importance attached to issues of Jewish spirituality. The Kabbalah Centre's attempt to replace particularistic, religio-ethnic-based views of Judaism with universalist, spiritual-based Kabbalistic teachings may also provide insight into larger trends within the Jewish community in the future.

The great twentieth-century scholar of Jewish mysticism Gershom Scholem, while skeptical of some modern manifestations of Kabbalistic thinking also understood that secular and nonhalakhic Jews were themselves distant relatives of the antinomian thread in Jewish mysticism, which sometimes served as an "anarchic breeze" that blows through the "well-ordered house" of halakhic Judaism.[55] As David Biale observed, Scholem's fascination with Jewish mysticism was related to the necessary disruption and destruction of fixed assumptions about legitimate Jewish tradition. Scholem understood "that there is no single voice of authority in the Jewish tradition. Where others saw a monolithic Judaism, Scholem found an anarchistic struggle between competing traditions."[56] What this means is that authenticity also must be seen as a product of anarchist energies and competition reflecting the endless interpretability of tradition, revelation, and truth, and the truth that emerges through each person's experience. Kabbalah serves an essential function in providing a point of view outside of convention and tradition that clears the way for new interpretations and attitudes toward tradition.[57]

6 The Messianic Heresy and the Struggle for Authenticity

Any illusion of consensus among Jews about the essential requirements for being a member of the Jewish people or practicing Judaism was clearly exploded with the advent of modernity and the fracturing of the Jewish community into a variety of competing and often incompatible religious subgroups, not to mention the emergence of nonreligious or secular forms of Jewish identification. In many ways, changing expressions of Jewishness have stretched traditional assumptions about religious beliefs and practices to the breaking point and repeatedly raised questions about what is authentically Jewish. Yet some of these questions are not new, and conflicts between different conceptions of Judaism can be found throughout Jewish history. When such tensions challenge what had seemed to be a consensus about Jewish laws, beliefs, or practices, struggles to assert the parameters of Jewish authenticity are an inevitable result.

Heresy and the Roots of Messianic Judaism

Questions about authenticity have often arisen in Jewish history in response to what one part of a community considers a deviant form of communal identity or religious practice. In its traditional religious form, deviance is a manifestation of the problem of *heresy*. Heretics are those who hold to religious beliefs or practices that are at odds with the "majority position" held by most Jewish religious leaders or authorities at a particular moment in time. Of course, Jewish heretics usually insist that the authorities who question them are actually the ones who got things wrong and that their own beliefs and practices are the authentic ones.

Within Jewish history, groups such as the Samaritans, the Karaites, and the Sabbateans have each insisted at various times that their group alone represented "true" Judaism. The fact that these groups are probably unfamiliar to most Jews today reflects the fact that the challenges each of these groups made to mainstream Judaism were largely unsuccessful, and they became progressively marginalized from the rest of the Jewish community.

Heresy is usually considered to be the foil to authenticity, the embodiment of what is inauthentic and illegitimate. Yet it is nearly impossible to pinpoint the boundaries of what is authentic and what is heretical with any precision for very long. Charges of heresy only represent a conflict with the perspectives of contemporaneous authorities. Although such charges may be intended at the time they are made as a sentence of permanent exclusion or banishment from the Jewish people, later authorities may evaluate the alleged offenses or infractions differently. Jewish history shows that what is accepted as authentic Judaism or condemned as Jewish heresy refuses to remain fixed for long and tends to vary with historical developments. What is normative at one point in religious history can become heretical at another. What is heretical to some Jews may be entirely acceptable to other Jews. For example, Jewish mysticism, Hasidism, and Reform Judaism are three very different developments in Judaism that were initially condemned as heretical by other Jews. Thus heresy, like authenticity, is not an inherent quality of particular ideas or practices but rather a fluid process that reflects the relationship between the dominant position of the community at a particular moment in relation to conflicting or challenging alternatives that exist. It occurs at the intersection where nonnormative, nonconforming religious beliefs or behaviors are faced with varying degrees of recognition or nonrecognition that occur at different moments in time.

While Judaism never developed compulsory creeds like the ones that characterized the early Christian church, important rabbinic figures from Rabbi Akiva to Maimonides have proposed lists of the foundational religious propositions, or articles of faith, that they insisted were essential to Judaism and distinguished it from the two other western religions that have developed out of Jewish concepts and stories. They were attempts to codify what were authentically Jewish beliefs and what elements were alien to Judaism. Among Maimonides's list of the Thirteen Principles of Jewish Faith were a number of religious ideas that clearly were intended as a rebuttal to some of the basic doctrines of Christian faith, without mentioning the latter by name. For example, Maimonides's emphasis on God as absolutely singular and incorporeal made clear that the Christian separation of God into a Father and an incarnate Son who is equally God, violated a basic Jewish principle. His assertion that the Torah is perfect and complete and will never need replacement or additions clearly challenged the validity of any new scriptures like the New Testament or Quran. The principle that Moses is the greatest prophet who ever lived or ever will live directly rejected claims that had been made about Jesus and Muhammad as newer and more perfect prophets. Finally, the faith that the Messiah is yet to come and will be accompanied by a resurrection of the dead made clear that Jesus could not have been the Messiah of the Jews.

Of course, Maimonides's Thirteen Principles were more of a snapshot of medieval Jewish thinking about God rather than a creed that all Jews understood and accepted, either then or now. Indeed, most Jews today would be hard-pressed to identify, much less affirm, these articles of faith. Liberal Jews, for example, have specifically disavowed a number of Maimonides's principles, including his ideas about the coming of a personal messiah and the resurrection of the dead. At the very least, however, Maimonides's principles laid out the argument Jewish authorities had developed to explain why the central doctrines of Christianity were totally unacceptable to Jewish faith, positions that continue to be asserted by traditional Jewish authorities today.

At the same time, modernity has produced new constructions of Judaism and Jewishness, each of which positions itself in a particular way in relationship to Jewish tradition and what is recognized as a legitimate version or interpretation of that tradition. This results in a relativizing of heresy. As Reconstructionist rabbi Carol Harris-Shapiro observed, "We are all, from a Jewish perspective somewhere, heretics."[1] Yet if we are all heretics to someone, then heresy is just another term for pluralism, and it no longer offers an enforceable standard for maintaining group boundaries.

Messianic Jews, however, are a notable exception in which a rare consensus of all major denominations of Judaism exists. Albeit for different reasons, all of them refuse to recognize Messianic Jews as Jews. They all agree that anyone who has accepted the Christian theological claim that Jesus is the divinely ordained messianic savior has placed themselves outside the bounds of acceptable Jewish beliefs and thereby cast their very Jewishness in doubt. Jews who accept the central claims about Jesus professed by Christianity for nearly two millennia trigger a radically different response compared to Jews who accept the basic religious ideas of Buddha, practice yoga, or simply reject the entire Jewish religious worldview.

What is it about Jews believing in Jesus's messianic status that causes so many other Jews to stop recognizing them as Jews? In the 1960s, Albert Memmi wrote, "To the Jew who still believes and professes his own religion, Christianity is the greatest theological and metaphysical usurpation in his history; it is a spiritual scandal, a subversion and blasphemy. To all Jews, even if they are atheists, the name of Jesus is the symbol of a threat, of the great threat that has hung over their heads for centuries and which may, any moment, burst forth in catastrophes of which they know neither the cause nor the prevention."[2] In other words, not only is Christianity theologically offensive to religious Jews; it is also in the name of Jesus that all Jews, religious and nonreligious alike, have suffered centuries of antisemitic persecution. Philip Roth made a similar point when he suggested that one of the few things that connects Jews together is "an ancient and powerful disbelief, which, if it is not fashionable or wise to assert in public, is no less powerful for being underground: that is, the rejection of the myth of Jesus Christ."[3]

Although atheism would seem to be no less serious a religious threat to Judaism than belief in "false messiahs," Jewish atheists are of less concern than "Messianic-Jews" for a simple reason. It is not lack of belief that threatens to dislodge one's Jewishness or even belief in Asian religions like Hinduism or Buddhism. A Jew who admires Jesus, much less believes that he is the Messiah or Son of God, risks violating a primordial taboo of Jewishness. For most Jews, Jesus has always represented the radioactive core of "goyishness" (non-Jewishness) that can be approached only by converts who wish to escape their Jewishness or others ready to commit ethnic/cultural suicide. Due to the historical tension between Judaism and Christianity, including the persecution and forced conversions of Jews at the hands of Christians, the rejection and denial of Christian doctrine have become paramount ingredients of Jewish self-definition.

There are several hundred thousand Jews in the world today who do not consider their faith in Jesus, or Yeshua (the Hebrew name many prefer to use), to be in conflict with their commitment to either Judaism or the Jewish people. Over the last fifty years or so, they have taken to calling themselves "Messianic Jews" and followers of "Messianic Judaism." The point of these terms has been to counter opposition from the mainstream Jewish community and make an argument for their own Jewish authenticity. They suggest that modern Judaism has been refracted through a variety of religious lenses that have produced the perspectives of different Jewish denominations. While none of these denominations are in complete agreement with one another, there is a general acceptance of the idea that they represent different forms of Jewishness today.[4] This means that there is no total consensus about what Judaism is or is not. Rather, there are different ways of being Jewish and different forms of Judaism, including Hasidic, Orthodox, Conservative, Reform, Reconstructionist, Renewal, and Humanistic. Messianic Jews believe that regardless of whether other Jews agree with their beliefs, they should be included in this list and recognized as real Jews practicing a legitimate form of Judaism. They claim to be perplexed about how following a Jewish rabbi named Jesus, all of whose original followers were Jews, would jeopardize their Jewish status.

To fully understand the Messianic Jewish position, it is first necessary to consider the evolution of this religious movement and its followers' desire to combine Judaism with ideas and beliefs that are at the heart of Christianity. Present-day Messianic Jews are the result of a rebranding and reconceptualization of earlier groups from the late nineteenth and early twentieth centuries who were known as Hebrew Christians. Hebrew Christians were the product of missionizing to Jews by various church groups who thought that Jews might be more open to accepting Jesus if they did not think it would require them to give up being Jewish first. What this really meant was that Jewishness would be defined as a matter not of religion but rather of nationality or race. From this perspective, Jews could remain Jews regardless of what they may happen to believe or not believe. To be a Hebrew Christian, therefore, is to claim membership in the Jewish (or Hebrew) people but to hold faith in the Christian religion. By uncoupling Jewish ethnicity from Jewish religion, it became possible to be simultaneously ethnically Jewish and religiously Christian. The early Hebrew Christians were not invested in preserving Jewish practices, and many of them participated in churches alongside Christians. Any residual ties to Judaism disappeared within a generation or two. Their status as Hebrew Christians was more of a temporary transitional identity in the process of shifting from being Jewish to becoming Christian.[5]

The development of the phenomenon of Messianic Jews out of the Hebrew Christian movement was a reflection of growing interest among Christians in the latter part of the twentieth century in the Jewish roots of Christianity, combined with the intensification of Jewish ethnic pride among American Jews. As a result, Messianic Jews struggled to affirm that their acceptance of Jesus as the Messiah was consistent with being Jewish not just by ethnicity or descent but also as an expression of their Jewish *religion*. If Jesus and his original followers represented one of a number of recognized options for Jews in the first century, then perhaps, argue Messianic Jews, the same is true today. By embracing the deeply Jewish origins of Christianity, Messianic Jews want to avoid the doctrine of "supercessionism" or "replacement theology," which holds that Christianity has *replaced* the covenant with the Jewish people on which Judaism is based with a new covenant based on the redemptive sacrifice of Jesus on the cross. Such theology has provided justification for the persecution and forced conversion of "faithless Jews" throughout the history of Christianity, since the continued existence of Jews was an ongoing irritant and a challenge to the unquestioned universal truth of Christianity.

When Christians Were Still a Jewish Sect

It is certainly true that in the century leading up to and following the life of Jesus, there was a proliferation of competing sects within Judaism. At that time, a single normative Jewish tradition shared by all Jews did not exist. Competing sects disagreed on issues of theology, law, interpretation, politics, and so on, but they generally recognized one another as different kinds of Jews. The majority of Jews in the world at the time were common people who probably had little sense of affiliation to any specific sect at all. The most prominent sects were the Pharisees (forerunners of rabbinic Judaism), the priestly Sadducees (who had rejected the concept of the Oral Law), and the ascetic Essenes (an eschatological group who were awaiting God's cataclysmic intervention in history). Fortunately for the later rabbis, both the Sadducees and the Essenes disappeared by the second century, so they provided no further competition to what became the dominant rabbinic form of Judaism.[6]

After the descendants of the Pharisees had become the controlling influence in Judaism, the positions of other groups of Jews were retroactively condemned as heretical. It is not really accurate to say that these groups had somehow strayed from "true" Judaism. What really had happened was that "true" Judaism had developed in a different direction. One might even say that from the point of view of what Judaism had been before, it was the Pharisees whose ideas were heretical in their abandonment of the centrality of ritual animal sacrifice, which had characterized the priestly religion at the Temple when it stood. Indeed, yesterday's heretics often become today's religious authorities. This is one of the main reasons that determining what is authentically Jewish is always a provisional judgment taken from a particular perspective at a particular moment in time.

It is doubtless true that none of these various Jewish heretics lost their status as Jews nor were they excluded from the Jewish community. In the first century, Jewish followers of Jesus, or Nazarenes, worshipped according to Jewish law and were still recognized as a Jewish sect. In time, the Nazarenes were branded as heretics by the rabbis and barred from synagogues, most decisively after the Nazarenes' failure to support the Bar Kokhba revolt. Ironically, the Nazarenes had refused to accept a competing (and ultimately failed) messianic claim that Rabbi Akiva had made about Bar Kokhba. In the wake of the collapse of that revolt, the Nazarenes became dispersed. Rabbinical Judaism paid little more attention to them, and slowly they disappeared like the other heretical Jewish sects of the first century, as a more Gentile form of Christianity took root and had no interest in preserving Jewish customs. From this point on, Jewish authorities focused on developing explanations for why the doctrines of the hugely successful new religion of Christianity were problematic from a Jewish perspective.

At the heart of the present-day campaign of Messianic Jews to be recognized as an authentic Jewish option is the claim that Messianic Jews are merely the present-day equivalents of the first-century followers of Jesus, Jews who operated in a Jewish world before the full development of either rabbinic Judaism, the Catholic Church, or Protestant Christianity. It was a time before a chasm of theological incompatibility and contradiction had solidified into the Jewish-Christian binary.

It is certainly true that during the life of Jesus and in the early years after his death, the Jesus movement was still regarded as a Jewish movement, albeit one increasingly regarded as heretical by dominant rabbinical authorities. Judaism itself was changing during the first century at the same time that ideas about Jesus were morphing in directions far beyond the actual teachings of Jesus that can be discerned in New Testament accounts. By the time the New Testament was written decades after Jesus had died, nascent Christian theology was developing ideas about a divine-human savior and a theory of salvation that diverged from traditional Jewish ideas. It is probably safe to assume that emerging theological concepts about the Trinity and the divinity of Jesus, incarnation, and the sacrificial meaning of the crucifixion of Jesus as atonement for humanity's sins were not yet firmly in place among the original Jewish followers of Jesus.

While Messianic Jews' argument is seemingly based on an appeal to Jewish *history*, it is actually dependent on a particularly *ahistorical* view of Jesus and the religious ideas that developed about him. Messianic Jews' belief in Jesus as the Messiah today cannot avoid an understanding of Jesus that has been filtered through centuries of Christian theology, popular religion, and culture. Faith in this Jesus is not at all identical with the experience of first-century followers of Jesus, who thought about him in terms of fairly primitive messianic concepts and theories. In other words, to be a follower of Jesus in the years immediately before and after his crucifixion by the Romans is arguably an internal Jewish matter, while being a follower of Jesus several centuries later, when Christian creeds have stabilized and Christianity has become the official religion of the Roman Empire, is to be a member of a different religion from Judaism. So it is not surprising that for the majority of Jews today, belief in Jesus as the Messiah is understood as a declaration of Christian faith. The question for Messianic Jews is whether this binary can be rolled back to create space for what is effectively a Jewish-Christian hybrid.

Jews Who Believe in Jesus

For modern Messianic Jews, focusing on the Jewishness of the first followers of Jesus is a crucial step in turning back the clock and normalizing Jesus as a figure in Jewish history rather than the center of a new religion that will be marked by a long history of antagonism toward Jews and Judaism. If only they can imagine themselves as part of the original community of followers of Jesus, when it was not yet a theological and sociological contradiction to be a Jew who followed Jesus, they can ignore the rupture between Jews and Christians that has existed for most of the last 1,900 years.

In 1979, when a case before the Israeli Supreme Court raised the question of whether a Messianic Jew's faith in Jesus constituted membership in another religion and invalidated the right to be legally recognized as Jewish in Israel, the court was unwilling to close its eyes to the centuries of fraught history between Jews and followers of Jesus. In explaining why a person who believes in Jesus as the Messiah has forfeited the right to be considered as a Jew for purposes of immigration (aliyah) to Israel, Justice Shagmar wrote that the appellant in the case "has made use of long and torturous arguments, regarding the possible tie of a Jew to belief in the messiahship of Jesus as though we were still in the beginning of the first millennium of the Common Era, as though nothing had happened since then in regards to the formation of religious frameworks and the separation from Judaism of all those who chose the other way."[7]

Justice Shagmar's point was that it may be true that Jesus and his original followers were all recognized as Jews. However, what is recognized as authentically Jewish changes over time, and ideas, beliefs, and groups that were once recognized as Jewish may cease to be recognized at a later time. There is normally a limited life span for sectarian movements as tolerated alternatives, after which they usually move to become separate traditions, are reabsorbed by the original tradition, or disintegrate.

In the decades since the Israeli Supreme Court's decision, the presence of Messianic Jews in Israel has grown in number to an estimated twenty thousand people, fueled by Russian Jews who came to Israel with histories of participation in Christian churches or at least openness to messianic claims about Jesus. While the Israeli Supreme Court's position on Messianic Jews still stands and Israeli rabbinical authorities remain overwhelmingly hostile, the attitudes of other Israelis are less clear-cut. Many take a hands-off attitude based on the idea that people should be free to believe, or not believe, whatever they wish, including ideas about Jesus as the Messiah. A survey of nearly 1,200 Israelis conducted in 1988 found that beyond the traditional religious requirement of having a Jewish mother, individual religious beliefs did not matter much in how people determined who should be counted as Jews. As long as someone was born to a Jewish mother, the majority of Israeli subjects would still consider that person a Jew, regardless of whether the person was an atheist (83 percent) or whether they celebrated Jewish holidays, followed the commandments, felt Jewish, and also believed that Jesus is the Messiah (78 percent).[8]

In the United States, the established Jewish community remains deeply hostile toward Messianic Jews. Since groups like Jews for Jesus were first active in the 1960s, around the time that a variety of religious "cults" were gaining traction among college students and other young people, Jewish organizations and leaders have tended to interpret the Messianic Jewish movement as a kind of religious cult that preys on vulnerable and religiously naïve young Jews. Although this has perhaps been true of some groups, Messianic Judaism cannot be so easily dismissed as a Christian trick or a trap in which innocent Jewish youth are ensnared. It may be more comforting for some Jews to believe the only way a Jew could believe in Jesus as the Messiah is if he or she were deceived, tricked, or somehow brainwashed. Yet for a variety of reasons, some Jews find the notion that Jesus really was the Messiah predicted by Jewish prophets to be believable and appealing.

Beyond concerns about deceptive recruitment practices by Messianic Jews in the early years of the movement, most American Jews consider belief in Jesus as a messiah to be incompatible with being a Jew and practicing Judaism. Research on American Jews conducted by the Pew Foundation in 2013 found that two out of three American Jews agreed that a person can be Jewish even if he or she does not believe in God.[9] However, only one out of three people in the survey reported that a person can be Jewish if they believe that Jesus was the Messiah. Although Messianic Jews puzzle at the reason why American Jews think belief in Jesus threatens a person's Jewish status twice as much as being an atheist, the fact that one in three Jews see nothing wrong with a Jew who believes in Jesus is itself notable. At a time when half of all Jews are marrying non-Jews, the vast majority of whom are Christians, there is an unprecedented amount of mixing between Jews and Christians, and Christians are far less likely to be encountered as threats or dangers as spouses, relatives, and friends. It may be that the adoption of messianic beliefs about Jesus will eventually become no more criticized than the adoption of Buddhist or Hindu practices.

The most common Jewish argument that has been used to dismiss the central claim of Messianic Jews that Jesus is the Jewish Messiah has not changed much since the origins of Christianity. The majority of Jews from the time of Jesus until today insist that Jesus could not be the Messiah because he failed to do the things that a messiah is supposed to do and that beliefs about Jesus exceed and distort who and what a messiah is. There has been no shortage of other figures in Jewish history who inspired messianic speculation. Yet in each case, the final verdict on messianic candidates was decided by historical events. If the Jewish Messiah, as described by biblical prophets to a despondent people living in exile, will be a triumphant figure who gathers the dispersed Jews together, defeats their enemies, and establishes a utopian theocracy on earth, then events that unfold during the life of a prospective messiah make clear to most members of the Jewish community whether such expectations have been fulfilled, regardless of whether that messianic candidate is Jesus, Bar Kokhba, Shabbatai Zevi, or the Lubavitcher Rebbe.

Unfortunately, identifying the Messiah, or rather disqualifying someone who had been thought to be the Messiah by some group of people, is not simply a task of checking off a messianic to-do list as completed or not completed. What we know about messianic movements that confront disappointed expectations and unfulfilled prophecies is that the most steadfast of the faithful will construct new interpretations of the Messiah's nature and role to enable them to continue in their faith. In most cases, even the most faithful followers either die off or are reabsorbed by the main group, but in some cases, like the followers of Jesus, they persist in the process of dramatically reinterpreting their notion of a messiah. Such reinterpretations may be dismissed by outsiders to the messianic group, and tensions between Orthodox and heterodox doctrines may continue for long periods of time.

It is this kind of conflict over what represents the legitimate traditions of the Jewish people that forms the basis on which some groups are excluded as not authentically Jewish. Yet Messianic Jews complain that religious definitions that are used to challenge their Jewishness are not equally applied to various people who have abandoned Jewish religious traditions. An example of the issue they are raising can be seen in the declaration by Charles Liebman, a prominent scholar of modern Jewish life, that the claims to Jewishness of Messianic Jews must be rejected because of "the absence of fidelity on their part to what we claim is the authentic tradition. Remove the conception of tradition . . . affirm the right of Jews to formulate Judaism as they see fit without regard to the past and there is no basis for argument with anyone's Jewish claim."[10] The question, of course, rests on who is the "we" referred to by Liebman who decide what "the authentic tradition" is and what are the limits of reconceiving it in new ways. Nor is it Messianic Judaism alone that offers a different formulation of Judaism than the traditional Orthodox form. Anything that could be said about a lack of fidelity to "authentic tradition" among Messianic Jews could equally be said about Reform Jews or Humanistic Jews. Liebman correctly identified the problem but offered no solution other than awarding Orthodox Judaism the authority to declare what is authentic Jewish tradition.

In his book on Messianic Judaism, Reform rabbi Dan Cohn-Sherbok focuses directly on the question of its Jewish authenticity. Although he presents the case against Messianic Judaism from mainstream Judaism and in Israeli law simply and objectively, he simultaneously acknowledges that if the pluralistic nature of modern Judaism is recognized and accepted, it is hard to single out one version of Judaism as more inauthentic than others.[11] As he further observes, Messianic Jews live intensely Jewish lives in many respects, remain invested in their Jewish identities, celebrate Jewish holidays, and feel connected to Israel: "They remain loyal to the Jewish people, even though they are rejected and condemned."[12] It is not that Cohn-Sherbok offers any kind of endorsement of Messianic Judaism or its interpretations of Jewish tradition, which clearly deviates from his own denomination's approaches to Judaism. Nonetheless, his book is widely quoted and referenced on Messianic Jewish websites as evidence of a glimmer of recognition by the mainstream Jewish world. In fact, it may be hard for Reform and Reconstructionist rabbis to defend the delegitimization of Messianic Judaism when they have also witnessed their own movements' encounters with this issue. Mordecai Kaplan himself, the founder of Reconstructionism, was excommunicated from the Orthodox rabbinate. Orthodox Jews reject Reform Judaism as "not Judaism" and Reform rabbis as "not rabbis"; questions were raised about including humanistic Jews in the Union for Reform Judaism. While different segments of every generation define some Jews as outside the realm of legitimacy, it is never possible to tell in advance who will prevail and how they will define authenticity in the future.[13]

After generations with high rates of intermarriage between Jews and Christians, the stigma attached to such unions has dissipated dramatically, and thousands of children in such families have grown up with exposure to both Judaism and Christianity. Some children of mixed marriages may identify primarily with just one of these religions, but others may feel comfortable with a mixture of elements from both of them. A clear demarcation between different types of identities has always been more of an ideal, compared to the actual field on which struggles for recognition play out, where boundaries between different group identities, cultures, and religions become messier. The sharp line that all segments of the Jewish community draw by refusing any recognition of the authenticity of Messianic Jews may reflect their anxiety over the larger issue of the breakdown of clear boundaries between Jews and Christians in many families and communities.

Postmissionary Messianic Judaism

Considering the enormous freedom to construct their identities and ways of being Jewish that has been available to Jews in the last half-century, including borrowing from other religious and cultural traditions, the uniform rejection of Messianic Jews from all quarters of the organized Jewish community is somewhat unique. Patricia Power has raised forceful objections to the reliance on indefensible essentialist definitions of Judaism "to anathematize the anomalous Messianic other" whose identity straddles the border between Jews and Christians.[14] She insists that some, though not all, forms of Messianic Judaism share more than enough "family resemblances" with other forms of Judaism to be recognized as potentially new, albeit controversial, expressions of Judaism.

Indeed, a particular segment of the Messianic Jewish movement in the United States has reimagined and reconstructed its identity in ways that it hopes will be sufficient not just for gaining recognition from the mainstream Jewish world but also for becoming integrated into the broader Jewish community. The umbrella organization for this segment is the Union of Messianic Jewish Congregations (UMJC), whose name is meant to parallel the organizational structure and names of other Jewish denominations like the Union for Reform Judaism or the Orthodox Union. This shift stems, in part, from the maturing of the Messianic Jewish movement from the founding generation that included mostly Jews who had been raised in traditional Jewish denominations and who switched to Messianic Judaism as adults to one in which many millennial Messianic Jews were raised in Messianic Jewish synagogues. This generation of Messianic Jews is looking to redefine its relationship to the Jewish community as a whole and to make the case that Messianic Judaism is an authentic form of Judaism "that does not invalidate or throw out all other Judaisms."[15] Leaders in this movement say it is time for Messianic Jews to sever their close connections with evangelical Christianity and focus on Jewish authenticity.[16]

In reclaiming the importance of Judaism, some millennial Messianic Jews turn to modern Orthodoxy for models while others look to more liberal perspectives in Judaism, seeking a balance between faith in Jesus and the practices of other branches of Judaism. They want to engage with Jewish tradition and halakha. And where they disagree with or challenge others' ideas, they insist that "we want to do so within the already established frameworks and boundaries of Judaism."[17] This means that they maintain traditional Jewish practices such as circumcision, keeping kosher, observing the Sabbath and Jewish holidays, and following Jewish halakha in general, as they understand it.

One of the leaders of the UMJC is Stuart Dauermann, a rabbi at Ahavat Zion Messianic Synagogue, who believes it is possible to establish a way for Jewish believers in Jesus to preserve a robust relationship to modern Judaism and Jews. Dauermann was born into a Conservative Jewish family and became a Messianic Jew in the 1960s. He acknowledges that the original Hebrew Christians were merely an offshoot of Christian missionary organizations. They included a little bit of Jewish seasoning to entice Jews to be open to their message, but their interest in Judaism was limited to the time of Jesus. They rejected the last two thousand years of normative Judaism as unnecessary and irrelevant.[18]

Other Messianic Jews also have tried to offer a "Jewish style" of Christianity, but Dauermann notes that it, too, lacks any real Jewish content or connection to the norms and values of present-day Judaism. He describes this kind of Messianic Judaism as "Jimmy Swaggart with Yarmulkes," the "B'nai First Baptist Church," and "ham and cheese on a bagel."[19] It remains fundamentally Christian in its underlying approach, despite its efforts at creating a Jewish atmosphere through the use of Jewish songs and dances, bearded "rabbis" with kipot and tallitot, as well as Jewish "props" such as Israeli flags and Stars of David. Dauermann rejects this approach as little more than superficial Jewishness without substance, integrity, or authenticity.

Dauermann thus starts by acknowledging the Jewish *inauthenticity* of much of the Messianic Jewish world and the legitimate criticism from the mainstream Jewish world. From the outset, Jewish leaders have mostly reacted with suspicion about Messianic Judaism, which they consider a Trojan horse for Christianity. Dressing up Jesus in Jewish terms, like calling him "Yeshua ha-Mashiach" ("Jesus the Messiah") or including Jewish melodies or prayers, has been dismissed as merely a deceptive marketing device that seeks to persuade Jews today that their first-century ancestors who rejected the message of Jesus two thousand years ago had made a mistake.

Dauermann hopes to offer a different perspective on Messianic Judaism and Messianic Jews, based on the efforts of people like him to develop a form of modern Judaism that shares as much as possible with the wider Jewish community, albeit with a central focus on "Yeshua," the Jewish Messiah. Rather than importing a few Jewish scraps into an evangelical Christian framework, Dauermann wants to import a few Christian ideas into a fully Jewish framework, as well as "to preserve every possible scrap of continuity with the wider Jewish community. We see the Jewish community as our primary community of reference. In this regard, we seek to develop not a Jewish version of Christianity, but a Judaism that reveals Yeshua's centrality."[20]

Dauermann is representative of the shift away from any affiliation with Christian groups or churches in some Messianic Jewish communities. These Messianic Jews think of themselves not as Christians with Jewish backgrounds but rather as Jews who happen to believe what a small group of Jews in the first century believed—that Jesus is the Messiah predicted in the writings of the Hebrew prophets. They insist that this is not just Judaism-lite, with some messianic beliefs mixed in, but a complete commitment to Judaism. They include people born and raised as Jews, who self-identify as Jews, wear yarmulkes, had bar/bat mitzvahs, read Hebrew, study Torah, observe Shabbat and Jewish holidays, keep kosher, want to raise their kids as Jews, have dreidels and menorahs in their living rooms, feel connected to and support Israel, *and* believe that Jesus is the Messiah.

Mark Kinzer, another leader in the UMJC, begins with a biological metaphor to describe the relationship between Messianic Jews and the rest of Judaism in his pamphlet titled "Judaism as Genus, Messianism as Species." He understands that believing in Jesus may not be a choice that most Jews will choose to make, but he denies that Messianic Jews have rejected or betrayed some fundamental part of their Jewishness. Judaism is the umbrella "genus" under which there are a variety of different "species" of Jewishness. The various species of Jews may be dramatically different from, and even incompatible with, one another, but they all nonetheless are related as members of the same genus. His point is that all Jews are part of the same family, no matter how deviant or heretical one Jewish group may seem to other Jews. In a family, not everyone will agree with one another or approve of their way of life, but certain bonds of connection still remain. The small detail he omits is that in response to behavior that seems radically unacceptable, even families may disown someone who claims to be a member or refuse to recognize claims that someone ever was a member of that family.

Kinzer regards the process of interpreting and reinterpreting the meaning of Torah as an essential part of the historical development of Judaism, to which Messianic Judaism merely wants to add its voice. He believes that being part of Jewish tradition means uncovering new layers of meaning by approaching Jewish texts from a messianic perspective. Kinzer compares this process with the way that Jewish mysticism also offered a new perspective on Torah and the fulfillment of mitzvot in light of its theories of unifying the fragmentation of divine light. In either case, "Judaism as a system of life and thought remains intact, but it is at the same time transformed by the new perspective from which it is considered."[21] It is true that Messianic Jews have inserted the name of Jesus into some prayers, which may bother other Jews, but they are not the only ones who introduced liturgical innovations that were greeted with resistance and rejection.

Jewish feminists have likewise reinterpreted the meaning of the Torah and transformed familiar stories, texts, and rituals by seeing them through new lenses that fundamentally change them. At first, some Jewish feminist innovations, midrash, and rituals were challenged by more traditional Jews as violations of authentic Judaism, yet over time many of them have been adopted as routine parts of liberal synagogues.[22] It is not unusual now to find some Reconstructionist synagogues where female pronouns for God have been introduced, references to the Jews' unique status as God's "chosen people" have been replaced with more universalist language, and additional changes have been made that other traditionalist Jews would reject.

The movement of some Messianic Jews to find a home within Judaism is described by some of their leaders as "Postmissionary Messianic Judaism" to signal their rejection of the earlier "mission to the Jews" stage of Messianic Judaism.[23] Now, they insist, they are just doing what many other groups of Jews have also done to reinterpret and reform Judaism in new ways. While their innovations may continue to be rejected by most other Jews, who remain adamant that this is not an acceptable form of Jewish expression, it is not impossible to imagine a time in the future when they are recognized as black sheep in the Jewish family, but family members nonetheless. "Hashivenu," one of the newer umbrella groups for Messianic Jews, states that its goal is to place equal emphasis on "Messianic" and on "Judaism." Their website states,

> Hashivenu envisions mature Messianic Judaism to be an authentic expression of Jewish life that maintains substantial continuity with Jewish tradition. But this is a Judaism that is energized by faith in Yeshua of Nazareth, whom we honor as both the promised Messiah and the fullness of Torah. Mature Messianic Judaism is not simply Judaism plus Yeshua, or Yeshua plus Judaism, but an integrated and seamless whole in which discipleship to Yeshua is expressed in traditional Jewish forms and in which the contemporary practice of Judaism is renewed in Yeshua and by the power of the Spirit.[24]

Authenticity and False Messiahs

Obviously, the label "Messianic Judaism" highlights the religious centrality of the doctrine of the Messiah within this particular understanding of Judaism. In this respect, Messianic Judaism has much more in common with Orthodox Judaism and fundamentalist Christianity than it does with either liberal Judaism or liberal Christianity. Both Messianic Judaism and Orthodox Judaism take literally the idea of a messiah that is described in the works of the Hebrew prophets. Messianic Jews see themselves as adhering much closer to Jewish tradition in their concept of a messiah, in contrast to most liberal Jews, who look at the Messiah as little more than a utopian metaphor, not an actual person whom they await.

Jewish authorities have traditionally regarded Jesus as a "false messiah," since his life ended without accomplishing the tasks normally associated with the Messiah. Just as Moses was sent by God to overcome the tyranny of Pharaoh and lead the oppressed Jewish slaves to a divinely promised land, where peace and prosperity would flourish, the Messiah was described as someone who would defeat the enemies of the Jewish people, gather them from the places to which they had been dispersed, and reestablish the line of Jewish kings in Israel. For most first-century Jews, the humiliating crucifixion of Jesus by the Romans without accomplishing the goals set for the Jewish Messiah was incontrovertible evidence that Jesus was not the Messiah. It should have marked the end of a failed Jewish messianic movement.

Of course, Jesus was not the last Jewish messianic figure whose followers struggled both to make sense of their leaders' apparent failures to bring about final redemption before their deaths and to find a way to explain that to skeptical Jews around them. It is not always the case that following a spiritual master who is eventually dismissed as a false messiah by most Jews is enough to threaten the followers' Jewish status.

In 1648, the year of the Chmelnitzky pogrom in Poland and other severe antisemitic persecution, a somewhat unbalanced man by the name of Shabbatai Zevi (1626–1676) proclaimed himself the Messiah. Slowly, despite the opposition of many of the rabbis, including excommunication by some of them, Shabbatai continued to gain followers and achieved widespread acceptance throughout many of the Jewish communities in the world. His disciple Nathan of Gaza predicted that the messianic age would arrive in 1666 and Shabbatai would become the new sultan of the Ottoman Empire. Many Jews sold their businesses and property to prepare for the messianic period and traveled to Jerusalem. When Shabbatai went to Constantinople to take the crown of the Turkish Sultan and inaugurate his messianic rule, he was arrested, jailed, and finally given the choice of conversion to Islam or death.

He chose to convert.

A messiah who converts to another religion clearly falls short of the expectations of the Jewish Messiah. Making sense of this development presented his followers with a challenge every bit as confusing as the one the followers of Jesus faced when their redeemer was crucified. But just as Christianity turned an awkward situation to its own advantage by saying that Jesus's humiliating execution had been part of God's plan all along, some of the followers of Shabbatai claimed that he *had* to convert in order to fulfill his messianic function. It was necessary for him to abandon following the Torah and convert to Islam in order to liberate sparks of divine holiness that had been trapped in realms of evil and impurity, like Islam. Although Shabbatai had converted, his apostasy was not real. He only seemed to be a Muslim, but he was really still a Jew.

While most of Shabbatai's followers stayed within Judaism, these "Messianic Jews" were still persecuted by the official rabbinic authorities. Other followers of Shabbatai, including some rabbis and mystics, felt that the conversion of the Messiah to Islam should serve as an example for them and that redemption required that they, too, pretend to be Muslims. They would not follow the worldly Torah and halakha but rather the mystical Torah revealed by the Messiah.

After the death of Shabbatai, different sects of his followers continued to try to understand the meaning of his messianic mission. This often meant combining a mixture of Jewish and Muslim ideas, including Kabbalistic and Sufi practices. Competing sects emerged, one claiming descent from the original followers of Shabbatai and others led by men who each claimed to be the reincarnation of Shabbatai. Today, only a few of their descendants continue to see themselves as Sabbateans. A Jewish-Muslim sect, the Donmes, still survives in Turkey. The members are formally Muslims, but inwardly they feel that they are Jews. Among younger Sabbateans today, there is an interest in reclaiming their Jewish roots and identities.[25]

The episode of Shabbatai Tevi's messianic career and the status of his followers, both after he converted to Islam and following his death, is instructive in considering the Jewish status of today's Messianic Jews. Messianic Jews raise the question of when the Jewish followers of Jesus ceased to be Jewish and why their present-day belief in Jesus should be treated any differently than the original Jewish followers of Jesus. In the case of the followers of Shabbatai Tevi, it would be hard to pinpoint a moment when they ceased to be Jews.

Gershom Scholem, perhaps the greatest expert on Jewish mysticism, has argued that the Sabbatean movement was Jewish from start to finish. He regarded it as symptomatic of a crisis of faith within the Jewish people at a time of weakening rabbinic authority. Scholem went so far as to suggest that the movement paved the way for nineteenth-century reform and haskalah by breaking the monopoly of rabbinic Judaism. From this perspective, the Sabbatean movement was not only authentically Jewish; it was a catalyst in bringing about needed religious change and innovation and pushing the development of Judaism in new directions.

Certainly, there is no question that Jesus and his followers were an authentically Jewish sect in the first century, one that likewise challenged the Jewish establishment of the time in ways that inevitably reverberated in the subsequent development of normative Judaism. While it is difficult to identify a precise moment when the movement that Jesus started ceased to be recognizably Jewish, it is also indisputable that in the aftermath of his death, a new non-Jewish religion emerged. Within a century of the crucifixion, the movement's doctrines about Jesus had become hellenized in ways that were incompatible with Jewish ideas, and the followers of the movement were overwhelmingly Gentiles. The Nazarenes, the Jewish followers of Jesus who remained committed to the observance of Jewish law, were increasingly marginalized and eventually rejected by other Jews as heretics and traitors and by Gentile Christians, whose religion had become increasingly de-Judaized, if not overtly anti-Jewish. Lacking recognition by either side, they gradually disappeared.[26]

The Rebbe Messiah

For many Jews, the epitome of an authentic Jew is the Chabad rabbi on a college campus or in a far-flung location where no other Jews can be found. They are fulfilling a vision of their greatest leader, the "Rebbe," Menachem Schneerson, who died in June 1994. While the Rebbe himself actively promoted the idea that the arrival of the Messiah was imminent, he also strongly opposed and discouraged speculation or declarations by those of his followers who were convinced that he was the Messiah. Many people would be inclined to dismiss the messianic speculation about the Lubavitcher Rebbe as merely an expression of the great admiration his followers had for his wisdom and righteousness, not a factor that could throw their Jewish status into question. Nonetheless, such messianic beliefs intensified among some of his followers in the final years of the Rebbe's life, and they underwent further transformation after his death.[27] Just as the shock of Jesus's crucifixion motivated his followers to give new meanings to the circumstances of his death, those who thought the Rebbe was the Messiah likewise needed to find new ways of understanding his death. Perhaps, said some, the Rebbe had not really died but was only in hiding, waiting for the right moment to announce his messiahship. Perhaps, said others, he would be miraculously resurrected, not unlike Jesus, to continue his messianic work and complete his mission of gathering the Jews to return to Israel and rebuild the Temple. Maybe his death had been atonement for others. Perhaps by freeing his soul from his body, he had become even more spiritually powerful than before. A few of his followers reportedly even claimed that the Rebbe is actually God, or at least has superhuman powers.[28]

Though such beliefs will seem heretical to some Jews, the role of the Rebbe in the Hasidic movement has always been suffused with messianic or messianic-like qualities. The Rebbe was seen as the human embodiment, or incarnation, of the Torah, a human manifestation of divine will and perfect righteousness, a vehicle for prophecies and miracles. Like Jesus, Schneerson accomplished little of what is traditionally expected of the Messiah in Jewish tradition. In both cases, the apparently unfulfilled requirements for a messiah become an impetus for new interpretations of the meaning of a messiah, including reports or expectations of resurrection or other means of completion of his messianic work in a future "second coming." In both cases, the claims were ignored or rejected by virtually all the rest of the Jewish people.

Like the first-century followers of Jesus, this segment of the Lubavitch Hasidim has focused on specific beliefs about their deceased leader that seem heretical to other Jews who do not share them. It is unlikely that a portion of Chabad will isolate itself from the rest of the Jewish world on account of these beliefs, since outreach and service to other Jews—Orthodox or not, observant or not—are central parts of the Chabad approach. Indeed, it is ironic for critics to accuse Chabad Messianists of not being authentically Jewish, since Chabad has done more to bring Orthodox Jewish perspectives and practices to a worldwide Jewish audience than any other group. The belief that a religious leader or master has messianic qualities that are not acknowledged by the rest of the Jewish world does not necessarily result in the loss of Jewish status until, as in the case of Jewish Christians, the chosen Messiah becomes the basis for a new religion. As with all messianic movements, Chabad Messianists will need to adjust their beliefs over time to accommodate the inevitable delay in the reappearance or return of the Rebbe. Some will doubtless abandon the messianic ideas and be reabsorbed by the nonmessianic part of Chabad, while others may persist in increasingly deviant ideas of the messianic meaning of the Rebbe. It is the aftermath of messianic beliefs about a particular figure that determines the degree to which continued recognition of their Jewish status by other Jews may be called into question.

PART III
AUTHENTIC JEWISH PEOPLEHOOD

7 Creating a National Jewish Culture in Israel

At the beginning of the Passover seder, Jews around the world have traditionally recited the line *"This year we are here; next year* may we be in the Land of Israel. *This year we are slaves; next year* may we be free men." This idea of exile and redemption has been interpreted in various literal and symbolic ways, but at the core of this understanding of "place" is the idea that Jewish life "here," wherever that place of exile may be, is insufficient, inadequate, and imperfect. It may not be clear just who and what it is that enslaves the Jews, or whether their slavery is political or psychological, literal or metaphorical; but what is clear is that the life they are living falls short in some important dimensions. In contrast, the life that Jews yearn for in the future, a life of freedom, is one that is associated with a specific location, the land of Israel. Out of this polarity between exile and redemption, between life in diaspora and life in their own land, it is easy to discern the outline of a powerful journey from inauthenticity to authenticity.

The sense of authenticity associated with life in the land of Israel has been understood in a number of different ways, expressing various political, cultural, religious, and existential forms of redemption that would blossom when Jews reclaimed their land. For religious Zionists, the return to Israel was the fulfillment of the divinely ordained mission of the Jewish people. Its realization has been taken as validation of the authenticity of divine promises made to ancient Israelites and of the possibility of authentic Jewish religious life rooted in the laws and rituals of ancient Israel. For cultural Zionists, Israel has offered Jews the freedom to create and express an authentically Jewish culture. Political Zionists generally have cared less about religious or cultural authenticity and more about Jews achieving the political legitimacy and authenticity associated with their own nation-state. Finally, there have been those who see life in Israel as a precondition for individual Jews creating their own personal visions of existential authenticity.

Zionism and Authenticity

The vague messianic fantasy of being rescued from exile and guided into a land of one's own became a concrete political platform once it was infused with the doctrines of modern European nationalism that pervaded nineteenth-century political thought. The assumption was that in order to constitute a real nation, a people needed to possess several essential ingredients—a land of their own, a common language, shared traditions and folkways, and a common historical situation. The origins of Zionism were based on the goal of restoring a national identity for the Jewish people that included these lost ingredients.

The Zionist platform was an attempt to answer the question, Is it possible for a Jew to remain authentic in a non-Jewish society, living in non-Jewish lands and speaking the national languages of other peoples? The answer offered by Zionism was an emphatic *no*. They began with the presupposition that the Jewish people needed to reinvent the conditions of their own authenticity, and that a normal, creative, and fulfilling life could only be lived in a land populated by one's own people. The romantic nationalism to which Zionism appealed was, in part, a reaction against the rootlessness and impersonality of modern urban industrialized society, where people lived among strangers and lacked any connection to traditional community, ancestral languages, and territorial roots. Many Zionists focused on a purer premodern era when people were tied more closely to one another and to the land where they lived. Whether one calls it an ethnic, tribal, or racial identity, the bond of shared language, culture, religion, land, and family histories that bind a people together held a powerful appeal that preceded and preempted any newly conferred rights associated with citizenship in European democracies. Such romanticized nationalism saw the unity of a people as a kind of transcendental essence or power that was also the source of their vitality and creativity.[1]

Since Jews had been excluded from this sense of national belonging in the places where they lived, the Zionist proposal of an autonomous nation for the Jewish people where their own creativity and culture could be expressed offered a solution that neither traditional diaspora Jewish life nor emancipation in European democracies could offer. On the one hand, many Zionists saw traditional Jewish religion as a weak and dying expression of the Jewish people. On the other hand, liberal emancipated Jews made religious reforms that had purged Jewish identity of its unique collective national or tribal cohesiveness. Reformers had wanted to minimize the importance of Hebrew and other cultural practices that set Jews apart. As a result, liberal Jews were becoming just people, not "a people."

True emancipation, Zionists argued, would require more than ossified religious traditions or newly legislated rights. It would require the liberation of the collective spirit of the Jewish people, which had been suppressed and distorted by diaspora life. Years later, Golda Meir wrote, "I have always believed that Zionism means Jewish emancipation in every sense, including the spiritual and cultural, so that a Jew who creates cultural values may do so as a free man. It may be assuming on my part, but I believe that there is no Jew in the *galut* creating as a free man and as a free Jew. Only a Jew in Israel can do so."[2] Zionist thinkers were convinced that Jewish diaspora life was a form of *galut*, or "exile," that was doomed to wither and die, if not because of outright persecution then because of assimilation and the loss of a raison d'être for remaining Jewish. Those who still believed in the promise of emancipation were victims of self-deception and false consciousness.

In his 1862 essay "Rome and Jerusalem," Moses Hess offered a description of what Sartre would later label the "inauthentic Jew": "The really dishonorable Jew is not the old-type, pious one, who would rather have his tongue cut out than utter a word in denial of his nationality, but the modern kind, who . . . is ashamed of his nationality because the hand of fate is pressing heavily upon his people. The beautiful phrases about humanity and enlightenment which he uses so freely to cloak his treason, his fear of being identified with his unfortunate brethren, will ultimately not protect him from the judgment of public opinion."[3]

As a minority in society, Jews could never be themselves, since they were always having to manage and respond to the real or imagined perceptions of non-Jews, for whom Jewish claims to a national identity shared with non-Jews were never pure enough. No matter how fluent Jews became with local language and culture, their claim to share the national spirit of the countries where they lived would never be recognized. They never could get rid of their "foreign accents."

In one of his most famous essays, "Slavery in Freedom" (1891), the great cultural Zionist Ahad Ha'am challenged the idea that political emancipation was sufficient for the Jews *as a people* to be free. While the assimilated Jews of Western Europe may have been granted civil rights and political freedom, he argued, it had come at a high price. Thinking that by becoming less Jewish, they would be considered more like everyone else, they had repressed the collective Jewish national spirit and succumbed to a kind of "spiritual slavery."[4] By trying to be what they were not and denying what they really were, the Jews in countries like France had condemned themselves to a servile, unnatural, and inauthentic life. The diaspora Jew, explained Ahad Ha'am, "works among an alien people, in a world that is not his own, and in which he cannot become at home unless he artificially change his nature and the current of his mind, thereby inevitably tearing himself into two disparate halves, and foredooming all his work to reveal, in its character and its products, this want of harmony and wholeness."[5]

The essentialist understanding of the collective Jewish national spirit proposed by Ahad Ha'am and others was rooted in the romantic nationalism, most famously articulated by Herder, which formed the core of European nationalism in the nineteenth century. By trying to explain the uniqueness of different national groups as a quasi-biological phenomenon, it was natural to turn to racial foundations for national differences. Against this background, it is not surprising that many Zionist thinkers sought to reclaim a similarly biological view of the Jewish people. Each people is united by its own special *volksgeist*, Herder had argued, which defines the essence of who they really are and provides the source of their cultural creativity and authenticity. In this perspective, authenticity is always defined at the collective level, where contributing to the growth of *the Jewish people as a whole* defines the purpose of an *individual Jew's* life. Ahad Ha'am explained, "When the individual thus values the community as his own life, and strives after its happiness as though it were his individual well-being, he finds satisfaction, and no longer feels so keenly the bitterness of this individual existence, because he sees the end for which he lives and suffers."[6] In short, the Jewish people, or perhaps more accurately, the Hebrew people, are like a single living organism in which each individual contributes to its overall survival and growth.

In an oft-quoted passage, Ahad Ha'am described Jewishness as resting on a familial bond with the Jewish people no less real and physical than a son's bond with his father. Those who disguise or deny their Jewishness as the price of acceptance by the non-Jewish world are no better than those who would disown their families. He wrote,

> I at least know "why I remain a Jew," or, rather, I can find no meaning in such a question, any more than if I were asked why I remain my father's son. I at least can speak my mind concerning the beliefs and the opinions which I have inherited from my ancestors, without fearing to snap the bond that unites me to my people.... In a word, I am my own, and my opinions and feelings are my own. I have no reason for concealing or denying them, for deceiving others or myself. And this spiritual freedom—scoff who will!—I would not exchange or barter for all the emancipation in the world.[7]

Spiritual freedom is only possible, according to Ahad Ha'am, by recognizing an inescapable collective bond. To the extent that emancipation encouraged Jews to sever this bond, they became detached from their authentic selves. Harmony, wholeness, and authenticity required a national center where Jewish culture could develop naturally and unfettered. From this center of Jewish culture, Ahad Ha'am proposed, "the spirit of Judaism will radiate to the great circumference, to all the communities of the Diaspora, to inspire them with new life and to preserve the overall unity of our people."[8]

The focus on the imperishable Jewish spirit, or *volksgeist*, in Zionist thinkers like Ahad Ha'am neither glorified ancient Israelite ancestors as the source of eternally valid texts and practices (as claimed by the strictly religious) nor disowned them as primitive and irrational in their beliefs and practices (as recommended by religious reformers).[9] It was important to be neither frozen in the past nor permanently disconnected from it. Ahad Ha'am understood that cultures grow, develop, and change in response to different situations and environments. Respect for traditions of the past does not require us to follow them. Indeed, Ahad Ha'am believed that the heyday of religion had already passed. Jews who had abandoned religious faith and practice were no less authentically Jewish, as long as they identified with the Jewish people and the changing expressions of the Jewish spirit. Each generation will reinvent its own expressions of the Jewish national spirit. He wrote, "Our outlook differs from that of our ancestors, not because we are essentially better than they were, but simply because our mental condition has changed, and our environment is different; . . . consequently, many of the sacred truths of every generation must become falsehoods and absurdities in the next, and they who judge to-day will not escape scot-free from the tribunal of to-morrow."[10]

The implication of this idea is that the expression of what is authentically Jewish requires a simultaneous connection to *both* the past *and* the future. Ahad Ha'am wanted to respect the connection that links Jews in any period of history with their ancestors, but those ancestors are not the authorities on what is authentically Jewish. Rather how the meaning of being Jewish is expressed in different moments of history is open to change, as the meaning of the past is reconceived in later periods of history. Most importantly, while Ahad Ha'am's position on the Jewish national spirit was inspired by the cultural essentialism rooted in European philosophers like Herder, he avoided a retrospective essentialism that romanticized the past. He demanded the independence of each generation of Jews to reconceive how the Jewish national spirit would be expressed and gradually change in different times and places.[11]

Other Zionist thinkers offered a more existentialist approach to Jewish authenticity building on Nietzschean iconoclastic ideas about Jewish religion and culture rather than Herder's ideas about a people's *volksgeist*. Misha Josef Berdichevski, for example, believed that collective identities, whether religious, cultural, or nationalist, were obstacles to the personal authenticity of individuals. While Berdichevski's background included a family lineage of rabbis, traditional yeshiva studies, and life in an Eastern European shtetl, he ultimately insisted that Jewish authenticity had little to do with traditional rabbinic teachings or beliefs. Indeed, he considered Jewish religious life in diaspora to be an unhealthy straitjacket on Jewish creativity and passion from which Jews needed to be liberated. In an essay titled "The Question of Our Past" (1900–1903) he wrote, "Among us, man is crushed, living by traditional customs, laws, doctrines, and judgments—for many things were bequeathed us by our ancestors which deaden the soul and deny it freedom."[12] Zionism would offer the opportunity for a new start for a new kind of Jew, a Hebrew who would create his own new path and his own values.

This existentialist approach to authenticity elevated the individual Jew to a lonely, if heroic, position as the sole authority for ethical values. Unlike Ahad Ha'am, Berdichevski did not propose any unifying collective spirit or common culture of the Jewish people. Rather he proposed a view of Judaism as "a conglomeration of constantly diverging groups and contradictory theories."[13] For Berdichevski, only the individual's own decision, independent of Jewish culture and heritage, could determine the basis for his authenticity: "The living man takes precedence over the heritage of his forefathers."[14] In other words, Jewish existence precedes Jewish essence. Without the idea of a Jewish *volksgeist*, or spiritual essence, Jewishness no longer exists apart from what individual Jews do or do not do and believe or do not believe. Berdichevski insisted on the concrete lives of individual Jews rather than any abstract concept of Judaism or Jewish spirit. His focus was on "the living man, before the legacy of his ancestors."[15] He insisted, quite simply, on the autonomous choices and actions of the individual Jew: "Whatever a Jew does and thinks, this constitutes his Jewishness."[16]

The Zionist project focused not only on a theory of collective authenticity that would be generated and expressed by a free people living in its own land. It also offered a theory of individual authenticity, embodied in a new mythic figure, the "new Jew" or Hebrew. Unlike the timid, weak, and ugly diaspora Jew who was forced to live without authenticity, the new Jew would embody the full promise of authentic Jewish life, characterized by strength, pride, and beauty.

The Re-creation of a Zionist Past and the Rebirth of the "Hebrews"

Like other nationalist movements, Zionism offered a selective historical narrative of the origins of the Jews as a national group that emphasized both their unity as a people and their distinctiveness—historically, culturally, and spiritually—from other peoples. The story focused on the classic myth of paradise, paradise lost, and paradise regained. In the Zionist version of Jewish history, the Jews had all lived together in ancient times in the land of Israel, where they spoke their own language, worked the soil, and were led by proud and strong leaders like King David. Nearly two thousand years ago, they had been forced out of their land and sent into exile, but now they were ready to return to their ancestral home. Thus Jewish life in exile had been merely a long hiatus in national existence that was about to come to an end.

While Zionism embodied typical nationalist fantasies about the restoration of the group's earliest cultural practices, this was a complicated goal that required deemphasizing centuries of actual Jewish life and culture in exile in favor of the imagined glory of the distant past. Rabbinic Judaism, the form of Judaism most directly responsible for the structure of religious practice in the Jewish diaspora, is an example of something that was deliberately ignored in the classic Zionist story. Unlike Orthodox Jews, for whom tradition and religious law are the barometers of authenticity, many Zionist thinkers rejected rabbinic culture and its traditions as obstacles to developing a new national cultural identity. To the extent that the Torah, the sacred text of Judaism, was mentioned at all, it was less as a revelation of divine law than as evidence, written in the Jews' original language, of their ancient claims to the land as well as of the prophetic predictions of their glorious return.

The archetype of the "New Jew" who would rise up in Israel was best embodied in the figure of the Sabra, or Hebrew, the heroic alternative to diaspora Jews. The Sabra was to be an embodiment of the Jewish *volk*, representing the dual connection to both the land where they lived and the people to which they belonged. These new Jews who were native to Israel were, like the sabra fruit, rough and tough on the outside but sweet on the inside. As Oz Almog describes it in his book *The Sabra*, the new strong and healthy Hebrew in Israel was defined in direct opposition to the weak and sickly Jews of the diaspora.[17] Almog saw the roots of this new Jew, ironically, in Jewish envy of the simple uncomplicated life of the Gentiles and an unconscious acceptance of a Gentile concept of masculinity and authenticity.[18]

The Zionist rejection of the life of the diaspora Jew as inauthentic also reflected an internalization of stereotypes about Jews that had developed within Gentile antisemitism.[19] The New Jew would not resemble the pale, unathletic, bearded, and hook-nosed Jew of European antisemitism. Rather he was, as Almog suggests, a figure of classical Greco-Roman perfection—clean-shaven, perfectly proportioned, tall, tan, with high cheekbones and an upturned nose.[20] The Sabra's muscular body and bearing represented physical strength, health, beauty, and the confidence of youth. His style of dress was simple, practical, with even a little cultivated messiness. Unlike the diaspora Jews who monitored themselves and had to be careful about what they said, the Hebrew Sabra spoke his mind directly, even rudely. He wore sandals, the footwear of his biblical ancestors, which allowed his feet to be in contact with both the soil and air.

Delegitimizing Palestinian Authenticity

The negation of the diaspora Jew in classic Zionist thinking represented the need for a clean break from the miseries of diaspora life in order to reestablish the broken connection of the Jewish people to their ancestral land and thereby restore their strength, health, and creativity. The inauthenticity of the diaspora was a necessary foil for asserting the authenticity of the "New Jew," which was based on the same kind of primordial connection that bonded national groups in Europe to their native lands. Unfortunately, these were also the same feelings that explained, as Sartre described in *Antisemite and Jew*, the French antisemites' insistence on their own rootedness in France and their rejection of the notion that others who lived among them, like the Jews, had any special rights or claims to belonging there. Sartre had condemned the inauthenticity at the heart of this kind of national identity. Despite his cautious support of Jewish nationalism, it is unlikely that he would have endorsed a Herderian form of nationalist identity for Jews in Palestine/Israel.[21]

As the waves of Jewish immigration (aliyah) from Europe to Palestine from 1882 to 1914 brought the Zionist dream of establishing a new national identity based on blood, land, and language closer to reality, it was necessary to come to terms with the presence of other people who lived in that land. How these "Others" were described in the Zionist narrative goes to the heart of the conflict between Jews and Palestinians over the last century. The purpose of the Zionist narrative has been to undermine any cultural or national authenticity associated with the Palestinians. It highlighted the young, strong, Jewish pioneers who were bringing the neglected wilderness back to life. Palestine was often portrayed as an empty place, "a land without a people," waiting for the return of the Jewish people for it to be reborn.[22] When they were considered at all, the indigenous people already in Palestine were seen as less developed, educated, and civilized, very much the way that native populations elsewhere were depicted by European colonial powers.

The enduring conflict between Jews and Palestinians has often played out as a struggle between competing national narratives that seek to establish or deny the authenticity of each side's claim to the same land. On the one hand, the Palestinians and the rest of the Arab world for the most part denied the legitimacy of Jewish claims to Israel as a national homeland. They have condemned Zionism as one more manifestation of European settler-colonialism and rejected the idea of a homeland expressly for Jews as racist. In addition, it faults Zionists for refusing to recognize the Palestinians as a people with what Edward Said called an "indissoluable bond with the land."[23] On the other hand, the Jewish narrative has challenged the idea that the Palestinians were actually an authentic national group until quite recently, and it accuses them of seeking the destruction of Israel and the Jewish people through terrorism and violence.

Conflict resolution specialist Herbert Kelman describes Israeli and Palestinian national identities as locked in a state of "negative interdependence" in which each side's affirmation of the authenticity of its own identity is intertwined with the negation of the legitimacy and authenticity of the other.[24] The intractability of the conflict, Kelman claims, is the result of the fact that "each group's identity becomes hostage to the identity of the other," and authenticity is a zero-sum game resting on the delegitimization of the other's claim to the land. Any movement toward a solution will require an ability to recognize the necessity and reality of "positive interdependence,"[25] a goal that resembles the "concrete liberalism" described by Sartre at the end of *Antisemite and Jew*, and the importance of "recognition" described by multiculturalists. For Kelman, this means that Israelis and Palestinians each recognize that their own identities can survive and be expressed only if they also find a way to allow the identities of the other to survive and be expressed.

The Authenticity of the Mizrahi/Sephardi Jews

The Zionist project to alleviate the alienation among the Jews of Europe was rooted both in European ideas of race and nationalism as well as the cultural tensions that enlightenment and emancipation had brought to European Jews and Judaism. Modernity had dealt a serious blow to the viability of traditional Jewish life in European communities. As a result, the Zionist model of Jewish authenticity was both dependent and counterdependent on European culture and the Ashkenazi Jews who lived there. In some cases, those more vehement voices for "negation of the diaspora" ruled out all aspects of diaspora Judaism and European culture as elements in a new authentic Hebrew identity. Others, such as Theodor Herzl, were content to appropriate European political, cultural, and philosophical ideas for the construction of a new authentic Jewish form of life.

In neither case, however, were the cultural ideas, religious practices, languages, or even physical appearance of non-European Jews given much attention. It was Ashkenazi immigrants to Israel in the early twentieth century who laid the foundation for the idea of reborn authentic Jews and planted the seeds of the idea of Israeliness. The Jewish diaspora of the Mediterranean and Arab worlds had developed a considerably different approach both to Jewish life and to relations with the surrounding non-Jewish world than that of the Ashkenazi Jews of Europe. While Zionist thinkers from Europe were attracted to the model of the New Jews who would initiate a renewal of Jewish society in Palestine, the unacknowledged cultural diversity of Jewish people from differing backgrounds undercut this project and its claims of authenticity from the start. If a new form of authentic Jewishness was to emerge in a Jewish homeland consisting of the experiences of a diversity of Jews and Jewish communities, it would have to take into account the lives and lifestyles of non-European Jews.

Many Zionist Jews from Europe had immigrated to Palestine in hopes of reclaiming the tribal or national culture of their biblical ancestors as a replacement for what seemed to be the bankrupt diaspora Jewish culture in Europe. When they imagined what those original Israelite "folk" were like, they often looked to the oldest Jewish immigrants to Palestine and to Jews living in the neighboring Middle Eastern countries. The New Jews who would spring from the soil of the land first tilled by their ancestors seemed to have more in common with Arab Jews than with diaspora Jews in Europe. Jews from Arab countries, particularly Yemenite Jews, were often idealized as embodiments of a kind of premodern pastoral existence that reminded Ashkenazi Jews of ancient biblical shepherds, whose customs and religious practices preserved the folk authenticity European Ashkenazi Jews were seeking.[26]

Yet there were limits to the romanticizing of Jews from traditional Arab cultures like Morocco, Iraq, and Yemen as the link to an ancestral past. Such Jews were also Arab in culture and language, an awkward fact that was eventually disguised under the umbrella labels "Mizrahi" or "Sephardi." Within this Zionist narrative, the attitude toward Arab Jews and Arabs as a whole was deeply ambivalent. On the one hand, Arab Jews and Arabs in general represented a premodern alternative to modern urban, European culture. They lived a simple life, untouched by the contamination and alienation of the diaspora life from which classic Zionists were drawn and seemingly connected to the world of the earliest Jewish ancestors. Their rootedness in the region and in a traditional lifestyle close to the land provided evidence of the continuous presence of Jews in the Middle East. For the pioneering generation of European Jews who immigrated to Israel, the goal was, in the words of a rabbi in Palestine at the time, "to become an Arab, to be in his total Hebrewness like them, for the Hebrew in him to be like the Arab in them."[27]

Zionist thinking was not immune to the orientalist ideas of other Europeans, especially those nations whose colonial empires extended into the Middle East in the first half of the twentieth century. But Zionism's connection to orientalism was more complex, since the land they proposed for Jewish settlement was itself part of the "oriental" world, and their own ancient roots in the oriental world provided the justification for their claim that they were entitled to relocate there. Indeed, one of the major complaints of European antisemites was that Jews were not like the Europeans among whom they lived. They were a different, *oriental* race of people.

Zionist orientalism particularly struggled with the meaning of Arabness as the authentic culture of long-standing inhabitants of the land. At the same time that European Jews wanted to orientalize themselves to some degree, to be as rooted in the land as the Arabs were, they also considered some aspects of the Orient as alien and other. Arab culture was seen as primitive and backward, with a history of violence and tribal conflict that made Arabs potentially untrustworthy and dangerous. The paradoxical situation of the Arabs was that they were seen as both models for the new Jews and also obstacles who would be displaced in the process of creating this new national group. Ammon Raz-Krakotzkin writes, "By appropriating the 'nativeness' of the Arabs, the Zionists assumed the role of natives and rendered the indigenous population obsolete."[28]

Whatever elements of Arab culture embodied by Mizrahi Jews would end up being incorporated into a newly invented sense of Israeliness, their Arabness had to be sanitized. Zionism struggled to hide or deny the obvious continuity between Jewishness and Arabness for Mizrahi Jews.[29] Just as Zionists used Hebrew to replace Yiddish as a legitimate Jewish language, they also strove to repackage the Arabness of Arab Jews. Nonetheless, Jews who spoke Arabic and Arabs who spoke Hebrew would continue to reveal the hybridization of cultures in Israel.

Since European Jews in Israel came to represent the dominant group, their European background was taken as an unmarked norm, while Arab Jews became a Jewish ethnic subgroup, known for their folklore, music, and oriental appearance. In this way, Arab Jews became a kind of internal "Other" within the Jewish community. By identifying them as Jews from specific (Arab) countries of origin—Yemenite Jews, Syrian Jews, Egyptian Jews, Moroccan Jews, and so on—their Arabness was effectively erased.[30] Ella Shohat explains that Israeli policy encouraged Arab Jews to claim only their Jewishness as an authentic identity while abandoning their Arabness. Arabness was seen as a contamination that could be eliminated through assimilation to Israeli constructions of Jewishness.[31]

Ironically, the Zionist promise that Jews in Israel could finally achieve the authenticity of being who they really were was not true for Jews from Arab countries. These Jews generally saw themselves as different from other Arabs on the basis of *religion*, not *Arabness*, which they shared as a cultural heritage and language as much as Arab Christians and Arab Muslims. In Israel, they discovered that becoming a real Israeli required that they abandon their Arab identities.[32] Thus they went from a place where their Arabness linked them with the larger society and their Jewishness marked them as "Other" to one where their Jewishness was what joined them with other Israelis, but their Arabness was suspect and delegitimized.[33] Great Jewish cultural and religious achievements, including the writings of Maimonides that were produced in Arabic and showed the evidence of Judaeo-Muslim cultural interaction, were downplayed in Jewish educational curricula that focused more on the Ashkenazi experience. Sephardi and Mizrahi Jews who immigrated to Palestine and later to Israel were confronted with Ashkenazi customs and ideas that they were expected to substitute for their own customs. They learned that "authentic Judaism" was the kind practiced by Orthodox immigrants from Eastern Europe, while Sephardi culture represented a collection of ethnic minorities.[34]

By using the European model of antisemitic hostility from the non-Jewish population as the template for understanding Arab Jewish history, the Zionist narrative magnified the victimization of Jews in all cultures and places outside of Israel, resulting in a distorted history of Arab Jews through a Eurocentric lens.[35] According to Ella Shohat, "Zionist history texts undermine the hyphenated, syncretic culture of actually existing Jews, rendering the non-Jewish side of the hyphen nonpertinent. This unidimensional categorization, with all Jews being defined as closer to each other than to the cultures of which they have been a part, is tantamount to dismembering a community's identity."[36] After centuries of Jewish experience as Arabs, Arab Jews nonetheless found it difficult to deny the hybrid parts of their identity, for the idea of an "Arab Jew" was no more illogical or paradoxical to them than an "American Jew" or "European Jew," each of whom participates in both Jewish culture and a broader cultural and linguistic tradition shared by non-Jews.[37]

Although the return of the Jews to their land was idealized by Zionists as a return to the place where their ancestors had lived in biblical times and to a more authentic way of life that had been lost, in reality, the Jewish immigrants were not returning to a way of life they had known once before. Rather they were inventing a new culture and establishing new "Hebrew" or "Israeli" values for themselves. The result would turn out to be part European, part Middle Eastern, part old, and part new invention.

Speaking Hebrew

The ideals of romantic nationalism in Europe emphasized the expression of a people's spirit in its language as well as in the folk traditions of music, dance, and festivals celebrating their connection to a particular land. Language in particular was understood as the primary expression of a people's *volksgeist* and their unique understanding of the world. Only their own language could express a people's earliest myths, memories, and ideas. So it was natural for Zionist thinkers to regard the revival of Hebrew as an indispensable element in the revival of the Jewish people and the reconstitution of their national identity. Ahad Ha'am wrote, "Hebrew is rooted in our very being, and neither has been nor ever will be ousted by any other language. All others, including Yiddish, gain a temporary footing under the stress of circumstances, and are forgotten when circumstances change and they are no longer needed. There is one language and one only that always has been, is, and will be forever bound up with our national existence, and that is Hebrew."[38] More than just a language, Hebrew signified a whole new culture and identity. Diaspora names would need to be changed to more authentic Hebrew names. Later, the word *Hebrew* would be replaced by *Israeli* to describe the Hebrew-speaking Jews living in the land of Israel. In either case, a new category—Hebrewness or Israeliness—had come into being as the new lifeblood of authentic life for Jews.

In his 1930 book *Hebrew Reborn*, Shalom Spiegel explored the meaning of the modern rebirth of Hebrew.[39] He began by asking the question, "Can a forgotten language actually be revived, made really alive again? Is the rebirth of such a language authentic?"[40] In referring to the authenticity of a language, Spiegel invoked the romantic nationalist idea dating back to Herder that a language is the natural expression of a healthy people. It sprouts and blooms when a people is rooted in the soil that nurtures and sustains them. According to Spiegel, "There is no redemption of the Jewish spirit unless it is rooted once again in the ancient mother earth whose clods are turned up by a Jewish plow."[41] The use of such biological images for a reborn Hebrew is striking. Spiegel described Hebrew as a veritable force of nature, a "living organism" containing "magic forces of nature and of blood" that expressed a Jewish connection to their own land and language comparable to any of the people of Europe.[42]

Spiegel emphasized the everyday secular Hebrew being spoken by Jews in Palestine as a source of healing, growth, creativity, and life itself. It spontaneously expresses "an untranslated genuineness of thought and feeling"[43] that made it more alive than the Hebrew language of sacred texts, which he found "remote," "narrow," "limited," "rigid," "barren," and "a language of abstractions, anemic, unimpressionable, unresponsive to current needs and experiences," "a toy, a pastime, a subject for unworldly pedants to busy themselves with."[44] The Hebrew spoken by Jewish farmers in Palestine was "rustic and dewy fresh." This was a Hebrew that "has recovered its faculties, its sight and its hearing, its senses of touch and smell, its capacity for motion. Again it pulsates, and plays up and down the whole color-scale of life."[45] The historical authenticity of liturgical Hebrew had been replaced by the expressive, even existential, authenticity of a contemporary spoken language.

The person most associated with the revival of Hebrew as a modern spoken language was a Lithuanian Jew named Eliezer Ben-Yehuda. He believed in the equal importance of Jews having their own language and their own land. Ben-Yehuda had changed his surname from Perelman to Ben-Yehuda ("son of Judah," "son of Jews") to express the new identity he was embracing, and also the diaspora language and identity he was renouncing. In changing his name to Ben-Yehuda, he remarked, "I felt reborn. The link between myself and the Diaspora was completely severed."[46]

Ben-Yehuda struggled to come as close as possible to feeling like he was both a native inhabitant of Israel and a native speaker of Hebrew. He broke off all ties with other countries and declared his undying love for Hebrew as the only language with which he would speak or think. In terms that almost sound like a marriage vow, Ben-Yehudah wrote, "I think in Hebrew by day and by night, awake and in dreams, in sickness and in health, and even when I am racked with pain."[47] Yet as much as he sometimes thought he had succeeded, he still felt a sense of loss over the fact that Hebrew had not been his first language, heard as a nursing infant.[48] He was able to provide that experience to his son Ben-Zion, who was raised with no other language besides Hebrew, making him the first native speaker of modern Hebrew.

Despite Shalom Spiegel's portrayal of Hebrew as a seed that merely needed to be dropped into the original fertile soil of the ancient Hebrews in order to effortlessly sprout and blossom, the authenticity of this revived language, as well as the culture it supported, had to be painstakingly constructed and invented. One issue that revealed the way a new authentic form of Hebrew was created was the issue of pronunciation. Ashkenazi Hebrew, like diaspora Jewish life in general, had deteriorated and been corrupted over time. It was weak and feminine, like the Jews of the diaspora, and even those Ashkenazi Jews who spoke Hebrew would need to relearn it correctly.[49] The Sephardi accent, in contrast, seemed more rugged, masculine, and therefore appropriate for the young strong Jews who were settling the land.[50] The Sephardim embodied Ben-Yehudah's image of true Hebrews: "Most of them were handsome, all were elegant in their oriental apparel, and their manners were impeccable." They spoke Hebrew "fluently and naturally, with a wealth of vocabulary and idiom, and their pronunciation so original [or authentic], so wonderfully oriental!"[51] It was obviously a more authentic way to speak Hebrew.[52]

Ironically, the form of Hebrew that became normative in Israel was neither Ashkenazi nor Sephardi. Ashkenazi Jews like Ben-Yehuda tried to establish their own ideas of what Sephardi Hebrew should be like. The result was a hybrid form of Israeli Hebrew, with characteristics from both Ashkenazi and Sephardi Hebrew as well as expressions from Yiddish.[53] It was the first generation of Israeli-born native speakers of Hebrew, mostly children of Ashkenazi immigrants, who set the gold standard of an authentic Hebrew accent, or "native Hebrew," further institutionalizing the Ashkenazi-Sephardi mixture, along with influences from Yiddish, Arabic, and Ladino.[54] Ironically, the gap between the new pronunciation and the original Sephardi pronunciation meant that the very community that had been held up as a model for authentic Hebrew speaking now found it necessary to adopt a new form of pronunciation based on a corruption of the way they had always spoken.[55] The growing political and cultural domination of Ashkenazi Jews in Palestine meant that they were the ones setting the norm for Sephardi-influenced Hebrew accents, and that accent was considered more prestigious. Whatever authenticity Sephardi and Yemenite forms of Hebrew might have had, it gradually was replaced by a new form of modern Hebrew, simultaneously a revival of ancient Hebrew but also a new creation.[56] The number of native speakers of Hebrew grew quickly in the twentieth century, from 40 percent of the Jewish population in 1914 to three-fourths at the time of statehood in 1948.[57] This was the generation of the Sabra, the authentic new Jew.

Israeli Folk Dance

Zionists held up the physical work involved in returning to a more agricultural lifestyle as an essential way for Jews to reclaim a healthy relationship to their bodies. This was the beauty and authenticity of life on the kibbutz, where physical labor produced strong, healthy bodies. The diaspora Jews' alienation from the strength of their own bodies had resulted from their focus on study rather than physical activity, as well as their lack of any real connection to land of their own. Once they had returned to life on their own land, it would also be possible to live more authentically in their own bodies.

Israeli folk dance emerged as a vehicle for celebrating Jewish life that was fully grounded in both one's own land and one's own body. It became an important expression of the reborn Hebrew culture springing forth from the newly planted Jews and the roots they were developing in the land of Israel. Like reclining at a Passover Seder, dance was also taken as a sign of a free people. To the creators and inventors of the new Israeli culture, Jewish life in diaspora had been joyless and timid. The kind of public dancing associated with folk traditions had been discouraged by Jewish communal leaders, who were concerned about how the Gentiles would react.[58] Accordingly, it was assumed that the Jews' own dance tradition had atrophied during Jewish life in diaspora, where the celebration of harvest festivals in Jewish holidays was only a faded image of the distant past.[59]

And yet the culture of Eastern European Ashkenazi Jews, and even non-Jews, provided some of the ingredients out of which Israeli music and folk dance would be created. Polish, Russian, and Romanian music and dance along with Jewish and non-Jewish culture of the Middle East would be fused together in a new Israeli culture. In other words, as much as Zionist pioneers wanted to create a new Israeli culture as an alternative to what they regarded as the inauthentic existence of Jews in diaspora, they nonetheless preserved both Jewish and non-Jewish elements of that rejected culture in their newly invented hybrid culture. The hora, perhaps the most iconic of Israeli folk dances, originated as a Romanian circle dance, but it was repurposed as an expression of the newfound equality and solidarity Jews enjoyed in their own land: "The tightly closed circle, with linked arms and hands on shoulders of the neighbors, was the exact expression of the close human relationship between all the members of the community; all of them with equal rights and equal value, regardless of sex or of dancing ability."[60]

The mothers of Israeli folk dance, Gurit Kadman and Rivka Sturman, were secular Zionists who had immigrated to Israel from Germany in the 1920s. They understood that an authentic people needed to have folk rituals and customs that expressed their collective essence. Since the original folk traditions of Israel had been lost over centuries of exile, they would need to be recreated. The goal, said Kadman, was to bring about a miracle, "the rise of a new unified Jewish culture."[61] Israeli folk dance would be an authentic expression and performance of this new culture, one rooted not in Europe but in Middle Eastern culture. Inventing new Israeli folk dances where none really existed immediately made Israeli folk dance different from the folk dances of other ethnic groups. It was not an anonymous expression bubbling up from the people. Rather, it was usually the creation of specific choreographers who blended and adapted both music and movements from other types of dances to create something uniquely Israeli.[62] And that was the problem. Deliberately creating folk dances, Kadman worried, "was against all the laws of the development of folk culture the world over. How can one create purposely, artificially, folk dances which usually grow slowly like trees out of deep roots, a process of hundreds of years?"[63]

Making the best of the situation, Kadman concluded that the absence of traditional folk authenticity was more than compensated for by the intense explosion of creativity in the emergence of new Israeli folk dances. Israeli folk dance was "a new kind of folk dance, shining with a concentrated brilliance which had taken other folk dances generations to attain. A new creation, it was also an alloy of many old cultures."[64] Thus the presence of European and Middle Eastern elements in Israeli folk dances did not matter, because these ingredients acquired a uniquely Israeli quality in the ways they were appropriated and performed.[65] Besides, the hybrid style of Israeli folk dance was appropriate for a culture that would need to unite Jews coming from a variety of cultures and countries.

Of course, the creation of a new Israeli folk dance tradition was never presented as something brand new. An origin story was also invented, which considered Israeli folk dance as a revival of something dating back to the biblical period, when the earliest community of the Jewish people established their rightful presence in the land.[66] A few scattered references to dancing among the ancient Israelites allowed new dancers to feel that they were merely resuscitating the authentic folk culture of their ancestors. Once again, both Arabs and Mizrahi Jews functioned as contemporary resources for tapping into something that felt like the remains of those ancestral traditions. Yemenite Jews were particularly appealing as the indigenous connection to an authentic folk tradition for Ashkenazi Jews settling in Israel. Although the Yemenite Jews had also been in diaspora in a nearby Arab country, they were thought to have preserved the original authentic Jewish folk traditions of the Jews' common ancestors. Their musical and artistic traditions were seen as both creative and authentic. Israeli folk dances absorbed some of the Yemenite customs as a way of placing themselves in a continuous, unbroken tradition and giving the impression that they were recovering the long-lost traditions of their biblical ancestors.[67]

While the traditional cultures of Arabs and Mizrahi Jews appealed to European Jews eager to distance themselves from their own culture, attitudes toward the cultural otherness of such groups were not without a sense of ambivalence. On the one hand, the lives of those associated with the folkways of the past appealed to those who are disenchanted with modern culture. Their lives were romanticized as more natural, authentic, and rooted in ancient practices that others of us have lost. But this unspoiled nobility was also accompanied by technological backwardness, intellectual parochialism, and religious superstition. In addition, even if Arabs were in some sense more authentic "folk" living in the land than newly arrived Jews, theirs was a kind of static authenticity. Elke Kaschl observes that Arab dance, while providing a connection to authenticity for Israeli folk dance, has also been regarded by some Israeli dance groups as stagnant and repetitive. The authenticity of Arab dances was understood as "old and boring," while Israeli folk dance was able to take the original dances from other groups and transform them into something "authentically inauthentic, that is, acceptably ever new, inventive and different."[68] In reality, the emergence of an "authentic" Israeli culture was a hybrid phenomenon from its very origin, rooted in both Jewish and non-Jewish sources.

Contemporary Israeli (Folk) Dance

The original Israeli folk dances were created by idealistic Zionists committed to the Jews' return to the land and the development of an indigenous Israeli culture inspired by both biblical and Middle Eastern customs. Over half a century has now passed since the golden years of Israeli folk dance. During that time, the original pioneering generations were replaced by new generations no longer committed to the values expressed in the original dances. Neither the centrality of socialist and collective values embodied in the kibbutz nor the importance of manual labor is the main focus of modern Israeli culture. On the contrary, Israeli folk dance has increasingly been influenced by commercialization and globalization.[69] In the early years, the creators and performers of Israeli folk dance declared themselves the "folk" who saw their own lives and values reflected in freshly created or recycled music and dance. Over time, Israeli folk dances became more of a nostalgic reminder of an earlier period than a reflection of the lives and experiences of people performing them. In the 1960s and early 1970s, Israeli folk dance was growing in the United States but waning in Israel. For American Jews, Israeli folk dance would continue to offer a connection to an idealized image of an Israel and its rugged "new Jews" that no longer existed, as kibbutz socialism and the pioneer spirit effectively disappeared as an important component in Israeli society. Nonetheless, Jewish camps in the United States continued to be places where American Jewish youth could pretend that they were sharing in the authenticity of Israel's pioneer spirit. Israeli folk dance offers a generalized feeling of solidarity with Israel, ideally represented by an Israeli dance instructor. Ironically, their Israeli peers are much more concerned with the latest developments in American music and popular culture.[70]

It is quite telling that for the most part, the word *folk* has been dropped from Israeli folk dance, which is now more often called simply Israeli dancing. *Folk* was the critical word in considering the original authenticity of Israeli folk dance, even though Israeli dance never originated from the folk in the same ways as other cultures' folk dances. Although the original creators and choreographers were well aware of the fact that Israeli folk dance was not like other folk dance traditions, they regarded this as a necessity in creating a new Israeli culture. Participants today note that the music is no longer folk music, and the steps are not the simple repetitive dances of folk traditions.

What is now called Israeli dance consists of choreographers who are usually Israeli and who usually use Israeli music, but they may not always be living in Israel, and the music may be non-Israeli music that happens to be popular in Israel, or any other music. Sometimes these dances by choreographers living outside of Israel are not ever danced in Israel but only in the circuit of dance camps outside of Israel. The "folk" who define the tradition now are simply the people who participate in Israeli dance, though sometimes this includes non-Israeli dances to non-Israeli music by non-Israeli choreographers. A new generation of dancers has wanted to develop Israeli dance in new ways. Choreographer Yoav Ashriel explains, "We can't freeze folk dances, because folk dance is something that's alive and continues to grow."[71]

The growth and change that occurred in Israeli folk dance triggered a struggle between those who want to uphold some standards for something to be considered an authentic Israeli folk dance and those who focus more on the inevitability of change in what constitutes Israeli culture and who and what composes it. From a traditionalist point of view, some feel that authentic Israeli folk dance requires Israeli music, Hebrew lyrics, Israeli choreographers, Israeli dance steps, and subject matter with a connection to themes from Israeli society and life, sometimes even biblical texts. But others reject the idea of preestablished standards when Israeliness itself has become more difficult to define, when Israelis enjoy a variety of kinds of music, when their culture is more cosmopolitan, and when Israeli dance is simply whatever dances Israelis are dancing at a particular moment. Indeed, some say that Israel is a country that is absorbing a variety of influences and that is precisely what makes it Israeli. After a long discussion about the authenticity of contemporary Israeli dance on the listserv "Rikud," one Israeli dance teacher summed up the issue like this: "The bottom line? Take what you like and leave what you don't. Don't analyze every new dance for its 'authenticity.' For the most part, we are still creating authenticity."[72]

Authentically Israeli

Classical Zionism was a secular ethnic and nationalist ideology that had proposed a new form of authentic being and cultural identity for "new Jews" in the revived nation of Israel. It selectively salvaged heroic moments of ancient Israelite history, but it was at best indifferent to traditional Jewish religion, and more often, overtly hostile. The emphasis on a new language, Hebrew, as well as the invention of a tradition of Israeli folk dance, were elements in the creation or renewal of a new "Hebrew culture." Indeed, the concept of something that could be called "Hebrew culture" or "Israeli culture" was offered as a rejection or transcendence of traditional Jewish culture. In other words, authentic Israeliness would replace inauthentic Jewishness. At the same time, a sizeable number of Israelis remained religious Jews, for whom living in Israel represented the most authentic form of Jewish life.

In the 1960s, a major social psychological study by Simon Herman titled *Israelis and Jews: The Continuity of an Identity* laid out the delicate relationship and potential tensions between Israeliness and Jewishness.[73] Although a fundamental premise of Zionism had been the inescapable tensions that existed between Jewish identity and a national or ethnic identification with the diaspora countries in which Jews lived, it hardly occurred to anyone that such a tension might develop among Jews in Israel as well. Herman found that among Israeli students in the late 1960s, being Jewish was much less important to them than to their parents, many of whom had moved to Israel after growing up as Jews in diaspora.[74] To be sure, in many cases, Herman found permeable boundaries between Jewishness and Israeliness—"The Jewishness is suffused with the Israeliness and the Israeliness is suffused with the Jewishness." But he also found that Jewishness was most important for Israelis who were religious, while Israeliness was less important. On the other hand, nonreligious Israelis identified more with being Israeli than Jewish.[75] Unlike American Jews, whose Jewish identities are an amalgam of ethnicity and religion, Israelis often differentiated the ethnic dimension (Israeliness) from the religious (Jewishness).

As Israeliness and Jewishness became disengaged and separate for different groups of Israelis, the definition and regulation of authentic *Jewishness* and Judaism fell upon Orthodox religious authorities, while *Israeliness* became associated with the nonreligious culture of Israel, one which is influenced by both Middle Eastern and Western cultures. As a result, the tension between Jewishness and the larger culture of the society in which Jews lived, a problem that the classic Zionists had hoped to solve, resurfaced in Israel.

Over time, the Zionist quest for a collective sense of national identity and authenticity began to fade, producing a crisis in the sources of authenticity for later generations of Israelis. In fact, the original Zionist vision of building a new unified culture in Israel had papered over a number of fault lines on matters of religion, ethnicity, and nationality. These stress points eventually led to fractures in Israeli culture in the decades following the Arab-Israeli wars in 1967 and 1973. With the Israeli occupation of the entire area that had been assigned to the Arabs when the British left the country in 1948, the new situation presented both opportunities and challenges, depending on one's perspective. The most consequential result, according to Baruch Kimmerling, has been the loss of societal consensus about the meaning of Zionism and the Jewish state.[76] Israel has splintered into a variety of social and cultural groupings, each with its own particularistic narrative of the country's origins, vision for its future, and definition of the meaning of Jewish and Israeli authenticity. Dormant tensions finally erupted into a simmering culture war between a largely secular middle class, modern traditionalist Jews, and a newly politicized Orthodox community. The fusion of religious Messianism and Zionist nationalism, inspired by earlier work by Rav Isaac HaCohen Kook, produced a politically powerful religious settler movement. Finally, Ashkenazi cultural and political dominance had been undercut by the political rise of previously disempowered groups such as Mizrahi Jews and Arab Israelis.[77]

Herder's recipe of a common language, shared traditions and folkways, and a connection to the land as the essential pillars of national identity lost much of their power in a rapidly modernizing society. The sense of identity from rootedness in the land was replaced by bourgeois materialism and consumerism. New inflows of immigrants from Russia and Ethiopia arrived with their own languages and cultures that proved harder to assimilate into the melting pot. The binary of the inauthentic diaspora Jew and the authentic new Jew in Israel gave way to cooperative, mutually respectful relations between Jews who live in Israel and those who do not. Hebrew is alive and well, but Hebrew-speaking is not a magical talisman, nor even something exclusive to Jews in Israel. In addition, life in a multilingual globalized world means there is distinct value, if not necessity, in being able to speak other languages as well. Israeli culture, music, and dance are not just the expression of a Jewish *volksgeist* but an increasingly cosmopolitan hybrid.[78]

Feeling like a tiny part of a larger collective project became seriously weakened as an adequate source of meaning for many Jewish Israelis, and they increasingly turned to more individualistic models of identity and self-fulfillment rooted in neither Jewish religion nor a secular commitment to ethnic nationalism. At an age when young American Jews have been traveling to Israel on so-called birthright trips for an experience of Jewish/Israeli authenticity, their Israeli counterparts have often felt a need to travel *away from Israel* to rediscover a sense of individual authenticity. The romantic orientalist image of Israel makes it an exotic destination of deep authenticity and spirituality for European and North American Jewish visitors to Israel, while many young secular Israelis have been attracted to different orientalist fantasies about non-Western cultures far from Israel. After their army service, many Israeli youths have been backpacking to places like India, Nepal, and South America in search of simpler, more "authentic" cultures where they can experience their "real selves."[79]

Finally, hundreds of thousands of Israelis have focused their quests for authenticity on the hundreds of New Age groups that have sprung up in recent decades, offering a variety of options for spiritual healing, transformation, and self-realization.[80] Some of these activities, groups, and products have nothing to do with Jewish religion or Israeli culture per se, while others have been constructed or packaged in ways that link them to Jewish traditions, such as Jewish yoga, Jewish meditation, or Jewish mysticism.[81]

In her nuanced and sensitive ethnography of several New Age Jewish groups in Israel, Rachel Werczberger concludes that the collapse of the original Zionist vision of Israel as a place where the collective authenticity of the Jewish people would be expressed and fulfilled left a vacuum that at least some Israelis have tried to fill with a "de-nationalized, de-ethnicized spiritual model in its stead."[82] Their alternative strategy has been not to return to the essentialist authenticity of traditional Orthodox Judaism but rather to rework Jewish origin narratives and traditions, blended with other generic spiritual ideas and practices, to create a new brand of Jewish authenticity that is simultaneously Jewish and spiritual as well as connected to their identities as modern, cosmopolitan Israelis.[83] Though it has been imperfectly achieved so far, the goal was to bring together their searches for individual spiritual authenticity within a model of collective, communal authenticity as Jews in Israel.[84]

8 Shtetl Authenticity

FROM *FIDDLER ON THE ROOF*
TO THE REVIVAL OF KLEZMER

For American Jews, the Jewish culture and religious life of Eastern Europe have become an important anchor of Jewish identity, particularly in the period after the Holocaust, when the catastrophic destruction of almost all of the Eastern European Jewish community relegated the lives they had lived to little more than nostalgic images of the past. To a great extent, the shtetl Jew, immortalized in American popular culture by the 1964 musical *Fiddler on the Roof*, served as an archetype eagerly embraced by an increasingly assimilated and intermarried American Jewish community. The idealization of Eastern European Jewish culture enabled American Jews to reclaim a sentimental image of Jewish authenticity overflowing with life and pathos. Alisa Solomon notes that *Fiddler*'s portrayal of shtetl life "felt tender, elegiac, even holy."[1] It was treated as a piece of multicultural history about the Jews "as if *Fiddler* were an artifact unearthed from a destroyed world rather than a big-story musical assembled by showbiz professionals."[2] The imagined joy of shtetl life, purged of the worst of its squalid poverty, would also offer American Jews a vicarious experience of a cohesive Jewish community, of life that was, if nothing else, authentically Jewish. For several hours in the darkness of a Broadway theater, the children and grandchildren of Jewish immigrants from Eastern Europe could see, hear, and almost taste the daily life of their ancestors.

The romanticization of the Eastern European shtetl for consumption by modern American Jews began only a few years after the Allied victory against Hitler put an end to the Nazi horror that effectively had obliterated the Jewish communities and culture of Eastern Europe. In 1953, Mark Zborowski and Elizabeth Hertzog published *Life Is with People: The World of the Shtetl*. Pieced together from a variety of sources, the book offered a composite picture of everyday life in a shtetl. The reception from Jewish academics was lukewarm, and they quibbled about the historical authenticity of many of the details described in the book. Renowned cultural anthropologist Raphael Patai complained that the book lacked historical depth and context and also ignored the cultural interchange between the shtetl and the surrounding non-Jewish world.[3] Yet the book was immensely popular with the general Jewish reading audience. Its appeal to American Jews at various stages of assimilation, according to Jonathan Boyarin, was in presenting "a place and time when Jews were truly themselves, when they possessed the resources for full expression of selfhood and had no substantial motivations to try to be anything less or anything else."[4] The shtetl, in other words, was a self-enclosed world where no one had to "search for authenticity," since they were authentically Jewish without having to think about it.

Over the last century or more, Eastern European Jews have been represented in a number of contradictory ways. On the one hand, as Jews in Western European democracies received political rights of citizenship, access to modern culture and secular knowledge, and the ability to assimilate to the society around them, they saw themselves as the model of Jews for the future. Jews from Eastern Europe, or "Ostjuden," were considered unsophisticated, vulgar, culturally backward, and intellectually stunted by religious superstitions.[5] On the other hand, European Zionism arose out of a disillusionment with the assimilationist strategy of liberal bourgeois Western Jews, whose identities seemed not only shallow but also contaminated by non-Jewish culture. As a result, some Zionists looked to Eastern European Jews as "the embodiment of Jewish authenticity and exemplars of the unfragmented self."[6] It was they who were "real Jews" and who still preserved and expressed the Jewish "volksgeist" in all its premodern purity and wholeness.[7] Yet at the same time, Zionists had also rejected the Jews of the Eastern European diaspora as weak, helpless, and clinging to a religious faith that was powerless against the forces of antisemitic oppression and eventually genocide.

For American Jews, *Fiddler on the Roof* quickly acquired an almost sacred status as a collective Jewish origin story. It should therefore come as no surprise that a Broadway revival of the play in 2004 that cast a non-Jewish actor, Alfred Molina, in the lead role of Tevye triggered a number of debates about the Jewish authenticity of the production. At the heart of the debate was the emotionally loaded question of whether a non-Jew could give an authentically Jewish performance in this title role or whether it was a more egregious case of "Jew-face" than Al Pacino playing Shylock.[8] This casting decision represented quite a change from the original portrayal of Tevye by Zero Mostel, a child of Eastern European Jewish immigrants who had been raised as an Orthodox Jew, or Haim Topol, an Israeli actor and son of a Russian Jewish immigrant to Palestine, who played Tevye both on stage and in the acclaimed 1971 film. Some critics complained about the lack of Jewish soul in the new production. It seemed as though the mere knowledge of an actor's non-Jewish roots interfered with the illusion of being in the presence of an authentic ancestor of many American Jews. *New York Times* critic Ben Brantley abstained from the controversy, conceding that he lacked standing to judge: "Being a goy myself, I won't try to assess the Jewish authenticity of this Fiddler."[9] Molina was soon replaced by Harvey Fierstein, who had been excited about Fiddler from the time it opened during his childhood and had even included songs from it at his bar mitzvah.[10]

Assessing the Jewish authenticity of *Fiddler on the Roof* in general raises some complicated issues that go beyond the ethnic or religious background of the leading actor. *Fiddler on the Roof* was based on a story by Sholem Aleichem, "Tevye the Milkman," published in 1895, right in the middle of the largest emigration of Jews out of Eastern Europe, many of whom settled in the United States. When the musical *Fiddler on the Roof* opened in 1964, some of the Jewish American children and grandchildren of those immigrants embraced its celebration of Yiddishkeit as a vicarious journey to an imaginary place of origins. Although the highly publicized trial of Adolph Eichmann in Jerusalem for his crimes against the Jewish people had occurred two years earlier, the full impact of the Holocaust had not yet been absorbed and processed by American Jews. American Jewish life was moving away from urban immigrant enclaves into the suburbs and their Americanized synagogues. Fewer and fewer American Jews understood Yiddish, a relic of immigrant parents or grandparents that many left behind as they became increasingly assimilated into American culture.

Much of the popularity of *Fiddler* stemmed from the assumption that it offered an accurate and realistic glimpse of Jewish life in Eastern Europe. The thick ethnic flavor and joyful traditions of shtetl life that had been destroyed by the Nazis could now be safely savored on Broadway as both entertainment and spectacle. Many members of the audience felt that their Jewish roots had been restored beautifully. But the show also became the target of heated debates about its authenticity. Almost immediately, the production was condemned by some critics as an inauthentic and exploitative exercise in nostalgia and sentimentality. Irving Howe famously described its setting as "the cutest shtetl we never had." He called the play a tasteless, slick, and sterile travesty of Sholem Aleichem's portrayal of Jewish life in Eastern Europe.[11] Although the musical's title had been inspired by Marc Chagall's iconic paintings, Chagall himself declined an invitation to design sets for the show and is reported to have disliked the production.[12] Later, with the success of *Fiddler* as an international cross-cultural hit that appealed to audiences in Japan, Russia, Finland, Poland, Germany, and many other places, other critics complained that this overwhelming response from non-Jews was evidence that the show had been cleaned up so as not to be "too Jewish."

Certainly, *Fiddler on the Roof* was never presented as a documentary reenactment aiming at absolute historical precision in its re-creation of life in a nineteenth-century shtetl, nor is that the only way to talk about its authenticity. To the extent that it has come to represent an origin story for Ashkenazi American Jews, it demonstrates a particular way in which the shtetl experience was reimagined and reconstructed. Today, there can be no doubt that *Fiddler* has become a legitimate part of American Jewish culture, where singalong screenings of the film and amateur productions of the show allow audience members to more fully transport themselves into the world of the shtetl, whether or not the place celebrated is historically accurate in all respects. Certainly, this process of appropriating important group experiences in ways that reflect communal issues and concerns of later periods is true of all cultural traditions and group narratives. It is as much true of the ways that Jewish tradition established an origin narrative about the Jewish people's exodus from Egypt as it is of this re-creation of the Jewish exodus from Eastern Europe.

The Jewish authenticity of *Fiddler on the Roof* demonstrates how determinations of authenticity are not static and can be transformed as successive generations of American Jews have interrogated their past and its relationship to the present. *Fiddler*, suggests Alisa Solomon, underwent a transformation from "a show dismissed alternatively as an inauthentic, even kitschy, portrayal of the Jewish past and as a too-Jewish piece of schmaltz . . . into genuine Jewish-American folklore."[13] It reflected not only the upheavals of the nineteenth century but also the upheavals of the 1960s: "The show's rebellious daughters carried a flame of women's liberation; its decrial of bigotry reverberated with the civil-rights movement; its offering of a plucky Ashkenazi origin story correlated with a shift toward a national self-definition of the United States as a country of immigrants."[14]

Appearing at a time when Americans were reclaiming ethnic roots, *Fiddler* retrieved the world of the shtetl from the ashes of the Holocaust as the symbol of a lost past. Even if it was not exactly the world their ancestors had actually lived in, American Jews still developed a connection to the world of Anatevka. It served a whole generation of assimilating Jews as "a sacred repository of Jewishness,"[15] a Jewish soundtrack for weddings, summer camp productions, and other celebrations and a symbol of ethnic and religious authenticity. Fifty-some years after its opening on Broadway, *Fiddler*'s legacy permeates American Jewish life, and its homage to traditions of another time and place has become the basis for new expressions of Jewish tradition in America. "The show about tradition has become tradition," says Alisa Solomon.[16] For that reason, perhaps, a non-Jewish actor playing Tevye, or a production in another country, such as Japan, including a Japanese cast and a Japanese audience may seem like a violation of its Jewish authenticity, no matter how talented or skilled the actors involved. To be sure, the show's success was to some degree a result of the universality of its story. The producer of the show in Tokyo wondered why Americans had flocked to a show whose story was "so Japanese."[17] This is perhaps true, but the Jewish particularity of the story, not its universality, is what made American Jews feel a special claim to *Fiddler*.

The Jewish particularity that gives *Fiddler on the Roof* its power does not assume some kind of essentialist Jewish authenticity in the past. On the contrary, the main tension in the story focuses not on the timeless beauty of shtetl life but rather on the inevitability of change and the fact that the shtetl was far from paradise. True, the shtetl, like the ghetto, was a place of community cohesion, but it was also marked by deprivation and oppression. *Fiddler* showed a world not only of tradition but also of the inability of tradition to protect against either the ravages and hostilities of the external world or the inevitability of change that was unfolding in the situation of the Jews in Eastern Europe. It is a wistful story about the impermanence of Jewish tradition witnessed by audiences who have experienced the rapid changes in some traditions and the decay of others.

Klezmer: Authentic Jewish Music

Questions about Jewish authenticity often arise in explicitly religious contexts that involve competing sources of authority and models of tradition to determine which Jewish doctrines and practices are "authentically Jewish" and which people can be identified as "authentic Jews." In considering the concept of authenticity in the realm of Jewish folk culture, many aspects of the shtetl world of *Fiddler* go beyond questions of religion and religious authorities into areas of Jewish food, music, humor, and sensibility. They reveal the tensions in a diaspora culture whose history is one not only of separation from surrounding cultures but also contact and interaction.[18]

The eponymous fiddler in *Fiddler on the Roof* offers a useful entry point for exploring such questions of authenticity in Jewish folklore and folk music. The fiddler embodies the precarious situation of all the Jews of the shtetl, struggling for a secure footing in a world of uncertainty and change. Tevye explains, "In our little village of Anatevka, you might say every one of us is a fiddler on the roof, trying to scratch out a pleasant, simple tune without breaking his neck. It isn't easy. You may ask, why do we stay here if it's so dangerous? We stay because Anatevka is our home. And how do we keep our balance? That I can tell you in a word—tradition! Without our traditions, our lives would be as shaky as a fiddler on the roof."

But what about the fiddler himself and the music he played? In Yiddish, the itinerant male musician was known as a "klezmer," though it was not until the late 1970s that a specific genre of music associated with Ashkenazi Jews in Eastern Europe became known as "klezmer music." The revival of klezmer music in the last fifty years picks up the story of one aspect of shtetl culture as it was transplanted and revived in new lands. It is something that continually balances a respect for musical traditions of the past with a recognition of the invigorating yet disorienting process of change. As a part of Jewish culture that thrives outside the domain of the rabbis and the synagogue, klezmer music does not trigger the same halakhic standards of authenticity that are invoked in debates between Orthodox and non-Orthodox forms of Judaism. Rather, it raises questions about what is authentically Jewish in the context of musical performance and folklore and the ways that concepts of authenticity are defined and deployed. In this respect, it has much in common with the ways that the authenticity of Israeli folk dance is understood.

The underlying theoretical issue regarding klezmer as authentically Jewish music cannot be answered by treating authenticity as an intrinsic or unchanging quality of any particular cultural practice or idea. Rather, the question involves how to understand the multiple ways in which klezmer's Jewish authenticity is attributed, constructed, or asserted. The authenticity of klezmer music can only be analyzed and defined in relation to the particular moments in time when it is relocated, reclaimed, and reinvented. Just as tradition is central to Jewish religious life, it is also essential to Jewish music. In both cases, it involves the particular ways of preserving the parts of the past that respond to the issues and needs of the present.

As ethnomusicologist Mark Slobin points out, the concept of klezmer as a genre of specifically Jewish music rooted in Eastern European Jewish culture is somewhat misleading, since it is the particular American construction of klezmer that standardized this form of music and established its canon in the 1970s.[19] Indeed, the most important and influential klezmer bands during that period have been American. As a result, Europeans often see klezmer music as an American import, albeit one with European roots.[20]

The music produced by Jewish musicians in Eastern Europe was itself a hybrid phenomenon from the outset, and klezmers were not required or expected to be musically "monogamous." Their travels brought them in contact with non-Jewish musicians with whom they shared and exchanged music. The result was traces of cultural influence from gypsy, Ukrainian, Greek, Turkish, and Bulgarian sources among others.[21] During this original period, the musical repertoire of klezmer musicians was an oral tradition passed from one musician to another.[22]

As Eastern European Jews immigrated to the United States, the music produced by klezmers underwent a variety of changes as it became adapted to an American cultural setting. On the one hand, the original klezmer repertoire from Europe became systematized and "canonized," establishing certain common experiences and expectations about the material Jewish musicians played.[23] The canon was not exactly what this music had previously been like in Europe. Recordings permanently enshrined particular performance styles, including mistakes. Wind instruments recorded better than string instruments and were used more often.[24] The music was structured by the marketing and technical demands of the recording industry. Longer medleys needed to be reduced to individual three-minute selections on 78 rpm records.[25] Songs were named and numbered in ways that had never been done before.[26] Records also meant that the music was used for individual listening more than as background at social functions.[27]

On the other hand, klezmer in America was not static. As Jewish immigration to the United States from Eastern Europe slowed to a halt in the 1920s, the original generation of klezmer musicians was followed by subsequent generations of American Jewish musicians who had learned from them. But these musicians performed at weddings and parties where audiences also appreciated and expected American dance music, Latin American music, and swing music in addition to klezmer.[28] So klezmer musicians drew on these other musical traditions, and klezmer continued as a dynamic, changing genre, developing in a distinctively American way. Since it lacked regular renewal from its Eastern European source, it gained new energy from elsewhere, including, for example, American jazz, with which it was frequently mixed.[29]

The function of Jewish folk music as a means of connection to Jewish roots or heritage underwent an upheaval in the period after the Second World War. The extermination of European Jews meant that the original cultural home of klezmer music was gone. There were few klezmer musicians among the survivors of the Holocaust to carry it on, and most survivors immigrated to Israel to participate in the birth of a new strong and hopeful Israeli culture.[30] In place of klezmer and shtetl culture, Israel and Israeli music offered a different source of authenticity. Moreover, the postwar embrace of Israel and Zionism resulted in a devaluation of European Jewish culture. Zionism had been founded on the inadequacy of European Jewish culture, a culture of diaspora rather than one grounded in a real homeland. Yiddish was seen as a relic of that doomed culture, weak and inauthentic compared to the heroic rebirth of Hebrew.[31] In Israel, a new culture based in Hebrew represented authentic Jewish life for the present and future, with a link to an ancient past. Meanwhile, as the children of Jewish immigrants in the United States became increasingly suburbanized, Americanized, and assimilated, the connection to the language and culture of the "old country" in Europe began to fade and disappear.

When young musicians rediscovered klezmer in the 1970s and 1980s, they wanted to breathe new life into a kind of music that had become moribund, except in small pockets of the Hasidic community in America. Many Americans had begun to search for their ethnic roots, and for most American Jews, this meant the European Ashkenazi culture that had been effectively erased by the Holocaust. This reevaluation of authentic Jewish culture represented a challenge to the dominant Jewish narratives of the rebirth of Hebrew and Israeli culture as the foundation of Jewishness, especially for those who were increasingly troubled by developments in Israel and the nature of Zionism. Hank Sapoznik writes, "Yiddish culture and music today can be an overt political act, a show of resistance to Jewish homogeneousness . . . and the artificial monolith of Israeli = Jewish."[32] Zionism and the rebirth of Israel had already demonstrated the possibility of an identity for Jews tied as much to language, culture, and land as to the religious practice of Judaism.

Mark Slobin and others characterize klezmer as an example of "heritage music," a type of music that enables members of respective cultural groups to reclaim, and reconnect to, their cultural roots, and to transport themselves to another place and/or time. The use of Yiddish lyrics, for example, would have been unremarkable for Eastern European Jews, for whom it was simply the language of everyday life. However, when it reappears during the revival of klezmer, Yiddish immediately becomes a touchstone of Jewishness or Yiddishkeit for American Jews who lack fluency or even knowledge of that language. Yiddish and the folk culture attached to it also offered a vehicle for expressing the ethnic identity and spirit of the Jewish people in nonreligious terms, dependent on neither Zionism nor Orthodox Judaism.

Of course, secular European defenders of Yiddish who had earlier proposed it as an expression of Jewish identity that required no ideological or religious commitment were living in a world where Yiddish could serve as the lingua franca of Jews from different European countries.[33] For American Jews rediscovering it, Yiddish was more a symbol of ethnic heritage than an actual means of communication. When used in klezmer music, it provides a kind of ethnic seasoning that pushes back against assimilation, re-creating a sense of cultural distance vis-à-vis hegemonic American culture yet without requiring actual linguistic competence.

Jonathan Rosen notes that a revived Yiddish culture has offered a blank canvas on which a variety of alternative forms of Jewishness could be perceived. It was more egalitarian than official Jewish (Hebrew) culture, and it was associated with populist and alternative perspectives from socialism to anarchism. Rosen writes, "Because Yiddish culture in Europe was essentially destroyed, learning Yiddish in America has a surreal aspect, like planning a trip to a country that doesn't exist. The culture of the country can be anything you want—gay, feminist, secular, religious—and no one can tell you that you don't belong. . . . The more comfortable Jews feel in America, the more open they are to reclaiming a culture of exile."[34] The Jewish authenticity of klezmer was an expression of the desire to preserve Jewish difference in the face of the overall movement of assimilation and acculturation to American society.[35]

The revival of klezmer demonstrates the unstable and fluid nature of authenticating the musical traditions associated with Eastern European Jews, and the new musicians who were reclaiming this music took different approaches to this process. For some, authenticity meant trying to reproduce earlier samples of music as closely as possible. Taking a page from the revival of American folk songs, they looked to the earliest available recordings of klezmer music, the 78 rpm records produced in New York in the 1910s to 1930s, and the few tattered musical scores remaining from that period. These became the sacred canon of klezmer and the standard against which some would judge the authenticity of newly produced music. At the same time, approaching the music across a gap of half a century meant that klezmer revivalists were deprived of contact with actual klezmer musicians from Europe.

Of course, this body of music had already been hybridized through its contact with other American musical traditions, so the assumption that early-twentieth-century recordings were the motherlode of authentic Eastern European Jewish music in its original purity overlooked the dynamic nature of this musical tradition. Other musicians recognized that Jewish musical tradition, even in the "old country," had never been fixed or static but rather reflected particular historical and cultural periods. It was inevitable that the revival of klezmer in the United States would produce music that was not only connected to a tradition of Eastern European Jewish music from another era but also reflected a substantial amount of new creative invention inspired by its reemergence in the context of Jewish culture in America.[36]

If reviving authentic klezmer music had been based on a goal of reproducing Eastern European Jewish music in an idealized pristine form, then much of the new klezmer music produced in America and elsewhere missed the mark. However, if the authenticity of klezmer is understood in the context of a vibrant and ever-changing process of cultural interaction, then American klezmer had merely resumed a process consistent with its evolution. Prominent klezmer bands have infused their music with the musical styles and vocabularies of American culture, including influences from jazz, ragtime, blues, bluegrass, rock, reggae, Latin, Israeli, and even hip-hop. Changes in instrumentation occurred as pianos, guitars, and saxophones were introduced to klezmer ensembles. These changes, along with greater roles for female klezmer musicians, reflected a significant Americanization of klezmer. A band called Davka is described as "neo-Jewish-roots-fusion, the acoustic equivalent of a Chagall painting, new klezmer-Middle-Eastern-jazz fusion, Middle-Eastern Ashkenazi jazz, fiddler-on-too-much-Turkish-coffee."[37] A band from Toronto named Beyond the Pale describes itself as "boundary-busting Eurofolk fusion. Inspired by klezmer and Balkan styles but influenced by everything from jazz and classical music to bluegrass, newgrass and reggae."[38] Its leader, Eric Stein, recently explained that the band includes both Jewish and Serbian musicians. They value musical diversity, not some particular standard of "authentic klezmer." He said the band is "about expressing ourselves and not being too slavish about trying to be authentic to something.... We're true to the spirit of the music, but not necessarily to the specific characteristics."[39]

The new Jewish music scene that has emerged is one of hybridity and syncretism, incorporating a diversity of musical traditions, arguably a comparable process to the way that Judaism has absorbed elements from surrounding cultures throughout its history. Seth Rogovoy says, "In some ways, the more diverse and experimental the music becomes, the more authentic it really is in relation to Jewish culture."[40] There can be no doubt that the musical hybridity of klezmer is a reflection of the postmodern cultural hybridity of its American producers and consumers. In this sense, authenticity is associated not with a frozen moment from the past, but with a more fluid, improvisational phenomenon whose authenticity lies in the continual reconstruction of itself and its shifting boundaries. For many bands, it is this creative fusion that composes "the real, authentic spirit of klezmer and forms part of its attraction."[41]

For many young Jews, klezmer offered a more authentic, emotional, even spiritual, connection to Jewish culture, religion, and history, but without a commitment to Jewish religious dogma or practice. Those who felt alienated from the world of the synagogue found ethnic roots in klezmer and the possibility of reclaiming cultural heritages from their places of origin. Seth Rogovoy called it "a middle-finger raised to the demon of assimilation, a shout-out to the world that said, 'Jewish is hip.'"[42] This experiential understanding of Jewishness and Jewish spirituality, this way of reconnecting to Jewish life apart from traditional synagogue attendance or religious observance, can be understood in relation to larger trends in contemporary American religion which have emphasized individual experience rather than conformity to established ritual and doctrine.

For others, klezmer legitimated not Jewish spirituality but a more secular form of Jewish identity, an alternative way to affirm Jewishness aside from Zionism or traditional Judaism. Initially, this gave klezmer the cachet of being countercultural, outside of mainstream American Jewish culture.[43] Of course, by now, klezmer has gone mainstream, and there are few Jewish kids growing up who have not been exposed to it at bar and bat mitzvahs, parties, and weddings. Klezmer is now taken for granted as a part of American Jewish culture, particularly at the college level, where other forms of Jewish identification often weaken.[44]

Authenticity and Experiential Access

Since klezmer is a form of heritage music associated with a particular ethnic group, questions about authenticity quickly became intertwined with the identities and backgrounds of the musicians who produce and perform it. One particularly thorny problem has been what Joel Rudinow has labeled the "experiential access argument." This is the idea that genuine heritage music can only be produced by members of a particular group, because only they have access to the experience that produced it, and only they can fully appreciate everything that the music expresses.[45] Just as the blues are seen as an expression of the collective experience of the African American community, so klezmer has often been described as an expression of the collective experiences of the Jewish people. The musical style of klezmer is said to reveal the historical travails of Jewish life, which can be expressed authentically only by those with some access to this group's specific experiences. Seth Rogovoy writes, "At its foundation, it is the expression of the Jewish heart and Jewish soul, filtered through the conversation tones of the violin and the clarinet, and reflective of the very rigors, pains, and joys of Jewish life in the diaspora at any particular moment."[46]

Indeed, many young Jews have felt as though klezmer touched them in a profoundly personal place, providing a connection to an ethnic self that had become threadbare in the process of assimilation to American culture. If klezmer is understood as the expression of certain essential qualities or experiences that bind the Jewish people together, then claims to this musical tradition rest not merely on the basis of musical ability, experience, or competence but also on one's standing as a member of the group. A Jewish musician, one might say, is able to understand or relate to klezmer on a more authentic level than a non-Jew, and the performance of a Jewish musician would be more authentic than that of a non-Jewish one when it comes to giving expression to the spirit of the Jewish folk or people. Whether or not blindfolded audiences would be able to distinguish the music produced by Jewish klezmers in contrast to non-Jewish ones, the musical qualities of klezmer performances cannot be so easily disentangled from the ethnic identities of the actual klezmer composers and performers.

A non-Jewish musician or two within a band of Jewish musicians might be tolerated or overlooked, without their presence jeopardizing the Jewish authenticity of the music. However, the degree to which performances of klezmer music can be considered authentic when none of the musicians are Jewish is more complicated. In *Virtually Jewish: Reinventing Jewish Culture in Europe*, Ruth Ellen Gruber described the growing fascination with Jews and Jewishness among non-Jewish Europeans, resulting in klezmer groups with mostly non-Jewish members performing for mostly non-Jewish audiences.[47] Some groups like the Klezgoyin in Germany made no secret of their non-Jewish identity, and they admitted that while they like klezmer music, they recognize that it is not their music and they cannot own it in the same way that Jewish bands might claim.[48]

The experiential access argument is the idea that the collective experience of a group has molded their values and perspectives in unique ways that are expressed in their cultural activities. Like Herder's earlier model about the essential characteristics of particular ethnic or national groups, the suggestion that mere membership in a group confers privileged access to ancestral group experiences and restricted ownership of the group's cultural traditions is both appealing and problematic. On the one hand, it offers a firm foundation to group identity and its expressions. On the other hand, however, it easily slips into essentialist assumptions about identity that ignore the heterogeneity and dynamic changes within group identities.

It may be more useful to understand ethnic authenticity as an emergent process rather than a preexisting characteristic. As Simon Frith argues, members of a group may get to know and consolidate a particular aspect of their identities through the cultural activities they share.[49] From this perspective, playing klezmer music or listening to it is not so much an *expression* of a prior inborn Jewish identity but rather a way of *bringing* such an identity *into existence* and giving it form. That is, the identity is as much a product of involvement with a particular musical tradition as it is a product of a preexisting identity. This means that a kind of Jewish identity is being performed, constructed, expressed, and affirmed in activities like klezmer music. And the form this identity will take may have tremendous variation.

To be sure, some Jewish musicians may have had childhood memories or contact with earlier klezmer tunes or lyrics or may have a reservoir of lived experience in Jewish culture or Yiddish language. However, for many assimilated Jews, it was the absence of such a connection that drew them to klezmer in the first place. They cannot make any claims to personal experience of European shtetl life or its musical culture. The klezmer experience does not magically access unconscious group memories of shtetl life, but it offers an experience in the present around which a connection to that past can be built.

While klezmer offers a bridge to Jewish roots in a cultural context that no longer exists, many klezmer musicians resist essentialist notions of klezmer authenticity that would imprison them in a futile effort to resurrect the precise forms of music that were produced by Jews in another place and time. That would reduce it to a static and fixed tradition. Mark Slobin calls klezmer "a constantly morphing and expanding musical system with no surviving homeland."[50] It is being reinvented and revitalized by people with no direct experience of the original. In place of authenticity defined in terms of nostalgia and recovery, the focus has turned to an existential authenticity rooted in freedom from tradition. Liner notes for a 1997 album of a band named Brave Old World read, "For us, this recording is a liberation from endless debates about authenticity, history, and social significance, and an affirmation of music which simply celebrates its own freedom: New Jewish music." It is Jewish but it is new, unencumbered by the ghost of the past.

Most klezmer musicians today define authenticity as a balance between a desire to respect and preserve tradition and an insistence on freedom to create and innovate new forms. They reject the idea of simply reproducing some image of the past as a recipe for artistic atrophy. Frank London of the Klezmatics has warned that discussions of authenticity are inevitably struggles over who has the power to define the contours and boundaries of recognized tradition: "For me, to be traditional is to be 'in the tradition.' To sound like a 1925 Jewish band in New York is to be traditional, but for me it means to be informed by the past and to be part of it, but to be moving into the future, to be both part of the music, but also part of the grander scheme in which the music functions."[51]

Ironically, for some musicians, it is precisely their Jewishness that buys them enough authority to experiment with klezmer in new ways without being questioned in the way that innovations made by a non-Jew might be. Alicia Svigals of the Klezmatics insists that klezmer is "authentic Jewish folk music," but it is not powered by nostalgia about the music of her grandparents' generation.[52] Rather, she said, it is "our music; having inherited it, we can now do with it whatever we wish."[53] Accordingly, her group has deliberately experimented with new forms, rhythms, and instruments: "We made new tunes sound old, and old tunes sound new."[54] Elsewhere she says, "We're not about authenticity. We're not about folk fetishes and fetishizing what's supposed to be a Jewish band."[55] Of course, not everyone accepts the degree of freedom and change claimed by Svigals here, and some question whether groups like the Klezmatics have sacrificed some degree of klezmer authenticity.

Although Svigals is typical of many klezmer musicians in rejecting what she calls a "fetishized" form of authenticity, she does think that a different kind of authenticity remains important. It is based on learning the style and musical vocabulary of earlier Jewish musicians but not becoming frozen in the past. Authenticity becomes a matter of merging respect for the past with one's own personal integrity, or, in other words, "to go beyond simply reciting a received text to speak spontaneously in our own voices."[56] She wants to merge the collective authenticity of tradition with the personal authenticity of individual voices or those of her band members and herself. By making a claim to the music as a Jew, Svigals's performance, however creative or innovative it may be, becomes simultaneously a performance of her Jewish identity, and the music produced by Klezmatics ultimately must become a believable addition to the Jewish folk music tradition known as klezmer. This means it will eventually be accepted and recognized by Jewish fans as belonging to the klezmer tradition in some sense or other and contributing to its canon, or not.

This does not preclude the possibility that non-Jews also enjoy klezmer, both as performers and listeners. Christina Baade, a non-Jewish klezmer clarinetist from Wisconsin, has addressed the ways that Jewish ethnicity is woven into the authenticity of klezmer music, and her apprehension that no matter how Jewish her playing sounds or how skilled her musicianship, she remains an outsider among Jewish musicians. Amid the incredible variety in the styles and approaches to klezmer music, the only unifying element that establishes the music's authenticity, Baade insisted, is a connection to the Jewish identity of the members and their sense of being part of a Jewish tradition. Baade writes, "The questions of ethnicity and authenticity haunt me as I play this music—and I've been assured that I 'sound Jewish' enough times to think that I really *can* play it. . . . While we struggle with what we mean by 'authenticity' and question who should and should not perform the music, we are left with the fluidity, the boundary-crossing, the uncontainability of music and what musicians can do with it. Let's celebrate good music and honest performances, and then interrogate our musical motivations again."[57] It is not that Jewishness is a prerequisite to klezmer authenticity but rather that in the process of creating and performing klezmer music, one is creating and performing a new understanding of Jewish identity.[58]

The debates over klezmer authenticity are a microcosm of the often-indeterminate nature of Jewish authenticity in general. There is something oddly paradoxical in Baade's juxtaposing the hybridity and cultural fluidity of klezmer music with the essentialist Jew/non-Jew binary. Surely, it makes little sense to insist on halakhic standards of Jewishness, such as having a Jewish birth mother, to determine whether or not a musician can produce authentic klezmer music in an authentically Jewish way. Insisting that Ashkenazi Jews with established Eastern European roots make more authentic klezmer musicians than, say, blond Anglo-Saxon Jewish converts may seem more sensible, but it still leads to equally problematic racial definitions of Jewish authenticity. On the other hand, there are likely to be additional questions of authenticity when controversial groups such as Messianic Jews decide to incorporate klezmer into their own traditions.[59]

Ethnicity, historian Dell Upton has proposed, needs to be understood as dynamic rather than static. He describes it as "a synthesis of imposed and adopted characteristics that is forged through contact and conflict. It is a role played for the benefit of others. Ethnicity is a creolized identity and a highly volatile one."[60] When culture is commodified in food, crafts, rituals, and music, it is easy to slip into the assumption that those who produce it are merely expressing some deep core of Jewishness within themselves that stabilizes their identity as Jews. However, modern klezmer music is best understood as an "invented tradition" that reveals "the process by which ethnic groups form themselves by choosing to commodify their identities and to attach them to equally consciously chosen material signs. The connection is arbitrary rather than 'authentic.'"[61] Perhaps, one way to understand the issue raised by Baade is to say that Jewish authenticity is not an immanent quality of a specific performance of klezmer music nor something that is guaranteed or disqualified by the performer's background. It becomes authentically Jewish when it is experienced by the performers and audience members as an element in a process that forms and sustains their own sense of Jewishness.

9 Becoming Jewish

INTERMARRIAGE AND CONVERSION

Throughout the last century, communal and rabbinical leaders from all Jewish denominations and organizations, as well as sociologists and demographers, have discussed and debated the "problem" of intermarriage. The challenges posed by both intermarriage and conversion have often been a proxy for broader tensions in modern Jewish life. These include the conflicts between Orthodox and more liberal forms of Jewish observance and belief, relations between Jews and non-Jews, and questions about ethnicity and acculturation. Underlying all of these issues is a more fundamental dispute—the conflict between competing models of authenticity and conditions for the recognition of Jewishness.

Boundaries and Religious Authenticity

The traditional religious approach to Jewish authenticity most often rests on a need to maintain strict boundaries not only between Jews and non-Jews but also between those Jews who are recognized as normative by a particular Jewish sect or denomination and those who are not. Attitudes toward intermarriage and policies about conversion to Judaism reflect particular assumptions about who and what will be recognized as authentically Jewish. For the more traditional Jewish leaders, endogamous marriage is essential to the perpetuation of both the Jewish people and the Jewish religion in their purest forms.

An essay titled "What Is Wrong with Intermarriage?" posted on an ultra-Orthodox (Chabad) website offers a good example of their analysis of the far-reaching implications of individual marital choices: "We are all the product of bygone generations; in the case of Jews, descendants of Abraham, Isaac, and Jacob. . . . To be a Jew today is not an accident of birth but the sum total of over 3300 years of ancestral self-sacrifice, of heroes who at times gave their very lives for their beliefs. . . . The indomitable Jewish spirit survived and clung to its traditions despite all odds. And now, the very latest link of that glorious tradition has the option of severing the chain in one fell swoop—or not!"[1] The language here invokes a dual sense of obligation to the past that consists of both a *biological* chain of generations going back to the Jewish patriarchs and a *religious* and *cultural* chain of tradition preserved by heroic sacrifice and perseverance. Both of these chains can be threatened "in one fell swoop" by intermarriage. This is the reason why rabbinic authorities throughout the centuries, notes Orthodox rabbi David Bleich, concluded that intermarriage was prohibited even before the revelation of the Torah at Sinai: "From the early dawn of history, the people of Israel sought to preserve their ethnic purity and legislated against intermarriage."[2] Bleich added that "among Jews, no practice is more widely abhorred than is intermarriage."[3] Bleich emphasizes that the Jewish community has long considered intermarriage to be more than merely a private personal decision made between individuals. It can either strengthen collective bonds within the community or present a rupture in those bonds that reverberates through the Jewish people as a whole.

The Chabad website's essay expresses the required subordination of the individual Jew to the collective Jewish people in a literary metaphor. Individual members of the Jewish people are like letters in a Torah scroll. Just as the integrity and authenticity of a Torah scroll require every letter to be correctly placed within the larger whole, so too does the integrity of the Jewish people depend on the choices and actions of individual Jews. Those who intermarry are like errant letters whose loss threatens the whole meaning of the sacred text that is the Jewish people.

It has not been uncommon, even in the modern era, for statements about intermarriage to mention Exodus 34:12–16 or Deuteronomy 7:1–4 as the fundamental Jewish religious texts on the subject. These verses describe the ancient Israelites' neighbors as idol worshippers whose gods should be smashed and whose daughters are to be avoided as potential wives for Jewish sons, since they will tempt them to the worship of false gods. Invoking such passages is intended to link the modern possibility of Jews marrying Christians who may believe in mainstream Christian doctrines like the incarnation, the Trinity, and the divinity of Jesus with the idolatrous neighbors surrounding the Jews in ancient Israel.

From the traditionalist perspective, rising rates of intermarriage are symptomatic of weakening commitments to normative Jewish traditions and the lure of assimilation. Indeed, for many years, intermarriage was regarded as tantamount to abandoning the Jewish people. In the first half of the twentieth century, Orthodox and Reform rabbis, who generally agreed on few things, shared the view that Jews who intermarried were guilty of not only treason to Judaism but also desertion from the Jewish people. In his classic work from 1934, *Judaism as a Civilization*, Mordecai Kaplan observed that "even those who have abandoned all Jewish religious beliefs and observances think twice before they give their sanction to intermarriage. Though not condemned as vehemently as apostasy, intermarriage is regarded as equivalent in a measure to deserting the Jewish people."[4]

Peoplehood and Endogamy

While it is no longer common to accuse an intermarrying Jew of either self-loathing or treason, it is not hard to find those who consider intermarriage indicative of weakness, selfishness, and a betrayal of the primordial tribal connection of individuals to their religious or ethnic group identity. This tribal connection implicitly establishes membership in a people as a consequence of being born to members of the group. Although a biological or racial concept of Jewish peoplehood is frowned on by most Jews today, racial understandings of Jewishness were common among American Jews in the late nineteenth century and early twentieth century. Jews saw themselves as unique not just because of their religion or culture but also because of something deeper, rooted in "biology, shared ancestry, and blood."[5] Increased acceptance and contact with non-Jews raised concerns among Jewish leaders, rabbis, and the Jewish press about the impact of intermarriage and the threat it posed to Jewish racial cohesion.[6] It is not surprising that nervousness also arose about the Jewish authenticity of those who claim to be Jews but who were not born that way.[7] If Jews were ultimately united by their Semitic blood, then intermarriage could undermine the strength of the race since non-Jews, even if they converted to Judaism, could never really become authentic Jews at the level of blood and race. Eric Goldstein notes that "for those Jews whose commitments had slipped, race served as an anchor in a time of changing boundaries."[8] Even some Reform rabbis, who tended to emphasize universal religious ideals as the essence of Judaism, still used ethnic terms like *Hebrew* or *Israelite* to refer to Jews and continued to support the importance of in-marriage for the sake of Jewish racial purity: "More than perhaps any other single issue, intermarriage provoked discussions that revealed the strong emotional attachments Jews still had to a racial self-understanding during the early twentieth century."[9]

Intermarriage and Conversion

When the focus of discussion about intermarriage pivots to the issue of non-Jews who convert for the sake of marriage to Jews, it signals the likelihood that the Jewish partner intends to continue to affirm a Jewish identity rather than employ intermarriage as a strategy of escape from association with the Jewish people. When this happens, the issue of authenticity is displaced from the intentions of a Jew who intermarries to the conditions necessary to authenticate the Jewish identity of a non-Jewish partner who converts. In other words, apart from the question of whether a Jew who intermarries can remain an authentic Jew is the further question of whether and how a non-Jew can ever truly be transformed into someone authentically Jewish.

The idea of conversion implies the possibility of changing, or "converting," a fundamental aspect of a person's identity. Popular nineteenth-century ideas about the bonds of kinship, shared history, and culture that establish membership in a people, nationality, or ethnic group also created doubts about how malleable and mutable certain core elements of a person's social identity may be. In the early twentieth century, David de Sola Pool, a prominent Orthodox rabbi and president of the New York Board of Rabbis, argued against intermarriage by appealing to the need of both Jews *and* Gentiles to remain true to their own histories and traditions—that is, to preserve their authenticity as individuals and as members of their ethnic and religious communities: "We have little respect for one who is so characterless as to submerge his own personality in that of his brother. Be yourself, be true to yourself is as sound a counsel to religious groups as it is to individuals. Let each be loyal to his own traditions *of birth*, his own religion and God."[10] Rabbi de Sola Pool understood the essence of a person's identity as grounded in "profound race memories which centuries of race tradition have woven into the very fiber of our natures."[11] Since he believed that marital happiness depends on a couple's shared racial memories, marriage between a Jew and a non-Jew, or any mixed marriage for that matter, was doomed to failure. The pool of suitable potential mates was determined at the moment of one's birth, when it became clear to which group one belonged.

Rabbi de Sola Pool's position blends together an essentialist model of individual authenticity (being true to yourself) with a similarly essentialist approach to group authenticity (being loyal to the group into which one is born). The boundaries between Jews and non-Jews must be maintained, he argued, since any attempt to adopt or convert to another group or religion would be a violation of the identity and group into which one had been born. To even think of converting would be an inauthentic act of weakness, lack of character, and lack of self-respect. When authenticity is defined in this way, conversion is a poor option, not only for the Jewish people, but also for the integrity of any prospective convert.

Of course, many Jewish authorities reject the notion of racial definitions of Jewish peoplehood and recognize the possibility of non-Jews becoming part of the Jewish people. Among Orthodox leaders who have been willing to consider conversion as an option, a clear distinction is usually made between those prospective converts who want to become Jews for the sake of their Jewish partners and those who seek conversion *l'shem shamayim*—that is, for the sake of heaven. Conversions that are made for pragmatic family considerations, like getting married to someone who is Jewish rather than out of a *sincere* personal commitment to living a Jewish life, are unacceptable. This requirement for sincerity and purity in the potential convert's motivation for conversion presents an important intertwining of two kinds of Jewish authenticity. Accepting the obligations and responsibilities associated with traditional Jewish law (essentialist Jewish authenticity) is insufficient by itself for conversion. In addition, the convert's intentions must be pure, and the decision must be an expression of his or her own inner commitment to *being* a Jew (expressive Jewish authenticity). In other words, a conversion that represents a genuine change in a person's identity from non-Jew to Jew can only happen when there is a sincere choice to realize it in the convert's life. Only then is a convert worthy of recognition as a real Jew. Even when both of these conditions are met, there may still remain questions about recognizing a convert as a "real Jew." Many converts report a subtle, and often not so subtle, difference in how they are regarded within the Jewish community. They feel their motives and sincerity in converting are often cause for suspicion.[12]

Full recognition of a convert remains difficult when, as Gary Tobin describes it, there is a mostly unspoken assumption among many Jews that "true membership in the Jewish community can only be achieved by birth. All other comers can never be like us, not really, not in their hearts. But we cannot say this out loud."[13] Thus a hierarchy of essentialist authenticity remains embedded in the idea of Jewish peoplehood that presents an insurmountable obstacle for a potential convert. No matter how devout they may be in their practice of Judaism, newly adopted religious observance cannot transform them into "biological Jews."[14] Rather, a person who tries to join the Jewish people is not magically changed into a Jew but is actually treated more like an immigrant. This is how converts were regarded in ancient Israel.[15]

The Hellenistic Jewish philosopher Philo described the importance of caring for proselytes, since they have left behind "their country, their kinfolk, and their friends, for the sake of virtue and religion. Let them not be denied another citizenship or other ties of family and friendship"[16] According to Peter Borgen, Philo understood that a convert "made a sociological, judicial, and ethnic break with pagan society and joined another ethnic group, the Jewish nation."[17] The identity of a convert is therefore more complicated than simply being transformed, or "converted," from a non-Jew to a Jew like all other Jews. To convert to being Jewish is to abandon parts of one's identity that may have deep emotional resonances from childhood. Like an immigrant, the convert never quite feels the same degree of comfort and fluency as the native and always worries that someone will detect in him an accent or mannerism that reveals that he or she came from another place, culture, language, or religion.

Jewish Souls in Non-Jewish Bodies

There are some Jewish communities who remain steadfast in their opposition to the idea of religious conversion to Judaism, since their essentialist understanding of Jewishness renders impossible the notion of being *transformed* or *converted* into a Jew. As Chabad rabbi Aron Moss explains in a kind of origin myth of Jewishness itself, the essence of Jewishness can be traced to the moment of the original divine creation of the first human being. At that moment, the fundamental polarities of human life were established—body and soul, male and female, and Jew and non-Jew. This divine intention determines who every person really is and must remain: "Jews should be Jews, non-Jews should be non-Jews, men should be men and women should be women. And every individual has to be himself."[18] By locating the origin of the Jewish people at the moment of creation, the question of whether or not someone is Jewish has already been predetermined and cannot change.

Jewishness, then, is described as an indelible, immutable essence that resides in every Jew. This essence, which Rabbi Moss calls the "Jewish soul," is the ultimate guarantor of Jewish authenticity. Most of the time, people with Jewish souls are raised as Jews, so there is an effortless expression of their Jewish souls in their lives. But perhaps, proposes Rabbi Moss, there are also cases where Jewish souls occasionally show up in the bodies of non-Jews, or more precisely, people who only outwardly *seem* to be non-Jews. While it is not at all clear how these Jewish souls became stranded in non-Jewish bodies, once it happens, they produce a subtle attraction among some non-Jews to Jewish religion, culture, and people.

It might be that a Jewish soul wound up in a non-Jew's body because at some point in the past a Jewish forebear converted to another religion. Converting *back* to being a Jew would simply be restoring the natural order to its intended balance. In such cases of misplaced souls, conversion is not a matter of *transforming* a Gentile into a Jew but rather of *returning* the Jewish soul within the Gentile to its rightful home within the Jewish people. A potential convert's initial decision to embrace Jewish religion and the Jewish people could be interpreted as evidence that they already have a Jewish soul. Kabbalistic concepts of reincarnation have also been enlisted to provide a convert with a hypothetical prior connection to the Jewish people. Thus, people who decide to convert to Judaism may be assumed to have already been Jews in their previous lives.

Obviously, the legal fiction of Jewish souls in non-Jewish bodies permits non-Jews to be recognized as Jews without describing the process as a literal conversion or change from one identity to another. No one can be changed into a Jew who was not one already, but those with latent or buried Jewish souls can be assisted in finding out who they already really are. Successful "converts" are as authentically Jewish as born-Jews, since they are not really converts at all, just Jews who are coming home. It is as if they found an old box in their attic that contained their Jewish citizenship papers. According to this explanation, there is no need to encourage non-Jews to convert because only those with Jewish souls will pursue a path of restoring their rightful Jewishness.

While the idea of lost Jewish souls may seem quaintly appealing, particularly for those who insist that "once a Jew, always a Jew," taking this perspective seriously would most likely create more problems than it solves. For if Jewish souls can be stranded in non-Jewish bodies, then presumably non-Jewish souls might have become trapped in Jewish bodies. Perhaps some Jews who find themselves romantically involved with non-Jews were never *really* Jews at all, but rather non-Jewish souls that wound up in Jewish bodies by mistake. Moreover, the transmission of souls, Jewish or otherwise, from one generation to the next seems to occur as a result of biological procreation, bringing us back to a kind of racial essentialism. Although this whole approach talks only about souls and not genes or blood, the simple fact is that the same process that gave a person their Jewish soul would also have established a biological and genetic tie to the Jewish people as well.

Moving from Nonrecognition to Outreach

In the non-Orthodox world, rabbinic responses to the issue of intermarriage have undergone substantial changes in recent decades. Over a century ago, Rabbi David Einhorn, one of the early leaders of the Reform movement in the United States, warned that "mixed marriages are the nail in the coffin of the small Jewish race."[19] In 1989, Rabbi Jerome Epstein expressed the unequivocal opposition of the Conservative movement to intermarriage, noting that "an inter-marriage has no authenticity in Jewish law" and should not be publicly acknowledged in any way.[20] If intermarriage lacks *legal recognition* by Jewish law, it is not entitled to any form of *social or public recognition* either, argued Epstein.

Epstein's responsum was adopted by the Conservative movement by an eight to four vote. The decision was published with an ironic, misleading title—"Congratulations to Mixed Marriage Families." The actual decision, however, was that synagogues are *not* to provide congratulations to members *either* on the marriage of their children to non-Jews *or* on the arrival of grandchildren born to their intermarried children. The real doctrine should have been titled "*No* Congratulations to Mixed Marriage Families." Conservative rabbis, moreover, were not permitted to participate in any ceremonies or receptions for a mixed marriage. Even as acceptance of intermarriage in the Conservative movement and outreach to non-Jewish partners was increasing, Epstein remained firm in the view that Conservative Judaism should continue to withhold any recognition or congratulations for marriages or births of children who lack "authenticity in Jewish law."[21] His position illustrates the multiple levels on which recognition operates and the efforts of Conservative religious leaders to control any possible leakage of recognition for intermarriage from rabbinic leaders.

Twenty years later, the Conservative movement's rabbinical association proposed "a delicate balance" to *recognize* the reality of interfaith families and non-Jews in synagogue communities. The new position combined "the unconditional welcome of interfaith families and non-Jews within the community alongside the prospect of conversion to those who sincerely feel moved to join the Jewish people." This position, focused on *keruv*, or "outreach," dramatically shifted the discussion away from legal principles toward other things that constitute the "delicate balance." It acknowledged that the boundaries of the Jewish community are increasingly porous. Indeed, there are already many non-Jews present within Jewish families and synagogues. The only issue is whether or not to accord them any recognition within the Jewish community.

Outreach presupposes the importance of recognition of the non-Jew as a member of interfaith families who will not be ignored or shunned. "Unconditional welcome" suggests a certain level of acceptance of the non-Jew as such, without pressure or expectation to change or convert. Conversion is still held onto as a "prospect," but one that is contingent on the "sincere feelings" of non-Jews to make this decision, not the result of social pressure or fear of ostracism.

The focus on "unconditional welcome" to non-Jewish members of interfaith families represents an important shift in the understanding of authenticity. The Conservative Rabbinical Assembly's statement established a new attitude toward the non-Jew: "Our first priority is always that the non-Jew experiencing our way of life, do so at a pace and in an environment where he or she feels comfortable. Moreover, the unconditional welcome we extend to non-Jews is heartfelt and enthusiastic wherever they are on their journey."[22] The statement is notable for several reasons. First, it refers to Jewishness not in legal (halakhic), religious, or ethnic terms but simply as "a way of life." While that term obviously will include elements of religion and ethnicity, a way of life focuses on various experiences of individuals and allows for both personal and group attitudes, values, and identities. Second, it understands the development of a way of life, Jewish or otherwise, as something that emerges as part of a personal "journey."[23]

Of course, some leaders in Conservative Judaism think that the gesture of welcome to non-Jewish partners should nonetheless include a strong sales pitch for conversion. In an op-ed column in the *Wall Street Journal* titled "Wanted: Converts to Judaism," Arnold Eisen, Chancellor of Jewish Theological Seminary, suggested that rabbis and Jewish institutions "actively encourage" non-Jewish family members to convert, since "Judaism needs more Jews." Rabbis should "use every means to explicitly and strongly advocate for conversion, bringing potential converts close and actively making the case for them to commit to Judaism" rather than remain on the sidelines.²⁴ Robyn Frish, the director of InterfaithFamily/Philadelphia, quickly objected to Eisen's suggestion and insisted that recognition of interfaith families should express that they are welcome "just as they are (rather than trying to turn them into what we want them to be)."²⁵

If liberal Judaism has increasingly come to understand that an authentically Jewish life has less to do with a preordained set of rules than with the acceptance and recognition of each person's own path or process for realizing the Jewish dimension of their lives, its policy of outreach for the intermarried is just one part of a broader strategy of outreach in general. The idea of a journey includes other elements in a person's life than just Jewish elements. Genuine recognition of the non-Jewish members of Jewish families and communities requires an appreciation that this is a person with a history and previous culture and religion that may need to be integrated in a new Jewish one. An understanding of Jewishness as both journey and way of life means that there are no preset destinations for either intermarried or other Jewish families.²⁶

Nonreligious Alternatives to Conversion

The situation of the Jewish people today has changed in many ways from the situation described by Sartre in the 1940s. In the United States, there are now hundreds of thousands of people who were not born and raised as Jews yet who are living in families that observe Jewish customs, rituals, and holidays. Just as there are people who are *officially recognized* as Jewish but who are not at all involved in Jewish life, there are people who are technically *not recognized* as Jewish but who are deeply involved in the Jewish life of their families, active in synagogues and other Jewish organizations, and knowledgeable about Judaism and Jewish culture. In some cases, they keep kosher, fast on Yom Kippur, send their children to Jewish day schools, and are as observant as many Jews.²⁷ The most common situation probably involves spouses or live-in partners of Jews who maintain some degree of participation in Jewish cultural and religious activities. They may have agreed to raise children, if any, as Jews, despite their own hesitation or disinterest in formal conversion. They may or may not have a connection to other religious traditions. Jewish demographer Gary Tobin estimated that "people living as Jews without converting far outnumber the amount of people who convert to Judaism."²⁸

Sometimes conversion is not an option either because a particular community refuses to recognize its authenticity or because a potential convert lacks any interest in a process predicated on commitment to a new religious system. A variety of proposals have been made to offer some degree of participation in, and recognition by, a Jewish community without the need for religious conversion. It generally moves the process of recognition out of the hands of religious authorities and religious definitions of Jewishness.

By resurrecting a category from the history of ancient Israel, Orthodox rabbi Steve Greenberg has tried to circumvent the contentious issue of the sincerity and purity of motivation of potential converts who may be acting only for the sake of marriage.²⁹ He suggests that a non-Jew who participates in Jewish life and the raising of Jewish children without ever converting may be seen as a *ger toshav*, a "resident alien"—that is, someone who loves the Jewish people without really being one of them. In a loose sense, the only religious requirement is that a *ger toshav* forgoes all idolatry, which would probably include any Christian belief about Jesus. If he or she is willing to follow the seven Noahide laws or most Jewish mitzvot, so much the better. It is not at all clear whether atheism would be tolerated in a resident alien, an option that was probably not envisioned at the time this category was formulated.

This alternative would allow non-Jews "to become not converts, but committed fans of the Jewish people," and more importantly to make a commitment to Jewish parenthood.[30] Greenberg recognizes that this proposal would not legitimize the marriage of a Jew and a non-Jew, nor prevent the child of a Jewish father and non-Jewish mother from requiring conversion to become a Jew recognized by the Orthodox community, but he feels it is a more humane response than complete rejection or ostracism of a non-Jewish spouse.

While this approach may satisfy those who want a more accommodating attitude toward those non-Jewish partners in intermarriages who are supportive of maintaining the Jewish atmosphere of their homes and child-rearing, there can be no question that it offers only limited recognition without loosening the boundary between Jew and non-Jew in any real way. Worth noting is that the *ger toshav* category makes a shift from a religious category to an immigration status. In this formulation, the non-Jew permanently remains a non-Jew, a "non-citizen" of the Jewish people, an alien without any path to citizenship or recognition, short of traditional Orthodox conversion (with its demand for proof of "sincerity"). This label confers no Jewish authenticity, and children of a female *ger toshav* will continue to lack recognized Jewish status in the absence of formal conversion, despite having been born and raised in the Jewish community. The *ger toshav* solution may be well-intended, but it remains problematic in creating a liminal status between Jewish and non-Jewish. It resolves an Orthodox halakhic insistence on preserving Jewish purity by preventing "insincere" converts from joining the Jewish people without the harshness of complete rejection. But it still withholds recognition of any meaningful status within the community.

At the other end of the denominational spectrum, Reconstructionist rabbi Steven Carr Reuben offers a similar solution as Greenberg but one that recognizes people whose lives are deeply connected to the Jewish people as a kind of Jews—"Jews by association." He uses this category to describe people who were not born Jewish ("Jews by chance") and have not become Jewish through conversion ("Jews by choice") but who live with Jews, share in Jewish life, and, to one degree or another, feel part of the Jewish community. The addition of this category is aimed at loosening the entrance requirements for claiming some degree of Jewish authenticity and at offering a form of recognition that is dependent neither on birth nor on formal religious conversion.

Participating in the evolving religious civilization of the Jewish people now includes multiple points of entry and forms of participation.[31] What is intriguing about the idea of "Jews by association" is that it dramatically shifts the locus of authenticity away from any individual and onto the family system where individual Jewish identities emerge out of a network of relationships and associations. It is certainly likely that many Jews may consider "association" an inadequate basis for assigning Jewish status, but others may recognize that this is the Jewish reality of everyday life for some people. When a family observes Jewish customs, rituals, holidays, and is involved in raising Jewish children, there need to be alternative ways of defining their Jewish authenticity aside from any irregularities in the Jewish status of individual family members.

Of course, there are many people whose connection to Jewish culture and community is not involved with religious and ritual observances. Indeed, some may be indifferent or explicitly hostile to religious practice, though still deeply committed to being Jewish. Yossi Beilin, a former prime minister of Israel, suggested that a significant portion of the Jews in the world are no longer religious. This indicated to him the need to offer nonreligious methods to become part of the Jewish people. Otherwise, if religious conversion controlled by religious authorities is the only way non-Jews are permitted to become part of the Jewish people, they are faced with the difficult choice of remaining outside the Jewish people or being forced into inauthenticity by promising to do something they do not believe in or intend to do.

Beilin proposed that it is time to formally recognize the authenticity of nonreligious, or secular, Jewish identity: "Judaism is also a nation, and an existential culture. Many Jews, maybe most Jews, are either atheists or agnostics, yet no one questions their Jewishness. Why is someone like me allowed to be an agnostic Jew while a convert to Judaism is not? Why must a non-Jewish atheist or agnostic go to a rabbi in order to become a Jewish atheist or agnostic?"[32] Beilin argues that people who are not already members of other religions should be recognized as Jews and members of the Jewish people largely on the basis of their own self-definition, subject to communal review of their Jewish references, their identification with the Jewish people, their knowledge of Jewish history, and their motivations.[33] Becoming Jewish in Beilin's model is a bit like joining a club or fraternity. Even though the rules and definitions of Jewishness might be left to individual discretion, Beilin is not saying that anything goes. The individual process of extracting meaningful elements from Jewish culture and communal life is always going to require a mechanism of recognition from some component of the community to formalize membership in the Jewish people.

Despite his sympathy for a normative approach to Judaism as a vehicle for Jewish continuity, sociologist and demographer Steven M. Cohen has also acknowledged that such an approach does not resonate in "post-modern, post-ethnic, post-religious, post-collective America." He suggests that a more welcoming approach to intermarried couples and families that includes some degree of recognition and acceptance may be in order.[34] Like Reuben and Beilin, Cohen's suggestion is to provide a path for non-Jewish spouses (and others) "to consider themselves as belonging to the Jewish people without taking the extra step of a religious conversion." According to a recent study of New York Jews, about 5 percent of the subjects claim a Jewish identity that they arrived at without either Jewish parents or religious conversion. Cohen recommends that such people might still be recognized as members of the Jewish people and participate in the Jewish culture among friends and family, if not necessarily in a formal religious setting. To do so would require recognizing what clearly already exists for some people—a "Jewish social identity." They could be officially recognized as members of the Jewish people by virtue of a process he names "Jewish Cultural Affirmation."[35]

What forms of Jewish authenticity and recognition, if any, might be assigned to those who were neither born Jewish nor converted to Judaism, but who share in a Jewish way of life and participate in the Jewish community? Obviously, to call such people Jews would not be completely accurate, but to simply label them non-Jews would be to ignore the Jewish dimensions and activities in their lives. If one were willing to deconstruct the Jew/non-Jew binary a bit, it might be possible to find new ways to talk about this growing population. Perhaps it is necessary to separate the use of the word *Jewish* as an essentialist dimension of identity from *Jewish* as a more fluid description of aspects in a person's life that connect them to Jewish life, culture, and community. Granting some form of recognition to a group of people we might call "Jewish non-Jews" or "non-Jewish Jews" is a first step in weaning ourselves from more essentialist definitions. Such terms will be condemned as illogical, paradoxical, or oxymoronic, but only as long as a rigid boundary between Jew and non-Jew is maintained.

Authenticity and Jewish Grandchildren

Discussion of Jewish survival and continuity moved to the top of the Jewish communal agenda in the final decades of the twentieth century in response to an apparently skyrocketing rate of intermarriage. As that happened, the prime venue of authenticity shifted from the Jewish and non-Jewish partners involved in intermarriage to their progeny. The real problem of intermarriage, Jewish demographers lamented, is its failure to produce significant numbers of children with strong Jewish identities. Jewish authenticity became a measurable and quantifiable phenomenon to be evaluated not by rabbis according to halakhic principles of matrilineal descent nor nonhalakhic alternatives, but rather by Jewish demographers and other social scientists looking at intergenerational patterns. Concern about the next generation of Jews represented the most important question for many Jewish leaders. This sentiment was well summarized in the title of Rabbi Jonathan Sacks's 1994 book *Will We Have Jewish Grandchildren?*[36] Recognition and welcoming of non-Jewish partners may be all well and good, but if the children of such unions do not identify with being Jewish, then what is the relevance of the recognition?

The uncertainty of the Jewish identity of one's children and their children is not an issue unique to the intermarried, of course. At the same time, the Jewish identity outcome in children and grandchildren is more complicated than a dichotomous choice of Jewish or not, as suggested by Sacks's book title. Judging the strength or authenticity of the Jewishness of the next generation raises a thicket of problems. How exactly does one measure the Jewish identity of the offspring of the intermarried: by their level of observance, by their inner sense of Jewishness, by their level of synagogue affiliation, by the intensity of their attachment to Israel, by their own choices for marital partners? We immediately tumble into questions that have vexed demographers and sociologists of contemporary Jewry about just how to measure and analyze Jewishness.

Nonetheless, this shift of the locus of authenticity from a static past to an unpredictable future is quite useful, for it is also a reminder that whatever debates about who is a true Jew and whose Judaism is authentic occur in the present, the final judgment is always suspended, always awaiting the as yet undetermined ways that Jewishness may be constructed, experienced, and expressed in future generations.

The resistance that prevents complete recognition from being extended to Jewish families that include intermarriage or conversion likely stems from the long-standing reflex to police communal borders against the threat posed by outsiders who may bring unwanted religious ideas and values with them that are hard to eradicate. Efforts to preserve what is considered authentically Jewish by enforcing essentialist ideas of Jewish peoplehood are unable to reverse or halt the trend away from exclusively endogamous Jewish family formation. Surely, the reality of intermarriage has challenged the ways of understanding Jewish identity and Jewish authenticity, as well as how the parameters of the community will be defined, redefined, and reconstructed. This is a process in which policies about recognition and inclusion will require continued negotiation and renegotiation.

10 Authentically Jewish Genes

A sixteenth-century peasant named Martin Guerre abruptly left his small French village one day, leaving behind a wife and infant. Eight years later, when a man claiming to be Martin Guerre returned, neither the villagers nor his relatives could be sure whether he was the real Martin Guerre or just an imposter. Although the villagers had lived with the original Martin, they weren't able to identify or recognize him with complete certainty. They scrutinized his appearance, which did look familiar, and they listened to his stories, which included detailed information about Martin. Most of them accepted Martin as who he said he was, and his wife welcomed him back into her home. Things became a bit complicated, however, when the real Martin Guerre returned to his village years later.[1]

If this story were happening today, perhaps the villagers would appeal to the tools of modern forensic science to make a positive identification. They might examine fingerprints, or dental records, or DNA before agreeing to recognize this person's claimed identity as authentic. All three methods depend on a comparison of two samples to see whether there is a match. There would need to be a previous record of the fingerprints or dental X-rays of the real Martin Guerre against which the new Martin Guerre's fingerprints or dental X-rays could be compared. The third method, a DNA sample, is a bit more complicated. To be sure, a sample from the new Martin Guerre could be compared with any preserved genetic material of the original Martin Guerre, if it were available. But DNA also leaves a genetic trail within all the kin of the person in question. So comparing DNA from the new Martin Guerre with a sample from his biological son or biological father would probably enable us to determine with a very high degree of certainty if this is indeed his real identity.

A Genetic Basis for the Jewish People?

The use of genetic analysis to establish a person's identity with near-perfect certainty in situations where one is trying to establish paternity, identify rapists, or exonerate people waiting on death row has certainly been refined with impressive results in recent years. It is these kinds of cases that have created an expectation or presumption that the data in our genes can not only confirm innocence or guilt but overturn criminal convictions and set us free. It may also be the source of truth about who we really are and who our distant relatives are.

The preoccupation with genetics as an instrument for determining Jewish identity or Jewish ancestry reflects the hope for a scientifically based standard of evidence to establish the boundaries of the Jewish people and to judge the Jewish authenticity of various individuals and groups who claim a connection to the

Jewish people. The idea that there might be distinctive Jewish genes is reminiscent of earlier biological theories of Jewishness, grounded in pseudoscientific ideas about uniquely Jewish racial characteristics, facial features, fingerprint patterns, or blood types. Such theories have offered a counter-balance to the consequences of more than two millennia of Jewish diaspora. They promise to demonstrate some essential quality of Jewishness underlying the incredible diversity of Jews in terms of their physical appearances, ethnicities, and languages, not to mention their cultural and religious practices.

Unlike race, which normally implies some kind of observable phenotypical characteristics (such as eye color, skin complexion, or hair texture) that differentiate members of one racial group from those of other groups, Jewish genetics provides a way of establishing a biologically inherited difference between Jews and non-Jews even when there are no observable physical differences. In fact, some Jewish geneticists have argued that Jews are genetically more similar to each other than to the surrounding non-Jewish populations where Jews have lived.[2] Even if they look similar to their non-Jewish neighbors, the links between them are hidden in their DNA. As one Jewish geneticist concludes, "We are really a single ethnic group coming from the Middle East. Even if you look like another European, with blue eyes and light skin, your (male) genes are telling that you're from the Middle East."[3] In other words, he is claiming that Jews throughout the world are still part of the same family, linked together by strands of DNA that have been passed down throughout the centuries, despite having been separated from one another for thousands of years.

As Harry Ostrer declares in *Legacy: A Genetic History of the Jewish People*, "Having a 3000-year genetic legacy can be a source of group identity and pride in the same way that having a shared history, culture, and religion can be sources of pride."[4] Indeed, Ostrer insists that this "genetic legacy" or "biological Jewishness"[5] will increasingly become a factor in allowing people to be recognized as Jews and claiming a "shared cultural legacy."[6] This new focus on a biological or genetic aspect of Jewishness also means that outward appearances, religious practices, or cultural traditions are merely variable expressions of this hidden aspect of Jewishness. Genetic authenticity makes all Jews into involuntary biological Marranos, outwardly different because of the influence of a variety of surrounding cultures, languages, and traditions but genetically interconnected inside. On this level, a person who has a genetic link to Jewish populations but does not have substantial cultural or religious participation can arguably claim a connection as deep, or possibly deeper, as a Jewish convert with a high degree of religious and cultural engagement but no genetic connection to prior Jewish populations.

Yet most Jewish geneticists reveal a profound ambivalence between their sense that, on the one hand, "the Jewish people" is a genetically recognizable and distinct population and, on the other hand, Jewishness is a matter of more than DNA. Just a few paragraphs after declaring the reality of biological Jewishness, Ostrer acknowledges the possibility of genetic mixing between Jews and non-Jews and admits that "there is no rigorous genetic test for Jewishness" nor any common set of genetic markers shared by all Jews.[7] As a result, the excitement over Jewish genetics needs to be tempered with the realization that the results of genetic research and analysis are easily distorted or exaggerated. Ultimately, the meaning of genetic markers may not be simply inherent within them but rather something that will be manifested in different ways to different people as they express particular group identities.

The Descendants of Aaron the Priest

The eureka moment in the emergence of Jewish genetics was the discovery of a combination of six genetic markers on the Y chromosome that has become known as the Cohen Modal Haplotype (CMH). The term *Cohen* in this label is ambiguous in a crucial way. On the one hand, it simply refers to how the initial group of subjects tested by Karl Skorecki—one of the earliest researchers—and subsequent researchers were selected. For Jews, the last name *Cohen* and a number of related names are indications that the fathers in these families have traditionally identified themselves as direct patrilineal descendants of the priests (*kohanim*) who worked in the ancient Temple in Jerusalem. Jewish geneticists wanted to see whether there were genetic clues about the distant past beneath this tradition. Since the Israelite priesthood was established by Moses's brother, Aaron, according to the Bible's account, was it possible that Jewish men whose family traditions tell them that they are of the priestly Cohen lineage might actually be distant relatives of Moses and Aaron?

What was intriguing about the discovery of the CMH in present-day *kohanim* was the possibility of estimating the time and place that these genetic markers first showed up. Such data might give greater plausibility to the reality of a Jewish tradition of a patrilineal priesthood, even though the religious and ritual duties of the Jewish priestly caste mostly ceased after the destruction of the Temple by the Romans during the first century CE. Today, "Cohens" retain some special privileges and duties in Orthodox Judaism, but far less, if any, special recognition in liberal Judaism. Skorecki, who is himself a Cohen (i.e., of priestly lineage; the last name of a "Cohen" isn't necessarily *Cohen*), reasoned that if there were any truth to the tradition of "Cohen" status being assigned through patrilineal descent from Israelite priests to subsequent generations of Jews, it might have left a genetic trail on the Y chromosome that fathers pass on to their sons.

It did not take long before the term *Cohen* in "Cohen Modal Haplotype" stopped being merely a descriptive term for the present-day religious status of the research subjects whose families claimed a priestly lineage indicated by their last names. It quickly slipped into two much more controversial hypotheses about the ancestry of any people possessing this set of markers. When this same genetic marker known as the CMH has been discovered in other individuals or groups with less established connections to traditional Jewish communities, the marker has often been interpreted as evidence of Jewish ancestry. Even more provocative was the suggestion that people with the CMH marker may actually be descendants of ancient Israelite priests, including possibly Aaron himself. According to British geneticist Neil Bradman, men who have tested positive for the CMH take it as an important piece of evidence about their ancestors: "The men walk a little taller after learning that they are Cohanim, members of the priestly caste."[8]

The genetic evidence that supports the Middle Eastern origins of Jews throughout the world is based on a comparison of particular genetic markers that appear among some portion of Jewish people with the genetic profiles of current inhabitants of the areas in the Middle East where Jews may have lived thousands of years ago. If, for example, a genetic marker found at a high frequency among some Jews is likewise found at a similar or higher frequency among peoples from a certain geographical area, it is possible that certain Jews also originated from that area. This means that the proof of Jewish roots in the Middle East is substantiated by the degree of common ancestry with Palestinians and other Arabs whose ancestors presumably remained in that region when the Jews who had lived there were dispersed throughout the world. The most common genetic studies that are said to establish Jewish roots in the Middle East have noted greater genetic overlap that many, though not all, Ashkenazi Jews have with Palestinians, Syrians, Lebanese, and Kurds compared to Europeans.[9]

Tracing contemporary Jews to Middle Eastern ancestors, perhaps even to ancient Israelites, is not the end of the story, since it is likely that those ancestors were themselves related to older Semitic and Mediterranean peoples. The common ancestors that many Jews as well as other Middle Eastern and Mediterranean populations share are probably people who predate the Israelites by thousands of years. The genetic origin of the haplogroup to which CMH belongs may go back far earlier than to Israelites, perhaps by ten thousand years or more.[10] In other words, the presence of particular genetic markers among certain Jews does not prove that all Jews are members of a single family, nor does the presence of the same markers among non-Jews prove that they were originally descended from Israelites.[11] As Wesley Sutton has noted, the CMH mostly likely reflects a Middle Eastern ancestor for both the Jewish and non-Jewish people who have it, not that both groups share specifically Jewish ancestors.[12] The same realization led some of the early researchers to acknowledge that the original CMH could not be used by itself as an identifier of either *kohanim* or Jews. Instead, they proposed a modified CMH that is more exclusive to Jewish populations.[13]

The Mixed Genetic Makeup of the Jews

But the genetic records of some Ashkenazi Jews also show a substantial admixture of European populations.[14] Levy-Coffman notes that "Jews do not constitute a single group distinct from all others. Rather, modern Jews exhibit a diversity of genetic profiles, some reflective of their Semitic/Mediterranean ancestry, but others suggesting an origin in European and Central Asian groups. This blending of European, Semitic, Central Asian, and Mediterranean genetic heritages over the centuries has led to today's Jewish populations."[15] Some genetic studies were preoccupied with establishing a Middle Eastern strand of Jewish genetic history, although some so-called Middle Eastern haplogroups found in both Ashkenazi and Sephardi Jews and Middle Eastern groups are also found in Greek, Italian, Albanian, Georgian, and other populations.[16] The excitement at a possible ancient Israelite connection in Jewish DNA results overshadowed and ignored the fuller genetic picture of Jews.[17] The fact that Jews in most geographical regions share some traits with neighboring populations suggests that the wall of endogamy was permeable as a result of intermarriage and conversions and included inflows of other genes with both Middle Eastern and European sources.

Indeed, one should be careful when referring to "the Jewish people" as though the term refers to a biologically or genetically distinct population that can be scientifically differentiated from other Middle Eastern groups or other people among whom Jews have lived. Over the centuries, genetic outsiders have joined with "the Jewish people," and likewise, many people with Jewish backgrounds may have become members of other religious and cultural groups.

Whatever the ultimate connections of the CMH to Middle Eastern ancestors, however, the amount of genetic material from this strictly patriarchal genetic lineage comprised exclusively of genes passed from fathers to sons becomes a vanishingly small part of the overall genetic picture of Jews, representing only a tiny fraction of the total ancestral population of the Jewish people while ignoring the vast majority of other ancestral lines. Going back just five generations, there are thirty-two possible genetic lines traceable to each of a single person's thirty-two great-great-great-grandparents. Yet only two of the genetic lines, one maternal and one paternal, are the sole focus of virtually all Jewish genetics. Whatever claims might be made about one hypothetical ancestor from thousands of years ago as the defining factor in one's identity, it also means that using one single genetic line out of thousands as the foundation for a present-day identity is more a reflection of cultural attitudes about kinship than it is a biological fact.

Ultimately, genetic relatedness represents only a small part of what constitutes the ties that create a family, a tribe, or a people. The question of who belongs or is recognized as a member of a family remains a social and cultural fact as much as a biological one. Jonathan Marks points out that "Genetic ties, in fact, form a relatively small part of what composes a family: all those aunts and uncles—some blood relatives, some related by marriage; all those step-, foster, and in-law relations; all those ex-spouses and ex-families; all those unacknowledged offspring."[18]

The questions of where families or tribes stop and others begin, or how many different families or tribes someone can belong to, are not simply issues of genetics or of facts out there waiting to be discovered. Distinctions people make, the meanings they attribute, who they recognize as related, or not, are cultural facts, "units of cultural meaning, not units of biology."[19] What the genetic record tells us is that Jews have a complex relationship of mixing with a wide variety of peoples.[20] This means that DNA testing results often serve as a genetic Rorschach picture onto which individuals can project and embrace different versions of themselves and the groups to which they belong.

The idea that Jewishness is solely determined by a continuous paternal lineage also overlooks the fact that definitions of Jewishness that began with an exclusive focus on paternal lines in the Bible gave way to later halakhic preoccupation with maternal lines as the determining factor in the Jewish status of a child. However, recent studies of mitochondrial DNA, through which the maternal line can be traced from mothers to daughters, do not supply evidence of roots in ancient

Israel/Palestine. Rather they indicate a significant amount of ancestry of Ashkenazi Jews in prehistoric Europe, suggesting early mixtures of Jews who originated in the Middle East with other non-Jewish neighbors.[21] Mitochondrial DNA from Jewish women more closely resembles that of neighboring non-Jewish women than Jewish women in other places.

All this introduces new levels of ambiguity in using genetics to determine who is authentically Jewish. If a Jewish man whose DNA had the CMH genetic marker married a non-Jewish woman, their son would not be Jewish according to Jewish law, even though he would have the CMH from his father, regardless of whether he personally identified himself as Jewish. So cultural and religious definitions of Jewishness do not line up precisely with genetic traces.

More importantly, the preoccupation with the paternal CMH as the yellow brick road leading back to ancient Israel ignores the fact that the vast majority of Jews who are not *kohanim* have no trace of the CMH, and their genetic records show a history of genetic mixing with other groups. Tudor Parfitt warns of the danger that genetic studies "will help buttress and even create essentialist constructions of ethnic minorities and a multitude of 'others' rather than contributing to a sane realization that important genetic or biological differences between peoples and groups simply do not exist."[22]

One of the greatest dangers of Jewish genetics is that it creates an illusion of scientific precision that then gets associated with details of religious history. Genetic analysis cannot confirm, for example, that a person is or is not an authentic "priest," that the common ancestor of those having this marker is the biblical first priest, Aaron, or that any other person having this marker, or a group with a significant percentage of people having this marker, are descendants of Jews or accurately described as "genetically Jewish."[23] Many people made an enormous leap by insisting that genetic connections to the Middle East in some Jews also represent empirical confirmation of Jewish historical narratives in the Bible, despite the fact that genetic evidence has little bearing on whether or not specific details about biblical narratives are historically accurate.

The frequency rate for the CMH among modern Jews who identify as *kohanim* is hard to pinpoint since it varies considerably in different studies. While the numbers of male subjects tested have been relatively small, it does appear that around half of the *kohanim* tested do have this set of markers. Since about 5 percent of Jewish men identify as *kohanim*, this means the number of Jewish *men* affected is about 2 to 3 percent or 1 to 2 percent of the total Jewish population. If there is a "genetic legacy" within the Jewish people, it is probably one of many legacies, including the one that produced blue eyes and light skin among some other Jews. There is nothing unusual about this, and it does not mean that only people with the CMH marker are the "real Jews," or that the Jewishness of Jews who do not have these markers is somehow in question.[24]

History and the Israelite Priesthood

The idea of being a direct descendant of the family of Moses and Aaron has an obvious romantic appeal and seems to validate some important details of the origin story of the Jewish people and religion. But the actual historical likelihood that such a clearcut lineage back to biblical ancestors exists rests less on scientific analysis of genetic markers and more on a set of tenuous hypotheses and speculations. There is no "scientific" way to prove that Moses and Aaron really existed, much less that Aaron is the progenitor of a line of Jewish priests related to present-day *kohanim*. There are no genetic samples of Moses, Aaron, or any other Israelite that lived three thousand years ago. Instead, conclusions are drawn by connecting some genetic dots, mixing them with speculation about dating genetic founders, and integrating them with an uncritical acceptance of biblical history.

Ironically, recent efforts to use up-to-date genetic research to establish connections to individuals and groups who may have lived thousands of years ago rely more on traditional religious narratives than on the perspectives and analyses of academic historians of those periods of history. For example, the CMH hypothesis presumes the existence of an unbroken line of hereditary priests going back to the time of Moses and Aaron. However, modern biblical and historical scholarship suggests a much more complex and messy process by which the Israelite priesthood emerged and priests were selected in different periods. There were times when priests had no sons to inherit their positions, there were periods of corrupt priests who were removed and replaced by others, and there were certain kings, such as Herod, who appointed priests of their own choosing. Each of these situations would entail breaks in the genetic lineage of the original Israelite priests. The story of the creation of the priesthood under the authority of Aaron provided a powerful retrospective narrative of the establishment of an important religious institution in ancient Israel. At the same time, most scholars date the parts of the Torah that describe the creation of the priesthood under Aaron and the principles of patrilineal succession anywhere from the seventh to fifth centuries BCE; that is centuries after the estimated time of both Moses and Aaron, as well as long after the early monarchies and the time of the Temple in Jerusalem.

Based on this reconstruction of the history of the Israelite priesthood, one might expect a very different genetic background among present-day *kohanim*. In fact, more than half of the tested *kohamin* do not have the extended CMH and represent twenty-one different haplogroups.[25] This suggests that the biblical account of a hereditary priesthood was presented as a tradition to ensure legitimacy to the priesthood, even if, or perhaps because, a pure patrilineal lineage did not actually exist. The tradition of linking all priests to Aaron, the symbolic, if not literal, "father" of all Jewish priests, emerged at a time of religious reform of priestly corruption as a way to restore the prestige of the priesthood. To simply take the biblical account at face value would be to ignore not only the historical development of that institution in Israelite religion but also the function served by origin myths when they are used to sanctify religious institutions by linking them back to the period and practices of the religious founders. There is no reason to believe that only *kohanim* with CMH are part of genuine lineages to ancient priests while those who lack it are altar outsiders. If the priesthood was a heterogeneous group from the start, then the presence or absence of a single marker cannot prove who is the real descendent of an Israelite priest and who is not, or more importantly, why it matters.[26]

Genetic Essentialism and the Role of Choice

The claims of Jewish genetics contain clear echoes of earlier romanticist notions of race, ethnicity, and nationality. All of these concepts routinely reject the diversity among different groups of Jews as only superficial differences that mask an underlying commonality within. Rather than seeing Jews as a racially and ethnically mixed group, genetic essentialism posits an invisible thread tying all Jews together as a group with links going back to the founding ancestors from ancient times. It creates an almost metaphysical idea of a people as something that exists once and for all and remains dimly decipherable beneath any later mixing and changing. The fact that cultural and biological mixing inevitably brought not only new customs but also new genes into the Jewish group, not to mention those Jews who left the group and brought their genes wherever they went, makes the total genetic picture of the Jews far more complex than presented by single markers like the CMH.[27]

What is often lost in the discussion of genetic approaches to Jewishness is the fact that the interpretation of genetic evidence and its incorporation into one's identity represents a particular individual *choice*. A person is not a Jew because an AncestryDNA or 23andMe genetic test says so. But these tests do force people to make decisions about the meaning or significance they want to attribute to their DNA reports and the genetic ancestry they represent. When human agency is reintroduced to the meaning of Jewish genetics, the discovery of "Jewish" genetic markers in a DNA test only offers a kind of "stock option" for Jewishness. In a sense, it offers preauthorization to exercise the option by embracing Jewish cultural practice, identification, and association to establish or reaffirm Jewish identity. People can also ignore or reject the option and continue with business as usual with regard to their identity.

The dramatic impact that genetic data can have on individuals' identities is therefore not preordained or inevitable. Unlike essentialist claims about race or blood being determinant of group membership, genetic data lacks any particular deterministic power of its own. Rather, genetic data provides the raw material out of which a person's sense of self can be modified, changed, or reinforced in line with the genetic fingerprint uncovered within the cells of their body. As Nadia Abu El-Haj explains in her excellent study of Jewish genetics, something remarkable happens in the process of incorporating genetic data into a new sense of one's Jewish authenticity. There is an opportunity to choose to define oneself in a new way that is also in some sense simply stating who one already was.[28]

The power of this genetic evidence, argues Abu El-Haj, lies in the fact that it "generates, grounds and authenticates . . . narratives of origins, kinship, and history."[29] These are the narratives that establish the collective authenticity of the Jews as a people or ethnic group. The origin story of the Jewish people describes the shared history of a group held together by kinship bonds through which they were able to maintain their identity during centuries of life in diaspora. Genetic data that establish connections leading back to common ancestors for present-day Jews throughout the world are only possible because earlier generations were able to preserve the boundaries of the group. This required a commitment to endogamy and the transfer of cultural and religious traditions from one generation to the next. What our DNA really shows, says Abu El-Haj, are the tracks left by the choices these ancestors made repeatedly to create new Jewish families and raise new generations of Jewish children to carry forward the collective identity of the people. The choices of these earlier generations that bound together the identities of the Jews as a single people had to be renewed in each generation. Otherwise, the lines of kinship and shared culture, as well as the genetic clues they left behind, would have unraveled.[30]

Just as genetic data cannot by itself certify anyone as authentically Jewish, neither does Jewish ancestry alone guarantee that someone will either identify or be recognized by others as a Jew. An authentically Jewish sense of self is always to some degree unstable and unsettled. It only emerges through a process Abu El-Haj describes as "a dialectic between the genetic facts and the practices of self-fashioning" that incorporate ancestry into an active dynamic sense of self.[31] Only in this way is it possible to transform an essentialist kind of genetic and cultural authenticity rooted only in the past into an existentialist one based on continually reaffirming the meaning of being a part of this group. As mentioned earlier, Sartre insisted that "Jewish authenticity consists in choosing oneself as a Jew—that is, in realizing one's Jewish condition," whether in response to the antisemitic judgments on which Sartre focused or the results of a DNA test. Existentialist authenticity emerges at the nexus between the meaning someone constructs out of the origin stories and kinship lines they choose to privilege. It is only in these narratives that genetic data about some aspect of one's genealogy is transformed into a record of the ancestral choices that one accepts as defining who one is today.

For a person who learns about their possible genetic lineage to particular Jewish ancestors, the choice is whether to maintain, or reclaim, the chain of generations leading up to the present moment by practicing endogamy, literally and culturally, or letting it lapse. The discovery of possible Jewish descent reinforces a sense of authenticity that is defined in terms of fidelity to the culture of one's ancestors and its survival. In other words, genetics establishes authenticity only in relation to the process of retrospective self-recognition and retrospective recognition by others that becomes part of an individual or group origin narrative. Here, Abu El-Haj suggests that biological discourse is combined with a liberal discourse of human agency: "We must *choose* to be true to those origins (and history) if we are to be—and we are to remain generations hence—who we have always already been."[32]

Whether or not we qualify the meaning of genetic evidence for establishing Jewish authenticity along the lines that Abu El-Haj suggests, there are many people who remain attracted to the idea that the tiny biological thread that connects a person to certain ancestors who were the founders of their tribe, people, or folk is what makes a person authentically Jewish. However, this elevation of endogamous genetic ancestors as the gold standard of Jewish authenticity places undue emphasis on the importance of genetic and cultural homogeneity. What gets lost or erased are the inevitable cultural mutations that occur along with genetic mutations over time as a result of migration and mixing with other populations. There is a whole different set of metaphors that can be used to describe this other dimension of identity and the kind of narratives through which it would be expressed. It is telling that the most common of these is probably the idea of *hybridity*, a biologically rooted idea that embraces the reality of mixture, intermingling, and impurity, as a more realistic foundation for understanding the nature of cultural identity and the complicated qualities that make up a people. Cultural theorists like Paul Gilroy, Stuart Hall, Kwame Appiah, and others have emphasized the importance of other origin stories in which the fluidity and messiness of cultural identity is highlighted in opposition to popular essentialist narratives.

PART IV
STRUGGLES OVER AUTHENTICATION AND RECOGNITION

11 Lost Jewish Tribes in Ethiopia

Early Myths of Lost Tribes in Africa

In the ninth century, a traveling merchant by the name of Eldad, whose background remains shrouded in mystery, arrived at a Jewish community in northern Africa with whom he shared stories about his travels throughout the world, but especially south of Egypt, presumably in parts of Ethiopia. Medieval Jewish travelogues, including Eldad's, have been described as "a marvelous blend of observation, empirical authenticity, and aggadic imagination."[1] Whatever encounters travelers may have had with unfamiliar people, they were usually filtered through the lens of popular Jewish legends and folklore.

Eldad not only claimed himself to be a member of the lost Israelite tribe of Dan, but he also recounted the heroic exploits of the various lost tribes he said he had encountered in remote places at the edges of the known world, stretching from China to Africa. According to Eldad, several of the tribes, including his own tribe of Dan, were living in the region of Ethiopia, on the other side of the Sambatyon River, a legendary river with magical qualities described in Jewish folk traditions. The tribes were protected by both water and fire and remained basically invisible and inaccessible to outsiders.[2] With careful analysis of these reports, it becomes clear that Eldad was a bit of a "trickster." He was able to cleverly weave together familiar legends and stories into a compelling first-person account of what he had learned about the alleged lost tribes, including an invented dialect of Hebrew with strange and unfamiliar words that he claimed to have learned from them.[3]

The appeal of Eldad was that he offered an opportunity to hear stories about Jews who had remained strong and independent during the centuries that other Jews had been forced to adapt to life in exile characterized by powerlessness and subjugation to other rulers and cultures. Eldad provided a glimpse into an alternate reality, one in which Jews were "uncorrupted by years of encounters with foreign peoples, untainted by the yoke of non-Jewish rules."[4] His accounts gave vicarious expression to a kind of lost authenticity for Jewish audiences, who could relive their earlier moments of glory as Israelites through his stories.

Despite the fantastical quality of much of Eldad's accounts and the apparent influence of legendary material about descendants of lost tribes of Israel, most people, even many today, stifled their skepticism about his inconsistencies and implausibilities. On the contrary, Eldad became the nucleus around whom others proposed the possibility of isolated pockets of descendants of lost tribes in Ethiopia. Eldad's account continued to be cited as the earliest piece of evidence of the continuous presence of Jews in Africa since biblical times. In subsequent centuries, rabbinical authorities routinely referred to Eldad as eyewitness proof of the idea that there were Jews in Ethiopia from the tribe of Dan.

In the sixteenth century, the chief rabbi of Egypt, David ben Solomon ibn Avi Zimra, also known as Radbaz (1479–1573), declared on the basis of Eldad's much earlier account that the Black Jews reported to be in Ethiopia were without question not only of "the seed of Israel" but also direct descendants of the lost tribe of Dan. He acknowledged that, not surprisingly, the Ethiopian Jews' understanding of Torah was undeveloped. After all, they had supposedly survived in complete isolation from the great sages and rabbis, which left them unfamiliar with the developments in Judaism that had occurred in the rest of the Jewish world. At the same time, Radbaz's recognition of the Jewish authenticity of Ethiopian Jews came with an important clarification that has set the tone for many subsequent cases of groups who claim to be related to lost tribes of Israel. Radbaz accepted the *genealogical* connection of Ethiopian Jews to the lost tribe of Dan at the same time that he insisted that their connection to *Jewish religion* had mostly been lost and needed significant remediation.

Ethiopian Jews, reasoned Radbaz, are "comparable to a Jewish infant taken captive by non-Jews. . . . And even if you say that the matter is in doubt, it is a commandment to redeem them."[5] Aside from the obvious paternalism, if not subtle racism, in comparing the Ethiopian Jews to infants, Radbaz implied that their religious ideas were tantamount to those of non-Jews, among whom they had lived for centuries. While they might be members of one of the original tribes of Israel, they were ignorant about traditional Judaism and would need to learn how to be Jewish all over again.

Lost Jews in the Colonialist Imagination

Despite the occasional references during the Middle Ages to possible groups of descendants of the lost tribes, it was not until European colonizers and Christian missionaries began to reach remote areas of the African continent in the seventeenth century that many more groups of Africans were identified as possible relatives of Israelite tribes. As Tudor Parfitt has documented, missionaries interpreted the religious and cultural practices of the African tribal groups they encountered through a biblical lens, so it was not surprising when they claimed to find remnants of biblical rituals in most everything they observed.[6] As Europeans spread across Africa, indigenous cultures repeatedly were interpreted through familiar biblical categories, a process that produced the "invention and construction of Jewish and Israelite identities throughout the African continent."[7] Parfitt has done a magnificent job in cataloging many of the African tribes throughout the continent who have been claimed or claimed themselves to be descendants of ancient Hebrews or lost Israelite tribes. These include the Yoruba, Igbo, and Fula in Nigeria; the Ashanti in Ghana; the Baluba in the Congo; the Banyankole in Uganda; the Tutsi in Rwanda; the Masai in Kenya; the Khoisan, Xhosa, and Zulu in southern Africa; and the Shona in Zimbabwe.

When racial models in the nineteenth century designated Jews as a distinct race, European travelers to Africa regularly claimed to discover groups with "Semitic" racial features, such as "Jewish" noses or lips.[8] The biblical lens and the myth of lost

Israelite tribes provided missionaries and their Christian supporters with handy tools by which they could transform the puzzling strangeness of Africans into the more familiar otherness of the Jews.[9]

The translation of indigenous cultures into biblical categories surely did not represent a discovery of their *authentic* identity, who they *really were* in their own eyes, but rather an explicit *denial* of their own linguistic, cultural, and religious identities.[10] European visitors assumed that indigenous crafts and other cultural products must have been influenced by earlier Middle Eastern prototypes. When they observed tribal customs such as circumcision, rules of purity, and animal sacrifices or heard tribal stories about the origins and heroic adventures of the ancestors, it was easy for them to imagine that all this had been inherited from ancient Hebrew forebears. Indigenous languages were scanned for familiar-sounding words. Any similarities between local languages and Hebrew words supplied a pretext for various folk etymologies linking African languages to Hebrew, or at least to remnants of it.

In Ethiopia, the legends about a connection to ancient Israelites have a much longer history than elsewhere in Africa. Unlike other African countries where people only learned about the saga of the Israelites when missionaries arrived during the European colonial period, Ethiopia has long had a connection to biblical stories, and there is early evidence of Judaic influence. Its national epic identifies Menelik, the founding king of Ethiopia, as the son of King Solomon and the Queen of Sheba. According to this story, Menelik brought the Ark of the Covenant back to Ethiopia with him, representing the continuation of the Israelites' story. For at least the last four centuries or so, certain groups of Ethiopians known as the Beta Israel ("House of Israel") have distinguished themselves from other Ethiopians by claiming themselves to be not only the descendants of ancient Israelites but also the sole preservers of the Israelite religious system.

In the discussion of the Beta Israel, there are two radically different ways of analyzing their authenticity as Jews. The first and more traditional approach is to treat authenticity as an empirical quality resting upon certain historical evidence from the past. The Beta Israel's claim to being authentic Jews, for example, can be read as an affirmation that they are in fact biological descendants of some identifiable group of ancient Jews. If this claim is accepted as true, not only are the Beta Israel defined as authentic Jews, but their differences in physical appearance as well as in religious practice from mainstream Jews do not detract from a deeper biological connection with the Jewish people, with whom they finally have been reunited after thousands of years of separation and isolation. In this case, people can embrace the Beta Israel's story as an inspiring affirmation of unwavering Jewish faith and unity, told through the experience of "a heroic, long-suffering, and loyal branch of the Jewish people whose exile is in the process of ending with its redemption."[11]

This kind of historical or objective authenticity is a fixed and stable quality of a person or group, established in the past and enduring unchanged over time. The members of a group either are authentic Jews or they are not, and a determination will be made based on the available evidence for this connection to the past. Authenticity in this sense is not something the Beta Israel could lose if they already possessed it, nor could they acquire it if it was not already there. This same conception of authenticity has been assumed not only by those who support the Jewish authenticity of groups like the Beta Israel but also by those who want to challenge their Jewish authenticity. Accordingly, if critics judge that the historical evidence for a connection to Jewish or Israelite ancestors is flawed, problematic, or in doubt, then any claims of authenticity automatically become invalid.

Supporters of the Jewishness of the Beta Israel generally have staked their authenticity claims on acceptance of the traditional Beta Israel origin story and the connection to a lost tribe of Israelites. As such, the Beta Israel are seen as a group that had preserved a form of ancient Judaism for thousands of years until they were rediscovered by the world Jewish community and reunited with their fellow Jews in Israel in the late twentieth century. From this point of view, the members of the Beta Israel deserve to be recognized as Jews today because they have always been Jews.

The debate over the Jewish authenticity of the Beta Israel is a relatively recent phenomenon that arose only when European Christians and Jews began to have increased contact with the Beta Israel in the nineteenth century. Christian missionaries who met the Beta Israel were concerned about what they considered the nonbiblical elements of Beta Israel religion, such as animal sacrifice and practices of ritual purity. Hoping to bring the Beta Israel closer to Christianity, the missionaries established schools where they taught the Beta Israel to read and write, and they distributed large numbers of printed Bibles in Amharic.[12] One of the missionaries, Henry Aaron Stern, was a converted Jew. When he visited the Beta Israel in 1860, Stern was struck by the fact that they "looked Jewish," with what he perceived as lighter skin than other Ethiopians and features that reminded him of European Jews.[13]

Reports about these missionary activities among the Beta Israel were sent back to the London Society for Promoting Christianity and soon brought the situation of the Beta Israel to the attention of European Jews, who were upset by the prospect of Beta Israel communities succumbing to Christianity.[14] Once again, the question of whether or not the Beta Israel were real Jews quickly resurfaced, because if they really were Jews, then the next question was what could be done to rescue them from conversion to Christianity.

Jewish Authentication of the Beta Israel

In 1864, a Hungarian Orthodox rabbi named Esriel Hildesheimer issued an appeal on behalf of the Beta Israel that circulated in the Jewish press in Europe. Hildesheimer, like others before him, affirmed that the Beta Israel were authentic members of the Children of Israel who had been exiled from Israel with only twenty-four books of the Bible. He acknowledged "a thicket of doubts" about this group, including some of his own: "Are the Jews of Abyssinia truly the Children of Abraham, Isaac, and Jacob? . . . At first, we genuinely wavered between two poles on the question of the genuine origin of the Jews of Abyssinia—are they Children of the Household of Israel or not?" Hildesheimer resolved the question by simply referring readers back to the ruling of Radbaz that "we are brothers, children of one father" as well as to contemporaneous essays that concurred that the Beta Israel "have truly sprung forth from the loins of Israel."[15] Hildesheimer concluded by echoing Radbaz's exhortation to rescue the Beta Israel, since they are "our brothers and our flesh." He recommended sending books and religious objects to the Beta Israel to strengthen the connection between the Beta Israel and world Jewry.[16]

Several years later, Joseph Halevy, a scholar of Judaica as well as Ethiopian languages, received funding to travel to Ethiopia to meet with the Beta Israel. He spent several months with them in 1867. When Halevy asked the Beta Israel if they knew of other Israelites in the world like them, they indicated that they thought they were the only Israelites left. Halevy explained to them that they were part of a larger world Jewish community, whose religious practices had advanced beyond the Beta Israel's. He emphasized the need for them to "catch up" with the "white Jews."[17] Halevy's reports reaffirmed the authenticity of their Jewishness. At the same time, he recommended steps to help the Beta Israel resist missionaries and connect themselves to world Jewry.[18]

The person most associated with bringing the issue of the Beta Israel to the attention of Jews in Israel, Europe, and the United States was Jacques Faitlovitch, a student of Halevy's who devoted his life to the struggle to gain recognition for the Beta Israel not only as "real Jews" but also as descendants of a lost Israelite tribe. After a visit to the Beta Israel in 1904, Faitlovitch lobbied rabbinic leaders to support the Beta Israel and convinced forty-four prominent rabbis to send a letter of support to the Beta Israel embracing them as "our brethren, sons of Abraham, Isaac, and Jacob, our flesh and blood."[19] Faitlovitch organized committees in Europe, the United States, and Israel to help the Beta Israel.

Of course, as generous and committed as Faitlovitch was to the cause of the Beta Israel, he also envisioned that the ultimate goal for the Beta Israel was to be integrated back into the religious practices and laws of rabbinic Judaism. In some ways, Faitlovitch's project was a version of the same colonialist agenda that Christian missionaries had been advancing, and the introduction of normative Judaism to the Beta Israel would have been almost as alien to them as the ideas of Christian missionaries.[20] Despite his good intentions to rescue the Beta Israel from the danger of Christian missionizing, his own missionary activity aimed not only at changing the Beta Israel's religious practices but also at changing their understanding of themselves as Jews.

Faitlovitch urged the Beta Israel to abandon long-standing practices he considered alien to modern Judaism. He, likewise, hoped to rescue the Beta Israel from their "primitiveness" by introducing them to a superior western culture and European rabbinic Judaism. Like other cases of newly discovered Jews in Africa, recognition of their Jewishness could only proceed by *not* recognizing, in fact, by erasing as much as possible, their Black Africanness. In order to make the Beta Israel more acceptable as Jews, Faitlovitch minimized any connection between them and the actual Africans among whom they lived. He wrote,

> When I was in Africa among the Falasha, surrounded by tribes of semi-savages, I felt an inexpressible joy in recording their energy, their intelligence, the lofty

moral qualities which distinguish them. We can be proud to count among our own these noble children of Ethiopia, who, with a no less legitimate pride, boast of tracing [themselves] back to our origins, worshipping our God, practicing our cult. The eagerness with which they seek to regenerate themselves, to leave this African Barbarism which envelops them and suffocates them, proves that the instinctive character of [their] race persists in them. . . . How different is that from the other Abyssinians, so contemptuous toward the education, progress and civilization of the Europeans to which they naively believe themselves to be superior.[21]

Faitlovitch wanted to claim the Beta Israel as fellow Jews, but he could only do so by imagining them as intellectually and morally superior to other Ethiopians, whose lives remained, in his view, at a level of barbarism and degeneration. For Faitlovitch, this process was not about changing the Beta Israel; rather, it was about restoring them to their original Israelite selves. To recognize the Beta Israel as Jews, he needed to heighten their difference from other Ethiopians and Africans, to show that the Africanness apparent in their physical appearance was just a superficial outer layer that could be peeled away. If the Beta Israel could be traced to non-Ethiopian outsiders, say, an Israelite tribe that had become lost and had wandered into Ethiopia, then they could more easily be accepted by the rest of the Jewish people.[22] Indeed, Faitlovitch even suggested that the Beta Israel had originally had white skin but that their skin had darkened after years in the Ethiopian sun.[23]

Due to the efforts of Faitlovitch and the organizing he did on their behalf, the Beta Israel became westernized enough so that their religious practices were more recognizable to other Jews, and other Jews became more recognizable to them. Both the Beta Israel and the outside Jewish world could look at each other as members of the same group. From repeated contact with modern Jews, the Beta Israel learned many elements of traditional Judaism, including observance of the Sabbath and dietary laws and beliefs about one God, the chosen people, and the Messiah. Gradually, the Beta Israel's dietary rules shifted to become in line with mainstream Judaism's system of kashrut, and they began to adopt iconic ritual objects from European Judaism, such as tefillin, tallitot, kippot, and mezuzot.

In addition to resocializing the Beta Israel into modern forms of rabbinic Judaism, Faitlovitch encouraged the Beta Israel to understand themselves as a people in exile. Supported by other Jews who were determined to redeem their Jewish brethren who had been ensnared by Christian missionaries, the Beta Israel became more assertive about the idea that they were descendants of a lost tribe who did not truly belong in Ethiopia. They needed to return to their original homeland in Israel. Israel and Jerusalem had changed from being merely mythical places in their ancient past to real places in the world today where they could live among other Jews.

Beta Israel in Israel

After the creation of the state of Israel in 1948, the status of Beta Israel as Jews took on a new significance, since recognition of their Jewish authenticity was a prerequisite for their possible resettlement in Israel. The Zionist project of gathering together the dispersed Jews of the world provided motivation for some Zionist Jews to seek out and identify long-lost descendants of ancient Israelites and other pockets of isolated Jews around the world. Israelis and other Jews visited some of the groups and brought them Jewish books and ritual objects, set up schools to teach Hebrew, and helped them organize more traditional western Sabbath services.[24] All this served to consolidate their Jewish identity.[25] By the 1960s, the clinics and schools opened among the Beta Israel by Jewish organizations from Israel and the stream of visitors from the outside Jewish world had left their mark on the Beta Israel. Hebrew prayer books and mainstream Jewish holiday observance became commonplace. Some of the Beta Israel now knew Hebrew, and they were yearning to move to Israel. As the reconstruction and reinvention of their Jewishness proceeded, recognition of the Jewish authenticity of the Beta Israel also grew, and as recognition grew, efforts to bring the Beta Israel to Israel to complete their transformation into "real Jews" also intensified.

During the 1960s, many rabbis still refused to recognize the Beta Israel as authentic Jews, primarily based on skepticism about their origin stories and concern about their religious deviance from normative Judaism. In 1973, Israel's Ministry of Absorption issued a report that argued the Beta Israel were "completely foreign to the spirit of Israel" and could not be considered part of the Jewish people in either culture or ethnicity. The ministry sided with historical and ethnographic research that considered the ethnic and cultural background of the Beta Israel as firmly rooted in the history of the Ethiopian people.[26]

Only one month later, however, Israel's Sephardi chief rabbi, Ovadia Yosef, declared that the Beta Israel were indeed Jews and should be brought to Israel and introduced to normative rabbinic Judaism. He was joined in this ruling several years later by the Ashkenazi chief rabbi, Shlomo Goren, who similarly proclaimed to the Beta Israel, "You are our brothers, you are our blood and our flesh. You are true Jews." The chief rabbis were aware that the conclusions of modern academic research raised doubts about the claims of the Jewish origins of the Beta Israel, particularly their alleged connection to the lost tribe of Dan, whom Eldad had claimed to find in Ethiopia. Ovadia Yosef insisted that when modern secular research contradicts the opinions of Jewish sages and rabbinic authorities as well as a group's own self-perception, Jewish religious decisions must respect the tradition. In this case, Eldad's account had been affirmed by rabbinic authorities like the Radbaz and others and embraced by the Beta Israel. Accordingly, the Beta Israel's claim to be Jewish descendants of the tribe of Dan must be accepted.[27]

Although the position of Ovadia Yosef could be taken to mean that when secular historical research conflicts with rabbinic tradition, that research may be rejected as mistaken, it is probably more accurate to say that in matters such as the authenticity of a group as Jews, there are other factors besides such research to consider. It is not so much a question of whether such research is factually correct or not but rather by what criteria will issues of authenticity be resolved. For Ovadia Yosef, Jewish authenticity was a question of Jewish law, or halakha, an area in which rabbinic authority trumps secular history or ethnography. When rabbis like Yosef and Goren make a decision based on their appraisal of earlier rabbinic literature, traveler's accounts, or the Beta Israel's own traditions about their origins, their ruling validates "community traditions" and constitutes "halakhic truth," which may or may not correspond to "historical truth" about the Beta Israel.[28] Indeed, Michael Corinaldi suggests that the Jewish authenticity of Beta Israel requires a "value judgment" about traditional sources, not a determination of their historical reliability.[29] He admits that beliefs about the ten lost tribes are "of a legendary nature" in rabbinic literature, but he insists that such beliefs are nonetheless reflected in the "subjective reality" of groups who identify with the Jewish people and religion.[30]

Obviously, the racial otherness of the Beta Israel could not be ignored, but the recognition of their bodily "flesh and blood" connection to an ancient tribe of Israel, whether historically accurate or not, provided a conceptual bridge between white Jews from Europe and Black Jews from Africa.[31] Although the declarations of the chief rabbis of Israel regarding the authenticity of the Beta Israel as Jews, descended from the tribe of Dan, resolved the issue in terms of the necessary legal status for the Beta Israel to be relocated from Ethiopia to Israel, it has not prevented continuing questions to be raised about Beta Israel authenticity among other Orthodox authorities, who surprisingly turned to secular historians to support the position that the Beta Israel were exposed to the Hebrew Bible by way of the Ethiopian Church, which accounted for the presence of practices alien to Judaism, such as having monks, and the absence of any evidence of post-biblical rabbinical Judaism.

Approaches to the Beta Israel Origin Story

So, does recent anthropological and historical research about the origins of the Beta Israel matter or not in determining their Jewish authenticity? For the chief rabbis, apparently not, at least not enough to invalidate their determination that the Beta Israel are authentic Jews. Whether or not origin stories are historically accurate or literally true is not always the most important factor, nor can authenticity be reduced to simple criteria that can be verified and settled once and for all. It is more useful to look at origin stories as part of an ongoing process of construction, enactment, performance, and recognition of identities that occurs in the present.

In the years since the Beta Israel were officially declared to be Jews by Israel's chief rabbis, academic scholarship has continued to raise questions about the historical evidence for seeing the Beta Israel as descendants of Israelite tribes and their religious system as an actual relic of pre-rabbinic forms of Judaism. Steven Kaplan, one of the most important figures in this reassessment of the roots of the Beta Israel, rejects the idea that Beta Israel religion represents a sample of early Judaism frozen at an earlier stage of religious and cultural development. The insistence on interpreting Beta Israel as a form of primitive Judaism has usually ignored the more direct relationship between the Beta Israel and the surrounding history, culture, and religion of Ethiopia.[32]

Kaplan thinks it is a mistake to impose narratives of persecution, exile, and return derived from mainstream Jewish communities on the Beta Israel, as though their identity as Jews in their own eyes and in the eyes of others has been fixed and constant throughout their history.[33] For Kaplan and many other historians, it is far less likely that the Beta Israel are actually descendants of Jews who migrated to Ethiopia long ago than that their group identity was shaped by the Jewish religious influences of biblical stories and ritual practices of ancient Jews that are held sacred by most Ethiopians.[34] Most likely they were a heretical group led by renegade monks around the fifteenth century who may have called themselves Jews as a way of distinguishing themselves from Christian Orthodoxy.[35] These monks probably were responsible for major elements of Beta Israel religion such as the focus on monasticism, laws of purity, and particular festivals, liturgy, and sacred texts, out of which the unique Beta Israel culture and religion began to emerge. At the same time, however, much of their culture, dress, diet, and religion remained similar to that of Ethiopian Christians.[36]

It was only after their contact with Halevy, Faitlovitch, and other Jews from the mid-nineteenth century that the Beta Israel began to see themselves as part of world Jewry. Far from being embodiments of Israelite religion that had remained unchanged for over two millennia, they *became* "Ethiopian Jews" who resembled other Jewish communities only in the last century or so.[37] Whatever the original form of Beta Israel culture, it became transformed into a form of "Ethiopian Jewish culture" that could be accepted by others as an authentic form of Jewish tradition. Paradoxically, in the name of *preserving* Ethiopian Jewish culture, the Beta Israel adjusted to *new* traditions. Sometimes even the efforts to preserve the original form of Ethiopian Jewish culture produced surprising new results. As tourists visiting the Beta Israel looked for souvenirs of their visits, they created a new market for Jewish-themed trinkets. In response, the Beta Israel provided newly designed and crafted folk art, including clay figurines that had little real connection to Beta Israel religion and culture.[38]

Understandably, Kaplan's doubts about the traditional origin story of the Beta Israel have resulted in anger and resentment from present-day members of the Beta Israel as well as from the rabbinic and political leaders and other supporters in Israel and elsewhere who support the recognition of the Beta Israel as Jews.[39] But Kaplan suggests that this response is based on a misunderstanding of historical research and its place in how communities determine the credentials for belonging. He insists that the process of *historical authentication* is distinct from that done for religious and political purposes: "Government policy and rabbinic Halakha are based upon considerations far removed from those of the historian."[40] Kaplan's point seems to be that such critics are holding on to a mistaken static and essentialist view of Jewish authenticity, which links present-day recognition as Jews with confidence in the literal truth of a particular origin story of the past.

For Kaplan, recognition of the present-day authenticity of the Beta Israel as Jews, in Israel and elsewhere, is not something to be determined by historians, and it does not depend on the determination that the Beta Israel have maintained the same identity, culture, and religious practice since biblical times. To understand the Beta Israel as authentically Jewish is a judgment regarding dramatic changes in the identity, culture, and religious practice that the Beta Israel have internalized and appropriated in response to the intervention of Western Jews and the later resettlement of most of them in Israel.[41] Their origin narrative about descent from ancient Israelites remains intact, but it required decades of enacting and performing the standards of normative Judaism for their recognition as Jews to become established, though pockets of skepticism about their story continued.

Transformation from Beta Israel to Ethiopian Jews

In the 1980s and 1990s, a series of airlifts resulted in the relocation of almost the entire population of the Beta Israel from Ethiopia to Israel. By 1993, nearly forty-five thousand Beta Israel were living in Israel. Today, the number of Beta Israel immigrants to Israel, along with their Israeli-born children and grandchildren, has more than tripled. Immigration to Israel resulted in dramatic changes to Beta Israel culture, as they simultaneously sought to become integrated into Israeli culture and mainstream Judaism and preserve their cultural and religious identities as Beta Israel from Ethiopia. The result has been a gradual hybridization of Beta Israel culture and Orthodox Judaism in Israel.[42]

Once in Israel, many Beta Israel, especially children, were placed in religious institutions that focused on bringing Beta Israel religious life in conformity with rabbinic Judaism in the name of "returning them to Judaism," even though this meant erasing some of the unique qualities of Beta Israel culture.[43] Kaplan and Rosen observe the intrinsic contradiction between the goals of preserving Beta Israel's Jewish culture and correcting it to be in line with mainstream Judaism in Israel. Relocation to Israel was the final step in the transformation of "Beta Israel" cultural identity to that of "Ethiopian Jews." The path that led the Beta Israel from their initial contact with Halevy in the mid-nineteenth century to emigration to Israel in the late twentieth century resulted in a remarkable reconstruction of their religious and cultural identities. This reconstruction was necessary to establish the authenticity of their Jewish identity in the eyes of a wider Jewish community and within Israeli society. It involved adjustment on multiple levels of identity.

While Orthodox authorities sometimes rejected the Jewish authenticity of the Beta Israel, the Beta Israel's long history of thinking of themselves as Jews and their desire to live as Jews in Israel were acceptable, as long as they underwent halakhic conversions that included ritual immersion, symbolic recircumcision for men, and acceptance of rabbinic halakha. Within a few years, the Beta Israel began to resist the necessity of these rituals to establish their Jewishness, and they were eventually discontinued. Beta Israel activists pushed for the recognition of their own religious leaders, who had been stripped of much of their power and status as communal leaders, no longer permitted to officiate at public rituals and ceremonies like marriages and funerals. Some accommodations were slowly made to give the Beta Israel priests, or *qessim*, bigger roles, but it took decades until, in 2018, Beta Israel religious leaders received government recognition to perform religious functions and make religious rulings.[44]

The recognition and acceptance of the Beta Israel as Ethiopian Jews in Israel has proceeded in fits and starts for a variety of religious, cultural, and racial reasons. The Israeli government belatedly understood the importance of helping the Beta Israel to preserve some of their traditional Ethiopian culture, but it has been undercut by competing efforts to encourage acculturation and assimilation to Israeli society. Beta Israel communities have struggled to find a comfortable balance between maintaining their cultural and religious traditions from Ethiopia while simultaneously needing to adapt to the normative practice of Judaism in Israel, with which most had very little familiarity before arrival in Israel.[45] Their adjustment to Israeli society has been complicated by high rates of poverty and unemployment, as well as racial discrimination. Being officially accepted as Jews did not change the fact that the Beta Israel had gone from being a religious minority in a racially homogeneous society in Ethiopia to a society in Israel where they instantly became a stigmatized racial minority. Kaplan and Salamon write, "Although groups of differing complexion, on a continuum from light to dark, live together in Israel, it is only the Jews of Ethiopia who, as a group, are seen as 'black.'"[46] Despite their excitement over arriving in Israel, the Beta Israel were unprepared for the racism they confronted there.

For most of its history, the Beta Israel lived as one Ethiopian group among others, all of whom shared in the Ethiopian foundation story of their connection to the Israelites through the legendary union of King Solomon and the Queen of Sheba. While the Beta Israel believed that they were the sole remaining Israelites following the Jewish religion of the Bible, there was nothing problematic about their racial background. As the Beta Israel began to be defined by the predominantly white Jewish world outside of Ethiopia, they now had to confront the anomaly of their Blackness within the rest of the Jewish world, especially in Israel, where they were seen not so much as Jews like everyone else but as Blacks whose Jewishness was not fully accepted by everyone.

The Beta Israel have responded to these challenges in a number of ways. In her ethnography of the Beta Israel in Israel, Tanya Schwarz found that when questioned about their Jewishness, many of the Beta Israel assert that their own particular cultural traditions are more pure and authentic than those of other Jews in Israel. She writes, "The Beta Israel consider themselves to be the last 'true Jews' who follow strictly the scriptures of the Bible and unashamedly know nothing of subsequent Rabbinical writings."[47] At the same time, the Beta Israel realize that living in Israel requires them to adapt their Judaism to the way it is observed in Israel, which means accepting at some level the message of Western Jews that the Beta Israel's own Jewish traditions are incomplete or inauthentic compared to normative Judaism.[48] The result is a mixture of partial accommodation to Israeli Judaism along with maintaining a strong Ethiopian ethnic/religious identity.[49] This balance is likely to change with younger generations of Beta Israel who have not only been socialized earlier and more easily into Israeli culture but who also embraced a more particularistic Black culture separate from Jewish culture that includes new connections to things like African American music, reggae, and so on.[50] While recognition of their Jewishness at first displaced the racial identity of the Beta Israel, the evolution of their relation to Israeli culture has involved a more hybrid sense of the authenticity of both their Jewishness and their Blackness.

Black and White Authenticity

Regardless of the problematic nature of the Beta Israel's origin story from a historical perspective, the insistence of the Beta Israel on their direct connection to ancient Israelites nonetheless offers a challenge to the role of white European Jews as the guardians of Jewish authenticity. Rabbi Sholomo Ben Levy, of the Israelite Board of Rabbis, an organization of Black Jews in the United States, sees the questioning of the legitimacy, validity, or authenticity of Ethiopian Jews and their religious practice as just an example of the general delegitimization of Black Jews by "the white Jewish world." Levy notes that when Joseph Halevy first visited the Beta Israel in the late nineteenth century, they were incredulous that a white European could claim to be linked to ancient Israelites: "Imagine the irony of that moment: black Jews questioning the Jewishness of white Jews; and the white Jew trying to convince them of his authenticity. The levity of that scene is surpassed by a far more serious point: when different Jewish communities come together, one will usually occupy the superior position; the one of dominance, authority, and control. Not surprisingly, the dominant group is in a position to judge the subordinate."[51]

Although the evidence for the standard narrative of mainstream Jewish history is doubtless of greater historical reliability than the origin narrative of the Beta Israel, Levy's point about the assertion of authority by more powerful Jewish groups to determine the Jewish authenticity of weaker groups is true. Ultimately, the acceptance of the Jewish authenticity of groups like the Beta Israel is not really a question of some kind of objective analysis. What has become increasingly clear in the modern world is that there are a variety of approaches to issues of Jewish authenticity and Jewish identity. As Eric Maroney observes, "We must see the Jewish experience as not a monolithic entity, finding expression in a few well-worn and comfortable paths, but as something as multiform and varied."[52]

Ephraim Isaac, a Harvard-educated scholar of African languages and culture, of Ethiopian Jewish background, argues that it is dangerous to use "historical, halakhic, or genetic" definitions of Jewishness to challenge the authenticity of any particular group of Jews and that both the unity and the diversity of the Jewish people must be embraced.[53] To assume that white Jews may "look Jewish" (either physically or in their attire) in a more authentic way than the Beta Israel is increasingly difficult to defend. Isaac writes, "We take the self-claim of most Jewish groups from the West for granted. We do not scrutinize their identity or the authenticity of their history. Would most Jews indeed tolerate such a far-reaching and unsettling ethnoreligious inquisition into their origins?"[54] Most Jews, he insists, cannot really verify their Jewish lineage for more than a few generations into the past. Accordingly, he says that "they should be the last to defend unrealistic Jewish authenticity or the concept of non-existing racial or ethnic purity or uniformity."[55]

There are indeed dangers in relying on any particular historical, legal, or biological criteria for determining Jewish authenticity, and yet these elements are inevitably invoked by different groups as central to the recognition of authenticity. If origin stories of certain groups rest on historical claims that are shown to be weak, that fact will need to be taken into account. If Jewish religious authorities find halakhic problems in the claims of some groups to be Jewish, that also will matter to certain parts of the Jewish community. And if lineage and descent are presented as major arguments for Jewish authenticity, then biology, genetics, and ideas about race may come into play.

At the same time that Isaac rejects these factors in deciding authenticity, he proposes his own kind of geological metaphor that remains connected to some of the same issues he questioned in other contexts. While he celebrates, on the one hand, the racial diversity of Jews who have gathered together in Israel today, he describes them less as a mosaic than as a color-coded microcosm or "core sample" of Jewish history, with Africans representing the oldest slice. He offers a racial color spectrum that ties Ethiopian Jews to the earliest period of ancient Israelite religion, while the white European Jews who act as authorities among the Jews are the most recent arrivals: "pinkish-white-skinned Ashkenazim of post-industrial Jewish culture, light-brown skinned Sephardim and Middle Eastern Jews of medieval culture, the varied but often medium brown skinned Yemenite Jews of late Second Temple period culture, and the coffee-brown-skinned Beta Israel Ethiopians of the First Temple period culture."[56]

Given this dating of different racial groups of Jews, it is no wonder that Isaac challenges the basis on which American Ashkenazi Jews think that they are what Jews look like, that their religion is "normative Judaism," and that their culture of borscht, bagels, and gefilte fish is real Jewish culture rather than the Ethiopian and Yemenite specialties that are probably closer to the those of the biblical period. Isaac insists that the Beta Israel "are Jews no more and no less than other Jewish groups in different regions of the world."[57]

At the same time, it is fair to say that the story of how the "Beta Israel" in Ethiopia became transformed into the community of Ethiopian Jews living today primarily in Israel is not at all comparable to the historical origins of European or Middle Eastern Jews. Indeed, it offers a complex case of the multiple factors at work in the process by which invented traditions of lost Israelite tribes in Ethiopia became established with the help of Eldad's legend of lost tribes in Ethiopia, European rabbis in earlier centuries, and chief rabbis of Israel more recently. Jewish organizations and activists like Faitlovitch helped resocialize the Beta Israel to more recognizable forms of Jewish identity and practice, while indigenous aspects of their culture were systematically uprooted and removed. Eventually, the Beta Israel became recognizable to themselves and others as Ethiopian Jews. At the same time, their racial otherness as Africans in a Jewish world of European and Middle Eastern Jews has meant that doubts still linger among some Jews about whether they truly are authentically Jewish, and they face the challenge of reconciling the tensions between the two sides of their identities, as both Jews and Ethiopians.

12 Recognizing Black Jews in the United States

At the same time that Jewish organizations and rabbinical leaders provided a sympathetic audience to activists who were lobbying them on behalf of Black Jews in Ethiopia, groups of African Americans were forming Jewish congregations of their own. Such groups of Black Jews in the United States have faced a much harder struggle than Ethiopian Jews in gaining recognition and acceptance by the broader Jewish community. The debate over recognizing newly emerging groups of Black Jews from the early part of the twentieth century until today has focused directly on the question of the basis on which these newly declared Black Jews can be considered authentically Jewish and entitled to recognition as Jews. Are they related to the Ethiopian Jews, who have been recognized as Jews and welcomed as such to Israel? Are their claims of descent from the original Israelites plausible? What do their group origin narratives reveal about the connection between race and Jewishness?[1]

The Origin Story of Black Jews

There are a variety of ways in which African Americans became involved with elements of the Hebrew Bible and Judaism and have come to identify as Jews. Many of them were introduced to the biblical stories of the ancient Israelites as part of the Christian education they received from slave owners and which became a central element within the Black church in the United States. The biblical story of the Israelites' slavery and redemption, as well as their exile and return, has always resonated with African Americans and has become a popular theme within gospel music and Black Christian theology. Many African Americans saw themselves as a new Israel that had been enslaved in a new Egypt.

In the early twentieth century, the affinity between African Americans and the biblical narrative of the ancient Israelites took a dramatic turn as some African American groups began to claim that Black people were more than *metaphorically* linked to the enslaved Israelites in the Bible; they were the *actual descendants* of the lost tribes of Israel. The assumption of many historians and other scholars was that this shift from metaphorical to literal identification was less the result of firm evidence of Israelite roots or other connection to ancient Judaism and more a matter of using the narratives of Jewish bondage and liberation as a template for their own experiences of slavery. This theoretical framework has been described as "symbolic identity formation" or "symbolic identification."[2]

According to this approach, Black Judaism emerged when the Israelites saga of liberation was viewed through the lens of the Black nationalist ideas of Marcus Garvey, which presented a glorified idea of Africa as the source of all civilization.

The resulting premise of the African-Israelite roots of Black people offered a more authentic religious and racial identity than the Christian religion of white oppressors could provide. No longer an inferior, enslaved people, Blacks could now claim kinship with the original chosen people in the Bible, from whom the Christian savior himself had come.[3]

In 1919, Wentworth Arthur Matthew opened a synagogue for Black Jews named "The Commandment Keepers Congregation of the Living God." Matthew had begun as a Pentecostal minister in a church that believed that most biblical prophets, as well as Jesus himself, were Black.[4] A variety of Black Jewish sects were forming in New York at the same time as news of the "Falashas," Black Jews living in Ethiopia, became more widely known through organizations that had been formed to help them. The connection of African Americans to Ethiopia had already been proposed to Harlem residents when some Ethiopian merchants joined with local African Americans to establish the Abyssinian Baptist Church in 1808, using the ancient name for Ethiopia. With the discovery of Black Jews in Ethiopia, it was natural for Matthew's group to claim kinship with them, declaring themselves to be "Ethiopian Hebrews." Much as many early Zionists distanced themselves from identification with the culture and mentality of diaspora Jews, Matthew's group eschewed being identified as "Negroes," a category they saw as a creation of white slave owners.

During the 1920s, at least eight different Black Jewish groups emerged in New York alone, building on this story of having roots in ancient Israel and Africa as well as their personal familiarity with white New York Jews.[5] This was a time when Marcus Garvey had made Harlem the world center of the organization he had formed—the Universal Negro Improvement Association—and the international movement he inspired to bring African Americans pride in their racial and cultural heritage. Over time, groups of Black Jews or "Black Hebrews" went in a variety of directions. Some maintained Christian elements along with Old Testament rituals, some continued to mention Jesus (but only as a prophet), and some purged Christian elements while also adopting more traditional Jewish practices. Most groups also retained or incorporated other Black cultural traditions.[6]

Matthew's understanding of Jewish rituals was doubtless informed by his acquaintance with Jews in New York, in addition to rituals of divine healing that he brought from his Pentecostal background. He assumed the title of "rabbi," a status that he claimed had been conferred on him by the chief rabbi of the Falasha Jews in Ethiopia. Matthew embellished his biography with African roots, saying he had been born in Africa to an Ethiopian Jew. Later, he elevated his title to "chief rabbi" and in 1925 established the "Ethiopian Hebrew Rabbinical College." Its goal was to train and ordain rabbis for Black Jewish communities and to educate African Americans in this strand of Jewish or "Israelite" practice. Renamed the Israelite Academy in 2001, this institution claims to "have brought back more Israelites to the worship of the one, true God of Israel whose ancestors were formerly scattered among the nations of Africa and then slaves in the western hemisphere than any other institution, movement, or organization."[7]

Over time, the various connections that Matthew and others asserted between African Americans and ancient Israelites multiplied and became genealogically more elaborate. On a very general level, Matthew saw all Blacks as "lost sheep of the House of Israel."[8] Biblical stories were combed for evidence of specific African connections. Moses, for example, was born in Egypt, which is located in Africa, so Moses must be considered an African, thought Matthew. No matter that the Jews who were enslaved in Egypt at the time of Moses's birth may have come from elsewhere in the ancient Near East. Moses's wife, the "Cushite woman" referred to in Numbers 12:1, was obviously an Ethiopian, according to Matthew and others. If Moses and his wife had African roots, moreover, this meant that their descendent King Solomon did as well. Not only that, Matthew embraced the legend that the Queen of Sheba, whose kingdom is thought to have been in the region of Yemen or Ethiopia, may also have been related to Moses's Ethiopian wife. He likewise adopted the origin stories of the Ethiopian people, which suggested that during a visit to King Solomon by the Queen of Sheba, she became pregnant with Menelik, the legendary first emperor of Ethiopia. Thus in Matthew's historical reconstructions, Ethiopia was the nexus of both African and Israelite lineages.

In addition to Menelik, the tribes of Judah and Benjamin eventually settled in Ethiopia as well, according to Matthew, providing African Americans yet another path of ancestry leading back to the Israelites. He believed that African Americans were not just *related* to Israelite ancestors; they had also maintained, in some form, the religious traditions of the Israelites from that time forward, secretly keeping the Israelite faith alive throughout the ordeal of slavery and up until the present.

By encouraging African Americans simultaneously to see themselves as Jews and to see the original Jews as people of color with roots in places in Africa like Egypt and Ethiopia, Matthew and others at this time provided a powerful new origin story. Matthew's story elevated African Americans from being "Negroes," a stigmatized, racial underclass, to being "Ethiopian Hebrews," the direct descendants of God's chosen people.[9] Not only that, it challenged the idea that white Europeans and their American descendants were the rightful owners and heirs to the religious ideas of ancient Israel.[10] If the central biblical characters are recast as African in origin, and if Black people were the true descendants of Judah, then Black Jews do not require their authenticity as Jews to be recognized or validated by traditional white Jews.

In Matthew's version of history, African Americans were both genealogically and racially linked to the biblical Israelites, while white Ashkenazi Jews were portrayed as latecomers and converts to the Judaism of the original African Jews. They were useful, perhaps, for having preserved Jewish practices during the last two thousand years, but they lacked the same depth of authenticity as Black Jews.[11] To the extent that so much of Jewish tradition, customs, food, and music have been adapted from European and American influences, those expressions of Jewishness were not as useful to, or resonant with, Black Jews, whose Judaism is based on their own experiences as Black people.[12]

Racializing Jewish Authenticity

The emergence of Black Jewish groups thus created an unusual challenge to the authenticity of traditional or "mainstream" Jews, whose own racial origins were now highlighted. Merely raising the possibility of *Black* Jews who are part of a tradition that is inflected through their identification with roots in Africa raises the question of whether the religious and cultural traditions of "normative Judaism" need to be seen as the practices of *white* Jews with roots in central and eastern Europe. In other words, if Black Jews are not simply Jews who happen to be Black but rather a form of Judaism in which Blackness is a central element, then perhaps other forms of Judaism will need to acknowledge the underlying, if unspoken, racial and cultural hyphenation implicit in all understandings of Jewishness. As Janice Fernheimer points out, just having other groups claim to be Jewish, whether they are recognized by mainstream Jews or not, forces a reevaluation of the idea of Jewishness and the hybrid identities of different communities of Jews.[13] The desire of Black Jews to be considered legitimate members of the Jewish people, Fernheimer observes, "complicated questions about the conceptualization and authentication of not only Black Jewish identity but also about the ways the American, Israeli, and Jewish identities are imagined and authenticated." They force the defenders of "mainstream" or "normative" Judaism to articulate the criteria by which different forms of Jewishness and Jewish practice are accepted as authentic.[14] Doing so requires contextualizing normative Judaism as a reflection of the historical developments in specific white or European or Ashkenazi communities and considering other possibilities of Jewish cultural and religious life for non-white Jews.

For African Americans who began to claim a lineage to the original Hebrews in the Bible, a fissure quickly opened between their attitudes toward two different kinds of Jews: the ancient Israelites with whom they identified and the present-day American Jews among whom they lived. For the Black community of Harlem, for example, biblical Jews' experience of bondage and oppression mirrored the experience of Blacks in America, whereas modern American Jews were associated more with racist oppressors. In a 1948 essay published in *Commentary* titled "The Harlem Ghetto," James Baldwin wrote that the bitterness felt by Blacks in Harlem over the injustice and oppression they had suffered at the hands of white America was filtered through their relations with Jews—the small merchants, landlords, and pawnbrokers who, according to Baldwin, "operate in accordance with the American business tradition of exploiting Negroes, and they are therefore identified with oppression and are hated for it."[15] At the same time, the Harlem Blacks readily identified with the historic suffering and mistreatment of the biblical Jews, Baldwin noted: "The Negro identifies himself almost wholly with the Jew. The more devout Negro considers that he *is* a Jew, in bondage to a hard taskmaster and waiting for a Moses to lead him out of Egypt."[16] Thus there were two opposing kinds of Jews: the oppressed African Israelites, whose descendants were the Blacks in America, and the white Jews from Europe who were on the side of the oppressors.

Obviously, the delegitimization of "mainstream" American Jews as inauthentic imposters in Matthew's origin story of the Black Jews did not provide much incentive for a warm embrace from American Jews with European ancestry. An article appeared in the Yiddish daily *Forward* on October 2, 1920, with the headline "These Negroes Say They Are the Real Jews." With a bit of tongue-in-cheek sarcasm, the author tells the white Jewish readers of this venerable Jewish newspaper that they are not "real Jews" after all, but rather usurpers, just as fair-skinned Jacob had usurped his swarthy brother Esau's place and blessing.[17] The Black Jews' origin narrative proposed a new way to understand who was authentically Jewish that did not require any recognition from white Jews. On the contrary, it created a head-on collision of dueling claims about who are the "real Jews."

Indeed, Matthew's revisionist version of biblical history established the need for a more intersectional understanding of the connection between Jewishness and racial identity. According to Roberta Gold, the resistance of white Jews of European backgrounds to recognize the authenticity of new groups of Black Jews in Harlem and elsewhere was rooted in the shifting racial status of European Jews in American culture during the early part of the twentieth century. At a time when recent immigrants from eastern and southern Europe to the United States, including Jews, were slowly becoming accepted as white in American society, the boundary between white Americans and Black African Americans was hardening.[18] To accept Matthew's contention that Jews have some kind of primordial tie to Africa and that the original Jews were people of color would threaten the acceptance of Jews into the community of other white Americans. Walter Isaac writes, "The more Euro-American Jews became 'white,' the more they had to prove that Black Jews were not related to them, that those Blacks claiming to be Jews were somehow tainted, false, or essentially different from themselves."[19]

Although the Black Jews brought the racial dimension of Jewishness out into the open, it had never really been absent in ideas about Jewish peoplehood at the time. Early Zionist social scientists, explains Mitchell Hart, had been influenced by the prevailing racial ideas about the Jewish people, which saw the Jews' strictly enforced endogamy as a tool for maintaining their racial purity and distinctness from other peoples.[20] On the one hand, some argued that the Jewish people had survived as a distinct group by avoiding racial mixing. On the other hand, certain Jewish anthropologists from the early twentieth century challenged the idea of Jewish racial purity as a myth. Maurice Fishberg said that there were no common physical characteristics shared by all Jews, since Jews had always mixed with local people, including Asians, Africans, and Europeans. They were not all members of a single Semitic race but had been influenced, culturally and racially, by the people around them. In America, Jews were increasingly seen as white, like the majority of other people in the United States.[21]

Black Jews, however, appealed explicitly to racial purity as evidence of their Jewish authenticity. In the lyrics of a song popular among Black Jews, the Jewishness of Blacks, and, implicitly, the Blackness of Jews, is understood as something in their blood. The song, "Ethiopia, Land of Israel," which has been described as the

"Hatikvah" of Black Jews, refers to lost Israelite tribes that fled to Africa and later were taken to America as slaves. According to the song, "Jews you are now, Jews were you before. Time has not changed your blood."[22]

In general, mainstream Jewish organizations, Jewish leaders, and the Jewish press did not take the claims of Black Jews very seriously, and they made few, if any, efforts to recognize them as an authentic part of the world Jewish community. Those who spoke to Matthew or visited his synagogue found his knowledge of Jewish religious practice and traditions quite superficial.[23] His claims that African Americans were descended from the Falasha of Ethiopia were regarded with skepticism. There was no evidence that most African Americans were originally brought to North America from Ethiopia, nor did Matthew's group have familiarity with any of the traditions and practices of the Falasha, as might have been expected if they were really related. When the white head of the American Pro-Falasha Committee visited the Commandment Keepers in 1931, he dismissed the Black Jews of Harlem as inauthentic: "The services are hybrid and mongrel, but they are faked . . . based on a mixture of superstition and ignorance that has nothing to do with Judaism."[24] He suggested that "Jews" in Harlem really are Black, whereas the Falasha had actually been white like other Jews until their skin darkened because of centuries in the tropical sun. In response, a newspaper article in the *Afro-American* applied the same logic in reverse. It insisted that all Jews were originally people of color and that Abraham and Moses were Black men. This fact might explain why even if most American Jews were racially lighter today, their African roots were evident in their hair and the fact that many of them went to "colored beauty shops" to get it straightened.[25]

Despite the claimed connection of Black Jews to either ancient Israelites or Ethiopian Jews, the actual practices found in Matthew's synagogue were clearly based on the Ashkenazi traditions to which Matthew would have been exposed by New York Jews in Harlem and elsewhere. Howard Brotz's description of a visit to Shabbat services at the Commandment Keepers in the 1960s included fairly common elements from mainstream American synagogues: people kissed the mezuzah on entering the building, men wore yarmulkes, women were seated separately in the back of the sanctuary, and there was a Torah scroll in an ark. The service included such standard ingredients as Torah blessings, the Shema, and the mourners' Kaddish, all recited in Hebrew. It concluded with Reform Judaism's version of the hymn Adom Olam.[26]

Ironically, the reproduction of some version of the practices of American Ashkenazi Jews only served to undermine the Commandment Keepers' claim to be carrying on the traditions of their Ethiopian ancestors. Aside from the fact that white Jews could not easily imagine a direct African lineage to Israelites, there seemed to be a much more obvious source for the group's Jewish knowledge, such as it was. The debate over the authenticity of the Black Jews was most often framed in terms of their knowledge of Jewish law, or halakha, and their observance of a halakhic standard in Jewish ritual and observance. At the same time, as Roberta Gold points out, "Black Jews were scrutinized in a way that whites were not."[27] Indeed, it was odd to disqualify Black Jews as authentic Jews based on a halakhic standard of authenticity at a time when many mainstream Jews were already taking a much more flexible approach to religion that reduced the focus on Jewish law.

Walter Isaac argues that the implicit racial dimension of Jewishness makes it easy to assume that white Jews have greater authenticity than Black ones and that doubts about the possible Jewish legitimacy of Black Jews are natural and reasonable.[28] The result is a tendency to denigrate the Judaism of Black Jews as "primitive and heretical" and to affirm the normative status of white Euro-Ashkenazi Judaism. The unchallenged presupposition is that "Judaism with European roots is normal while other Judaisms are not."[29] Isaac suggests that the situation of Black Jews is similar to that of Sephardi Jews in the face of Ashkenazi hegemony, which orientalizes and exoticizes them and rejects their Judaism as distorted, false, imitative, and inauthentic. The underlying issue in Isaac's critique is whether or not Judaism must be conceived as a singular object with preestablished boundaries policed by mainstream religious authorities, or whether it is possible to consider not only different denominations within mainstream Judaism but different conceptions of Judaism itself, and different paths leading to connection with it.

Christian and Black Roots of Black Judaism

While some would argue that the racial otherness of Black Jews has been the biggest stumbling block in the recognition of their authenticity by other Jews, others insist it is the characteristics of the religious system of Black Judaism and its likely Christian origins that are most problematic.[30] In *Black Judaism: Story of an American Movement*, James Landing differentiates between Blacks who decide to convert to traditional Judaism or who have been adopted and raised as Jews, on the one hand, and the specific religious movement of Black congregations who identify as Jews, Hebrews, or Israelites, on the other hand.[31] He locates the origin of Black Judaism in Christian sects that found particular meaning for African Americans in Old Testament stories about the Israelites, to which they added "a veneer of Jewish belief, practice, and ritual."[32] If the original members of many of Black Jewish groups were raised within Protestant Christianity, it is more appropriate, argues Landing, to see Black Judaism as a manifestation of "black social protest" rooted in a Christian focus on the Old Testament rather than as a movement that developed *within Judaism*. In other words, Landing considers Black Judaism more an authentically Black movement than it is an authentically Jewish one. He writes, "Black Judaism had nothing to do with contemporary Jews or Jewish life."[33] He sees Black Jews as largely unaware of, and indifferent to, modern Judaism, so it is little surprise that white Jews mostly rejected their claims to be a legitimate or authentic form of Judaism.

Landing is doubtless correct that Black Judaism did not emerge as a movement within traditional Judaism, nor can its origin story be taken at face value. Indeed, it is easy to poke holes in its historical plausibility on many levels. Landing's focus on the specific historical conditions that produced Black Judaism leaves little if any possibility for considering anything about Black Judaism as authentically Jewish. It pays little attention to how the movement has developed and its shifting relationship with mainstream Jews. For this reason, his conclusions seem inadequate. As discussed in the last chapter, Steven Kaplan confronted a similar issue in evaluating evidence for the origin story of the Beta Israel (Ethiopian Jews). In that case, however, Kaplan carefully differentiated the process of historical authentication from the process of political or religious recognition of Jewish identity. In that case, rabbinical authorities recognized the Beta Israel as Jews in spite of the historians' doubts.

In the same way, the absence of professional historians' imprimatur on the origin story constructed by Wentworth Matthew does not settle the question of Jewish authenticity. To be sure, the story requires a remarkable suspension of disbelief regarding the survival of ancient Israelite tribes, their migration to Ethiopia, their arrival in North American, and their final migration to Harlem. Embracing the "invented tradition" of this connection with the biblical Israelites testifies simultaneously to a desire for rootedness in a glorious past and a belief in the persistence of that identity over thousands of years. It is a manifestation of what Tudor Parfitt calls "a longing for a lost past and a desperate desire to be reunited with the beginning."[34] Black Jews are hardly alone in finding expression for those desires through reconstructing their group narratives through the lens of their own group experience. How those expressions are regarded by other groups of Jews is an unfolding story, as the boundaries of Jewishness are stretched in new ways.

Is Halakha White?

In the latter half of the twentieth century, the circumstances of the Jewish status of Black Jews and their relations with the mainstream Jewish community shifted to some degree. Congregations of Black Jews had now been in existence for two or even three generations. This meant that their members were not primarily former Christians with a strong attraction to the biblical saga of the Israelites. The children who had been raised within these congregations knew of no other ethnic or religious identity for themselves than that of being Black Jews. The civil rights movement had brought together African Americans and Jews in other contexts, so the question of why Black Jews were still marginalized outside the mainstream Jewish community engendered greater attention and discussion, particularly of the racial implications underlying this issue.

As the civil rights movement pushed discrimination against African Americans to the top of the country's social agenda in the 1960s and 1970s, some Jewish leaders denied that their refusal to recognize Black Jews as Jews was racially motivated. In a 1970s volume, Conservative rabbi Harold Goldfarb insisted that Judaism does not have any kind of "race test" while he simultaneously reaffirmed the halakhic authority of traditional rabbinic Judaism. Blacks, he insisted, are as readily recognized as authentic Jews as anyone else, as long as "they fulfill the Halakhic requirements of authenticity. But where there is reason to question an individual's status as a Jew, he must submit proof of his Jewish legitimacy or, if such proof is lacking, undergo the conversion procedure required by Halakha, if he wishes to be recognized as a Jew."[35]

Whether or not there is an official race test for Jewish legitimacy, the issue of race was nonetheless embedded in how Goldfarb explained when there was a basis for questioning a person's Jewish status. It turns out that people of color will automatically be scrutinized more closely than whites when it comes to their Jewishness. Since the "historical Jewish community" has always consisted of whites (of European ancestry), there is a natural presumption, Goldfarb argued, that white Jews' claims of Jewishness are true unless there is a concrete reason to doubt them. Presumably, Sephardi or Mizrahi Jews, who might not necessarily be considered white, can also claim lineage in well-established historical Jewish communities. In other words, it is more plausible for people of European descent to claim a connection to the communities that have historically constituted the majority of Jews in the world. However, since Blacks, Asians, or other non-whites were never part of these historical Jewish communities, there is always a need to verify their Jewish status. They are more than welcome to become part of the Jewish community, but in most cases, they must first undergo conversion according to halakhic standards.

Without accepting traditional halakha and its rules for conversion, there was no way for Black Jews' claims of Jewishness to be recognized, according to Goldfarb. Because we live in a "troubled and changing era"[36] where there is little agreement among Jews about religion, Goldfarb stressed the importance of maintaining "the age-old rules for establishing Jewish authenticity" to ensure "the unity and well-being of the Jewish community as a whole."[37] Only in that way can everyone's "full and authentic Jewish identity" be guaranteed. Of course, Goldfarb's solution to the question of Black Jews quickly slips into a circular argument. On the one hand, he suggests that we can recognize authentic Jews by their willingness to accept both halakhic authority and the process of conversion, if it is indicated. On the other hand, we can assume that when anyone refuses to recognize the authority of halakha, as many Black Jews do, this in itself is evidence of their Jewish inauthenticity and deviant understanding of Judaism.[38]

J. David Bleich, an important Orthodox authority on halakha at Yeshiva University, argued that the census referred to in the book of Numbers in the Bible establishes the conditions for establishing one's Jewish identity. It requires offering genealogical proof of one's lineage. Bleich wrote, "An authentic claim with regard to genealogical identity, then as now was the *sine qua non* for recognition as a member of the Jewish faith-community by virtue of birth. The sole—but crucial—condition which must be met by a claim to Jewish identity by virtue of birth is that it be predicated upon authentic Jewish parentage."[39] Accordingly, in order to prove oneself to be Jewish, one has to establish Jewish lineage. This is why genealogies are so important not only in the Bible but also today, when those who are authentically Jewish can point to Jewish parents, grandparents, great-grandparents, and so on, to establish their Jewishness and place them within a particular origin narrative.[40]

In the absence of such genealogical evidence of Jewishness, conversion is the only option that Bleich allows. The problem with Black Jews in the United States is that before claiming their new Jewish identities, they, their parents, or their grandparents were Christians. This nullified any claim to Jewish lineage in his mind: "In view of their earlier known identification with Christianity any claims advanced by, or on behalf of, these groups to descent from the ten lost tribes of Israel or to being the only authentic descendants of the original ethnic Jewish community must be dismissed as sheer fabrication."[41] Even for second- or third-generation Black Jews, who were raised from birth as Jews, Bleich would presumably still insist on going back to their grandparents or great-grandparents to locate the break in their lineages when earlier relatives abandoned Christianity and embraced their new Jewish identities.

Having rejected the Black Jews' claimed connection to ancient Israelites, Bleich insisted that the only way they might be able to claim to be Jewish is if they could demonstrate a conversion to Judaism by some of their forebears. Lacking either a convincing story of connection to Israelite tribes or previous conversion, Bleich concluded, "any claim to Jewish identity on their part must be rejected as spurious."[42] Even if Black Jews could make a case for having been converted, they would also need to demonstrate observance of all commandments and be able to claim "recognition of the entire community without question or reservation."[43] Bleich could barely contain his sense of the absurdity of Black Jews' case for being recognized as Jews. They could present no convincing evidence of Jewish lineage (especially for descent from the Falasha), of Jewish conversion, of halakhic Jewish observance, or of recognition by the Jewish community of their Jewishness.[44]

Intersectional Jews and Multiple Judaisms

In an essay about Black Jews titled "Who We Are," Rabbi Sholomo Ben Levy, president of the International Israelite Board of Rabbis, emphasized the importance of recognizing the "true racial diversity that exists within the Jewish world."[45] Because of the dominance of white Jews from Europe within the Jewish world in the United States, he argues, the presence of other kinds of Jews has been made invisible. Demanding that Black Jews abide by conversion according to Orthodox halakha to establish their Jewishness makes little sense to Levy when the vast majority of American Jews themselves do not observe halakha and yet are still considered Jews. From Levy's point of view, the standards of rabbinic Judaism are simply the practices and ideas of one particular community of Jews that has tried to assert hegemony over others and ignore the possibility of other Jewish communities with their own traditions and histories.

The strategy of pluralizing "Judaism" into "Judaisms," proposed by Black Jews, resembles the arguments made by Messianic Jews. It is intended to accomplish two goals. First, it is meant to expand the generic concept of Judaism as an umbrella under which groups outside the established Jewish community can lay claim to being alternative forms of Judaism, and their members can see themselves and be recognized by others as one variety of Jews. Second, by relativizing the different forms of Judaism into different *Judaisms* followed by different kinds of Jews, it aims to decenter established authorities as gatekeepers to Judaism. In this decentered view of Jewish religion, forms of Judaism developed by groups of Jews who have often been excluded become part of the mosaic of expressions of Jewish experience, culture, and religion. The delegitimization of Black Jews and Black Judaism is replaced by a recognition of the existence of a "black Jewish culture" based on "black Jewish experiences, rituals, myths, laws, and traditions."[46]

An important point in this approach is recognition of the specific experience that people bring to their understanding of Judaism based on their gender, race, culture, and history. Just as feminists have offered new midrash and interpretations of Jewish texts based on their experience as women, Black people will have their own midrash and traditions, as Judaism is approached through the lens of their specific historical experiences of racial oppression, their cultural resources as Black people, and their unique adaptation of Jewish texts to condemn racism and validate their identities.[47] Andre Key proposes that Black Judaism can be "in conversation with" mainstream Judaism but not subordinated to it, as though Western rabbinic tradition is the gold standard against which all forms of Judaism must be judged. He emphasizes that Black Judaism should be understood within the broader context of African American religious traditions that focus on the racial oppression of Black people as a central moral and theological issue.[48]

Jews as a Mixed Multitude

In the century since Wentworth Matthew founded the Commandment Keepers Congregation of the Living God, some efforts have been made to bridge the gap between Black Jews and mainstream white Jews. This has often required a difficult balancing act between adopting some elements of mainstream Jewish traditions into the services of Black Jews, organizing activities that bring mainstream Jews together with Black Jews, and preserving the uniqueness of the Black Jews' perspective. One person who stands out in this area is Rabbi Capers Funnye. He has worked hard to both honor the traditions of Black Judaism that he inherited from Rabbi Wentworth Matthew and his successors and to build cooperation with the white Jewish world without conceding to them the role of gatekeepers for who and what is authentically Jewish.

Rabbi Funnye grew up in the African Methodist Episcopal Church, but he became involved with an Afrocentric African American Jewish congregation in college. This offered him both an alternative to Christianity and an expression of Black nationalism. He later studied with the successor to Wentworth Matthew, Rabbi Levi Ben Levy, and was ordained in 1985 by the Israelite Rabbinical Academy, one of the main training schools for Black Jews. He is currently the rabbi at Beth Shalom B'enai Zaken Ethiopian Hebrew Congregation in Chicago, an offshoot of the Commandment Keepers, and was recently appointed as the chief rabbi of the Hebrew Israelites in the United States. At the same time, his children attended a traditional Jewish day school, and he was accepted as a member of the Chicago Board of Rabbis.[49]

In addition to his education in the Israelite Rabbinical Academy, Rabbi Funnye also underwent a traditional Conservative Jewish conversion to express his respect for traditional halakha and to distance himself from the racial separatism of certain other Black Israelite groups. Newer members of his congregation become Jewish and join the congregation by means of "the exact processes laid out in *halakhah*," explained Rabbi Funnye. These include study, examination by a rabbinical Bet Din, and the rituals of *mikveh* and circumcision.[50] All this is consistent with normative Judaism.

The website of Rabbi Funnye's congregation explains that its members often identify themselves as "Hebrews" or "Israelites" rather than as "Jews," since it seems more biblical, and the term *Jew* has commonly been associated with whiteness. His image of the Jewish community is one that embraces a variety of different ways of understanding the identities of people who look back to the ancient Israelites as their ancestral role models. The result is a multiracial, multiethnic approach that allows for more than one form of Judaism, not just the particular form that was developed by white European Jews. "A genuinely inclusive Jewish community," he insists, "would have within it every color of the rainbow of humanity."[51]

There are a number of different rhetorical strategies that Rabbi Funnye has employed to establish not only his own Jewish authenticity but also that of Black Jews within a multiracial Jewish people. Like most Black Jews, Rabbi Funnye grounds his case for the Jewishness of African Americans like himself and the members of his congregation in the Africanness (and Blackness) of the original Jews and the centrality of Africa to the biblical narrative. He notes that the two most important events in Jewish history—the miraculous exodus from Egypt and the revelation of the Torah to Moses at Mount Sinai—both occurred in Africa. This connection between the original Israelites and the origins of Judaism in Africa offers a powerful reimagining of biblical history, although it also requires considerable blurring of the overall consensus of historians of the ancient world. Most of them agree that the Israelites were most likely not indigenous to Africa in general, or Egypt in particular, but rather were more likely related to western Semitic tribes such as the Canaanites.[52] An even more fundamental question is whether any discussion of the racial characteristics of the Israelites as either white or Black is an anachronistic imposition of a modern racial binary that cannot be neatly applied to either ancient Israel or Egypt. To a great degree, this issue reveals more about the racial dynamics of the contemporary world than that of ancient Israel.

The idea that the revelation of the Torah at Mount Sinai occurred in Africa certainly provides an emotionally and symbolically appealing connection to Black Jews, though the status of the Sinai Peninsula as part of Africa is murky at best, and most geographers consider it to be part of Asia. The Sinai Peninsula's location is probably more significant as a kind of liminal space between enslavement in Egypt and liberation in the promised land of Israel. It is not only the place of revelation to Moses and connection between God and the Israelites. According to the biblical narrative, it is also where the Israelites needed to wander for forty years before they were ready to enter Israel. This wilderness is the connector between Africa and Asia and between Egypt and Israel, symbolic of the dialectic of slavery and freedom and the complexity of the racial composition of the Jewish people.

Although Beth Shalom B'enai Zaken's website affirms their belief that the ancient Israelites were "people of African descent," Rabbi Funnye also rejects any idea of the racial origins of the Jewish people as homogeneous.[53] Rather, he sees the contemporary racial diversity of the Jewish people as a reflection of their racially diverse origins. He explained this diversity to his congregation: "There are Ashkenazi Jews of European descent, Sephardi Jews of Spanish descent, Mizrahi Jews of North African descent, and Yemenite Jews of Yemeni descent. We are Jews of African descent."[54] Similarly, in the biblical description of their flight from Egypt, the Israelites are said to be accompanied by "a mixed multitude" (*erev rav*; Exodus 12:38). Rabbi Funnye suggests this expression confirms the diverse nature of the people leaving Egypt, which he imagines included "every ethnicity."[55] The meaning of the Hebrew expression *erev rav* has been interpreted in many ways, but at the very least, it seems to suggest that some non-Israelite Egyptians (i.e., Africans) chose to join the Jewish people at the outset of the exodus.[56] Even if the Israelites were not themselves Africans, it does seem reasonable to assume that some people from Africa were among the various tribal groups that were being consolidated into the Jewish people.

Besides his sense of the original racial diversity of the Jewish people, Funnye had also mentioned a personal genealogical connection. Long after he had converted to Judaism and become a practicing Jew, he discovered that his great-grandparents' last name was Cohen. Not only is Cohen the quintessential Jewish name, but it signifies those Jews who trace their lineage back to the priesthood in the ancient temple in Jerusalem. As if to cover all bases, the Cohens he discovered in his family tree were on the halakhically important *maternal* side of the family.[57] This possibility of Jewish branches in his family tree transforms Rabbi Funnye from a former Christian with contested connections to ancient Israelites to a lost Jew being reunited with his original people.

At the same time that Rabbi Funnye's understanding of the origins of the Jewish people opens up a place for Africans and African Americans as Jews and his own family history suggests an even stronger connection, he is quick to insist that Judaism transcends racial identities and family trees. It is based on a common spiritual core. He notes, "Our faith cannot be based upon an ethnic or racial identity, but on our spiritual oneness."[58] As Ken Koltun-Fromm astutely analyzes, Rabbi Funnye simultaneously asserts and undercuts the traditional approach to Jewish authenticity by weaving together narratives of spiritual quest, possible genealogical connection, and cultural heritage that collectively, if not individually, present a powerful argument for the depth of his Jewish roots.[59] This shift to a focus on timeless spirituality offers a backup explanation that is not dependent on a specific historical narrative about Jewish origins in Africa for verification or authentication.

Funnye describes his connection to Judaism as part of a "spiritual quest" in which he followed inner sparks of Jewishness and the calling of a Jewish soul. By referencing the Kabbalistic notion of divine sparks implanted in people from the moment of creation, he suggests not only a primordial bond with the Jewish people, but he also offers a new line of explanation for how even those who lack connection to the present-day Jewish community may feel a pull toward Judaism as a result of errant Jewish sparks and souls that show up in unexpected people. Koltun-Fromm notes the importance of this rhetorical move: "A Jewish calling appropriates a spiritual rather than a cultural legacy, but confers recognition in equal measure, thereby legitimating religious reversion as authentic spirituality."[60]

The Black Jewish groups that emerged a century ago have developed in a variety of directions, from separatist ones who remain antagonistic toward mainstream white Jews to those that are seeking greater recognition and inclusion in the overall Jewish community and whose religious practice increasingly overlaps with that of other Jews. As Black Jewish groups have become more established with time, they are no longer composed of disgruntled Christians constructing new religious roots in ancient Israel. Today their members include at least three generations of people who have been Black Jews or Hebrews or Israelites from birth and have grown up with Jewish parents and grandparents. This fact alone, over time, will have an important impact on forms of mutual recognition between Black Jews and the broader Jewish community.

Rabbi Capers Funnye's Jewish journey serves as an excellent illustration of one of many ways Black Jews have tried to position themselves in relationship to the other parts of the Jewish community. On the one hand, it includes his particularist emphasis on the central importance of Blackness in understanding the origin and message of Judaism. On the other hand, he also embraces a multicultural and multiracial approach to the Jewish community as the modern manifestation of the original "mixed multitude" that constituted the Jewish people as they embarked on the journey from slavery to freedom. Finally, he offers a universalist model of Jewish peoplehood based on spirituality rather than race, culture, or ethnicity, an option that seems to undermine the basis of *Black* or multicultural Jewish identity. Each of these approaches is likely to present different possibilities for the broader recognition of Rabbi Funnye and his congregants as authentically Jewish by other Jews.

13 Authenticating Crypto-Jewish Identity

One way of understanding the question of authenticity in its simplest terms is as a response to the question of who I "really" am. Whenever anyone raises this question, the word *really* suggests that things are not always as they seem. People may think of themselves differently from how others see them. In some cases, they may prefer to keep their real identities secret, while in other cases, they may be determined to have their real identities recognized by others. While the notion of a person's real self or "true self" may suggest a core of identity that is relatively permanent and immutable, there are also cases when a person's sense of their true self undergoes a dramatic transformation. Sometimes, this is in response to the discovery that what they had previously believed about who they are did not tell the whole story. In response to new beliefs, new evidence, new experiences, or new stories about their past, a whole new conception of their real, authentic self may begin to emerge.

Reconstructing a Crypto-Jewish Origin Story

One such example of this transformation in a group of people's sense of cultural, ethnic, and religious identity in which the story people tell about themselves and their roots has been replaced by a dramatically different story of who they really are has unfolded in the latter part of the twentieth century among certain Hispanic families in New Mexico. These people have come to regard themselves as having a "crypto-"—that is, "hidden" or "secret"—identity as Jews, despite generations in which they and their families, to some degree, identified with and participated in the Catholic Church or, in some cases, other Christian denominations. They have become completely convinced of their Jewish ancestry based on the evidence they have pieced together from a variety of sources, including puzzling family customs and traditions, information passed on from grandparents and others, genealogical research, genetic testing, personal ambivalence about Catholicism, and in some cases an inexplicable attraction to Jewish traditions and Jewish people.

These crypto-Jews in the southwest United States see themselves as part of the massive dispersion of Spanish Jews who fled the Iberian peninsula in the fifteenth century. Many of the Sephardi Jews who left relocated to North Africa and the Middle East. Others, including conversos who had to be forced to convert to Catholicism, are presumed to have fled to Latin America, Mexico, and parts of the United States. As crypto-Jews began to reclaim their Jewish identities, it was as though a lost tribe of Israel had been found, a fragment of the Jewish people brought out of the shadows into the light. Jewish officials in Israel, who are always looking for new sources of immigration into the Jewish state, greeted the prospect of large numbers of newly discovered people with Jewish roots with delight. In 2014, Natan Sharansky, head of the Jewish Agency in Israel, recommended that the Israeli rabbinate be more lenient in allowing conversions of crypto-Jews to Judaism. He referred to estimates of "millions of descendants of conversos, including hundreds of thousands who are exploring ways of returning to their Jewish roots."[1]

While the Sephardi Jews were able to live openly as Jews with access to rabbis, synagogues, Jewish texts, and Jewish education, the crypto-Jews of the Americas had to survive for five centuries without any of these things, in complete isolation from the rest of the Jewish world. As a result, if any of them managed to preserve some residue at all of Jewish prayers, rituals, or traditions, it would be an amazing, almost miraculous, testimony to the tenacity and perseverance of the Jewish spirit, creating an unbroken chain going back to their Spanish Jewish ancestors. For those who have identified with the crypto-Jewish origin story, there is no question in their minds of their Jewish authenticity and their right to rejoin the rest of the Jewish community today. They insist that the evidence of their Jewish ancestry implies not just a present-day discovery of lost roots but a primordial connection to each of the generations leading back to their Jewish ancestors in Spain five centuries ago. To offer recognition and respect to present-day crypto-Jews implies equal respect and recognition for all the intervening generations and their efforts, conscious and unconscious, to preserve their Jewish heritage.

Crypto-Jewish identity requires a radical recalibration of the weight of one's public Catholic identity in relation to a newly emergent Jewish one. Crypto-Jews reconstruct their long detour away from the main body of the Jewish people and their centuries of living within the world of Catholicism as a rupture of mythic proportions that left them exiled from the rest of the Jewish people. If fifteenth-century Spanish Jews were *forced* to convert, however, then the legitimacy of the Catholic faith in every subsequent generation of their descendants is undermined, no matter how piously Catholic they may have become. This assumption is important to some crypto-Jews because it justifies the rejection of generations of Catholic devotion as merely ripples of the original violation caused by their earlier ancestors' forced conversion. If the origin of the non-Jewish or Catholic part of crypto-Jew's identity was not freely chosen, then in some ways all subsequent involvement in Catholic religious life for the next five hundred years can be shed as an invalid and illegitimate identity, the "fruit of a poisonous tree." Of course, this kind of retrospective reframing of the past in light of a newly claimed Jewish identity establishes a sharp new line of separation between the hidden Jewish side and the public Catholic side of family history, a new way of conceptualizing a past that was likely experienced much differently by earlier generations, if there was any awareness of this identity fissure at all.

Essentialism in Crypto-Jewish Experience

The personal narratives of crypto-Jews demonstrate not only a desire to vindicate the historical authenticity of a Jewish legacy passed on to them by distant ancestors. They also regularly invoke an argument based on experiential authenticity that is reminiscent of contemporary attitudes about sexuality and gender identity. In recent years, for example, the transgender community has normalized the idea that for some people, the outward form of their sexual anatomy does not conform with the gender identity they experience. This results in a sense of self-alienation or being trapped in a body and/or identity at odds with who they "really" are. Crypto-Jews often describe a comparable kind of experience in which they feel a profound mismatch between an emergent inner sense of being secretly Jewish and their families' outwardly Catholic cultural and religious traditions.

For many crypto-Jews, Jewishness is a timeless essence that persists in spite of conversion or assimilation. Even in the absence of any actual Jewish self-awareness, knowledge, or practice, a person can still be a carrier of this imperishable core of Jewishness. Sometimes it will be described in a quasi-biological way or as an actual genetic marker, and sometimes it is seen in the more metaphysical idea of a "Jewish soul." In any case, the rediscovery of this Jewish kernel within crypto-Jews is usually accompanied by a moral obligation to adopt more openly the supposed culture, religion, and ethnicity of ancestors who lived centuries before.

An inexplicable attraction to Jews and Judaism reported by some crypto-Jews was often the clue that led them to explore the genealogical evidence for their Jewish ancestry. In "My Fifty Year Search for My Portuguese-Jewish Self," Stephen Gomes describes becoming aware of and coming to terms with his Jewishness as a process that sounds remarkably like an LGBTQ person "coming out" about their sexuality or gender identity. He refers to years of "pain, challenges, and uncertainties," rooted in his realization since childhood that he did not fit in with the Catholic kids at his school. By the time he reached college, he reports, he felt that "something nameless, ineffable and undefined was calling me" and could no longer be ignored. His best friend asked him why all his friends were Jewish, and he slowly gravitated to the idea that he had a "Jewish soul" that was expressing itself in these ways.[2]

Although he had been raised as a Catholic, Gomes described his life as being incomplete and inauthentic until the transformative moment when he entered the *mikveh* and became reborn as a Jew. While many converts to a new religion may experience the final transition to a new religious identity as the resolution of a long struggle or search, the notion of formal conversion to Judaism as a process of reconnecting with one's true self is particularly highlighted in Gomes's narrative. Conversion normally implies the abandonment of an old identity and the embrace of a new one, yet Gomes described his conversion to Judaism less as a switch in identity and more as a return to who he had been and where he belonged all along. Like a number of other crypto-Jews, Gomes describes the process of *returning* to Judaism as one of "homecoming" and reclaiming his long-lost Jewish soul: "I was home at last. The feeling is still very new and very vivid for me; I am fully certain for the first time, I truly know who I really am at the core of my soul—without a trace of doubt or lingering hesitancy . . . I felt as if I had come home to where I belonged. It was my journey back to where I belonged."[3]

The model of authenticity displayed in this example privileges the idea of historical roots as the foundation of a person's true identity and the source of an imperishable, essential self, associated here with the soul. The Jewish soul introduces a metaphysical concept impervious to centuries of competing social identities. This inner core remains pure in its dormancy, while giving hints and clues of its presence. It is a lens through which the puzzle of one's "true identity" and "real roots" can be recognized.[4]

Although Gomes's reclaiming of his Jewish identity through the reconstruction of a past connection to Judaism and the persistent call of his Jewish soul results in a sharp fissure in his identity representing an earlier life of inauthenticity and confusion followed by his breakthrough into authentic Jewish identity, not all descendants of Spanish and Portuguese Jews understand the meaning of Jewish roots in the same way. In many cases, crypto-Jewish narratives combine puzzling family memories and traditions, historical or genealogical documentation, and feelings of attraction to Jews and Judaism. Sometimes, it is the discovery of a Jewish ancestor that validates a new interest in Jewishness and provides the primary anchor for building a crypto-Jewish narrative. Such data can be used to explain and/or motivate the claimed affinity for Jewish things among crypto-Jews.

Decoding Jewish Roots of Family Traditions

Some of the most intriguing aspects of crypto-Jewish narratives are the pervasive accounts of mysterious and usually unexplained family traditions that seem to resemble Jewish laws of kashrut, such as slaughtering animals in a particular way or avoiding pork; Jewish mourning customs, such as covering all the mirrors in the home after a relative dies; Sabbath rituals, such as lighting two candles on Friday nights; practicing circumcision for male babies; or playing a spinning top game similar to a Hanukkah dreidel. In addition, crypto-Jewish narratives often describe an early awareness of feeling different from other Catholic children or feeling uncomfortable and alienated from Christianity. There are reports of deathbed confessions from elderly family members who are said to reveal long-held secrets that the family was Jewish or just a general unspoken awareness of being Jewish.[5]

For most crypto-Jews, the development of an observant Jewish religious identity has to be recreated, often with the help of sympathetic rabbis, who quickly socialize these new Jews into a form of traditional Jewish practice. They may also offer special "rituals of return" or formal conversion according to Jewish law. Along with groups and organizations for crypto-Jews, supportive Jews from the mainstream Jewish community provide an important form of official "recognition." Such recognition is far from unanimous, however, as many mainstream Jews remain skeptical about the credibility of crypto-Jewish authentication narratives, and they regard tenuous claims of Jewish ancestry as an insufficient basis for being recognized as Jewish. The offer to permit crypto-Jews to undergo conversion has been a diplomatic way of handling these cases. The message is that even if a crypto-Jewish origin story cannot be reliably confirmed and some evidence may even dispute it, the debate over the historical authenticity of particular origin narratives becomes moot in the face of formal conversions to Judaism.

The crypto-Jewish phenomenon raises crucial issues about the complex elements that compose a person's cultural and religious identity and the ways in which it may in some circumstances become reconfigured and even reinvented in relationship to critical narratives about a family's roots and its connection to group history. The stories of crypto-Jews have been presented as discoveries of hidden pasts that contain the sources of their true identities and authentic selves. This process has been described as a "reawakening and reenergizing of memory," in which the crypto-Jews have "become aware of many more threads connecting them to their ancestors' Judaism—and in many cases, reconnecting them, after a lifetime of feeling disconnected from their innermost selves."[6] Yet more than a passive retrieval of a preexisting self, the process is an active reconstruction and retelling of a new personal origin story that gathers together details that will connect to a general crypto-Jewish master narrative. Other family narratives that have been accepted without question for generations will undergo a gradual or radical deconstruction, as they are now regarded as a superficial layer disguising their true family stories. With a change in one's origin story also comes a change in one's sense of religious, ethnic, and even racial identity. If crypto-Jews believe that they have "Jewish blood," then they have something in common with white Jews, even if their outward appearance seems non-white. They have Jewish bodies, even if they do not "look Jewish."

In the words of Ori Soltes, the stories of crypto-Jews "signify, in their marvelous, multiple ambiguities, the boundary between individual and group and the edge between true and false knowledge of one's roots, as well as between memory and forgetting."[7] Indeed, the ambiguities and questions raised by the crypto-Jews are even more complex than Soltes indicates, for the issue is not as simple as "true and false knowledge of one's roots" but also the ways in which belief in Jewish ancestry, regardless of its accuracy, transforms memories and creates new identities.

As certain as crypto-Jews may be in their new Jewish origin stories, the lack of recognition from much of the mainstream Jewish community, or an insistence on conversion that crypto-Jews read as a lack of belief in their ancestral narratives, is also a part of many of their stories. Rather than being welcomed and made to feel at home at mainstream synagogues, many encountered disbelief in their stories and rejection of their claims of Jewishness. One crypto-Jew lamented, "We had been in hiding hundreds of years, and when we finally came out, we were not accepted."[8] The hope of many crypto-Jews is for this doubt about their Jewish authenticity to be replaced in time by acceptance so that finally they will be able "to live fully authentic Jewish lifestyles and to rejoin the Jewish world."[9]

Many crypto-Jews regard the refusal of most Jewish congregations to recognize crypto-Jews as Jews unless and until they undergo conversion to Judaism as traumatizing and insulting. What a cruel irony that people whose ancestors, they believe, were compelled to convert to Christianity should be confronted with demands for a new required conversion when they seek to return to Judaism five centuries later. If mainstream Jews really believed the stories of the crypto-Jews, no conversions should be necessary to recognize them as Jews. So it is easy to read the insistence on conversion as a widespread doubt about the whole crypto-Jewish story in the larger Jewish community, or at least an unwillingness to ignore generations of Catholic observance in the background of most crypto-Jews. A requirement of conversion for anyone seeking membership in a synagogue and within the Jewish people side-steps the question of whether or not their story of Jewish ancestry seems credible or just an exercise in wishful thinking.

The Fifteenth-Century Expulsion of Jews from Spain and the Crypto-Jewish Phenomenon

To locate the roots of the crypto-Jewish phenomenon of the last quarter-century or so, it is necessary to look at events from half a millennium earlier, in the year 1492, when King Ferdinand and Queen Isabella of Spain had not only dispatched Columbus on a journey to the New World but had also ordered the expulsion of all the Jews from Spanish territory. It is this event that provides the foundation for the belief of growing numbers of Hispanics living in New Mexico that despite their families' long family histories within the Catholic Church, they are in reality the descendants of fifteenth-century Spanish Jews.

The history of religion is filled with episodes of forced conversions of individuals and groups. In the majority of cases, people subjected to forced conversion by conquering armies, ruling powers, slave owners, or missionaries eventually assimilate to a new cultural identity to some degree, and within several generations, children are being raised with little or no awareness that their ancestors, maybe their grandparents or great-grandparents, ever practiced a different religion. Much of the spread of Christianity has involved such compulsory conversions.

Although there are certain unique circumstances regarding this case, it also shares a number of features with the other groups discussed who have made claims about a previously unknown or unnoticed connection to the Jewish people. There are certainly parallels between the conquest and dispersion of some of the ancient tribes of Israel and the forced conversions and expulsion of the Jews from the Iberian peninsula in the fifteenth century. In both cases, it is likely that the majority of the Jews who abandoned their religion, whether against their will or by choice, were gradually assimilated into the surrounding populations. And it is also true that the idea of pockets of Jewish survivors secretly, even unconsciously, resisting assimilation and preserving some remnant of Jewish tradition has caught the imagination of many people, particularly American Jews. What is noteworthy in such cases is not simply whether or not there is convincing historical evidence for these stories but also why they are so compelling both for the individuals or groups who identify with them and for the mainstream Jewish community, which will determine what, if any, recognition to grant them.

During the fourteenth to fifteenth centuries, prior to their eventual expulsion, many Spanish Jews were either forced to convert to Christianity or willingly chose to do so rather than face continuing persecution as Jews. According to most accounts, the attitudes and beliefs of these erstwhile Jews, now Catholic, fell along a spectrum ranging from fully embracing their new Christian religion to secretly maintaining elements of their original Jewish beliefs, practices, and tradition beneath the public appearance of Catholic faith and practice. Some of these converted Jews, known variously as Marranos, conversos, New Christians, and more recently, crypto-Jews, eventually immigrated to the New World, where a remnant of their connection to Jewish tradition may have continued in disguised form, and some awareness of their Jewish ancestry may have survived.

This is the position of Stanley Hordes, one of the strongest advocates for the claim that there is a chain of continuous religious and cultural transmission linking present-day crypto-Jews in New Mexico with crypto-Jews from fifteenth-century Spain and Portugal. Based on connecting the dots between his historical research on the immigration of converted Jews to the New World and the data from interviews with crypto-Jews now living in the Southwest, Hordes has no doubt about the accuracy of crypto-Jewish accounts of their Jewish lineage. In her ethnography of crypto-Jews in the Southwest, Janet Liebman Jacobs acknowledged the controversy about the literal historicity of crypto-Jewish narratives and therefore was careful to select subjects who possessed persuasive documentation, genealogical research, and family history to confirm their crypto-Jewish lineage. Still, other scholars remain skeptical about most crypto-Jewish narratives and complain that crypto-Jewish supporters are only able to "connect the dots" by "leaps of logic, circular reasoning, conjectures built upon conjectures, and conclusions based on unverifiable oral testimony and material culture."[10]

The claim of continuous transmission of Jewish culture and identity from fifteenth century Spanish Jews through the centuries to crypto-Jews in New Mexico today is a matter of more than historical interest, since it is tied to implicit moral judgments in the interpretation of how conversos navigated between their original Jewish religion and their newly acquired Christian one. Hordes, for example, posits a straightforward binary between voluntary apostasy and coerced conversion—that is, the conversos *either* "converted sincerely and truly embraced their new faith" *or* they "converted in name only and secretly continued to practice their ancestral Jewish religion."[11] The latter group, which is the basis for the idea of present-day crypto-Jews, is of particular interest to many Jews because it represents a path that presumably was more difficult, heroic, and ultimately more authentic than the path of those who abandoned their religious heritage and ethnic group.

To some degree, the construction of this converso binary was sharpened by the perceptions of the two communities in the original conflict. For the religious Jewish community, any deviation from traditional belief and observance was apostasy, so conversos had already stepped out of the Jewish community and into a new Christian one. However, for the representatives of the Catholic Church in the Inquisition, whose job it was to root out any residual ties to Jewish tradition among the conversos, the suspicion lingered that many conversos were not apostates at all but still attached to being Jewish.[12] This left the conversos in a suspect position where they were not fully accepted either by the Jews whom they had left or by the Christian groups they had joined.

The responses of the conversos were doubtless more complicated and nuanced than the binary of genuine apostasy to Christianity vs. secret loyalty to Jewish tradition and the Jewish people. David Gitlitz describes the conversos as a group as "diverse and inconsistent" and observes that their beliefs and loyalties shifted and changed along the spectrum from those who remained wholly committed to being Jewish to those who became persuaded of the superior truth of Christianity. In some cases, they held on to beliefs and practices from both religions, engaging in some degree of syncretism. Others became skeptical about religion in general and failed to identify deeply with either tradition.[13] Not all the conversos had been forced to convert and some saw conversion to Christianity as an opportunity for social and economic improvement. Given all the possible permutations, it is hard to be definitive about people's motivations or the authenticity of their responses. Nor is there any easy way to even say which positions were the most "authentic" or what that might mean.

Whatever the original motivation of various conversos for becoming new Christians, the impact of those decisions would reverberate in the lives of their children, grandchildren, and future descendants. It is likely that most of the converso children and grandchildren became good Catholics, while a small number of them resisted giving their hearts over to Christianity and tried to preserve some residue of their Jewish identities and practices. In the absence of any contact with Jewish texts, rabbis, or opportunities for public Jewish observance, however, the connection to Jewishness among the smaller number of crypto-Jews inevitably became thinner and thinner, and even their self-awareness as Jews may have largely faded and disappeared over the generations.[14] Continuing efforts to eliminate "Judaizers" from the converso population in the New World meant that by the beginning of the eighteenth century, few (if any) crypto-Jews are believed to have been secretly preserving Jewish traditions or continuing to identify as Jews.[15]

According to some historians, the persecution and forced conversions of Spanish Jews leading up to the Inquisition were mostly successful in extinguishing Jewish observance in Spain. When these former Jews found that their transformation into "new Christians" through conversion did not protect them from continued persecution by the "old Christians," some conversos did flee, especially to Muslim areas, like Morocco and Algiers, where they thought they might return to Judaism. In these places that witnessed the arrival of small numbers of conversos "returning" to Judaism, rabbis expressed hope that it signaled a "large-scale Marrano 'revival.'"[16] This idea of a large pool of hidden Jews waiting to return to Judaism and rejoin the Jewish people has fueled fantasies about the descendants of the lost tribes of Israel for centuries and reinforced the idea of the indelible nature of Jewishness. To some degree, this model was also applied to the conversos.

Among the Jews remaining in Spain before the expulsion at the end of the fifteenth century, there was considerably less expectation for this kind of return. Historian Benzion Netanyahu has gathered evidence that conversos were regarded by other Jews as more than just apostates. They were seen "not only as followers of another religion, but also as members of another people." They were "complete aliens, totally cut off from the body of Jewry."[17] Needless to say, their return to be Jews was neither suspected nor anticipated. According to Netanyahu, the widespread idea that the newly converted Jews were secretly still practicing some parts of Judaism may likely have been less of a reflection of what actually was happening in this community than an invention of Christian authorities who refused to see the new Christians as anything other than Jews still surreptitiously practicing their heretical religion. Netanyahu deduces from Jewish sources from that period, like the Portuguese Jewish philosopher Abravanel, that the conversos "were not merely *affected* by [Christian] culture and religion and *yielded* to the natural processes of assimilation, but *consciously* and *willingly* participated in that process."[18] He suggests that they sought to be recognized not only as Christians in their religion but also as Gentiles in their ethnicity.

Whatever small number of crypto-Jews faithful to Judaism may have been among the conversos, most of those who were tortured, persecuted, and murdered by the Inquisition were nonetheless seen by Abravanel as "traitors to their religion like all *real* converts, and also betrayers and deserters of their people"[19] In Netanyahu's analysis, the biggest problem the majority of conversos encountered was having the authenticity of their *new Christian faith* recognized, not secretly preserving remnants of Judaism and holding onto an inner self-identity as Jews. The largely successful Christianization of the Spanish Jews produced people within several generations who were so fully socialized into Christianity that they had "no knowledge of the Jewish religion and no interest in its precepts."[20]

The degree to which any residue of Jewish belief and practice managed to be preserved among those who claim to be descendants of conversos goes to the heart of the unresolved debate among scholars over the "historical authenticity" of the narratives and evidence offered by the crypto-Jews of New Mexico. There are three different questions that need to be separated in addressing this issue. First is the question of whether it is likely that crypto-Jewish families in New Mexico are actual descendants of Spanish conversos. Second is the question of whether their family customs, rituals, or beliefs are correctly interpreted as remnants of their Jewish ancestors and centuries-old Jewish practices or whether such family traditions can plausibly be attributed to other more recent sources. And third is the question of the weight and relevance that the answers to these first two questions will be given in evaluating the ways in which the crypto-Jews' authenticity as Jews is recognized by other Jewish communities.

Challenges to the Crypto-Jewish Narrative

While it is not impossible that some contemporary crypto-Jews in New Mexico have Jewish ancestry or that there are traditions in their families that have a connection to Jewish observances from much earlier periods of history, it is equally true that elements of some of these crypto-Jewish narratives and/or the interpretations they give to specific customs and objects are historically dubious and open to alternative explanations for their origins. Without making any kind of final judgment in the heated scholarly debates about the origins of the crypto-Jews, a modest conclusion would have to acknowledge that the evidence supporting the historical accuracy of the crypto-Jewish narrative is far from incontrovertible. There are clearly inconsistencies and contradictions that do raise doubt about the actual origins of some of the crypto-Jewish practices reported.

The significance of the presence or absence of reliable historical evidence for the claims in crypto-Jewish narratives is a complex issue that has possible implications for the acceptance and recognition of crypto-Jews as part of the Jewish people by the mainstream Jewish community. For some scholars, like folklorist Judith Neulander, the problematic nature of crypto-Jewish claims casts a shadow over any possible authenticity associated with crypto-Jewish narratives. According to Neulander, crypto-Jewish claims about the Jewish ancestry of the founding Hispanic families in New Mexico are unfortunate fabrications with "superficial plausibility and popular appeal."[21] She expresses respect for the fact that most groups base their identities on their own special origin stories, in which the group's own collective memory and reconstruction of the past is privileged over the historical accuracy of individual details. Such stories are important for the ways they reveal the fundamental values and worldview of the group.[22] Yet Neulander seems to regard the origin stories of New Mexico's crypto-Jews as particularly contaminated and problematic. The result is that she portrays the crypto-Jews as more like naive and gullible victims of a scam than the actors in an incredible story of Jewish survival. She suggests that shoddy scholarship plus sensationalized and uncritical media reports have fed into an unconscious desire of some Hispanics in the Southwest to acquire a more prestigious racial lineage by identifying with Jews, who represent a whiter population than various mixed-race people in the Southwest.[23] As stories of crypto-Jews recovering their Jewish roots appeared in newspapers, magazines, and on TV, the phenomenon gained momentum, and larger numbers of Hispanics began wondering about their own potential Jewish roots.

For Neulander, the evidence linking ambiguous cultural customs and folk traditions in crypto-Jewish families to fifteenth-century Spanish Jews is unconvincing, and some of those customs and traditions may derive from other sources that are historically and geographically closer than fifteenth-century Spain and Portugal. Perhaps the use of a four-sided top has nothing to do with Spanish Jews, who did not use dreidels in the fifteenth century. Instead, it might have a non-Jewish origin, since similar tops are used in the Southwest, or its use may have resulted from exposure to customs of Ashkenazi Jews, who brought customs like the dreidel with them at least a century earlier.[24] Some Jewish customs may have been adopted from Christian sects in the Southwest that encouraged the observance of Jewish holidays and rituals that are described in the Old Testament. At the very least, there are multiple possible cultural sources for customs that crypto-Jews see only as evidence of their Sephardi Jewish roots.

Though crypto-Jews have often complained about the lack of recognition they received from mainstream Judaism, it is also true that their stories have a special resonance for many Jews that contributes to the fascination with crypto-Jews. According to Neulander, this fascination can be explained as a manifestation of Jewish wish fulfillment, "a beleaguered peoples' need to believe itself indomitable, as evidenced by a miraculous crypto-Jewish survival."[25] There is no doubt that the appeal of the crypto-Jewish story exists on a symbolic or allegorical level as well as a historical one. It is a miraculous story of survival in the face of persecution, a kind of modern-day

Hanukkah tale of something that lasted beyond all reasonable expectations. Like the oil that burned for eight days, the crypto-Jews' hold on their Jewishness has lasted for five centuries. Michael Carroll suggests that the fantastic story of the crypto-Jews' maintaining a secret loyalty to their authentic Jewish selves beneath their outward Catholic appearance offers a redemptive moment to contemporary Jews living in the shadow of the Nazi genocide of European Jews. Carroll claims that the possibility of crypto-Jews in New Mexico "allows us to envision a world in which the horrors of the Holocaust are a little less horrible than they were in the real world."[26] The crypto-Jew thus becomes a metaphor for Jewish survival and for the imperishable kernel of Jewishness that persists throughout the centuries.

New Forms of Recognition of Crypto-Jews

The desire for recognition by some crypto-Jews of what they consider their rightful place within the Jewish community appears to be based on the validity of their claims of Jewish ancestry as well as their seeming observance of Jewish customs and traditions passed on to them from those ancestors. If these claims are false or mistaken, some might claim that the problem posed by the crypto-Jews is not that mainstream Jews have withheld recognition of their Jewish status but rather that overly credulous advocates and supporters have been too quick to offer their recognition. If the crypto-Jewish sensation is merely a modern variation on a much older phenomenon of the dominant culture identifying lost or hidden Jews—for example, lost tribes of Israel—in remote places and groups of people and of such groups taking on customs and practices that enable them to believe in these connections, then the nature of the recognition they receive may need to be reconsidered.

However, as some crypto-Jews do become more integrated into Jewish synagogues and have contact with the mainstream Jewish community, as their children grow up with normative and nonnormative forms of Jewish identity, the question of recognition and authenticity will inevitably rest on more than just historical evidence about their Jewish origin stories. This leads us to the issue of whether some forms of recognition should be provided to crypto-Jews within Jewish communities, *even* when crypto-Jewish claims probably rest on at least some historical errors and misinterpretations.

Seth Kunin's helpful ethnographic analysis of the crypto-Jews of New Mexico offers an alternative way of framing the issue of authenticity that uncouples it from problems of historical accuracy. Kunin argues that the best way to look at the crypto-Jews is as a late-twentieth-century phenomenon in which a group of Hispanics in the southwestern United States has constructed a particular narrative about their past that emphasizes forced conversions and secret Jewish practices as the foundation and justification for their newly claimed identity as Jews.[27] They should be approached not so much as the bearers of fragments of earlier Jewish practice but rather as a contemporary living culture.[28] After reviewing the debate over the historical authenticity of crypto-Judaism in New Mexico, Kunin argues that *historical authenticity* is not essential to recognize the *cultural authenticity* of the crypto-Jews.

Jonathan Freedman makes a similar point in arguing that the crypto-Jewish phenomenon represents "a new form of Jewishness" based on an ethnic or cultural identity that is expressed "only through improvised, often invented cultural practices and constructed (and often fictitious) narratives."[29] Freedman concedes that crypto-Jewish identity is "fundamentally unverifiable, hence epistemologically unstable."[30] Given the syncretic mixture of Catholic tradition with remembered, or reinvented, forms of Jewish practices, crypto-Jewish identity "calls attention to the fluid and shifting boundaries that have defined and continue to define Jew and gentile alike."[31] Freedman's conclusions leave unresolved whether the crypto-Jews ought to be considered "authentically Jewish" in the absence of rabbinically supervised conversions. After first describing crypto-Jews as "a new form of Jewishness," he later suggests that the crypto-Jewish syncretism of Jewish and Christian elements has produced more ambiguous and unstable forms of identity that are something new, "neither 'Jewish' nor non-Jewish but somewhere in between."[32]

In making an argument for the cultural authenticity of crypto-Jews in New Mexico as a distinct cultural phenomenon, Kunin likewise avoids the question of whether or not they should be considered Jews. Some crypto-Jews may seek that form of recognition and others may not. Some have long family histories of crypto-Judaism, as well as genealogical documentation, while others simply feel a special affinity to Judaism and Jews. While all of them construct their present identities in ways that incorporate their belief in the Jewish origins of their families and their customs, the nature and degree of change in these reconstructed identities are quite variable. Ethnographers have interviewed some subjects for whom newly discovered Jewish lineage is merely a strand of their ethnic background but does not alter their families' long-standing Catholic identities. Others construct a syncretic hybrid of both Jewish and Christian traditions and beliefs that enables them to hold on to Jesus and Mary by Judaizing them in some of the same ways that Messianic Jews do. Finally, the groups that have received the most attention in the Jewish world are those whose identities undergo a complete transformation that rejects their previous Catholic background as inauthentic due to its roots in forced conversion and replaces it with exclusively Jewish religious practice and identity.[33] This process will often include formal conversion and "return" to Jewish synagogues and communities.

Kunin emphasizes that the forms of crypto-Jewish identities are cultural constructions subject to change and reinterpretation, even if the basic crypto-Jewish narrative suggests a more essentialist view of identity as fixed and unchanging. Kunin writes, "Culture is not inherited whole cloth in an unchanging form from one generation to the next; rather, it is learned and appropriated by each individual and generation and is changed, both consciously and, more important, unconsciously, by those who take it forward."[34] If this is so, then crypto-Jewish identity is no different from any other cultural or religious identity, in which cultural authenticity does not rest on the historical authenticity of every detail of its origin narrative.

Although Kunin rules out the likelihood that Jewish practices from the fifteenth century were passed down intact to the present day, he is agnostic about exactly how the crypto-Jewish identities were constructed.[35] Since crypto-Jews lacked contact with any Jewish groups or religious authorities, their customs would have developed in isolation and reflect each family's own interpretations and practices. Whatever historical origins there might have been, they would have been reshaped and reinterpreted in very individual ways.[36] Kunin acknowledges that some rituals or folk traditions that crypto-Jews interpret as based on Jewish practices are probably of non-Jewish origins.[37] Nonetheless, regardless of whether these practices have demonstrable Jewish roots or prototypes, "crypto-Jews interpret these practices as expressive of both Jewish past and crypto-Jewish present, and thus they are culturally authentic, expressing a real crypto-Jewish identity."[38] From this perspective, even if four-sided tops that were used in some crypto-Jewish families were just common toys found among others in the Hispanic community rather than relics of Jewish ancestors, what is important is that these objects have been interpreted as expressions of Jewish identity: "Thus as a Jewish ritual item, it has clear cultural authenticity even if its historical authenticity is in question."[39] Kunin's point is that the moment that crypto-Jews interpreted the top as a Jewish dreidel, regardless of where it originally came from, it became, retrospectively, an authentic Jewish object offering one small piece of a newly reconstructed history of a crypto-Jew's Jewish heritage. Similarly, even if the presence of six-pointed stars on tombstones, churches, or other places originated in non-Jewish sources, when crypto-Jews interpret its presence as a Jewish symbol, Kunin suggests, it is transformed into an authentic part of their culture. Thus, the fact that the Star of David was not a commonly used symbol for Jews in fifteenth-century Spain, and that it was used by other groups before it became associated with Jews, is not important if the contemporary crypto-Jews interpret its presence as part of their crypto-Jewish heritage.[40]

Kunin's argument is that the story of the Jews' persecution, forced conversions, and subsequent expulsion from Spain in the fifteenth century represents a compelling story on which crypto-Jewish identity has been constructed. Although critics like Neulander question whether crypto-Jews have any actual connection to Spanish Jewish conversos or Jewish customs derived from them, Kunin responds that "external validation of the collective memory is less important than its perception by those in the community."[41] The crypto-Jewish narrative of their origins may have little to do with any documented history. Seth Ward writes, "No doubt many claims of heritage, of survival, of tradition, or of genealogical purity, are too grandiose, but the primacy given Judaic heritage and identity is striking. It may be misplaced to some outside observers, yet still must be understood and appreciated."[42] Jonathan Freedman emphasizes that crypto-Jewish narratives of a hidden Jewish past, family secrets, and disguised identities "can serve as a source for this rooted yet flexible construction of social identification and cultural meaning," and "compose their own order of being with the power to shape and reshape both the sense of the past and that of the future."[43] It does not really matter whether they are literally or historically true, nor is there any way to ever settle the claims of the crypto-Jews. Ultimately, Freedman concludes, "all identities are in some respects malleable products of history and personal choice" expressed in narratives that are always open to revision and reinvention.[44]

The underlying conclusion of all these positions is that the crypto-Jewish origin narrative is a "myth," *not* because it is false (its historical truth remains indeterminate), but rather because its truth is of a different kind. It offers "a model by which we explain and give coherence to past, present, and future. As with any myth, a key part of its power is the perception of its essentialness—that is, both its validity and its permanence."[45] So even if the crypto-Jews lack convincing evidence for some observers, their story has become a foundational part of their self-understanding and identity.

Kunin sees the ability to continually reconstruct and reinvent one's identity as a characteristic of postmodern identities in general. The crypto-Jews are no different from any other Jews at this moment in time insofar as each of them will determine the meaning and nature of the practices and beliefs that compose their Jewishness.[46] Kunin says that cultural authenticity does not require external authorities to determine whether there is sufficient historical documentation. Cultural authenticity is about "shared self-definition."[47]

Kunin is certainly right to highlight the fluidity and freedom that characterize the process of defining, reinventing, and reconstructing one's cultural identity. At the same time, his position makes it hard to imagine how any identity that a person claims, regardless of historical evidence, would lack cultural authenticity in his eyes. His declaration that "crypto-Jewish culture and identity are as culturally authentic as any other culture or construction of identity" is based on his assumption that cultures and identities are ultimately whatever the people who claim them say they are.[48]

Kunin goes too far in detaching the process by which cultural meaning and identity are created from some tangible connection to a particular people, history, texts, artifacts, and so on. Surely, if a person read about the particular suffering of Jewish Holocaust survivors and totally identified with their plight, they could not on that basis alone plausibly declare themselves to be Holocaust survivors or to be recognized as such. Indeed, we would likely find historically unsubstantiated claims about something like this to be illegitimate and inauthentic, regardless of the self-definition of certain people.

In the final pages of his book, Kunin actually dials back his position, and it becomes clear that while he does not think that problematic details about historical evidence are enough to invalidate crypto-Jewish identity and culture, he does not see the crypto-Jewish phenomenon as completely untethered from questions of historical evidence and authenticity. After spending so much energy rejecting the relevance of historical authenticity, Kunin turns around and mostly endorses the controversial position of Hordes. Far from just making up their crypto-Jewish identity, Kunin concludes, the historical and genealogical evidence really do make it most likely that crypto-Jewish identity is a heritage that was passed down to them in some form or other by their crypto-Jewish ancestors.[49] The concluding paragraph of his book retreats a bit on his earlier dismissal of the importance of historical verification. He writes, "The evidence in favor of both the historical and the cultural authenticity of crypto-Judaism is very persuasive."[50] Kunin is surely right that the cultural authenticity of the crypto-Jews does not hinge on documentary or other evidence of their actual ancestry, whether persuasive or not. They are engaged in a process of cultural and identity transformation that will likely unfold and develop over time in relation to the Jewish communities with which they affiliate.

If crypto-Jews see themselves as a unique group, somehow inspired by, or somehow connected to, Spanish conversos but distinct from mainstream Jewry, then perhaps they and they alone will decide on the cultural authenticity of their particular origin narrative. Although not all of the crypto-Jews want a closer connection with the mainstream Jewish community or are anxious that their status as Jews is recognized, many of them do seek these connections, whether through conversion, rituals of return, or a general sense of identification not just as crypto-Jews but as Jews, tout court. For this reason, Kunin's approach to cultural authenticity, while useful in highlighting the process of continuous reinterpretation and reconstruction of postmodern identities, is insufficient.

At some level, we must also consider the creative and fluid process of recognition of crypto-Jews by others. Obviously, recognition is not a discrete legal determination that would declare crypto-Jews authentic Jews once and for all. The debate over the historical evidence supporting crypto-Jewish narratives in New Mexico is instructive in the ways that recognition is also a fluid process that involves reconstructing and reinterpreting the status of other groups. For the crypto-Jews, there are scholars as well as synagogues and religious leaders who both recognize and do not recognize them, just as other divisions in Jewish life may be recognized by some parts of the Jewish people and not by others. In a curious repetition of the original response to the first new Christians in Spain, some parts of the Jewish community are eager to welcome these people (back) into the community, while others see their claims are dubious and insist on the necessity of religious conversion in order to recognize them as Jewish.

In some ways, "crypto-Jew" is a transitional identity leading to participation in mainstream Jewish institutions, as well as religious and cultural life. For crypto-Jews who have undergone conversion or been recognized as Jews in certain synagogues without the need for conversion, it is easy to imagine that their children and grandchildren will eventually be educated as, and recognized as, members of the Jewish community, just like any others. In an increasingly diverse American Jewish community, their Hispanic, Native American, or other backgrounds will not seem remarkable. Kunin actually sees their assimilation into mainstream Jewish culture as a loss of the uniqueness of the crypto-Jewish identity. But the more important question for the future will be not only how Hispanics in New Mexico developed an idiosyncratic interpretation of their family histories but also how their version of Jewishness and their narrative of persecution and survival is integrated into the larger Jewish world.

14 Newly Found Jews and the Regimes of Recognition

The problem of *losing* Jews to assimilation and intermarriage has been the focus of discussion about Jewish identity among Jewish demographers and communal leaders throughout much of the second half of the twentieth century. This backdrop makes the prospect of *finding* Jews who had allegedly lost their connection to the Jewish people centuries or even millennia ago quite intriguing. Yet both the process by which remote groups in Africa and Asia, such as the Abayudaya Jews of Uganda, the Mizo ("B'nei Menashe") Jews of northern India and Burma, or the Bene Israel Jews from India, start to *recognize themselves* as Jews and the related process by which the established Jewish communities of Israel and the United States offer them recognition as Jews are tied to complex political issues and agendas. Recognition of others as "real" Jews simultaneously involves questions of religious and cultural authority, cultural norms, and mutually reinforced models of Jewish identity. For this reason, the contested nature of recognition of "newly found" Jews offers a microcosm of larger issues of recognition in the Jewish world today.

Unlike most Jews, who can trace their Jewish lineage back as many generations as they have records, the family history of newly found Jews usually includes a rupture in Jewish lineage and the fact that their identification as Jews by themselves and by others occurred relatively late in their community's history. With no actual historical records of continuous identification as Jews and little, if any, knowledge of Jewish customs or religious practices that match known forms of Judaism or Jewish life, it is not surprising that their recent claims of Jewishness have been met with not only fascination but also a degree of skepticism.

The decision to recognize (or not) the claim of some groups to being descendants of lost tribes of Israel can be interpreted in two different ways. It might be seen as a way to help the members of a group recover their authentic, though previously hidden, identities as Jews. The idea that one's true, or authentic, identity might lay in a newly discovered secret about the identities of one's ancestors requires a particular essentialist view of identity as stable and unchanging, even when it is unobserved or unknown. On the other hand, if identification as a Jew is something that is actively constituted and constructed, then newly claimed Jewish identities may reflect an authentic reformation of their identities, regardless of demonstrable historical evidence of their Jewish roots. To the degree that mainstream Jewish groups offer recognition of newly found Jews as Jews, they may be not only validating a narrative of Jewish origins but actively contributing to the performance of that narrative in the present.

Did Some Israelite Tribes Really Become Lost?

The story of the lost tribes of Israel is the most common origin myth utilized by groups seeking to justify their self-recognition as Jews, even when few historians or archeologists offer support for such a connection. We have already seen this in the case of the Beta Israel from Ethiopia and various groups of Black Jews in the United States who claimed to be related to ancient Israelites. Just how plausible is the claim of whole intact communities being descendants of actual Israelite tribes from biblical times?

It is generally assumed that many of the members of the ten tribes of Israelites from the northern kingdom of Israel were exiled by their Assyrian conquerors over 2,700 years ago and eventually were absorbed by the Assyrian population.[1] Archeological evidence also suggests that many others of the original Israelites in the ten lost tribes remained in the land or fled to the southern kingdom of Israel where they were absorbed by other Israelite groups. There is no evidence that any Israelite tribes migrated as cohesive groups to Africa, India, or elsewhere, or that ancient Israelite religious and cultural practices have been preserved in isolation for over two millennia. This lack of historical evidence of the continued existence of the lost tribes has not prevented their persistence as an "imagined mythical community" in the minds of many people. Tudor Parfitt observes that where the history of the original tribes left off, "the history of the myth of the Lost Tribes" takes over.[2]

Stories of the lost tribes are obviously deeply appealing testimonies to a faith that has allegedly been maintained for thousands of years despite a lack of contact with all other Jews. But if, as many historians assert, the story of the lost tribes is not really plausible, what kind of recognition can be given to those groups claiming lost Israelites as ancestors? Origin narratives straddle the boundary between verifiable history and imaginative constructions, and their effectiveness and importance seldom require empirical evidence. In many cases, the evidence for a connection to the ancient tribes of Israel is present-day residual practices that seem to correspond with descriptions from the Hebrew Bible. But such practices may merely reveal prior exposure to the biblical text rather than descent from the people described in the text.

The challenge in evaluating such claims is that the biblical text did not yet exist at the time that some of the Israelite tribes disappeared as distinct groups. Moreover, the Bible does not necessarily give an accurate portrayal of the Israelite tribes' earliest religious practices and traditions. Although the biblical narrative describes the consolidation of a nationalist religion focused in Jerusalem and its Temple, the tribes that eventually were considered "lost" were involved in a lot of other things that would hardly have been acceptable in the newly emerging Israelite religion. Archeologists Israel Finkelstein and Neil Silberman note that "there were countless fertility and ancestor cults in the countryside, and there was the widespread mixing of the worship of YHWH with that of other gods. As far as we are able to tell from the archaeological evidence of the northern kingdom, there was a similar diversity of religious practice in Israel."[3] Only after the fall of the northern kingdom did Jerusalem's influence become more focused on proper religious law and practice. So it may have been only in the late eighth and early seventh century BCE, after at least some parts of the northern tribes were exiled, that biblical monotheism really took root. The heightened monotheistic focus in the surviving state of Judah was read back into the earlier history of the Israelites as the origin narratives of the Hebrew Bible were composed. The biblical "history" that survived is a product of the proponents of the YHWH-only movement, which now emphasized the story of YHWH's revelation of divine law and liberation of the Israelites from Egypt.

Ironically, the very biblical practices that some present-day groups observe and point to as evidence of their connection to the ancient "lost tribes" are anything but evidence of such a connection. Such practices only became normative after the original tribal groups were supposedly lost. Many of the original religious practices of the northern tribes were interpreted by the new authorities in Jerusalem as Canaanite heresies. According to Finkelstein and Silberman, "What was old was suddenly seen as foreign and what was new was suddenly seen as true."[4] If any members of the northern tribes had somehow survived in isolation from the emergent forms of normative Judaism, their religious ideas and practices would still include some of the alien cultural elements that the religious leaders in Jerusalem had felt a need to purge from Judaism.

What all this means is that even if a hypothetical group of descendants of a lost tribe actually existed, their connection to Judaism as we know it today, or even to just the version of Israelite religion described in the Bible, would be far more tenuous than most people would think. Far from being a group committed to the same Torah as modern Jews, they would have been a syncretistic group unfamiliar even back then with much of what later became normative Judaism. To the degree that contemporary groups of newly found Jews follow practices or rituals described in the Hebrew Bible, it is more likely that they learned these things from being taught about the Bible many centuries later, not that they had secretly or unconsciously preserved some kind of biblical-era religion for thousands of years.

It is probably no accident that reported discoveries of pockets of lost tribes of Israel erupted around the time that global exploration and colonialism introduced new peoples, languages, cultures, and religious practices to Europeans. It was natural to make sense of them in terms of well-known elements of Israelite religion, especially food taboos, sacrifices, and rituals like circumcision. From there it was a short leap to conclude that Israelite tribes themselves had brought these practices straight from the biblical period as they wandered undetected to the far corners of the world. In addition, once Christian missionaries arrived to teach biblical stories to indigenous groups, it was easy for these people to adopt new origin myths that tied them into the central narrative of the powerful European culture.

This historical context for the discovery of possible lost tribes of Israel complicates the decision regarding whether or not to recognize lost tribe origin stories. On the one hand, the recognition of lost tribe status could be seen as a matter of respect for the autonomy of groups to define themselves and to construct their own origin stories. On the other hand, if the idea of being connected to the lost tribes of Israel was produced by the monocultural gaze of colonial European Christians, which saw alien cultural practices as evidence of an imagined Judaism frozen at the pre-Christian, tribal, sacrificial stage described in the Old Testament, then perhaps recognition only contributes to the erasure of the original cultural and religious identities of indigenous people.

The Jewish Search for "Lost Jews"

After the creation of the modern state of Israel, the phenomenon of lost tribes underwent a significant change as the political consequences of claiming an Israelite identity became clear and the existence of certain groups became more widely known to Israeli and other Jews. Many of these groups have been contacted, educated, encouraged, and converted by mainstream Jews who felt a mission to reclaim such "lost" Jews and bring them back to Israel, even when the evidence of a connection to lost tribes was thin at best.

Of course, merely identifying with the biblical saga of the suffering and triumphs of the Jews has always been available to converts, even if they were not personally part of that history. To claim "lost tribe" status places a group in a much different position than that of mere converts. It demands recognition of an actual biological, ethnic, or tribal connection that goes beyond merely an acceptance of Jewish *religion*. It involves actually being one of the original groups that composed the Jewish *people*.

In the last half-century, the discovery and recognition of "lost Jews" or "newly found Jews" have been taken up as causes by Jewish organizations specifically devoted to this issue. In 1975, Rabbi Eliyahu Avichail, an Israeli Orthodox rabbi, established one of the earliest organizations for retrieving "lost Jews." This was the same period in which the religious Zionist movement in Israel was confronting the issue of the new territories that had been conquered in the 1967 war.[5] Even earlier, in the 1940s and 1950s, various organizations appeared in Israel devoted to locating lost tribes and helping them move to Palestine/Israel.[6] Avichail's organization was called Amishav, meaning "my nation is returning" or "my people are returning." Amishav and its successor organization Shavei Israel ("Israel Returns"), founded by Michael Freund in 2004, both highlighted the idea of "return" in their names, presumably referring to the "return" of Jews both to traditional Judaism and to inclusion in the Jewish people. The additional agenda of both organizations was that the lost people of Israel must be located so that they can return *not only* to Judaism and the Jewish people *but also* to their ancestral home, the reborn country of Israel.

At its outset, Amishav received encouragement and support from Rabbi Zvi Yehuda Kook, the leader of the newly formed Gush Emunim. Gush Emunim promoted a messianic view of settlement in what it called "Greater Israel" (Israel proper plus the newly occupied territories) as part of a divine plan for the ultimate redemption of the Jewish people. Part of that redemption would involve the ingathering of Jews who had been dispersed throughout the world back to Israel and their settlement in the newly acquired territories, known in the group by the biblical names Judea and Samaria. Like Gush Emunim, Amishav and Shavei Israel were grounded in a religious Zionist ideology and the conviction that gathering exiled Jews from throughout the world also furthers the divine plan for the Jewish people and hastens their final messianic redemption. Thus the recognition of lost tribes was less about the groups themselves than it was seen as evidence of divine prophecies being fulfilled.

Recognition as Resocialization

The prospect of the return of potentially millions of lost Jewish souls living in Afghanistan, Pakistan, India, Burma, Ethiopia, and elsewhere to Israel where they can join the ranks of religious Zionists has represented a particularly exciting and urgently important mission for organizations like Amishav and Shavei Israel. It is not at all important whether people recognized as "lost Jews" have always lived or identified as Jews. In fact, they generally have not. Rather, there may be a variety of other indicators, such as names and words in their languages that sound like Hebrew, ritual practices like circumcision, or dietary rules that seem Jewish.[7] They may appear to have lighter skin or Semitic features (such as "Jewish noses") that set them apart from the other non-white, non-European groups in the area. Such factors are often described as evidence of the presence of a "Jewish soul," a timeless preexisting essence that establishes Jewish status even in the absence of any prior awareness of its presence. These factors are not sufficient to justify *full recognition* as Jews but rather are a necessary precondition to begin the process of returning to Judaism and to Israel.

Groups that were identified by Amishav or Shavei Israel as "lost Jews" received a crash course to bring them up to speed with contemporary forms of traditional Jewishness. They were encouraged to learn Hebrew and Orthodox Jewish beliefs and practices, to undergo Orthodox conversion, and ultimately to immigrate to Israel, where they could contribute to God's plan of redemption by settling in religious Zionist communities in "Greater Israel." Their current cultural practices and religious traditions might have been interpreted as residues of ancient Jewish practice, but they were also seen as having been garbled over time or buried under overlays of Christian, Muslim, or other religious traditions. So there was little need to preserve or recognize the actual cultural and religious experience that characterized the group's history for generations. Clearly, this is quite different from the multicultural approach to recognizing devalued or underappreciated practices and identities of marginalized groups in society. Amishav and Shavei Israel recognized only a distant origin myth of Jewish descent that was the basis for the group's claim to Jewish religion and culture regardless of their other cultural connections.

According to a small note at the bottom of Shavei Israel's mission statement, "Our work is in complete accordance with Jewish Law and under the ongoing supervision of the Chief Rabbinate of the State of Israel."[8] Recognition in this context is primarily a religious matter consisting of Orthodox authentication of Jewish status and final confirmation by Israel's chief rabbinate. The involvement of Israel's chief rabbis makes clear that the final outcome of the process of recognition includes not only return to Judaism and return to the people of Israel but also return to the land of Israel. Having this rabbinic certification of Jewish status also insulates organizations like Shavei Israel from the morally complicated issue of missionizing among these remote groups, a criticism to which they often have been subjected. They insist that their organization "does not proselytize nor does it support any form of missionary activity."[9] Since many candidates for lost tribe status were in fact already exposed to, and even converted by, Christian missionaries during the previous two centuries, Shavei Israel wanted to establish that its work was not an updated Jewish version of the same mission of civilizing the natives by introducing them to biblical beliefs and practices. Shavei Israel emphasized that helping people "return" to the Jewish people "does not and should not involve coercion or compulsion." On the contrary, the organization merely "opens the door to all who have decided that Judaism and a return to the Jewish people are central to their fate and their identity."[10]

Shavei Israel was also aware that bringing "lost Jews" to Israel at a time of dwindling numbers of other Jews immigrating to Israel was an important tool in the demographic race with the non-Jewish Arab inhabitants of Israel. Beyond just adding to the religious Zionist population of Israel, these "lost Jews" were recognized as direct descendants of the original Jewish inhabitants of Israel, thereby providing a powerful counterargument to the recognition of any Palestinian claims to land in Israel. Such recognition was expected to either erase or take precedence over other identities that lost Jews might have.

What made these groups authentically Jewish was nothing fixed or stable but merely an identity-grounding narrative that both they and Jewish representatives accepted as a framework for reconstructing their identities as Jews. Their Jewishness came into existence at the moment this mutual recognition and understanding occurred.

The Bene Israel of India

The Bene Israel are a group of Jews from western India who were "discovered" in the eighteenth century and who have been the subject of considerable research and some controversy regarding their origins and the revival of their awareness of themselves as Jews and their practice of Judaism. The majority of them immigrated to Israel after the creation of the state, though a sizeable community of Bene Israel still remains in Mumbai. Like other newly discovered Jews, the Bene Israel offers an excellent example of the process by which a group's claim to Jewish roots becomes established, an origin story becomes accepted, and their authenticity as Jews is recognized, or not, by other Jews, Jewish organizations, and the state of Israel.

The Bene Israel did not always use this name to describe their community, and for a long time, they were known simply as members of a lower caste in India called the "Shanwar Telis" or "Saturday Oil Pressers."[11] The process that transformed the Shanwar Telis into the Bene Israel can be described in relation to two very different kinds of narratives. In the most popular narrative, the one told by the Bene Israel themselves, the Bene Israel are direct descendants of a small group of Israelites stranded in India who, despite having lost or forgotten most of their original religious knowledge, retained clues of their origins in ancient Israel. It is a familiar story embraced by other newly discovered Jews that focuses on the dispersion of Jews long ago into remote areas where they became isolated from the rest of the Jewish world for centuries. Clinging to fragments of their Jewish or Israelite roots against all odds, they then were miraculously rediscovered by the outside Jewish world, thanks to which they were finally able to reunite with the world community of Jews.

A very different kind of narrative looks at the Bene Israel not through the lens of Jewish history but rather as an intriguing case of a small group of people in India who became increasingly identified with Judaism and Jewishness only in the last two and a half centuries as a result of a series of encounters with outsiders, both Jewish and non-Jewish.[12] This story tracks the changes that transformed the Shanwar Telis from a low-status Indian caste into an urban, educated, westernized Jewish group. In response to such outside contact, the Shanwar Telis may have been receptive to interpreting rituals and traditions derived from Hinduism and Islam as vestiges of their original Israelite religion. This process of increasing self-recognition of their Jewishness in conjunction with recognition of their Jewishness by others created a complicated relationship to their preexisting Indian identity. If the Bene Israel were really Israelites who had arrived from abroad long ago, then to what degree did they also understand themselves to be Indians and wish to be seen as such by others? The official story of their origins implied that the Indian part of their identity was just a veneer over their original Israelite identities.

By the end of the eighteenth century, the first Bene Israel synagogue had been completed in Bombay, but there still remained an overall lack of knowledge of Jewish history and scripture among the Bene Israel. Their lack of any awareness of rabbinic Judaism was taken as confirmation of the antiquity of the Bene Israel community, supposedly dating back to pre-rabbinic times in Israel but lacking any connection to Judaism since then. As they were gradually brought in line with modern Orthodox Judaism during the early nineteenth century, their sense of being Jews as well as their recognition as Jews by others strengthened. Over time, the Jewish identity of the Bene Israel became more "modernized, westernized and Hebrewized" at the same time that their sense of connection to Indian culture weakened and became less and less important.[13]

Every historical account of the Bene Israel routinely starts by explaining the absence of any specific evidence about the possible origins of the Bene Israel from outside of India or the length of time that they may have lived in western India. Their origins remain "shrouded in legend"[14] and "shrouded in mystery."[15] Such typical references to both legend and mystery as the shrouds that obscure any kind of reliable information about the Bene Israel are significant since they flag two interconnected elements—the absence of real evidence to resolve this mystery and the emergence of a variety of imaginative narratives that have been embraced by the Bene Israel themselves as well as by Jewish and non-Jewish outsiders who have encountered and studied them.

Although a variety of stories and theories have been offered about the arrival of the Bene Israel in India, dating it anytime from the tenth century BCE to the last millennium, the stories themselves are not nearly that old. Virtually all the speculation about and interaction with the Bene Israel has occurred only within the last 250 years. The process of reconstructing the Bene Israel's Jewish roots as well as the Bene Israel's self-discovery of themselves as Jews has involved a process that is less about uncovering specific evidence of the group's buried past and more about the central importance served by origin stories as the means of authenticating newly emerging claims of Jewish identity.

In this case, the authenticity of the Bene Israel's Jewishness was not a fixed and stable quality or characteristic that has persisted unchanged over time, nor was it something that rested on some kind of historical verification of their story. Rather, their authenticity as Jews was generated in the interactions between the Bene Israel and the outside world. If the people who were to become known as the Bene Israel had not encountered these various outside groups, the question of their authenticity as Jews would never have come up, nor would this particular origin story have become so widely accepted.

One of the earliest examples of the traditional approach to the origins of the Bene Israel community can be found in Haeem Samuel Kehimkar's *History of the Bene Israel in India*. Kehimkar (1831–1907) was himself a member of the Bene Israel community and a lifelong advocate of Jewish religious education and the study of Hebrew for Bene Israel children. According to the book's preface, Kehimkar completed his manuscript around 1897, but it was not until forty years later that Immanuel Olsvanger, a scholar of Jewish folklore and a Zionist activist who had emigrated to Israel in 1933, obtained the manuscript from the author's family in India and arranged for its publication in Jerusalem in 1937. In his preface to the book, Olsvanger addresses the Bene Israel community directly and tells them that the Jewish world

> will always remember with admiration and gratitude that you kept alive the torch of Judaism with a heroism and fortitude unparalleled by any other branch of our ancient and ever young nation. True, amidst the tolerant and hospitable people of India, you have never been subjected to any persecutions. But for nearly 2000 years you have lived in that country without any concrete symbol of our faith. Faint recollections of inherited customs have been your only guides. There was however that sentence never forgotten by you: "Hear O Israel, God our Lord, God is One."
>
> You have found, after having come into contact with the rest of Jewry, a wonderful synthesis between the ancient civilizations of Israel and India, and for that you are to be congratulated.[16]

Written at a time of accelerating antisemitism in Europe and the growing threat of Nazism, Olsvanger's praise offered a fascinating, and in some ways contradictory, combination of elements in the narrative of the Bene Israel, which were held up in contrast to the experience of Western Jews. He described their "heroism and fortitude" as "unparalleled" by other groups of Jews, while at the same time he acknowledged India as a tolerant country with no history of persecution of Jews.

Where exactly is the need for heroism when living among the "tolerant and hospitable people of India"? Perhaps it lay in the Bene Israel's resistance to assimilation and integration with the local population. As a result, they were able to retain an ember of their Jewish background, a single sentence emblematic of their Jewish faith, even when most of it has been forgotten.

According to the Bene Israel tradition, their original ancestors fled Palestine sometime in the second century BCE and were shipwrecked on the Konkan Coast, not far from Bombay (Mumbai). The fourteen survivors of the shipwreck swam or were washed to shore, where they collapsed. In some versions, they were miraculously revived on the shore by the prophet Elijah. These survivors, the seven founding couples of the Bene Israel community, settled in a nearby village and became established in the oil-pressing business, as a result of which they were known as the "Shanwar Telis," the oil-pressers who abstain from work on Saturday.

The story has the familiar feel of a founding myth linking a group to the dramatic story of their earliest ancestors from the distant past. There is little, if any, actual historical evidence to substantiate the story, or even any records of the presence of the Bene Israel as a Jewish group in India much before the eighteenth century.[17] The Bene Israel origin story serves a number of purposes. It establishes a connection to ancient Israelites and ancient Israel at the same time that it also explains the absence of any significant knowledge of Judaism, especially in the forms into which it has developed in the rest of the world. Cut off from other Jews for two thousand years, the Bene Israel simply "forgot" most of their ancient Jewish religion, with the exception of a few things such as circumcision, dietary laws, and Sabbath restrictions that outsiders were able to identify as having a Jewish, or at least biblical, basis. However, the fact that the Bene Israel have lived for thousands of years in India does not mean that their deepest identity is rooted there. Indianness is secondary to the kernel of Jewishness that has been preserved and passed on for centuries. This miraculous example of the primordial power of Jewish identity to persevere for centuries, even in the isolation of an alien culture, is one that has proven quite popular among Western Jews.

The transformation of the Bene Israel into Jews who practiced Judaism according to the standards of Western Jews brought greater interest and attention to their community, but it also resulted in increased questioning of their origin story and their claimed descent from ancient Israelites. For those who found the Bene Israel's story unsubstantiated, if not implausible, it was easier to imagine the Bene Israel as a small Indian community that had been encouraged to identify themselves as Jews and who had adopted the Jewish practices they had been taught. The questioning of their authenticity as Jews produced heated exchanges in Indian newspapers in the latter part of the nineteenth century between those questioning the Bene Israel's "purity" and Bene Israel leaders and supporters offering their own rebuttals.[18]

Many of the challenges to the Jewishness of the Bene Israel came from the Baghdadi Jews, who had only recently settled in India from Iraq and other Arab countries. Unlike the Bene Israel, who had been part of Indian culture for centuries and who looked and acted very much like other Indians, the Baghdadi Jews were lighter-skinned than the native Indian population, and they neither considered themselves to be real Indians nor desired to assimilate with Indian culture.[19] As the Baghdadi Jews became increasingly westernized and identified with the British, they did not want to be associated with non-white native Indian groups like the Bene Israel. Their effort to distinguish themselves from the Bene Israel, whose Jewish authenticity they questioned, was rooted in an implicit sense of racial superiority, which became manifest in accusations that the Bene Israel's Jewishness was "impure." The Bene Israel were as dark as other Indians, they charged, either because of earlier intermarriages with Hindu women, whose children were not really Jewish according to Jewish religious law, or because the Bene Israel were simply an Indian group who had informally decided to adopt Judaism.[20] Thus the Baghdadi Jews challenged the Bene Israel's authenticity on two fronts, both racial and religious. The Bene Israel looked like Indians, not Israelites, and their knowledge and practice of Judaism was flawed and incomplete.

Defenders of the Bene Israel reasserted the unquestioned authenticity of the Bene Israel as "direct descendants of the Hebrews who lived in Palestine about 2000 years ago."[21] The fact that the Bene Israel's racial characteristics appear more Indian than Israelite was attributed to the impact of the different climate, housing, food, and clothing in India compared to ancient Israel.[22] This was no different from northern European Jews becoming as white as the people among whom they live. It was also said that careful observers would still be able to pick out features in the faces of the Bene Israel that resembled Jews from Jerusalem and elsewhere in the Middle East.[23]

The twentieth century brought a dramatic upheaval in the Bene Israel community in the period after World War II, when both India and Israel gained independence from Britain within a year of each other. Initially, the Bene Israel had not been particularly interested in political Zionism or the idea of moving to Palestine, but as the political situation in India changed, many of the Bene Israel left the country, with most of them joining the flood of Jews returning to the new Jewish state. Some Bene Israel were prescient in worrying that objections about their religious status that had been raised by Baghdadi Jews would be revived.[24]

The experience of the Bene Israel in Israel is a dramatic example of the instability of recognition of their Jewishness by other Jews and the impact of that instability on attitudes toward their Jewish authenticity. Throughout their history, recognition of their Jewishness has wavered and been challenged, and questions about their "purity" as Jews that had been raised by the Baghdadi Jews in India in the nineteenth century resurfaced in Israel in the 1960s. Although the chief Ashkenazi rabbis in Israel had declared in 1944 that the Bene Israel were legitimately Jewish according to the standards of Jewish law, new concerns were raised by the Sephardi chief rabbi of Israel, a Baghdadi Jew named Itzhak Nissim, in 1960.[25]

The chief rabbi was responding to the long-standing charges that there was a distinct possibility of intermarriage in the past between the Bene Israel and non-Jews. If so, the Jewish status of the children of such marriages would be in doubt, and other Jews in Israel needed to be warned about marrying them.[26] What was presented as a dispute over Jewish law and the requirements for official Jewish status was also clearly about the "purity" of the Bene Israel, that is to say, about their racial history. When confronted with the Indian-looking Bene Israel, there were those who could not recognize, literally, the faces of the Bene Israel as Jewish. The debate over Bene Israel purity and the struggle to establish the authenticity of Bene Israel as Jews continued for four years. After extensive lobbying, protests, hunger strikes, and adverse publicity about the discriminatory nature of the rabbinic ruling, the Bene Israel were recertified as authentic Jews who could be married by other Jews. With public opinion clearly in favor of the Bene Israel, Prime Minister Levi Eshkol declared the Bene Israel worthy of recognition as "Jewish in all respects without qualification, no different from all other Jews and having equal rights, including those of personal status. . . . You are our brethren; to us you are the people of Israel."[27]

Unlike some earlier responses to the charge of racial impurity in the Bene Israel because of their physical resemblance to non-Jewish Indians, defenders of the Bene Israel, such as Benjamin Israel, did not attempt to discern any telltale Jewish physical features among the Bene Israel. Rather, he insisted that the notion of some normative set of Jewish racial qualities was an illusion. From the very start, he said, the Jews were not a "distinct race" but a "mixed people," and they inevitably continued to mix with local people wherever they lived: "Today, Jews display almost every physical characteristic that may be found in the nations among which they have dealt, and it should be no matter of surprise for an Indian Jew to resemble in many ways non-Jewish Indians rather than English or Russian Jews."[28] Benjamin Israel attempted to undermine the idea of a recognizable Jewish racial identity against which authenticity must be measured. He did this by tweaking the origin story of the Jews to one that includes racial mixture from the outset and assumes its continuation throughout Jewish history.

Benjamin Israel's defense of the authenticity of the Bene Israel does not treat their Indianness, either culturally or racially, as something that dilutes or compromises their authenticity as Jews. Rather, he implies that hybridity is itself the authentic characteristic of Jews from the beginning. From this perspective, Jews participate in forms of Jewishness that reflect the cultural values, food, music, and language of the places where they are living. It is no surprise that the generations of Bene Israel who have been born and raised in Israel still want to hold onto their Indianness in Israel, in terms of embracing their Indian ethnic identity, Indian cultural values, food, music, literature, theatre, and Marathi language.

The hybridity of Jewishness and Hindu or Indian cultural elements has been mentioned as a concern that might impact the Jewish authenticity of the Bene Israel in the eyes of some critics. While there is nothing unusual about Jewish communities absorbing local cultures, this process usually goes unnoticed in regard to European Jews, whose traditions and culture have clearly been influenced by the wider European culture. The declaration of the chief rabbi in 1964 about the authenticity of the Bene Israel heritage did not settle this issue, and questions continue to be raised about how people who look and dress like non-Jewish Indians could actually be from families who can trace their Jewish background back hundreds of years, at the very least.

In a recent study of Indian Jews who have settled in Toronto, the same questions about Bene Israel authenticity raised in India by the Baghdadi Jews in the nineteenth century were still being raised by white Canadian Jews, who struggled to understand "how Jews could be both Indian and brown." Bene Israel members reported that they were treated as "inferior and inauthentic Jews," and they continually had to demonstrate that they were "'real' Jews and not Hindu or Muslim Indians who had converted."[29] Origin stories that are part of Indian Jewish history and tradition receive less attention or credibility in places where the dominant version of Jewish history is Ashkenazi. Groups like the Bene Israel face the dilemma of either holding onto their Indian Jewish identities and traditions and struggling for acceptance and recognition in the white Ashkenazi world that questions the Jewish authenticity of Indian food, music, or customs or replacing their original cultural traditions from India with Ashkenazi customs and traditions in order to fit in and be recognized within the Ashkenazi Jewish world.[30]

The tendency to define Jewish authenticity primarily in terms of notions of peoplehood that presume common ancestry leads to an unfortunate and inevitable binary choice regarding the Jewish origin stories embraced by newly found Jews like the Bene Israel. Acceptance of the Jewish authenticity of the group becomes dependent on acceptance of the literal historical accuracy of the origin story. That is, if one accepts the story of Israelite shipwreck survivors from two thousand years ago as the progenitors of the Bene Israel, then a genealogical link has been established as a prima facie case for authenticity, even when evidence of continuous Jewish identification or practice is lacking. Jewishness becomes a biological essence that survives even in the absence of any self-awareness of Jewishness, Jewish faith, or Jewish practice.

On the other hand, there is often reasonable doubt that can be raised about the historical evidence for such origin stories and alternative explanations of how and when identification with the Jewish people may have begun. This leaves us with the question of whether Jewish authenticity claims must be withdrawn in cases where origin stories are questionable. If the origin story of the Bene Israel or the Beta Israel or Black Hebrews is lacking in reliable evidence, does that preclude the possibility of their being recognized as authentically Jewish by the rest of the world Jewish community? For mainstream Western Jews, origin stories are normally accepted without question or hesitation, even though specific individuals probably cannot provide evidence of their own family's ties to an ancient Jewish community.

Origin stories, whether they deal with the creation of the first human beings or just the origin of one's own specific group, are one of the standard ingredients in any group's identity. Authenticity is best seen not as a fixed quality that a person or a group has or does not have; this assumes that authenticity is determined in the past and merely discovered in the present. Authenticity, understood as feeling like a real member of a group and being recognized by others as one, is a fluid process that reflects the stories a person or group constructs to connect them to the group and, equally important, the forms of recognition that these constructions receive from others.

The Tribe of Menashe

In parts of Burma and northeast India, certain members of the Mizo or Shinlung tribes now consider themselves to be descendants of the lost Israelite tribe of Menashe. These people are from an area that was frequented by Protestant missionaries in the nineteenth century, at which time most of them were converted to Christianity. It was probably from these Christian sources that local groups learned about the Old Testament and some Hebrew words, the adventures of the Israelites, and the story of the ten lost tribes.

In 1951, not long after the creation of the modern state of Israel, a Mizo minister had a vision in a dream in which the Holy Spirit told him that the Mizo were really Jews from a lost tribe and were supposed to return to Israel, their ancestral home. At this point, many of them began to follow biblical laws and customs. Over the next twenty years, they adopted more and more Jewish practices, established synagogues and Jewish schools, and began to identify themselves as Jews. In other words, the dream about descent from a lost tribe initiated a process in which they were involved not so much in uncovering a dormant or lost identity as much as using that idea as the basis for constituting a new one, often based on rituals and traditions introduced by Jewish visitors. In a real sense, they became a lost Jewish tribe when they began to act like how they thought Jews should act.

The fact that the association of local groups with stories of lost tribes occurs in remote areas visited by westerners and missionaries obviously raises questions of whether recognizing these people as lost Jews is an important acknowledgment of who they "really are" or rather a misrecognition through European Christian lenses that negates these groups' authentic identities. It is likewise possible to recognize their self-identification as Jews as a newly constructed identity while suspending judgment about the literal historical claims made. Or perhaps there is a third possibility that avoids the usual binary options for validating these claims.

From the perspective of mainstream Jews, when the Jewishness of a remote group is recognized, their previous group or cultural identities are either erased or delegitimized. Residual inflections of Jewishness through these other cultural backgrounds sometimes serve to exoticize their Jewishness and other times are seen as illegitimate. Sometimes it is unwanted syncretism that needs to be uprooted and eliminated, but sometimes they are celebrated as part of the diversity and multiculturality of Jews.

The construction of the Mizos' new cultural identity received a tremendous boost when Amishav's Rabbi Avichail visited the group and identified the Mizo as "B'nei Menashe," members of the tribe of Menashe. Avichail was convinced that the name of the legendary founder of the Mizo people, Manmasi, was a corruption of the biblical tribe named Menashe, so he dubbed them B'nei Menashe, provided them with Bibles, Torahs, and other religious items, and prepared them to convert to Orthodox Judaism. Amishav's representatives insisted that certain Mizo customs predated their involvement with Christianity and were reminiscent of a festival like Passover. Like the Christian missionaries before them, Amishav's group was primed to see and hear residues of biblical names, words, and practices in Mizo customs. This recognition was not welcomed by all members of these tribes, and some pointedly reject the idea that there are descendants of the lost tribes among them.

Nevertheless, for those increasingly committed to their recognition as descendants of lost tribes, a unique Mizo story of exile emerged that described a long path of wandering from Assyria to Afghanistan, as far east as China and Vietnam, and eventually back to their present location in Myanmar and India. Like many of the newly discovered lost tribes, these were poor people for whom the idea of noble ancestry and a divine plan that would bring them to the new state of Israel may have proved very appealing.[31] Rabbi Avichail proceeded to convert the Mizo to Orthodox Judaism and then lobbied both for their recognition by the state of Israel as a lost tribe and for permission for them to immigrate to Israel. By 1989, Avichail persuaded the Israeli government to allow some of the Mizo to travel to Israel, where nearly a thousand of them eventually settled in religious settlements in Israel's occupied territories.

For members of the B'nei Menashe, recognition by Amishav and Israeli rabbinic authorities validated their belief in the inner core of their Jewishness, even in the absence of any knowledge about Judaism. This became their real, true, authentic self and the basis for acquiring more normatively Jewish identities. In this new identity narrative, the practice of Christian and other non-Jewish traditions for generations leading up to their claim of Jewish identity was dismissed as a foreign influence that had nothing to do with who they really are. Following their recognition as descendants of the tribe of Menashe provided by Rabbi Avichail and ultimately by the chief rabbi in Israel, it became easier for additional members to abandon Christianity and for the group to construct a new Jewish sense of self based on descent from Menashe's tribe.

Of course, the Jewish identity of the Mizo was mostly a modern invention, nurtured by Orthodox rabbis who encouraged the idea that the Orthodox Judaism adopted by the B'nei Menashe was directly connected to the original Judaism of the ancient Israelites. Their story, like those of other newly found and newly observant Jews, offers a deeply appealing account of the persistence of Jewish faith in some form, despite thousands of years of exile from the rest of the Jewish people, and their return to their ancestral home. When Michael Freund, head of Shavei Israel, visited the B'nei Menashe in 2002, he saw men wearing kippot and tzitzit and women with long sleeves and head coverings—that is, he saw a community dressed like Orthodox Jews, as well as singing Hebrew songs and waving Israeli flags. To see the B'nei Menashe observing Orthodox traditions in a new Jewish center built by Israelis or listening to Israeli music may strike some people as no more an authentic expression of "who they really are" than the Christian identity they had accepted from Protestant missionaries during the British colonial period.[32] Still, regardless of the tenuous historical foundation for their connection to ancient Israelites, the Mizo's self-image as descendants of a lost tribe has taken root in their identity. Whatever happened in their past, they now see themselves and want to be seen as "real Jews."

As inspiring as many people find the devoted practice of traditional Judaism by the B'nei Menashe, the model of recognition offered by Amishav and Shavei Israel illustrates the problems when cultural or religious identity is defined in essentialist ways within a hierarchical model of authority. Shavei Israel's recognition of a Jewish soul in certain members of the Mizo took place within a hierarchical model of power that worked to preserve and reinforce the authority of Orthodox Jews in Israel and elsewhere as both the arbiters of Jewishness and the embodiment of authenticity that is most consistent with the biblical roots of the Jewish people. For the Mizo, the price of recognition was acceptance of a program of assimilation to a particular model of normative Judaism that would replace who they had always been with a newly constructed identity as "real Jews." Where is the authentic cultural identity of a group that was converted by Protestant missionaries during the British colonial period, introduced to Judaism and the Old Testament, taught about Judaism by Orthodox Israeli rabbis, and today have a Jewish center built by Israelis where they listen to Israeli music?[33]

Lost Tribes and Jewish Diversity

The American-based organizations that have supported the recognition of "lost Jews" emerge out of a somewhat different cultural context and ideological framework from the Israeli organizations. Organizations like Kulanu ("All of Us") and Be'chol Lashon ("In Every Language") developed later than the original Israeli Amishav organization against the background of (1) rising concerns in the American Jewish community about the impact of assimilation and intermarriage on Jewish communal survival, and (2) the growing American conversation in the mid-1990s on issues of multiculturalism and diversity. "Newly found" Jews were not important to them as potential candidates for Orthodox conversion and immigration to Israel or in contributing to a messianic ingathering of Jewish exiles. Rather, the fundamental issues of these groups related to the challenges confronting the American Jewish community and the realities of Jewish diversity. For those concerned about the long-term survival of a Jewish population decimated by genocide, assimilation, and intermarriage, the potential influx of these newly found Jews represents a possible, if partial, solution to repopulating the Jewish people.

In Spring 1994, Amishav USA became Kulanu. Founder and president Jack Zeller explained that while Kulanu continued to support Amishav's mission of helping "lost Jews" return to Judaism, there was also a need to reflect an "American agenda and diverse membership" that included "American Jews of varied backgrounds and practices." Zeller apparently was referring especially to denominational, rather than ethnic or racial, diversity, since he continued, "We also believe that some who seek to return to Judaism may not be on the road to a connection to 'traditional' Judaism. We think they deserve support as well."[34]

American Jewish organizations engaged in efforts to support Jews from Asia and Africa often made a connection between this work and what they saw as the crisis in the American Jewish community. In contrast to the diluted Jewish identity of American Jews, "lost Jews" were often portrayed with a seemingly indestructible Jewish identity, a kernel of which has managed to survive for centuries despite complete separation from the Jewish people. This mythic notion of Jewishness as an imperishable kernel that may be dormant, hidden, or forgotten but that sustains an unbreakable connection to the Jewish people offers an obvious consolation for those concerned about Jewish survival. One of Amishav USA's leaders, Karen Primack, made explicit the contrast between the imperiled condition of modern Jewish identity and the imputed strength of the Jewishness of newly found Jews:

> Yes, we all know we are losing Jews to intermarriage, to cults, to other religions, to indifference.... What I have come to appreciate, though, is the irony that allows many Jews to wring their hands in despair over the intermarriage rate and yet to ignore the plight of our cousins, shown by impressive scholarship to be from the Ten Lost Tribes, who have maintained their identity through 27 centuries of hardship. Many are practicing Jews eager to study further in Israel, and some to relocate there. They deserve at least as much attention—and financial support—as those who are leaving Judaism.[35]

Despite the lack of any real evidence that the groups in question had any awareness of themselves as Jews until the modern age, Primack constructed a narrative based on the lost tribes' continuous, tenacious commitment to Jewishness from biblical times until today. The recognition of lost Jews' authenticity and Jewish commitment in spite of centuries-long persecution and adversity created an idealized binary of authentic and inauthentic Jews. The newly found Jews were idealized as the repository or embodiment of a religious and ethnic commitment that had become weak and fractured in modern Jewish life, where Jews lived in comfort and security yet were quick to abandon Jewish religious practice.

Aside from their indestructible Jewish identities, lost Jews also provided the exotic appeal of premodern folk cultures and the aura of authenticity that they represent. They offered a glimpse of a romanticized view of a Jewish past that had long been symbolized by the Eastern European shtetl. Yet in the aftermath of the obliteration of that form of Jewish life by the Nazis and the Zionist focus on ancient Israel, living communities of lost Jews have a unique appeal: a connection to an even older period of Jewish history, or at least the premodern lifestyle associated with that period.

The candidates for lost tribes are themselves usually described as members of some ethnic "tribe." This immediately helps construct their identity as already tribal, in contrast to Jews in developed countries, who usually are described as being in "communities" rather than tribes (e.g., Ashkenazi community or Sephardi community). At the same time, Kulanu takes a nonjudgmental approach to origin stories or verifiable historical evidence of Jewish lineage and connection to early Israelites. They tend to emphasize the intensity of the devotion and sincerity of the beliefs of these communities, which are seen as inspiring to Western Jews.

Even when outsiders recognized new Jewish groups as authentic Jews and respected their local forms of Jewish practice, the process of recognition inevitably introduced to those groups other forms of Jewish practice and culture and reshaped their practice.[36] When local cultural and religious customs were integrated into new forms of emerging Judaism, they were creating new forms of Jewishness, just as other parts of the Jewish community have done throughout history. And when groups accepted new traditions from outside rabbis and other Jewish visitors, they felt they were only reclaiming what they had forgotten but was already theirs. So they had to invent and construct a new way of being Jewish in order to reclaim who they think they already were.[37]

In contrast to the approach of religious Zionist organizations like Amishav and Shavei Israel, where recognition of lost tribes also validated the authority and authenticity of Orthodox Jews, for the more liberal American organizations, the recognition of newly found Jews and the imagined persistence of their Jewishness in the face of conquest, exile, and life among strangers offer a counternarrative to the story of assimilation, abandoning of traditional religion, and intermarriage in modern Jewish life that has made it hard to recognize some Jews as Jewish anymore. In both cases, recognition is a reciprocal process that includes the co-construction of interconnected narratives of Jewish authenticity.

Recognition, Authenticity, and Heritage Tourism: The Case of the Abayudaya

The elements of recognition involved in the case of seven hundred or so Abayudaya Jews of Uganda are somewhat different from other groups of newly discovered Jews, since the involvement of the Abayudaya's involvement with Judaism can be dated very specifically to the early twentieth century rather than some hypothetical link to lost tribes of ancient Israel. The Abayudaya Jews began in the early twentieth century as a separatist sect based on the Hebrew Bible in rejection of the Christianity of British colonialists. In 1919, the group's leader, Semei Kakungulu, circumcised himself and his sons and declared the community the "Kibina Kya Bayudaya Absesiga Katonda (the Community of Jews who trust in the Lord)" or Abayudaya for short. Embracing Jewishness was a form of cultural resistance against the religion of the British empire, though it was a while until all Christian elements from the group's religion had been eliminated.

When their leader died, the group split into one group that continued certain Christian beliefs, including recognizing Jesus as the Messiah, while another group tried to become more traditionally Jewish. A group of young Abayudaya revived the dwindling movement in the 1970s and 1980s and sought support from Jews in Israel and the West. Like many such groups, they have been visited by Jews from Israel and the United States interested in their claims of Jewishness. As a result of these visits, they have adopted the major ingredients of traditional Jewish practice in regard to issues like circumcision, ritual slaughter, Sabbath observance, and ritual purity. In 2002, Kulanu sent a *bet din* of Conservative rabbis to Uganda to formally convert about six hundred of them.

Despite the Abayudaya's undisputed lack of a lengthy Jewish history or origin myth about the lost tribes of Israel, Jewish groups have nonetheless attributed a special kind of premodern authenticity to them that serves as a revitalizing force for modern Jews. When American and Israeli Jews first visited the Abayudaya, they were transported to a world where people who also claimed to be Jews lived in mud huts with no electricity or running water. Today, much of this has changed, as electricity and running water have become available, thanks to the help of Western Jewish organizations.

It is no surprise that communities of newly found Jews have become destinations of heritage tours that began to be marketed to Western Jews in the mid-1990s. Kulanu organized trips to Uganda to visit the Abayudaya and to various groups of lost Jews in India. Heritage tours to the Abayudaya offer a hybrid journey consisting of both traditional African village life and an overlay of modern Jewish practices that villagers have learned from Jewish emissaries sent by groups like Amishav and Kulanu. The Jewish content makes otherwise unfamiliar-looking people seem like distant relatives, while the premodern village life offers heritage tourists the feeling of authenticity of a world from another time and place.

This peculiar combination of ancient and modern was evident on a 1995 trip to the Abayudaya Jews when visitors reported a joyous welcome from "50 Africans singing *Hevenu Shalom Aleichem* and *Hava Nagila* accompanied by a guitar and the ululations of women."[38] The fact that these are well-known songs from modern Western Jewish culture, not from a hypothetical Israelite tribe, does not seem to diminish their appeal. They reflect the impact of increasing contact with American and Israeli Jews after the 1980s and their introduction of Hebrew and contemporary Jewish music and liturgy. This accommodation to the practices of Western Jewish visitors, such as singing popular Hebrew songs, serves to authenticate the Jewishness of the Abayudaya both to Western Jews and to the Abayudaya themselves.[39]

A few years later, the Abayudaya were already beginning to develop a more indigenous form of Jewish practice, which Kulanu made available on a DVD of Abayudaya versions of Jewish liturgy with African melodies and rhythms. Kulanu described it like this: "Imagine the *Siddur* set to the music of Paul Simon's 'Graceland' album, and you'll get some idea of the sound, as well as of how moving and entertaining that sound is. The group sounds much like Ladysmith Black Mambazo in its phrasings and tight harmonies, while the many female voices recall Sweet Honey in the Rock."[40] It is paradoxically the *Africanness* of the Abayudaya that gives a special authenticity to their *Jewishness*. White American Jews can now claim and enjoy this kind of African musical tradition as part of their own Jewish culture and incorporate it into services of Reform and Conservative Jews, who see it "less as an object of exotic interest than as potential sources of spiritual renewal, an opportunity to affirm the richness and inclusivity of Jewish culture."[41]

For the Abayudaya, Kulanu's recognition has meant an active participation in the construction, promotion, and institutionalization of Abayudaya Jewish culture. Kulanu offers an online "boutique" of crafts on behalf of the Abayudaya of Uganda and the B'nei Menashe of India that includes locally produced kippot, tallitot, and hallah covers, gift items that Western Jews are likely to purchase as examples of Jewish folk arts, despite the fact that these Jewish ritual items have been introduced to the Abayudaya only recently from the West and are now produced for sale back to Jews in the United States and elsewhere.

In recent years, organized trips to the Abayudaya Jews have become increasingly more elaborate. The 2004 trip included visits to six Abayudaya synagogues, arts and crafts demonstrations, tours to national parks and baboon sanctuaries, with optional white water rafting and gorilla wildlife safaris.[42] The following year, Kulanu formalized its marriage of heritage tourism and ecotourism with a trip marketed as "Jewish Life in Uganda, Wildlife Safari and Mitzvah Tour."[43] Responding to Western Jews' interest in their community has become a significant part of Kulanu's economic development plan for the Abayudaya, providing both resources and employment for the community. Recent Kulanu tours also include the annual Abayudaya Music and Dance Festival, which allows performers from villages to share their music, dance, and stories.[44] Unlike groups whose recognition of newly found Jews focuses on assimilation to Orthodox Judaism and immigration to Israel, Kulanu is committed to preserving and developing the local culture of newly found Jews. By providing an audience for Abayudaya cultural festivals and customers for their Jewish crafts, Kulanu moves beyond recognition to an actual partnership in the establishment of Abayudaya Jewish culture.

Jewish Diversity and Multicultural Recognition

Be'chol Lashon ("In Every Tongue") is an initiative of the San Francisco Jewish think tank Institute for Jewish and Community Research founded by Gary Tobin and Dianne Kaufmann-Tobin in 2000. While supporting outreach to many of the same groups of "lost Jews" as Amishav or Shavei Israel, appreciation of Jewish diversity and multiculturalism, not halakhically correct conversions, is Be'chol Lashon's primary goal. In its vision statement, Be'chol Lashon attempts to sidestep all the fraught debates regarding the essential ingredients necessary to be recognized as a Jew, halakhic or otherwise. Their focus is on constructing a diverse, multiracial understanding of the Jewish people, not an ingathering of Jews around a religious Zionist ideology nor a sentimental return to the tribal past: "Imagine a new global Judaism that transcends differences in geography, ethnicity, class, race, ritual practice, and beliefs. Discussions about 'who-is-a-real-Jew' will be replaced with celebration of the rich, multidimensional character of the Jewish people."[45] An earlier version of the organization's mission statement builds on multicultural themes of diversity, difference, and inclusion: "*Be'chol Lashon* (In Every Tongue) grows and strengthens the Jewish people through ethnic, cultural, and racial inclusiveness. We advocate for the diversity that has characterized the Jewish people throughout history, and through contemporary forces including intermarriage, conversion and adoption. We foster an expanding Jewish community that embraces its differences."[46]

As an organization whose top priorities are Jewish diversity and inclusion, their narrative of the origins of the Jewish people places multiculturalism at the moment of creation: "The historical home of the Jews lies at the geographic crossroads of Africa, Asia, and Europe. Jews are an amalgam of many peoples and Jewish origins include a multitude of languages, nations, tribes, and skin colors."[47] Absent in this narrative of Israelite history are any genealogical or familial metaphors emphasizing common descent from the sons of a single patriarchal ancestor. Instead, Be'chol Lashon offers an image of the Jewish past as both racially and culturally diverse at its core. We are reminded that Moses was married to Zipporah, an Ethiopian; Solomon and David had African wives; and Joseph married an Egyptian—that is, an African.[48] Thus Jewish roots are arguably as much or more in Africa than in Eastern Europe.

This multicultural origin myth of the Jewish people is offered as justification for the recognition of non-white Jews as an authentic element of the distant Jewish past and a necessary component to be recognized as part of the Jewish people today. Although it recognizes "newly found" Jews throughout the world, Be'chol Lashon insists that traveling to remote villages in Africa or Asia to find such Jews of color is unnecessary. Many "diverse Jews," as they are called by Be'chol Lashon, can be found within the United States. Be'chol Lashon supports the recognition of these Jews as part of an effort to reconstitute the Jewish people in a different way. This kind of recognition will help liberate Judaism from restrictive membership norms and help it become what Lewis Gordon describes as "post-denominational and pan-denominational, post-racial, and pan-racial. It is what Judaism has always been—we are a people."[49] Of course, it is not at all clear who and what determines the boundaries of a people like this, other than self-identification with it.

This recognition of the multiracial foundations of the Jewish people is part of Be'chol Lashon's deliberate agenda to challenge the default association of Jewishness with whiteness and Judaism with the rabbinic system of European Jews.[50] Unlike the strategy of Amishav, Be'chol Lashon's goal is not the education and socialization of diverse non-white Jews into rabbinic Orthodoxy. On the contrary, the recognition of lost Jews, particularly in Africa, presents the possibility of many different forms of Judaism and Jewish life that also deserve respect and appreciation. This perspective has the effect of decentering the assumed authenticity and legitimacy of mainstream Judaism by treating it as only one of several legitimate forms of Jewish expression.[51] Gary Tobin explains, "There has never been, nor likely will there be any single authentic Judaism.... Liturgy, ritual observance, and social interaction all change and evolve, and there has been tremendous latitude and variety among Jewish cultures over time and place, with ongoing reinterpretation and adjustment. Beliefs and activities come and go, institutions are created and abandoned, great bodies of knowledge consistently added to and reconfigured."[52]

For Be'chol Lashon, the Jewish people are a perfect symbol for the ideals of global inclusion, acceptance, and diversity. Having lived among people in all parts of the world and adapted and adopted elements of those cultures, including marrying those people, Jews are "a people that is composed of relatives from practically every branch of the human family."[53] From this perspective, recognition is a kind of cosmopolitan appreciation of diversity in contrast to the more common essentialist group identities that a politics of recognition is in danger of reifying.

Faced with the option of extending recognition to hundreds of thousands of people who, Be'chol Lashon insists, may be interested in becoming Jews, Gary Tobin asks, "Are we ready to welcome them? Are we ready to grow and change? Are we willing to become who we have always been?"[54] In this last question can be found the paradox of recognition for Be'chol Lashon. To open the Jewish people to a more fluid, dynamic approach to the definition of who is a Jew will make the process of recognition disorienting, tenuous, and uncomfortable. But only by doing that, he suggests, can Jews likewise experience the recognition of who "we have always been." If authenticity is a recognition of one's true identity, then the true identity that Jews must recognize is one that lacks a fixed essence or reality, one that always remains an uncertain process of becoming in which any rules or definitions are subject to constant revision over time.

Conflicting Models of Recognition

Comparing the various organizations that have been devoted to outreach to newly found Jews reveals very different ways in which the idea of recognition can operate. The goal of Amishav and Shavei Israel to restore lost Jews to their true identities pays homage to the romantic ideal of Johann Gottfried Herder, and more recently Charles Taylor, that we are morally obligated to recognize who people "really are" and to affirm them in their own authentic cultural identities. Yet in the case of newly found Jews, whose actual connection and embeddedness in Jewish culture is limited to an origin myth about events over two millennia ago, this idea of a "real self" becomes a kind of metaphysical Jewish essence that actually has little to do with the actual historical experience of these people in any meaningful sense. Rather, through a process of religious education and socialization, culminating in conversion to normative Orthodox Judaism, they are able to create new religious and cultural identities and gain recognition based on traditional European rabbinic Judaism mixed with messianic Israeli religious Zionism.

The insistence on an unchanging Jewish core identity—a Jewish soul, if you will—guides their process of recognition and understanding of modern Jewish life. The essentialized Jewish identity ascribed to lost Jewish tribes by Amishav and Shavei Israel serves as a direct rejection of the fluidity and instability of postmodern Jewish identity. A sense of Jewishness that supposedly can survive for centuries despite its isolation from any other Jewish communities, that can resist all other cultural and religious influences and, at the appropriate moment, can resume authentic Jewish life in Israel offers a potent counternarrative not only to those who have abandoned strict Jewish religious practice but also to those who argue for more open-ended, flexible concepts of Jewishness today. It is, therefore, no surprise that Amishav and Shavei Israel may recognize some diversity in the origins of the Jewish people as reflected in the racial diversity of tribal groups of "newly found" Jews, but they offer no recognition of diverse ways of being Jewish, nor do they consider the potential openness of Jewish identity to change and transformation.

Kulanu's openness to greater flexibility in the denominational spectrum of Judaism as an option for newly found Jews, as well as an appreciation of some elements (mostly music and crafts) of the cultural diversity of these groups, reflects the greater autonomy offered by modern liberal forms of Judaism in constituting a Jewish identity. Nonetheless, there is no serious questioning of rabbinic Judaism as a cultural and religious system primarily developed among white European Jews. As a result, the recognition offered to newly found Jews remains tied to asymmetrical power relations that privilege an American denominational model of Jewishness.

The most expansive expression of Jewish diversity and the politics of recognition is found in Be'chol Lashon. Its agenda is to maximize the growth of the Jewish people by loosening the boundaries that exclude some people interested in being Jewish. There is little preoccupation with the intricacies of who is a Jew, concern with halakhic laws and rabbinic authorities functioning as gatekeepers, or focus on authenticity as a central characteristic of Jewishness. Rather, the priority placed on multicultural recognition as an open-ended process with a more welcoming attitude toward "diverse Jews" results in a redefinition of Jewishness that maximizes inclusion and deconstructs prevailing normative assumptions.

In this sense, Be'chol Lashon's understanding of Jewish identity avoids the pitfall of an essentialist assumption about a primordial Jewish core identity that defines one's real self. Rather, it offers recognition not only of different kinds of Jews and different ways of being Jewish but also of the dangers of reifying any single definition of Jewish identity. As Stuart Hall notes, a person's sense of her or his "real me" is a product of the narratives that she or he participates in constituting.[55] For this reason, recognition of any person's nationality, religion, or ethnicity is always to some degree a political act that remains "temporary, partial, and arbitrary."[56] But Hall also describes the need to acknowledge and accept "a politics in the recognition of the necessarily fictional nature of the modern self, and the necessary arbitrariness of the closure around the imaginary communities in relation to which we are constantly in the process of becoming 'selves.'"[57] It is a recognition that identity is always situated in relationship to culture, languages, and history but that those categories themselves are also changing and impermanent.

For Be'chol Lashon, the recognition of newly found Jews is a necessary part of creating a truly multicultural Jewish people. Whether they are actually members of some lost tribe of Jews is less important than the metaphorical power of this narrative. In its own way, the gathering of the lost tribes back into the Jewish people represents Be'chol Lashon's own redemptive narrative of an expanding Jewish people that welcomes all groups who feel lost and want to be welcomed into a group where they can feel that they belong.

Conclusion

In December 2019, President Donald Trump issued an executive order on "Combating Antisemitism," aimed in particular at curbing anti-Israel activism on college campuses. It did so by interpreting antisemitism as a potential violation of Title VI of the 1964 Civil Rights Act, which prohibits discrimination on the basis of race, color, or national origin. Anti-Israel activism, including the BDS ("Boycott, Divestment, and Sanction") movement, even if coming from Jews themselves, is presented as an attack on the nation of Israel, the self-proclaimed homeland of the Jewish people. According to this reasoning, it is therefore an attack on the Jewish people as a whole, including American Jews, not on account of their religion (which isn't protected under the Civil Rights Act), but on the basis of nationality. The Jewish people constitute a nationality because, according to biblical narratives, they were all once part of the ancient nation of Israel.

Although some American Jews appreciated this official condemnation of antisemitism, many others voiced concern at the order's definition of Jews as either a distinct nationality or a racial minority, neither of which may capture how most American Jews think of themselves. In doing so, the order illustrated a critical aspect in which Jewishness is at least partially constituted as a result of how Jews are "recognized" by others among whom they live. This was the controversial conclusion of Sartre's original analysis in *Antisemite and Jew* back in the 1940s, when he concluded that "the Jew is in the situation of a Jew because he lives in the midst of a society that takes him for a Jew."[1] Sartre was rightly criticized for minimizing the independent cultural and religious content of Jewishness apart from antisemitism, but his observations are a useful reminder of the role of *recognition*, or misrecognition, from non-Jews as constitutive of a very real dimension in how Jewishness is experienced.

By identifying Jews as a distinct race or nationality, the executive order inscribes an element of difference in American Jews that sets them apart from other Americans, which inadvertently reinforces part of the antisemitic worldview it is ostensibly intended to combat. In its simplest form, the definition of American Jews as a distinct race, nationality, or both presents Jews as a "people" in the essentialist tradition of Herder and modern nationalism, united by a connection to an ancestral language, culture, and homeland. It assumes that American Jewish support for Israel is a natural manifestation of Jewish patriotism, since Israel is their national homeland, while criticism of Israel is a form of ethnic and nationalist disloyalty. It ignores the diversity of opinions that Jews may hold about Israel and its political role in the world.

Jewish "Being" and Jewish "Nothingness"

The episode illustrates the persistence of the ethno-nationalist model of group identity and authenticity that Sartre attacked as a dangerous form of bad faith. His rejection of the underlying essentialism in this understanding of cultural or ethnic identity was greatly expanded and elaborated by the various antiessentialist critiques that developed in the feminist, social constructivist, and postcolonial theories in the latter part of the twentieth century. Of course, Sartre's critique was buried within his own complex philosophical system, much of which he had just laid out in his major philosophical work, *Being and Nothingness*. Without becoming entangled in the philosophical intricacies of that work, we can still use the two central terms in its title to recap the major approaches to defining authentically Jewish identities that have been discussed in the preceding chapters.

The philosophical tension between "being" and "nothingness" helps us see two very different ways of understanding identity and authenticity as well as people's cultural and nationalist sense of belonging. One way treats them as something firmly rooted in the world, as things that have weight, substance, fullness, and permanence. These characteristics are inherent or immanent within a person, simply parts of their essence or "being." The most important factor that determines Jewishness is out of one's direct control. It is a question of descent, or "roots," determined by the family, religion, and the ethnic group into which one is born.[2] Cultural identity based on this model emphasizes the sense of belonging to a group whose survival depends on ensuring the continuity from one generation to the next. The shape and boundaries of this identity are predetermined and predefined. There is an order that exists, as well as traditions and norms to which one must submit and conform.

Although people are attracted to the comfort and security they associate with the world of "being," it is a betrayal of one of the most important human characteristics—the ability to "uproot" themselves from the givenness of their lives (their "roots") and redefine their inherited roles, models, and values. It is the freedom and power to recreate meaning, reexamine values, and redirect the central narratives through which they understand their lives. This realization that meaning, identity, and authenticity are never permanently fixed, never a predetermined "thing" or being is the realization of "nothingness," the power of consciousness to break the spell of what already is, of being, and to narrate its own restless movement. When what is authentically Jewish is seen through the lens of being, it enjoys the aura of permanence and stability. When what is authentically Jewish is seen through the lens of nothingness, meaning is indeterminate, in process, unfolding over time, negotiable, coming into focus and then dissolving as something new emerges.

The challenge of all cultural identities is to manage the dialectic between "being" and "nothingness." To the extent that individuals and cultures are continually moving beyond where and what they have been in the past, there is an ongoing tension between continuity and discontinuity with the past. There is always a degree of slippage between the received cultural traditions and the way they are carried forward into the future. As they are reinterpreted, reintegrated, or rejected, what is authentically Jewish is always in a process of becoming. Stated in the Zenlike form of existentialism, this means that who and what the Jewish people *really are* is who and what they *are not* (yet). The reason that people are continually engaged in a search for authenticity, despite glimpses of it in their life experiences and relationships, is not because authenticity is an elusive entity concealed in the deepest recesses of their own selves. Rather, it is because authenticity describes an ongoing process that unfolds in time and history, describable but not contained only in terms of where it has been yet already moving forward toward what is not completely foreseeable.

To be authentically Jewish is to realize the "authentic" meaning of Jewishness, to understand that whatever comfort, meaning, and security "being Jewish" provides today already exists in a world of change where grasping too tightly on meanings forged in the past gives birth to essentialism and inauthenticity. The coherence of an individual's sense of self, as well as the identity of the group with whom they identify, is always provisional and emergent. It is both built on their past and present situation yet also freely transcends any permanent or fixed essence. It is not confined or limited by its point of origin, but rather it is continually reinterpreted in ever-widening spirals of new meanings that are pulled in different directions based on the gravitational pull of other dimensions of identity and the world around them.

Diaspora and Hybridity

Although many of the groups described in this book appeal to the essentialist myths of ancestral tribes, chosen people, and promised lands as the foundation of Jewish identity and the rationale for Jewish traditions, Sartre suggested that the nothingness of consciousness is also mirrored in the experience of the Jews. He took the Jewish experiences of homelessness, exile, and dispersion as metaphors for universal existential themes. This included the observation that the mystery of human consciousness, which includes the sense of a cohesive self without a permanent core at its center, is a "diasporic" phenomenon, analogous to the diaspora experience of the Jewish people, who feel a sense of cohesion despite the absence of a common essence uniting them.[3] There are real experiences of individual, religious, and ethnic identity, which are crucial to people's sense of security and belonging in the world, but their stability is also to some degree an illusion that obscures their own fragility.

Other theorists have also appealed to the concept of diaspora as a model for challenging essentialist cultural identities. According to Jonathan and Daniel Boyarin, the Jewish experience of diaspora emphasizes its nonattachment to fixed traditions and places. Jewish identity, they suggest, is best understood "not as a proud resting place . . . but as a perpetual, creative, diasporic tension."[4] Just like the continual process of uprooting from the rootedness of one's situation that Sartre described, the essence of Jewishness is to uproot all claims of essence. The Boyarins write, "Jewishness disrupts the very categories of identity."[5] Cultural theorist Paul Gilroy likewise has invoked the concept of diaspora as an antiessentialist antidote to the illusion of cultural identity as stable and bounded. Diasporas, Gilroy suggests, produce identities that are "creolized, syncretized, hybridized, and chronically impure cultural forms."[6] They are produced not by a fixation on specific "roots" but rather on the "routes" to the present and the transcultural and transnational encounters they involved. Such routes maintain a sense of continuity with the past while they also remain open to new movements, encounters, and changes in the future.[7]

The Jewish experience of diaspora, argues Jonathan Freedman in *Klezmer America*, was not one of purity, essence, and boundaries. On the contrary, it has been characterized by "relentless and even definitional hybridity."[8] Freedman argues that klezmer is a "resolutely impure cultural form" that is a microcosm of the Jewish experience of diaspora life, where Jews were called on "to engage in a syncretic, hybridizing engagement with a national culture in ways that transform both their own identity and experience and that of the culture at large."[9] Jews now contain a variety of races, cultures, sexualities, and philosophies.

The diaspora model's focus on *routes* rather than *roots* redirects the search for what is authentically Jewish in a new direction. The traditional paradigm sees the Jewish people as "a people apart" that has persevered in the face of hostility in their host countries and preserved their cultural heritage and community by remaining insulated and isolated from the surrounding cultures where they lived. According to this perspective, when the boundaries between Jews and non-Jews were lowered in the modern world, authentic Jewish life became weakened and eroded.

In a new paradigm for Jewish identity and authenticity, there is a recognition that boundaries between Jews and non-Jews have always allowed some degree of cultural mixing and cross-fertilization. Evidence of the resulting "hybridity" has become a new touchstone for Jewish authenticity. As discussed in previous chapters, klezmer music, Israeli folk dance, Jewish yoga and meditation, and many of the newly found Jews all demonstrate different degrees of cultural mixing and hybridity. Mixing between Jews and non-Jews is not confined to cultural exchange. It also involves increasingly heterogeneous personal histories and roots in multiple communities. Poet Adrienne Rich addressed this issue by describing herself as "split at the root," with a "recognizably Jewish" father and a "white southern Protestant mother."[10] The result was someone who was not Jewishly recognizable yet was strongly attached to some aspect of Jewishness. Her Jewishness rejected the path of Sartre's inauthentic Jew who survives by "trying to pass, deny, or escape from the wounds, and fears of the community," and embraced instead the model of "a Jew resistant to dogma, to separatism, to 'remembering instead of thinking,' in Nadine Gordimer's words—anything that shuts down the music of the future. A Jew whose solidarity with the exiled and the persecuted is unrestricted. A Jew without borders."[11]

New Understandings of Authentically Jewish

According to other observers, cultural mixing and hybridity as defining factors of the Jewish people are new developments of the modern world and the breakdown of the cohesion of premodern communities. This has resulted in new kinds of Jews, new ways of being Jewish, and new approaches to what is authentically Jewish. Cynthia Baker highlights a variety of "new Jews," a category she uses to flag the inadequacy of traditional ethnic, national, and religious definitions of Jewishness.[12] The term *new Jews* functions more as a negative space or emptiness from which major categories of Jewishness have been swept away. These new ways of thinking about Jewishness represent "a critique, a rejection, and dissolution of standard dichotomies—including us/them, homeland/diaspora, religious/secular, masculine/feminine, even Jew/Gentile."[13] Baker is typical of recent efforts to talk about Jewishness in ways that disrupt, challenge, and transcend essentialist categories, which have been replaced with various terms with the prefix *post-* that emphasize positions that reject preestablished categories yet still identify as Jewish.[14] Out of the postmodern decentering and deconstructing of old labels we arrive at new Jews who are described as "post-Zionist," "postethnic," "postdenominational," and even "post-Jewish."

From 2007 to 2008, Spertus Museum in Chicago presented an exhibit titled "The New Authentics: Artists of the Post-Jewish Generation."[15] The title implied that what is authentically Jewish is being redefined by a new generation without appealing to traditional group identities, which have been "replaced by an understanding of identity that identity has neither essential qualities nor clear boundaries but rather is permeable and constantly on the move . . . , identity is performative and self-renewing."[16] The result is that what is authentically Jewish is "either nowhere, or just as easily, everywhere."[17] It means whatever the "New Authentics" want it to. The absence of any essence has become its essence. To be a "rootless cosmopolitan" is no longer a Stalinist antisemitic epithet but a badge of authenticity. It is obviously hard to pin down any content associated with this kind of approach to authenticity, and perhaps that is its weakness. Nonetheless, the idea of Jewishness as a kind of floating signifier without any preestablished meaning does resonate with younger generations who are questioning all of the traditional parameters of identity.

Regimes of Recognition

While these examples of a Jewish "avant-garde" who are forging new approaches to what is authentically Jewish deserve attention, it would be an exaggeration to say that they have been endorsed or "recognized" by much of the Jewish community who remain attached to certain minimal norms and boundaries. There may be a general agreement that change and innovation are inevitable and often worthwhile, but some Jews are leery of approaches that seem completely untethered from traditional roots, all "nothingness" and no "being." For traditional Jews who still define what is authentically Jewish as a perfect balance of part religion, part ethnicity, part culture, and part attachment to Israel, all intertwined in an organic whole, the postmodern emphasis on fluidity, hybridity, and blurred boundaries is seen as a recipe for weakened commitment to communal continuity and a hollowing out of authenticity. Depending on the perspective one takes, the present moment may be seen either as a time of exciting change and radical new options or a period of decline, loss, and threats to survival.

These tensions remind us that discussions of what is authentically Jewish rarely result in consensus and test the limits of how much change is too much. Arnold Eisen, for example, argues that some innovations to Jewish tradition are legitimate but that "creating Judaism in our own image, and the image of our times" is not.[18] Eisen specifically objects to those who "cherry-pick" parts of Jewish tradition to support particular positions or policies. Yet the idea of a neutral reading of tradition not filtered through any particular lens, agenda, or ethical priorities is an illusion. The elements of Jewish tradition that have been preserved at different periods in history were themselves responses to contemporaneous issues and cultural influences.

Eisen's concern does raise the issue of how to handle innovations and reconstructions of Jewishness that are so abrupt and discontinuous with the traditions of other Jews that they risk isolation from other Jewish communities, who find them unrecognizable as something Jewish. There is nothing new about this process, and new "paradigms" for Judaism and Jewishness have arisen throughout Jewish history.[19] The impact and durability of any new ways of expressing or defining what is authentically Jewish depend to a significant degree on the extent to which they are eventually recognized by ever-widening circles of other Jews. Throughout this book, we have explored a variety of conflicts and struggles over recognition based on religious law, cultural traditions and representations, nationalist ideology, origin myths, and genetic history.

The process of recognition involves two major dimensions. One aspect of recognition is identification, as when one "recognizes" a person on the street as a friend. A second important dimension of recognition is judgment, which may be related to respect, rights, or status, as when one "recognizes" a person *as a friend*. Oftentimes, these two dimensions become intertwined, and identification is shaped by judgments. During the Nazi occupation of France, antisemitic propaganda exhibits and films offered information on how to recognize a Jew. In that case, recognition occurred through an antisemitic lens, the purpose of which was "to transform the way in which actual Jews would be seen. In its stereotypical representation, the Jew's body became a signifier that was meant not to correspond to a specific reality, but rather to create a reality."[20] This is a dehumanizing form of recognition that aims to stigmatize Jews and establish them as "other." Although the recognition of remote tribes and groups as Jews during and following the colonial period was not motivated by animus against Jews, the process nonetheless included judgments that helped "create" Jews as much as discover them.

For Jews who lived in small, mostly homogeneous communities in earlier periods, recognizing Jews was a simple matter. After the emancipation of European Jews in the nineteenth century, assimilation made Jews less recognizable. As a result, the recognition of authentic Jews became associated with those who were more recognizable, such as Eastern European Jews like those romanticized in *Fiddler on the Roof*, Hasidic Jews, or anyone with a beard and kippah. In the last fifty years, as various groups have embraced cultural and ethnic pride, some Jews claimed to be able to recognize certain facial features, physical gestures, and speaking styles as authentically Jewish. Some Jews even claimed to possess a special "Jewdar" that enabled them to recognize other Jews even in the absence of any obvious clues.[21]

Recognition is also involved in how people understand their own sense of Jewishness. Increasingly, groups who have not felt represented in normative Judaism have insisted on finding ways to recognize themselves within the Jewish narratives and traditions. The impulse to change the ways of expressing Jewishness often occurs when certain people neither recognize any complete representation of themselves in the existing narratives and traditions nor feel that all parts of themselves are recognized by others. There are many kinds of Jews—women, LGBTQ, of color, converts, Messianic, crypto, and so on—who feel unrecognized and unrepresented among those who are considered authentically Jewish.

The ideal form of recognition offers the opposite of antisemitic recognition. It avoids judgments that distort or demean a person's identity and affirms that a person really is the way that they see themselves. A key ingredient in the construction of identity from early childhood onward is the experience of simultaneously recognizing oneself and feeling recognized as such by others. To be deprived of this kind of reciprocal recognition can cause a person to lose the sense of who they are.[22] Thus recognition of what is authentically Jewish may be expressed in tolerance, acceptance, and celebration of diversity and hybridity in all its forms. Recognition can also become a tool of cultural enforcement that polices group boundaries and seeks to erase hybridity, difference, and deviance. The tension between these two poles will continue in the future as people forge new ways to live that stretch the limits of what they consider authentically Jewish and new demands for recognition emerge.

Notes

INTRODUCTION

1. Charles Lindholm, *Culture and Authenticity* (Malden, Mass.: Blackwell, 2008).

2. Irving Howe, "New Black Writers," *Harper's Magazine* 239 (December 1969): 131.

3. Irving Howe, "The Problem of Jewish Self-Definition," *Reconstructionist* (October 1983): 6.

4. François Gauthier, "Introduction: Consumerism as the Ethos of Consumer Society," in *Religion in Consumer Society: Brands, Consumers and Markets*, ed. François Gauthier and Tuomas Martikainen (London: Routledge, 2013), 52.

5. Thomas Luckmann, *The Invisible Religion* (New York: Macmillan, 1967), 99.

6. Joel Levine, "Why People in the Sunbelt Join a Synagogue," in *Contemporary Debates in American Reform Judaism: Conflicting Visions*, ed. Dana Evan Kaplan (London: Routledge, 2001), 58–63.

7. On the history of brand authenticity, see Jonatan Södergren, "Brand Authenticity: 25 Years of Research," *International Journal of Consumer Studies* 45, no. 4 (2021): 645–663, https://doi.org/10.1111/ijcs.12651.

8. Jessica Carew Kraft, "Design Thinking in Synagogues," Clergy Leadership Incubator, February 1, 2016, http://www.cliforum.org/2016/02/jessica-carew-kraft-design-thinking-in-synagogues/.

9. Sarah Banet-Weiser, *Authentic™: The Politics of Ambivalence in a Brand Culture* (New York: New York University Press, 2012), 14.

10. Jeremy Carette and Richard King, *Selling Spirituality: The Silent Takeover of Religion* (London: Routledge, 2004), 16.

11. Banet-Weiser, *Authentic™*, 11.

12. Andrew Potter, *The Authenticity Hoax: How We Get Lost Finding Ourselves* (New York: Harper, 2010).

13. Mark Toft, Jay Sunny, and Rich Taylor, *Authenticity: Building a Brand in an Insincere Age* (Westport, Conn.: Praeger, 2020), 11.

14. Wade Clark Roof, *Spiritual Marketplace: Baby Boomers and the Remaking of American Religion* (Princeton, N.J.: Princeton University Press, 1999), 4.

CHAPTER ONE — THE CHANGING FACES OF JEWISH AUTHENTICITY

1. Charles Lindholm, *Culture and Authenticity* (Malden, Mass.: Blackwell, 2008).

2. Nin Wang, "Rethinking Authenticity in Tourism Experience," *Annals of Tourism Research* 26, no. 2 (1999): 353; Deepak Chabra, "Authenticity of the Objectively Authentic," *Annals of Tourism*

Research 39, no. 1 (2012): 499–502; Yvette Reisinger and Carol J. Steiner, "Reconceptualizing Object Authenticity," *Annals of Tourism Research* 33, no. 1 (2006): 65–86.

3. Dennis Dutton, "Authenticity in Art" in *The Oxford Handbook of Aesthetics*, ed. Jerrold Levinson (New York: Oxford University Press, 2003).

4. See Charles Lindholm, "The Rise of Expressive Authenticity," *Anthropological Quarterly* 86, no. 2 (Spring 2013): 361–395.

5. One of the earliest and most influential analyses of the emergence of authenticity as an ideal is Lionel Trilling's *Sincerity and Authenticity* (Cambridge, Mass.: Harvard University Press, 1973).

6. Charles Taylor, *The Ethics of Authenticity* (Cambridge, Mass.: Harvard University Press, 1991).

7. Lindholm, *Culture and Authenticity*, 8–9.

8. For Rousseau's thoughts about Jews and Judaism, see Jonathan D. Marks, "Rousseau's Use of the Jewish Example," *Review of Politics* 72, no. 3 (Summer 2010): 463–481.

9. For the dilemma of authenticity caused by Jewish emancipation, see John Murray Cuddihy, *The Ordeal of Civility* (New York: Delta, 1974).

10. "Jean-Paul Sartre: A Candid Conversation with the Charismatic Fountainhead of Existentialism and Rejector of the Nobel Prize," *Playboy* (May 1965): 76.

11. Jean-Paul Sartre, *Antisemite and Jew: An Exploration of the Etiology of Hate* (New York: Schocken, 1995), 132–133.

12. Lindholm, "Rise of Expressive Authenticity," 364.

13. See Charles Taylor, *Sources of the Self: Making of Modern Identity* (Cambridge, Mass.: Harvard University Press, 1989), 376, 415.

14. Richard Handler and Jocelyn Linnekin, "Tradition, Genuine or Spurious," *Journal of American Folklore* 97, no. 385 (1984): 273.

15. Handler and Linnekin, 278.

16. Anthony D. Smith, *Chosen Peoples: Sacred Sources of National Identity* (New York: Oxford University Press, 2003).

17. Lindholm, *Culture and Authenticity*, 113; Steven M. Cohen, *American Modernity and Jewish Identity* (New York: Tavistock, 1983), 9–16.

18. Cf. Maiken Umbach and Mathew Humphrey, *Authenticity: The Cultural History of a Political Concept* (London: Palgrave Macmillan, 2018), 14.

19. Shaye J. D. Cohen, *The Beginnings of Jewishness: Boundaries, Varieties, Uncertainties* (Berkeley: University of California Press, 2001), 3.

20. Efraim Shmueli, *Seven Jewish Cultures: A Reinterpretation of Jewish History and Culture* (Cambridge: Cambridge University Press, 1980), 4.

21. Shmueli, 22.

22. Jonathan Webber, "Modern Jewish Identities: The Ethnographic Complexities," *Journal of Jewish Studies* 43, no. 2 (1992): 246–267.

23. Leonard Fein, *Where Are We? The Inner Life of America's Jews* (New York: Harper, 1988), 43.

24. Jacob Neusner, *Death and Rebirth of Judaism* (New York: Basic, 1987), 19–20.

25. Michael Lerner, *Jewish Renewal: A Path to Healing and Transformation* (New York: G. P. Putnam's Sons, 1994), xix.

26. Shmueli, *Seven Jewish Cultures*, 10, 250.

27. Cf. Jocelyn S. Linnekin, "Defining Tradition: Variations on the Hawaiian Identity," *American Ethnologist* 10 (1983): 241–252.

28. Neil Gillman, *Sacred Fragments: Recovering Theology for the Modern Jew* (Philadelphia: Jewish Publication Society, 1990), xxi.

29. Gillman, xxiii.

30. Cohen, *American Modernity and Jewish Identity*, 27.

31. Cohen, 33.

32. Wang, "Rethinking Authenticity," 358.

33. Jean-Paul Sartre, *Existentialism Is a Humanism* (New Haven, Conn.: Yale University Press, 2007).

34. Folklorist Dell Hymes questions even talking about "tradition" as a stable thing and prefers to focus on the active social process of "traditionalizing" elements of the past into a usable meaning for the present.

35. Sartre, *Existentialism Is a Humanism*.

36. Rajko Muršič, "The Deceptive Tentacles of the Authenticating Mind: On Authenticity and Some Other Notions That Are Good for Absolutely Nothing," in *Debating Authenticity: Concepts of Modernity in Anthropological Perspective*, ed. Thomas Fillitz and A. Jamie Saris (New York: Berghahn, 2013), 46–62; Andrew Potter, *The Authenticity Hoax: How We Get Lost Finding Ourselves* (New York: Harper, 2010).

37. Regina Bendix, *The Search of Authenticity: The Formation of Folklore Studies* (Madison: University of Wisconsin Press, 1997), 9.

38. Bendix, 9.

39. Jonathan Boyarin, "In Search of Authenticity: Issues of Identity and Belonging in the Twentieth Century," in *The Cambridge History of Judaism*, vol. 8, *The Modern World, 1815–2000*, ed. Mitchell Hart and Tony Michels (Cambridge: Cambridge University Press, 2017), 944, 960.

40. Dimitrios Theodossopoulos, "Laying Claim to Authenticity: Five Anthropological Dilemmas," *Anthropological Quarterly* 86, no. 2 (Spring 2013): 347–349.

41. The antiessentialist position is sometimes called "constructivist." See Edward M. Bruner, "Abraham Lincoln as Authentic Reproduction: A Critique of Postmodernism," *American Anthropologist* 96, no. 2 (1994): 397–415; Handler and Linnekin, "Tradition, Genuine or Spurious"; Erik Cohen, "Authenticity and Commoditization in Tourism," *Annals of Tourism Research* 15 (1988): 371–386.

42. See chapter 1, "The Nature of Consciousness and the Story of the Self," in Stuart L. Charmé, *Meaning and Myth in the Study of Lives: A Sartrean Approach* (Philadelphia: University of Pennsylvania Press, 1983).

43. Mendes-Flohr, "Secular Forms of Jewishness," in *The Blackwell Companion to Judaism*, ed. Jacob Neusner and Alan Avery-Peck (Malden, Mass.: Blackwell, 2003), 470.

44. Gillman, *Sacred Fragments*, xxvi.

45. Stuart Hall, "Minimal Selves," in *Studying Culture: An Introductory Reader*, ed. Ann Gray and Jim McGuigan (London: Edward Arnold, 1993), 136–137. Such arbitrary and provisional closures are also at work in what philosopher Judith Butler calls a "constructed, performative accomplishment," which constitutes a position of meaning in response to social and cultural norms. Judith Butler, "Performative Acts and Gender Constitution: An Essay in Phenomenology and Feminist Theory," *Theatre Journal* 40, no. 4 (December 1988): 520.

46. Boyarin, "In Search of Authenticity," 961.

CHAPTER TWO — RECOGNITION AND AUTHENTICITY: FROM SARTRE TO MULTICULTURALISM

1. Cf. Rajko Muršič, "The Deceptive Tentacles of the Authenticating Mind: On Authenticity and Some Other Notions That Are Good for Absolutely Nothing," in *Debating Authenticity: Concepts of Modernity in Anthropological Perspective*, ed. Thomas Fillitz and A. Jamie Saris (New York: Berghahn, 2013), 47.

2. Jean-Paul Sartre, *Antisemite and Jew: An Exploration of the Etiology of Hate* (New York: Schocken, 1995), 27.

3. Sartre, 83.

4. There has been a robust debate about the strengths and weaknesses of Sartre's essay that I will not relitigate here. These include the degree to which Sartre accepted the reality of Jewish culture, history, and religion; his depth of knowledge of Jews and Judaism; possible traces of antisemitism in his descriptions of Jews' personal and physical characteristics; and the coherence of his portraits of authentic and inauthentic Jews. For more analysis of these issues, see Susan Suleiman, "The Jew in Jean-Paul Sartre's *Réflexions sur la question juive*: An Exercise in Historical Reading," in *The Jew in the Text: Modernity and the Construction of Identity*, ed. Linda Nochlin and Tamar Garb (London: Thames and Hudson, 1995); Jonathan Judaken, *Jean-Paul Sartre and the Jewish Question: Anti-antisemitism and the Politics of the French Intellectual* (Lincoln: University of Nebraska Press, 2006); and the articles collected in Denis Hollier, ed., "Jean-Paul Sartre's *Antisemite and Jew*," *October* 87 (Winter 1999).

5. Sartre, *Antisemite and Jew*, 90, 136–137.

6. In January 1940, Sartre wrote to Simone de Beauvoir that Jews might struggle against antisemitism not only because of their generic human rights but also because they recognized "a cultural and religious value in Judaism." Simone de Beauvoir, ed., *Quiet Moments in a War: The Letters of Jean-Paul Sartre to Simone De Beauvoir: 1940–1963* (New York: Scribner's Sons, 1993), 32. Around this time, Sartre also told a Catholic priest he had befriended in a German prisoner of war camp that it would be a mistake for Jews to abandon their religious beliefs for the sake of assimilation. He offered his own image of a multicultural society: "If we were making our republic, we would have inspired ourselves with the Bolsheviks' primitive idea: a special statue for each 'nationality' which permits him not to be ashamed of his history,

his language, and his culture." Marius Perrin, *Avec Sartre au Stalag 12D* (Paris: Jean-Pierre Delarge, 1980), 70.

7. Sartre, *Antisemite and Jew*, 66. I have discussed Sartre's identification with Jews and the conditions for Jewish authenticity in Charmé, *Vulgarity and Authenticity: Dimensions of Otherness in the World of Jean-Paul Sartre* (Amherst: University of Massachusetts Press, 1991), specifically chap. 4, "Strangers on the Train: Jewish Marginality and the Rejection of Civility," 105–144.

8. Charmé, 233.

9. Jean-Paul Sartre, *Existentialism Is a Humanism* (New Haven, Conn.: Yale University Press, 2007), 24–25.

10. Sartre, *Antisemite and Jew*, 89.

11. Jay Michaelson, "The Myth of Authenticity," Forward, December 23, 2009, https://forward.com/articles/121663/the-myth-of-authenticity/.

12. Sartre, *Antisemite and Jew*, 59–60.

13. Stuart Hall, "Cultural Identity in Diaspora," in *Cultural Discourse and Post-colonial Theory: A Reader*, ed. Patrick Williams and Laura Chrisman (New York: Columbia University Press, 1994), 395.

14. Charles Taylor, *The Ethics of Authenticity* (Cambridge, Mass.: Harvard University Press, 1991), 38.

15. Will Kymlicka, *Multicultural Odysseys* (Oxford: Clarendon, 1995), 105.

16. Charmé, *Vulgarity and Authenticity*, 236.

17. Charles Taylor, similarly, insists that identity has a dialogical dimension marked by the degrees of recognition given or withheld by others. Cf. *Ethics of Authenticity*, 49.

18. Michael Satlow, *Creating Judaism: History, Tradition, Practice* (New York: Columbia University Press, 2006), 15.

19. Satlow, 6.

20. Sartre, *Antisemite and Jew*, 146.

21. Sartre, 147.

22. Susan A. Glenn, "The Vogue of Jewish Self-Hatred in Post–World War II America," *Jewish Social Studies* 12, no. 3 (Spring–Summer 2006): 100.

23. Lionel Abel, "The Existence of the Jews and Existentialism," *Politics* 6, no. 1 (Winter 1949): 37–40.

24. Clement Greenberg, "Self-Hatred and Jewish Chauvinism—Some Reflections of 'Positive Jewishness,'" *Commentary* 10 (1950): 426–433.

25. See Judith Friedlander's useful study *Vilna on the Seine: Jewish Intellectuals in France since 1968* (New Haven, Conn.: Yale University Press, 1990).

26. Judith Friedlander, "'Juif Ou Israelite?' The Old Question in Contemporary France," *Judaism* 34, no. 2 (Spring 1985): 223.

27. This strategy was eventually summarized in a line from the 1863 poem "Awake My People" by Judah Loeb Gordon: "Be a man in the streets and a Jew at home." Reprinted in Howard M. Sachar, *A History of Jews in the Modern World* (New York: Vintage, 2006), 189.

28. For a more extensive review of French Jews' philosophical analysis of Jewish identity after Sartre, see Erik H. Cohen's *The Jews of France Today: Identity and Values* (Boston: Brill, 2011) chap. 3; and Seth Wolitz, "Imagining the Jew in France: From 1945 to the Present," *Yale French Studies* 85 (1994): 119–134.

29. Albert Memmi, *Portrait of a Jew* (New York: Orion, 1962), 187.

30. Memmi, 262.

31. Memmi, 288.

32. Memmi, 293.

33. Albert Memmi, *The Liberation of the Jew* (New York: Orion, 1966), 284.

34. Memmi, 296.

35. Memmi, 299.

36. Memmi, 296–297.

37. Memmi, 297.

38. Memmi, 298–300.

39. Alain Finkielkraut, *The Imaginary Jew*, trans. Kevin O'Neill and David Suchoff (Lincoln: University of Nebraska Press, 1997), 36.

40. See Hillel Schwartz, *The Culture of the Copy: Striking Likenesses, Unreasonable Facsimiles* (New York: Zone, 1996).

41. Finkielkraut, *Imaginary Jew*, 178.

42. Finkielkraut, 21.

43. Finkielkraut, 39. For the relevance of Sartre's view of consciousness for a model of personal identity and the process of constructing a life story, see Charmé, *Meaning and Myth in the Study of Lives: A Sartrean Approach* (Philadelphia: University of Pennsylvania Press, 1983).

44. Finkielkraut, *Imaginary Jew*, 168.

45. Finkielkraut, 169.

46. Finkielkraut, 114.

47. Finkielkraut, 168.

48. Finkielkraut, 166.

49. Finkielkraut, 168–169.

50. Richard Handler and Jocelyn Linnekin, "Tradition, Genuine or Spurious," *Journal of American Folklore* 97, no. 385 (1984): 289.

51. Finkielkraut, *Imaginary Jew*, 169.

52. Finkielkraut, 179. Author and filmmaker Georges Perec similarly describes his own sense of Jewishness in similar terms of emptiness and absence:

> I do not know exactly what it is to be Jewish, what it does to me to be Jewish. It is something obvious, but of rather poor obviousness, a label that does not connect me to anything particular, to anything concrete; it is not a sign of belonging, it is not tied to a belief, a religion, observance, culture, folklore, history, destiny or language. It would more likely be an absence, a question, a questioning, a looseness, an anxiety; an anxious certainty behind which is silhouetted another certainty that is abstract, heavy and unbearable, that of having been singled out as a Jew, and because a Jew, a victim, owing life only to chance and exile (quoted in Cohen, *Jews of France*, 151).

53. Cf. Fran Markowitz, "Plaiting the Strands of Jewish Identity," *Journal for the Comparative Study of Society and History* 32, no. 1 (January 1990): 182–187.

54. Jean-Paul Sartre, *Being and Nothingness: An Essay in Phenomenological Ontology* (New York: Washington Square, 1993), 100.

55. Cohen, *Jews of France*, 64.

56. On the impact of North African Jews in France, see Michel Abitbol and Alan Astro, "The Integration of North African Jews in France," *Yale French Studies*, no. 85 (1994): 248–261.

57. Jacques Derrida, "Abraham, the Other," in *Judeities: Questions for Jacques Derrida*, ed. Bettina Bergo, Joseph D. Cohen, and Raphael Zagury-Orly (New York: Fordham University Press, 2007), 1–35.

58. Derrida, 10.

59. Derrida, 30–31.

60. Sartre, *Antisemite and Jew*, 136–137.

61. Sartre, 137.

62. Joseph Margolis, "Talking to Myself," in *Jewish Identity*, ed. David Theo Goldberg and Michael Krausz (Philadelphia: Temple University Press, 1993), 334.

63. Maria Damon, "Word-landslayt: Gertrude Stein, Allen Ginsberg, Lenny Bruce," in *People of the Book: Thirty Scholars Reflect on Their Jewish Identity*, ed. Jeffrey Rubin-Dorsky and Shelley Fisher Fishkin (Madison: Wisconsin University Press, 1996), 386.

64. Charles Taylor, "The Politics of Recognition," in *Multiculturalism: Examining the Politics of Recognition*, ed. Amy Guttman (Princeton, N.J.: Princeton University Press, 1994), 42.

65. Taylor, 33.

66. Erik Erikson, *Insight and Responsibility* (New York: Norton, 1964), 90, 93.

67. Terence Turner, "Anthropology and Multiculturalism: What Is Anthropology That Multiculturalists Should Be Mindful of It?," in *Multiculturalism: A Critical Reader*, ed. David Theo Goldberg (Malden, Mass.: Blackwell, 1994), 407.

68. Brenda Lyshaug, "Authenticity and the Politics of Identity: A Critique of Charles Taylor's Politics of Recognition," *Contemporary Political Theory* 3 (2004): 313.

69. Bhikhu Parekh, *Rethinking Multiculturalism: Cultural Diversity and Political Theory* (Cambridge, Mass.: Harvard University Press, 2000), 150.

70. Parekh, 175.

71. Patchen Markell, *Bound by Recognition* (Princeton, N.J.: Princeton University Press, 2003), 14–16.

72. Markell, 41.

73. Markell, 14.

74. Markell, 20. See also Nancy Fraser, "From Redistribution to Recognition? Dilemmas of Justice in a Post-socialist Age," *Theory, Culture & Society* 18, nos. 2–3 (2001): 21–42; and Nancy Fraser, "Rethinking Recognition," in *The Philosophy of Recognition*, ed. Hans-Christoph Schmidt am Busch and Christopher Zurn (New York: Rowman & Littlefield, 2010), 211–222.

75. Markell, *Bound by Recognition*, 189.

76. Erich Fromm, *Psychoanalysis and Religion* (New Haven, Conn.: Yale University Press, 1950).

77. David Hansen, *The Teacher and the World: A Study of Cosmopolitanism as Education* (New York: Routledge, 2011), 57.

CHAPTER THREE — ORTHODOXY AND THE AUTHENTIC JEW

1. Leonard Gewirth, *The Authentic Jew and His Judaism* (New York: Bloch, 1961).

2. Gewirth, 7.

3. Gewirth, 7.

4. Emil Fackenheim, "The 614th Commandment," in *The Jewish Return into History* (New York: Schocken, 1978), 21.

5. Fackenheim, 19.

6. Fackenheim, 21.

7. Fackenheim, 22.

8. Fackenheim, 23.

9. Emil Fackenheim, "The Dilemma of Liberal Judaism," in *Quest for Past and Future: Essays in Jewish Theology* (Bloomington: Indiana University Press, 1968), 130.

10. Fackenheim, 131.

11. Fackenheim, 140.

12. Jonathan Sacks, *One People? Tradition, Modernity, and Jewish Unity* (London: Littman, 1994), 65.

13. Sacks, 91.

14. Sacks, 146.

15. Sacks, 148.

16. Sacks, 154, 156.

17. Sacks, 31.

18. Sacks, 151.

19. Sacks, 157–158.

20. Sacks, 158.

21. Sacks, 252.

22. Emanuel Feldman, "Symposium on 'The State of Orthodoxy,'" *Tradition* 20, no. 1 (Spring 1982): 21.

23. Sacks, *One People?*, 133–134.

24. Sacks, 157.

25. Norman Lamm, "Seventy Faces: Divided We Stand, but It's Time to Try an Idea That Might Help Us Stand Taller," *Moment* 2, no. 6 (June 1986): 24.

26. Lamm, 25.

27. Elliot Abrams, *Faith or Fear: How Jews Can Survive in a Christian America* (New York: Free Press, 1997), 178.

28. Abrams, 183.

29. Jonathan Sacks, *Will We Have Jewish Grandchildren? Jewish Continuity and How to Achieve It* (London: Vallentine Mitchell, 1994), 110.

30. Sacks, 107.

31. Menachem Kellner, *Must a Jew Believe Anything?* (London: Littman, 1999), 125.

32. Kellner, 110.

33. Kellner, 114.

34. Charles Liebman, *Deceptive Images: Toward a Redefinition of American Judaism* (New Brunswick, N.J.: Transaction Books, 1988), 57.

35. Kellner, *Must a Jew Believe*, 9.

36. Lis Harris, *Holy Days: The World of a Hasidic Family* (New York: Summit, 1985), 11.

37. Jay Michaelson, "The Myth of Authenticity," Forward, December 23, 2009, https://forward.com/articles/121663/the-myth-of-authenticity/.

38. Martin E. Marty and R. Scott Appleby, *The Glory and the Power: The Fundamentalist Challenge to the Modern World* (Boston: Beacon, 1992), 116.

39. Marty and Appleby, 120.

40. Cf. Jonathan Cohen, "'If Rabbi Akiba Were Alive Today . . .' or the Authenticity Argument," *Judaism* 37, no. 2 (Spring 1988): 136.

41. Samuel Heilman, "Constructing Orthodoxy," *Transaction* 15, no. 4 (1978): 34.

42. Heilman's concept of "traditioning" is quite similar to the concept of "traditionalizing" popularized by folklorist Dell Hymes. Cf. Dell Hymes, "Folklore's Nature and the Sun's Myth," *Journal of American Folklore* 88 (1975): 345–369.

43. Moshe Samet, "The Beginnings of Orthodoxy," *Modern Judaism* 8 (1988): 249–269; Heilman, "Constructing Orthodoxy"; Michael Silber, "The Emergence of Ultra-Orthodoxy: The Invention of a Tradition," in *The Uses of Tradition: Jewish Continuity in the Modern Era*, ed. Jack Wertheimer (New York: Jewish Theological Seminary Press, 1992), 23–84.

44. Samet, "Beginnings of Orthodoxy," 264.

45. Jacob Katz, "Orthodoxy in Historical Perspective," *Studies in Contemporary Jewry*, 2 (1986): 4–5.

242   NOTES TO PAGES 53–58

46. Jenna Weissman Joselit, *New York's Jewish Jews* (Bloomington: Indiana University Press, 1990), 40.

47. Joselit, 20.

48. Zev Eleff, *Authentically Orthodox: A Tradition-Bound Faith in American Life* (Detroit, Mich.: Wayne State University Press, 2020), 22.

49. Etan Diamond, "The Kosher Lifestyle: Religious Consumerism and Suburban Orthodox Jews," *Journal of Urban History* 28, no. 4 (May 2002): 488–505.

50. Diamond, "Kosher Lifestyle," 489.

51. Diamond, 503.

52. Joselit, *Jewish Jews*, 23.

53. Joselit, 150.

54. Joselit, 150.

55. Menachem Friedman, "Life Tradition and Book Tradition in the Development of Ultraorthodox Judaism," in *Judaism Viewed from Within and from Without: Anthropological Studies*, ed. Harvey Goldberg (Albany: State University of New York Press, 1987), 245–246.

56. Lawrence Kaplan, "Daas Torah: A Modern Conception of Rabbinic Authority," in *Rabbinic Authority and Personal Autonomy*, ed. Moshe Sokol (Northvale, N.J.: Jason Aronson, 1992), 12–13.

57. Kaplan, 22.

58. Haym Soloveitchik, "Rupture and Reconstruction: The Transformation of Contemporary Orthodoxy," *Tradition* 28, no. 4 (Summer 1994): 75–77.

59. Silber, "Emergence of Ultra-Orthodoxy," 49–50.

60. Soloveitchik, "Rupture and Reconstruction," 68.

61. Soloveitchik, 86.

62. David Berger et al., "A Symposium: 'The State of Orthodoxy,'" *Tradition* 20, no. 1 (Spring 1982): 10.

63. Louis Bernstein, in Berger, "Symposium," 14.

64. Reuven P. Bulka, in Berger, "Symposium," 17.

65. Aharon Lichtenstein, in Berger, "Symposium," 48.

66. Efraim Shmueli, *Seven Jewish Cultures* (Cambridge: Cambridge University Press, 1980), 2.

67. Jacob Neusner, *Death and Rebirth of Judaism* (New York: Basic, 1987), 19–20.

68. Irving Greenberg, "Toward a Principled Pluralism," in *Towards the Twenty-First Century: Judaism and the Jewish People in Israel and America*, ed. Ronald Kroish (Hoboken, N.J.: KTAV, 1988), 189–193.

CHAPTER FOUR — REFORMING JEWISH TRADITION AND THE SPIRITUAL QUEST

1. Stefan Kanfer, *Stardust Lost: The Triumph, Tragedy, and Mishugas of the Yiddish Theater in America* (New York: Vintage, 2007), 264.

2. Jacob Neusner, "When Reform Judaism Was Judaism," in *Contemporary Debates in American Reform Judaism: Conflicting Visions*, ed. Dana Evan Kaplan (New York: Routledge, 2001), 70.

3. Neusner, 76.

4. Neusner, 77.

5. Jack Wertheimer, "Judaism without Limits," *Commentary*, July 1997, https://www.commentarymagazine.com/articles/judaism-without-limits/.

6. Wertheimer.

7. Charles Liebman, "When Judaism Gets Personal," *Forward* 98, no. 31 (1999): 9.

8. Bernard Susser and Charles S. Liebman, *Choosing Survival: Strategies for Jewish Future* (New York: Oxford University Press, 1999), 69, 89.

9. Quoted in Kaplan, *Contemporary Debates*, 9.

10. Simeon Maslin, "Who Are the Authentic Jews?" *Reform Judaism Magazine* 24, no. 4 (Summer 1996): 10–16; Balfour Brickner, "Orthodox Have No Lock on Authenticity," *Jewish Week* 209, no. 51 (1997): 31.

11. Brickner.

12. Maslin, "Authentic Jews?"

13. Maslin.

14. Alfred Gottschalk, "Reform Judaism of the New Millennium: A Challenge," in Kaplan, ed., *Contemporary Debates*, 237.

15. Cf. Bethamie Horowitz, "Reframing the Study of Contemporary American Jewish Identity," *Contemporary Jewry* 23, no. 1 (2002): 14.

16. G. W. Allport, *The Individual and His Religion* (New York: Macmillan, 1979); G. W. Allport, *The Nature of Prejudice* (Reading, Mass.: Addison-Wesley, 1954); G. W. Allport and M. J. Ross, "Personal Religious Orientation and Prejudice," *Journal of Personality and Social Psychology* 5, no. 4 (1967): 432–443.

17. Jack Wertheimer, Charles Liebman, and Steven M. Cohen, "How to Save American Jews," *Commentary* (January 1996): 170.

18. Erich Fromm, *Psychoanalysis and Religion* (New Haven, Conn.: Yale University Press, 1950), 26.

19. Cf. Erich Fromm, *Escape from Freedom* (New York: Henry Holt, 1941), 140–154.

20. Fromm, 255–258.

21. Fromm, *Psychoanalysis and Religion*, 49.

22. Fromm, 84–85.

23. Fromm, 47.

24. Jonathan Sacks "Creativity and Innovation in Halakhah," in *Rabbinic Authority and Personal Autonomy*, ed. Moshe Sokol (Northvale: Jason Aronson, 1992), 127.

25. Sacks, 129.

26. Fromm, *Psychoanalysis and Religion*, 85.

27. Fromm, 95.

28. Fromm, 114.

29. Fromm, 115.

30. Fromm, 95.

31. Mordecai Kaplan, *Judaism as a Civilization: Toward a Reconstruction of American-Jewish Life* (New York: Schocken, 1967), 178.

32. Mordecai Kaplan, *Judaism without Supernaturalism: The Only Alternative to Orthodoxy and Secularism* (New York: Reconstructionist, 1967), 13.

33. Mordecai Kaplan, *The Religion of Ethical Nationhood: Judaism's Contribution to World Peace* (New York: Macmillan, 1970), 5.

34. Kaplan, 7. In Mordecai Kaplan and Arthur Cohen, *If Not Now, When? Toward a Reconstitution of the Jewish People* (New York: Schocken, 1973), 96, Kaplan defines salvation as "the maximum, harmonious functioning of a person's physical, mental, social, moral, and spiritual power."

35. Kaplan, *Ethical Nationhood*, 10.

36. Kaplan, 48–49.

37. Kaplan, 53.

38. Kaplan, 66, 78.

39. Kaplan, 104.

40. Robert Wuthnow, *After Heaven: Spirituality in America since the 1950s* (Berkeley: University of California, 1998), 148–149.

41. Daniel Batson, Patricia Schoenrade, and W. Larry Ventis, *Religion and the Individual: A Social-Psychological Perspective* (New York: Oxford, 1993), 159.

42. Steven M. Cohen and Arnold Eisen, *The Jew Within: Self, Family, and Community in America* (Bloomington: Indiana University Press, 2000), 2.

43. Cohen and Eisen, 192.

44. William James, *The Varieties of Religious Experience: A Study in Human Nature* (London: Collier, 1969); Abraham Maslow, *Religion, Values, and Peak Experiences* (New York: Penguin, 1976).

45. Carol P. Christ and Judith Plaskow, eds., *Womanspirit Rising: A Feminist Reader in Religion* (New York: HarperCollins, 1992), 8–10.

46. Judith Plaskow, *Standing Again at Sinai: Judaism from a Feminist Perspective* (New York: HarperCollins, 1991), x.

47. Plaskow, 45.

48. Plaskow, xvii.

49. Plaskow, 72.

CHAPTER FIVE — THE EXPERIENTIAL AUTHENTICITY OF JEWISH MEDITATION, JEWISH YOGA, AND KABBALAH

1. A survey of some of these developments can be found in Jeffrey Salkin, "New Age Judaism," in *Blackwell Companion to Judaism*, ed. Jacob Neusner and Alan Avery-Peck (Malden, Mass.: Blackwell, 2000), 354–370.

2. Harvey Cox, *Turning East: The Promise and Peril of the New Orientalism* (New York: Simon & Schuster, 1977), 65.

3. Mira Niculescu, "'Find Your Inner God and Breathe': Buddhism, Pop Culture, and Contemporary Metamorphoses in American Judaism," in *Religion in Consumer Society: Brands, Consumers and Markets*, ed. François Gauthier and Tuomas Martikainen (London: Routledge, 2013).

4. Salkin, "New Age Judaism," 368.

5. Cox, *Turning East*, 65–66, 69.

6. Avram Davis, ed., *Meditation from the Heart of Judaism: Today's Teachers Share Their Practices, Techniques, and Faith* (Woodstock, Vt.: Jewish Lights, 1999), 10.

7. Davis, 9.

8. Aryeh Kaplan, *Jewish Meditation: A Practical Guide* (New York: Schocken, 1995), chap. 5.

9. Kaplan, 42.

10. "Q & A with Rabbi Daveed El Harar," *Nefesh Haya* (blog), accessed August 6, 2021, http://www.nefeshhaya.com/qa-with-rabbi-daveed-el-hara.html.

11. Kaplan, *Jewish Meditation*, 42.

12. Kaplan, 45.

13. Kaplan, 46.

14. Zvi Zavidowsky, "Restoring the Meditative Side of Judaism: A Beginning," accessed December 14, 2021, http://www.angelfire.com/pe/ophanim/Olam3.htm.

15. Kaplan, *Jewish Meditation*, 41.

16. Mark Verman, *The History and Varieties of Jewish Meditation* (New York: Jason Aronson, 1977), 7.

17. Goldie Milgram, "Introduction to Jewish Meditation," Reclaiming Judaism, accessed August 6, 2021, http://www.reclaimingjudaism.org/teachings/introduction-jewish-meditation.

18. Erich Fromm, *Psychoanalysis and Religion* (New Haven, Conn.: Yale University Press, 1950), 94–95.

19. Jeff Roth, *Jewish Meditation Practices for Everyday Life: Awakening Your Heart, Connecting with God* (Woodstock, Vt.: Jewish Lights, 2009), 1.

20. Verman, *Jewish Meditation*, 2.

21. Brenda Shoshana, *Jewish Dharma: A Guide to the Practice of Judaism and Zen* (New York: Da Capo, 2008), 3.

22. Shoshana, 280.

23. Roger Kamenitz, *The Jew in the Lotus* (New York: HarperCollins, 1994), 255.

24. Louis Sahagun, "At One with Dual Devotion," *Los Angeles Times*, May 2, 2006, https://www.latimes.com/archives/la-xpm-2006-may-02-me-jubus2-story.html.

25. Rebecca Spence, "Meditation Hits the Jewish Mainstream," *Jewish Forward*, August 11, 2006, http://www.forward.com/articles/623/.

26. Matthew Gindin, "Above the Sun: The Ancient (and New) Riches of Jewish Yoga," Jewish Yoga Network, September 2011, https://vuvuzela-orchid-mfa9.squarespace.com/blog/above-the-sun-the-ancient-and-new-riches-of-jewish-yoga.

27. Gindin.

28. Of course, there are some Jews, particularly Orthodox, who battle against yoga as a dangerous and forbidden example of idolatry or "avodah zarah." The Lubavitcher Rebbe is reported to have taken this position. And other religious Jews who like the benefits they get from yoga still struggle with the question of its legitimacy for Jews. Cf. Taffy Brodesser-Akner, "Kosher Yoga: How a Modern Orthodox Jew Struggled to Reconcile Her Yogic Practice with Her Judaism," *Jewish Journal*, https://jewishjournal.com/community/76195/.

29. Yoga Alliance, "2016 Yoga in America Study Conducted by Yoga Journal and Yoga Alliance Reveals Growth and Benefits of the Practice," 2016, https://www.yogaalliance.org/Get_Involved/Media_Inquiries/2016_Yoga_in_America_Study_Conducted_by_Yoga_Journal_and_Yoga_Alliance_Reveals_Growth_and_Benefits_of_the_Practice.

30. Cf. Celia Rothenberg, "Jewish Yoga: Experiencing Flexible, Sacred, and Jewish Bodies," *Nova Religio: The Journal of Alternative and Emergent Religions* 10, no. 2 (November 2006): 57–74.

31. Jodi Falk, "Rocking and Rolling through Judaism," 614: HBI eZine, http://614ezine.com/rocking-and-rolling-through-judaism/.

32. Rothenberg, "Jewish Yoga," 61–62.

33. Falk, "Rocking and Rolling."

34. Falk.

35. Eleanor F. Odenheimer, Rebecca Buchanan, and Tanya Prewitt, "Adaptations of Yoga: Jewish Interpretations," in *Muscling in on New Worlds: Jews, Sport, and the Making of the Americas*, ed. Raanan Rein and David Sheinin (Leiden, Netherlands: Brill, 2014), 57.

36. Diane Bloomfield, *Torah Yoga: Experiencing Jewish Wisdom through Classic Postures* (San Francisco: Jossey-Bass, 2004), xiii.

37. Rami M. Shapiro, "The Teaching and Practice of Reb Yerachmiel ben Yisrael," in Davis, *Meditation*, 31.

38. Bloomfield, *Torah Yoga*, xiv.

39. Steven J. Gold, *Yoga and Judaism: Explorations of a Jewish Yogi* (Morrisville, N.C.: Lulu.com, 2007).

40. *Torah-Veda* (blog), accessed December 12, 2021, http://yajcenter.blogspot.com/.

41. Joseph Dan, *Kabbalah: A Very Short Introduction* (New York: Oxford University Press, 2007), 70.

42. Audi Gozlan, "Kabalah Yoga," accessed August 6, 2021, http://www.kabalahyoga.com/kabalah-yoga.

43. Ron Feldman, "My Mystical Encounter," *Moment* 22, no. 1 (February 1997): 14.

44. Feldman, 19 (emphasis added).

45. Feldman, 47.

46. Jody Myers, "The Kabbalah Centre and Contemporary Spirituality," *Religious Compass* 2, no. 3 (2008): 412–413.

47. Kabbalah Centre, "Frequently Asked Questions," accessed June 2010, http://www.kabbalah.com.

48. Boaz Huss, "Kabbalah and the Politics of Inauthenticity: The Controversies over the Kabbalah Centre," *Numen* 62 (2015): 210.

49. Huss, 207.

50. Aron Moss, "Is New-Wave Kabbalah Authentic?," Chabad.org, accessed August 6, 2021, https://www.chabad.org/library/article_cdo/aid/160990/jewish/Is-New-Wave-Kabbalah-Authentic.htm.

51. Huss, "Kabbalah," 208.

52. Huss, 218.

53. Jody Myers, *Kabbalah and the Spiritual Quest: The Kabbalah Centre in America* (Westport, Conn.: Praeger, 2007), 121.

54. Myers, 125.

55. Gershom Scholem, "Toward an Understanding of the Messianic Idea in Judaism," in *The Messianic Idea in Judaism: And Other Essays on Jewish Spirituality* (New York: Schocken, 1995), 21.

56. David Biale, "Gershom Scholem and Anarchism as a Jewish Philosophy," *Judaism* 32, no. 1 (Winter 1983): 76.

57. Biale, 71.

CHAPTER SIX — THE MESSIANIC HERESY AND THE STRUGGLE FOR AUTHENTICITY

1. Carol Harris-Shapiro, *Messianic Judaism: A Rabbi's Journey through Religious Change in America* (Boston: Beacon, 1999), 17.

2. Albert Memmi, *Portrait of a Jew* (New York: Orion, 1962), 189.

3. Norman Podoretz, "Jewishness and the Younger Intellectuals: A Symposium," *Commentary* 34, no. 1 (June 1961): 350–351.

4. Of course, as described in chapter 3, while Orthodox Jewish leaders do not recognize liberal Judaism as a legitimate form of Judaism, they at least recognize liberal Jews as Jews.

5. Ira O. Glick, "The Hebrew Christians: A Marginal Religious Group," in *The Jews: Social Patterns of an American Group*, ed. Marshall Sklare (Glencoe, Ill.: Free Press, 1958), 415–431.

6. However, the Karaites, like the Sadducees, also rejected the concept of the "Oral Torah," which became the foundation for rabbinical Judaism. There are still a small number of Karaites in the world today, in Israel and elsewhere, and their relationship to mainstream Judaism raises some of the same issues as Messianic Jews.

7. Quoted in Dan Cohn-Sherbok, *Messianic Judaism* (London: Continuum, 2000), 196.

8. Cohn-Sherbok, 197.

9. Pew Research Center, "A Portrait of American Jews," October 1, 2013, http://www.pewforum.org/2013/10/01/jewish-american-beliefs-attitudes-culture-survey/.

10. Charles Liebman, *Deceptive Images: Toward a Redefinition of American Judaism* (New Brunswick, N.H.: Transaction Books, 1988), 103.

11. Cohn-Sherbok, *Messianic Judaism*, 213.

12. Cohn-Sherbok, 211.

13. See Stuart Charmé, "Heretics, Infidels, and Apostates: Menace, Problem, or Symptom," *Judaism* 36, no. 1 (Winter 1987): 17–33.

14. Patricia A. Power, "Accounting for Judaism in the Study of American Messianic Judaism" (PhD thesis, Arizona State University, 2015), 28.

15. FFOZ Staff Writer, "The Messianic Jewish Millennials," First Fruits of Zion. September 9, 2015, https://ffoz.org/discover/messianic-judaism/the-messianic-jewish-millennials.html.

16. Gabriela Reason, "Competing Trends in Messianic Judaism: The Debate over Evangelicalism," *Kesher: A Journal of Messianic Judaism*, January 2, 2005, https://www.kesherjournal.com/article/competing-trends-in-messianic-judaism-the-debate-over-evangelicalism/.

17. FFOZ Staff Writer, "Messianic Jewish Millennials."

18. Stuart Dauermann, "Varieties of Messianic Believers (Part Two)," *Messianic Agenda* (blog), July 1, 2011, http://www.messianicjudaism.me/agenda/2011/07/01/varieties-of-jewish-yeshua-believers-part-two/.

19. Dauermann.

20. Dauermann.

21. Mark Kinzer, *The Nature of Messianic Judaism: Judaism as Genus, Messianism as Species* (West Hartford, Conn.: Hashivenu Archives, 2000), 12, http://hashivenu.org/.

22. The story of how the new practice of placing an orange on the Passover seder plate became an accepted tradition is a good example, including folkloric justifications that later appeared. Susannah Heschel, "An Orange on Plate for Women—and Spit Out Seeds of Hate," March 19, 2013, https://forward.com/opinion/172959/an-orange-on-plate-for-women-and-spit-out-seeds/#.

23. Cf. Mark Kinzer, *Postmissionary Messianic Judaism: Redefining Christian Engagement with the Jewish People* (Grand Rapids, Mich.: Brazos, 2005).

24. Hashivenu, "A Vision for a Maturing Messianic Judaism," accessed December 15, 2021, http://www.hashivenu.org/.

25. Jacob M. Landau, "The Dönmes: Crypto-Jews under Turkish Rule," *Jewish Political Studies Review* 19, nos. 1–2 (Spring 2007): 109–118, https://jcpa.org/article/the-donmes-crypto-jews-under-turkish-rule/.

26. On the de-Judaization of early Christianity, see Paula Fredriksen and Oded Irshai, "Christian Anti-Judaism: Polemics and Policies," in *The Cambridge History of Judaism*, vol. 4, *The Late Roman Rabbinic Period*, ed. Steven T. Katz (Cambridge: Cambridge University Press, 2006), 977–1034.

27. Simon Dein, "Moshiach Is Here Now: Just Open Your Eyes and You Can See Him," *Anthropology and Medicine* 9, no. 1 (2002): 24–36.

28. Dein, 33–35.

CHAPTER SEVEN — CREATING A NATIONAL JEWISH CULTURE IN ISRAEL

1. George L. Mosse, *The Crisis of German Ideology* (New York: Schocken, 1981), 4.

2. Golda Meir, "What We Want of the Diaspora," quoted in Jeffrey Rubin-Dorsky, "Philip Roth and American Jewish Identity: The Question of Authenticity," *American Literary History* 13 (2001): 79–107.

3. Moses Hess, "Rome and Jerusalem," quoted in Arthur Hertzberg, *The Zionist Idea: A Historical Analysis and Reader* (New York: Atheneum, 1970), 121–122.

4. Ahad Ha'am, "Slavery in Freedom," in *Selected Essays of Ahad Ha'am*, trans. Leon Simon (New York: Atheneum, 1962), 177.

5. Ahad Ha'am, "The Jewish State and the Jewish Problem," in Simon, *Essays of Ahad Ha'am*, 267.

6. Ahad Ha'am, "Flesh and Spirit," in Simon, *Essays of Ahad Ha'am*, 147.

7. Ha'am, "Slavery in Freedom," 194.

8. Ha'am, "Jewish State," 267.

9. Ahad Ha'am, "Ancestor Worship," in Simon, *Essays of Ahad Ha'am*, 207.

10. Ha'am, 209.

11. Ahad Ha'am, "Past and Future," in Simon, *Essays of Ahad Ha'am*, 80, 90.

12. Berdichevski, "The Question of Our Past," quoted in Hertzberg, *Zionist Idea*, 299.

13. Arnold Band, "The Ahad Ha'am and Berdyczewski Polarity," in *At the Crossroads: Essays on Ahad Ha'am*, ed. Jacques Kornberg (Albany: State University of New York Press, 1983), 52.

14. Quoted in David Ohana, "Zarathustra in Jerusalem: Nietzsche and the 'New Hebrews,'" in "The Shaping of Israeli Identity: Myth, Memory and Trauma," ed. Robert Wistrich and David Ohana, special issue, *Israel Affairs* 1, no. 3 (Spring 1995): 38–60.

15. Berdichevski, "Question of Our Past," quoted in Hertzberg, *Zionist Idea*, 294.

16. Berdichevski quoted in Ehud Luz, *Parallels Meet: Religion and Nationalism in the Early Zionist Movement* (Philadelphia: Jewish Publication Society, 1988), 165.

17. Oz Almog, *The Sabra: The Creation of the New Jew* (Berkeley: University of California Press, 2000), 6.

18. Almog, 78.

19. Almog, 76.

20. Almog, 78.

21. Sartre had a strong record of writing in support of decolonization in Algeria and other African countries. Yoav Di-Capua's *No Exit: Arab Existentialism, Jean-Paul Sartre, and Decolonization* (Chicago: University of Chicago Press, 2018) describes the attraction of Arab intellectuals in the 1950s and 1960s both to Sartre's existentialism and his anticolonialist and postcolonialist work but also their total disillusionment at Sartre's support for Israel at the time of the 1967 Arab-Israeli War. He declined to criticize Israel for the situation of the Palestinians and clearly thought that a socialist country set up by refugees from the Holocaust was different from the many countries undergoing decolonization during the same time.

22. This expression was widely used within the early Zionist movement, but its source is uncertain. For more information about this expression see Adam M. Garfinkle, "On the Origin, Meaning, Use, and Abuse of a Phrase," *Middle Eastern Studies* 27, no. 4 (October 1991): 539–550.

23. Edward Said, *The Question of Palestine* (New York: Vintage, 1994), 8.

24. Herbert C. Kelman, "The Interdependence of Israeli and Palestinian National Identities: The Role of the Other in Existential Conflicts," *Journal of Social Issues* 55, no. 3 (1999): 589.

25. Kelman, 598.

26. Yehouda Shenhav, *The Arab Jews: A Postcolonial Reading of Nationalism, Religion, and Ethnicity* (Palo Alto, Calif.: Stanford University Press, 2006), 28.

27. Quoted in Almog, *Sabra*, 188.

28. Ammon Raz-Krakotzkin, "The Zionist Return to the West and the Mizrahi Jewish Perspective," in *Orientalism and the Jews*, ed. Ivan Davidson Kalmar and Derek J. Penslar (Waltham, Mass.: Brandeis University Press, 2005), 169.

29. Shenhav, *Arab Jews*, 146.

30. Shenhav, 194–195.

31. Ella Shohat, "Dislocated Identities: Reflections of an Arab Jew," *Movement Research* 5 (Fall 1991 / Winter 1992): 8. https://www.academia.edu/11961837/_Dislocated_Identities_Reflections_of_an_Arab_Jew_Published_simultaneously_in_Emergences_Movement_Research_5_Fall_1991_Winter_1992_p_8.

32. Ella Shohat, "Rupture and Return: Zionist Discourse and the Study of Arab Jews," *Social Text* 21, no. 2 (Summer 2003): 52.

33. Shohat, 54.

34. Daniel Elazar, *The Other Jews: The Sepharidim Today* (New York: Basic, 1989), 186.

35. Ella Shohat, "The Invention of the Mizrahim," *Journal of Palestinian Studies* 29, no. 1 (1999): 6.

36. Shohat, 6.

37. Shohat, "Rupture and Return," 49–74.

38. Ha'am, "Two Domains," in Simon, *Essays of Ahad Ha'am*, 94.

39. Shalom Spiegel, *Hebrew Reborn* (New York: Macmillan, 1930).

40. Spiegel, 5.

41. Spiegel, 23.

42. Spiegel, 21, 22.

43. Spiegel, 15.

44. Spiegel, 12, 22.

45. Spiegel, 12.

46. Eliezer Ben-Yehudah, *A Dream Come True* (Boulder, Colo.: Westview, 1993), 91.

47. Ben-Yehudah, 16–17.

48. Ben-Yehudah, 17.

49. Benjamin Harshav, *Language in Time of Revolution* (Berkeley: University of California Press, 1993), 163.

50. Harshav, 21.

51. Ben-Yehudah, *Dream Come True*, 65–66.

52. Harshav, *Language in Time of Revolution*, 153.

53. Harshav, 164, 169.

54. Itamar Even-Zohar, "The Emergence of a Native Hebrew Culture in Palestine, 1882–1948," *Poetics Today* 11, no. 1 (Spring 1990): 175–191.

55. Shelomo Morag, "The Emergence of Modern Hebrew: Some Sociolinguistic Perspectives," in ed. Lewis Glinert, *Hebrew in Ashkenaz: A Language in Exile* (New York: Oxford, 1993), 214.

56. Morag, 218.

57. Morag, 217.

58. Benjamin Zemach, "The Beginning of Jewish Dancing," in *Ha-Rikud: The Jewish Dance*, ed. Fred Berk (New York: Union of American Hebrew Congregations, 1972), 6–7. According to some, the joyous Chassidic dance introduced by the Baal Shem Tov finally had offered for some an escape from ghetto life, which had become "drab, miserable, colorless, and hopeless." Dvora Lapson, "The Chasidic Dance (1937)," in Berk, *Ha-Rikud*, 16.

59. Zemach, "Jewish Dancing," 6.

60. Gurit Kadman, "Folk Dance in Israel," in Berk, *Ha-Rikud*, 26–27.

61. Gurit Kadman, "Yeminite Dances and Their Influence on the New Israeli Folk Dances," *Journal of the International Folk Music Council* 4 (1952): 27.

62. Kadman, 14.

63. Kadman, 9.

64. Cf. Ayalah Kaufman, "Indigenous and Imported Elements in the New Folk Dance in Israel," *Journal of the International Folk Music Council* 3 (1951): 56.

65. Judith Brin Ingber, "Shorashim: The Roots of Israeli Folk Dance," *Dance Perspectives* 59 (Autumn 1974): 14.

66. Kaufman, "Folk Dance in Israel," 55.

67. Sara Levi-Tanai, "Treasure Out of Yemen," in Berk, *Ha-Rikud*, 12.

68. Elke Kaschl, *Dance and Authenticity in Israel and Palestine: Performing the Nation* (Boston: Brill, 2003), 199.

69. Kaschl, 61.

70. Kaschl, 85.

71. Ingber, "Shorashim," 46.

72. April, "Re: Rikud 244 (choreographers)," Groups.io, March 30, 2001, https://groups.io/g/rikud/message/1800?p=%2C%2C%2C20%2C0%2C0%2C0%3A%3ACreated%2C%2CTake+what+you+like+and+leave+what+you+don%E2%80%99t%2C20%2C2%2C40%2C65595700.

73. Simon Herman, *Israelis and Jews: The Continuity of an Identity* (New York: Jewish Publication Society, 1971).

74. Herman, 48.

75. Herman, 57.

76. Baruch Kimmerling, *The Invention and Decline of Israeliness: State, Society, and the Military* (Berkeley: University of California Press, 2001).

77. Kimmerling, 172.

78. Donna Robinson Divine, "Zionism and the Politics of Authenticity," in "Zionism in the 21st Century," special issue, *Israel Studies* 19, no. 2 (Summer 2014): 94–110.

79. Chaim Noy and Erik Cohen, eds., *Israeli Backpackers: From Tourism to Rite of Passage* (Albany: State University of New York Press, 2005), 7; Ayana Shira Haviv, "Next Year in Katmandu: Israeli Backpackers and the Formation of a New Israeli Identity," in Noy and Cohen, *Israeli Backpackers*, 71.

80. Cf. Rachel Werczberger and Boaz Huss, eds., special issue, *New Age Culture in Israel, Israel Studies Review* (Winter 2014); Marianna Ruah-Midbar, "Current Jewish Spiritualities in Israel: A New Age," *Modern Judaism* 32, no. 1 (February 2012): 102–124.

81. Ruah-Midbar, 104.

82. Rachel Werczberger, *Jews in the Age of Authenticity: Jewish Spiritual Renewal in Israel* (New York: Peter Lang, 2017), 146.

83. Werczberger, 149.

84. Werczberger, 151.

CHAPTER EIGHT — SHTETL AUTHENTICITY: FROM *FIDDLER ON THE ROOF* TO THE REVIVAL OF KLEZMER

1. Alisa Solomon, "On Jewishness, as the Fiddler Played," *New York Times*, October 17, 2013, https://www.nytimes.com/2013/10/20/theater/fiddler-on-the-roof-its-production-heritage.html.

2. Alisa Solomon, *Wonder of Wonders: A Cultural History of* Fiddler on the Roof (New York: Metropolitan, 2013), 2.

3. Raphael Patai, review of *Life Is with People: The Jewish Little-Town of Eastern Europe*, by Mark Zborowski and Elizabeth Herzog, *American Anthropologist* 54, no. 4 (October–December, 1952): 544.

4. Boyarin, "In Search of Authenticity," 951.

5. Steven Aschheim, *Brothers and Strangers: The East European Jew in German and German Jewish Consciousness, 1800–1923* (Madison: University of Wisconsin Press, 1982), 3, 6. Cf. John Murray Cuddihy, *The Ordeal of Civility: Freud, Marx, Levi-Strauss, and the Jewish Struggle with Modernity* (New York: Basic, 1974).

6. Aschheim, 84.

7. Aschheim, 84, 102, 108, 187.

8. For further discussion of the issue of non-Jewish actors cast as Jewish characters, see Ted Merwin, "Jew-Face: Non-Jews Playing Jews on the American Stage," *Cultural and Social History* 4, no. 2 (June 2007): 215–233.

9. Ben Brantley, "A Cozy Little McShtetl," *New York Times*, February 27, 2004, https://www.nytimes.com/2004/02/27/movies/theater-review-a-cozy-little-mcshtetl.html.

10. Solomon, *Wonder of Wonders*, 223.

11. Irving Howe, "Tevye on Broadway," *Commentary* 38 (November 1964): 73–74.

12. Solomon, *Wonder of Wonders*, 298.

13. Alisa Solomon, "How 'Fiddler' Became Folklore," Forward, September 1, 2006, https://forward.com/culture/1710/how-e2-80-98fiddler-e2-80-99-became-folklore/.

14. Alisa Solomon, "Tradition! The Indestructible 'Fiddler on the Roof,'" *New Yorker*, October 8, 2015.

15. Alisa Solomon, "Tevye, Today, and Beyond," Forward, September 8, 2006, https://forward.com/culture/2422/tevye-today-and-beyond/.

16. Solomon, *Wonder of Wonders*, 343.

17. Solomon, 305.

18. Amnon Shiloah, *Jewish Musical Traditions* (Detroit, Mich.: Wayne State University Press, 1992), 37.

19. Mark Slobin, ed., *American Klezmer: Its Roots and Offshoots* (Berkeley: University of California Press, 2002), 1.

20. Slobin, 2.

21. Yale Strom, *The Book of Klezmer: The History, the Music, the Folklore* (Chicago: A Capella, 2001), 110–111, 150.

22. Strom, 111.

23. Strom, 111.

24. Christina Baade, "Jewzak and Heavy Shtetl: Constructing Ethnic Identity and Asserting Authenticity in the New Klezmer Movement," *Monatshefte* 90, no. 2 (1998): 211.

25. Seth Rogovoy, *The Essential Klezmer* (Chapel Hill, N.C.: Algonquin, 2000), 55.

26. Henry Sapoznik, *Klezmer! Jewish Music from Old World to Our World* (New York: Shirmer Trade, 1999), 89; Slobin, *American Klezmer*, 16.

27. Baade, "Jewzak," 211.

28. Peter Sokolow, "Mazel Tov! Klezmer Music and Simchas in Brooklyn, 1910 to Present," in *Jews of Brooklyn*, ed. Ilana Abramovitch and Sean Galvin (Waltham, Mass.: Brandeis University Press, 2002), 180.

29. Sapoznik, *Klezmer!*, 116.

30. Strom, *Book of Klezmer*, 171.

31. Strom, 246.

32. Sapoznik, *Klezmer!*, 291.

33. David H. Weinberg, *Between Tradition and Modernity: Haim Zhitlowski, Simon Dubnow, Ahad Ha'am and the Shaping of Modern Jewish Identity* (New York: Holmes and Meier, 1996), 139.

34. Jonathan Rosen, "A Dead Language, Yiddish Lives," *New York Times Magazine*, July 7, 1996, 26–27.

35. This, of course, was quite similar to the dynamic of the "imaginary Jew" described by Finkielkraut.

36. Shulamis Dion, "The Klezmer Revival," *Humanistic Judaism* 20, no. 3 (Summer 1992): 55.

37. "Bands and Performing Groups: Klezmer, Jewish, and Related or Derivative Musics," KlezmerShack, accessed August 7, 2021, http://www.klezmershack.com/contacts/klezbands_d.html.

38. Beyond the Pale, "Bio," accessed August 7, 2021, https://www.beyondthepale.net/about.

39. Ruth Schweitzer, "Beyond the Pale Creates Ruckus with New Album," Canadian Jewish News, June 19, 2017, http://www.cjnews.com/culture/beyond-the-pale-ruckus-new-album.

40. Quoted in Gaby Alter, "The Arts: A Musical Coat of Many Colors," *Hadassah Magazine*, October 2005, http://www.hadassahmagazine.org/2005/10/10/arts-musical-coat-many-colors/.

41. Ruth Ellen Gruber, *Virtually Jewish: Reinventing Jewish Culture in Europe* (Berkeley: University of California Press, 2002), 230.

42. Rogovoy, *Essential Klezmer*, 2.

43. Strom, *Book of Klezmer*, 224.

44. Slobin, *American Klezmer*, 61.

45. Joel Rudinow, "Race, Ethnicity, Expressive Authenticity: Can White People Sing the Blues?," *Journal of Aesthetics and Art Criticism* 52, no. 1 (Winter 1994): 132.

46. Seth Rogovoy, "The Klezmer Revival: Old World Meets New," Berkshire Web, accessed ca. May 2009, http://www.berkshireweb.com/rogovoy/interviews/klez.html (site discontinued).

47. Gruber, *Virtually Jewish*, 6, 185.

48. Gruber, 188.

49. Simon Frith, "Music and Identity," in *Questions of Cultural Identity*, ed. Stuart Hall and Paul du Gay (London: SAGE, 1996), 111.

50. Mark Slobin, *Fiddler on the Move: Exploring the Klezmer World* (New York: Oxford University Press, 2000), 5.

51. Frank London, "An Insider's View: How We Traveled from Obscurity to the Klezmer Establishment in Twenty Years," in Slobin, *American Klezmer*, 210.

52. Alicia Svigals, "Why Do We Do This Anyway: Klezmer as Jewish Youth Subculture," *Judaism: A Quarterly Journal of Jewish Life and Thought* 47, no. 1 (Winter 1998): 47–48.

53. Svigals, 48.

54. Strom, *Book of Klezmer*, 229.

55. Rogovoy, *Essential Klezmer*, 118.

56. Svigals, "Why We Do This," 219.

57. Christina Baade, "Can This White Lutheran Play Klezmer? Reflections on Race, Ethnicity, and Revival," *Sonneck Society for American Music Bulletin* 24, no. 2 (Summer 1998): 37–38.

58. Baade, "Jewzak," 208.

59. "Joyful Joe" Miterko, "Re(Jew)vinating Jazz Part II: Klezmer and Messianic Worship," *Meuchad* (blog), June 27, 2017, http://meuchad.org/blog?offset=1528322008761.

60. Dell Upton, "Ethnicity, Authenticity, and Invented Traditions," *Historical Archaeology* 30, no. 2 (1996): 4.

61. Upton, 5.

CHAPTER NINE — BECOMING JEWISH: INTERMARRIAGE AND CONVERSION

1. Nissan Dovid Dubov, "What Is Wrong with Intermarriage?," Chabad.org, accessed August 7, 2021, https://www.chabad.org/library/article_cdo/aid/108396/jewish/Intermarriage.htm.

2. David Bleich, "The Prohibition against Intermarriage," *Journal of Halacha and Contemporary Society* 1, no. 1 (1981): 7.

3. Bleich, 5.

4. Mordecai Kaplan, *Judaism as a Civilization: Toward a Reconstruction of American-Jewish Life* (New York: Schocken, 1967), 50.

5. Eric Goldstein, *The Price of Whiteness: Jews, Race, and American Identity* (Princeton, N.J.: Princeton University Press, 2006), 11.

6. Goldstein, 19, 22.

7. Among nonobservant Jews, there is a tendency to see Jewishness as a fact of birth unrelated to religious practice, which makes them feel more authentically Jewish than even the most observant convert. Shelly Tenenbaum and Lynn Davidman, "It's in My Genes: Biological Discourse and Essentialist View of Identity among Contemporary American Jews," *Sociological Quarterly* 48 (2007): 435–450.

8. Goldstein, *Price of Whiteness*, 22.

9. Goldstein, 29–30, 102.

10. David de Sola Pool, "Intermarriage" (New York: National Jewish Welfare Board, 1958), quoted in Albert I. Gordon, *Intermarriage: Interfaith, Interracial, Interethnic* (Boston: Beacon, 1964), 187 (emphasis added).

11. De Sola Pool, "Intermarriage," 5.

12. Cf. Nan Fink, "Stranger in the Midst: A Memoir of Spiritual Discovery," *Tikkun* 12, no. 1 (January 1997): 31–34.

13. Gary A. Tobin, *Opening the Gates: How Proactive Conversion Can Revitalize the Jewish Community* (San Francisco: Jossey-Bass, 1999), 99.

14. Steven M. Cohen and Charles Liebman, *Two Worlds of Judaism: The Israeli and American Experiences* (New Haven, Conn.: Yale University Press, 1990), 24.

15. Nicholas de Lange, *Judaism* (New York: Oxford University Press, 1987), 20.

16. Philo, *The Special Laws*, vol. 7, bk. 1:52, *Loeb Classical Library*, ed. Jeffrey Henderson, trans. F. H. Colson (Cambridge, Mass.: Harvard University Press, 1937), 129.

17. Peder Borgen, "The Early Church and the Hellenistic Synagogue," in *Philo, John, and Paul: New Perspectives on Judaism and Early Christianity* (Atlanta: Scholars, 1987), 213.

18. Aron Moss, "What's This 'Jewish Soul' Thing? Aren't We All One," Chabad.org, accessed August 7, 2021, https://www.chabad.org/library/article_cdo/aid/166900/jewish/Whats-this-Jewish-soul-Thing-Arent-We-All-One.htm.

19. K. Kohler, "David Einhorn: The Uncompromising Champion of Reform," in *Yearbook of the Central Conference of American Rabbis*, vol. 10 (New York: Central Conference of American Rabbis, 1910), 265.

20. Eliot Sala Schoenberg, "Intermarriage and Conservative Judaism: An Approach for the 1990s," *Conservative Judaism* 43 (Fall 1990): 13.

21. Jerome Epstein, "Congratulations to Mixed Marriage Families," *Rabbinical Assembly: Committee on Jewish Law and Standards* 16 (1989): 457–466, http://www.rabbinicalassembly.org/sites/default/files/public/halakhah/teshuvot/19861990/epstein_congratulations.pdf.

22. Rabbi Julie Schonfeld and Rabbi Jeffrey A. Wohlberg, "A Delicate Balance: The Rabbinical Assembly's Position on Outreach and Conversion," Leadership Council of Conservative Judaism (LCCJ), Keruv Commission, 2009.

23. On the idea of Jewish identity as a journey, see Bethamie Horowitz, "Connections and Journeys: Shifting Identities among American Jews," *Contemporary Jewry* 19 (1998): 63–94.

24. Arnold Eisen, "Wanted: Converts of Judaism," *Wall Street Journal*, July 24, 2014, http://online.wsj.com/articles/arnold-m-eisen-wanted-converts-to-judaism-1406244075.

25. Rabbi Robyn Frish, "Converts Not Necessarily Wanted—an Open Letter to Arnold Eisen," 18Doors, accessed August 7, 2021, http://www.interfaithfamily.com/blog/iff/conversion/converts-not-necessarily-wanted-an-open-letter-to-arnold-eisen/.

26. Stuart Charmé, Jeffrey Kress, Tali Hyman, and Bethamie Horowitz, "Jewish Identities in Action: An Exploration of Models, Metaphors, and Methods," *Journal of Jewish Education* 74, no. 2 (2008): 115–143.

27. Debra Nussbaum Cohen, "A Slice of America: Judaism among Non-Jews," *New York Times*, May 31, 2003, https://www.nytimes.com/2003/05/31/nyregion/religion-journal-a-slice-of-america-judaism-among-non-jews.html.

28. Cohen.

29. Rabbi Steve Greenberg, "Between Intermarriage and Conversion: Finding a Middle Way," Spirit and Story, accessed August 7, 2021, http://www.rabbiswithoutborders.net/ss43.html.

30. Greenberg.

31. Steven Carr Reuben, *A Parent's Guilt-Free Guide to Raising Jewish Kids: Understanding Judaism in the Modern World* (Bloomington, Ind.: Xlibris, 2002).

32. Yossi Beilin, *His Brother's Keeper: Israel and Diaspora Jewry in the Twenty-First Century* (New York: Schocken, 2000), 99.

33. Beilin, 100.

34. Steven M. Cohen, "Yes, Something Can Be Done: A 'Purple' Solution to Intermarriage," Mosaic, September 15, 2013, https://mosaicmagazine.com/response/uncategorized/2013/09/yes-something-can-be-done/.

35. Steven M. Cohen and Kerry M. Olitzky, "Op-Ed: Conversion Shouldn't Be the Only Path to Joining the Jewish People," Jewish Telegraphic Agency, November 29, 2013, http://www.jta.org/2013/11/29/news-opinion/opinion/op-ed-conversion-shouldnt-be-the-only-path-to-joining-the-jewish-people.

36. Jonathan Sacks, *Will We Have Jewish Grandchildren? Jewish Continuity and How to Achieve It* (London: Vallentine Mitchell, 1994), 110.

CHAPTER TEN — AUTHENTICALLY JEWISH GENES

1. Natalie Zemon Davis, *The Return of Martin Guerre* (Cambridge, Mass.: Harvard University Press, 1984).

2. Doron M. Behar et al., "The Genome-Wide Structure of the Jewish People," *Nature* 466 (2010): 238–242.

3. Michael Hammer, quoted in Jon Entine, *Abraham's Children: Race, Identity, and the DNA of the Chosen People* (New York: Grand Central, 2007), 211. Cf. M. F. Hammer et al., "Jewish and Middle Eastern Non-Jewish Populations Share a Common Pool of Y-Chromosome Biallelic Haplotypes," *PNAS* 97, no. 12 (June 6, 2000): 6769–6774.

4. Harry Ostrer, *Legacy: A Genetic History of the Jewish People* (New York: Oxford University Press, 2012), xviii.

5. Ostrer, 217.

6. Ostrer, 215, 222.

7. Ostrer, 218.

8. Ostrer, 96.

9. Susan M. Kahn, "Are Genes Jewish? Conceptual Ambiguities in the New Genetic Age," in *Boundaries of Jewish Identity*, ed. Susan A. Glenn and Naomi B. Sokoloff (Seattle: University of Washington Press, 2011), 16; Susan M. Kahn, "Who Are the Jews? New Formulations of an Age-Old Question," *Human Biology* 85, no. 6 (December 2013): 919–924; J. E. Elkins et al., "An Updated World-Wide Characterization of the Cohen Modal Haplotype," American Society of Human Genetics Annual Meeting, Salt Lake City, October 2005, http://www.smgf.org/resources/papers/ASHG2005_Jayne.pdf.

10. Ostrer, *Legacy*, 97.

11. Ornella Semino et al., "Origin, Diffusion, and Differentiation of Y-Chromosome Haplogroups E and J: Inferences on the Neolithization of Europe and Later Migratory Events in the Mediterranean Area," *American Journal of Human Genetics* 74, no. 5 (2004): 1023–1034; Avshalom Zoossmann-Diskin, "Are Today's Jewish Priests Descended from the Old Ones?," *HOMO: Journal of Comparative Human Biology* 51, nos. 2–3 (2000): 156–162.

12. Wesley K. Sutton, "'Jewish Genes:' Ancient Priests and Modern Jewish Identity," in *Who Is a Jew? Reflections on History, Religion, and Culture*, ed. Leonard J. Greenspoon (West Lafayette, Ind.: Purdue University Press, 2014), 108–9.

13. Sutton, 109.

14. Gil Atzmon et al., "Abraham's Children in the Genome Era: Major Jewish Diaspora Populations Comprise Distinct Genetic Clusters with Shared Middle Eastern Ancestry," *American Journal of Human Genetics* 86 (June 2010): 850, 854, 855, 857.

15. Ellen Levy-Coffman, "A Mosaic of People: The Jewish Story and a Reassessment of the DNA Evidence," *Journal of Genetic Genealogy* 1 (2005): 13.

16. Levy-Coffman, 24.

17. Levy-Coffman, 31.

18. Jonathan Marks, *What It Means to Be 98% Chimpanzee* (Berkeley: University of California Press, 2002), 135.

19. Marks, 136.

20. Levy-Coffman, "Mosaic of People," 31.

21. Raphael Falk, "Genetic Markers Cannot Determine Jewish Descent," *Frontiers in Genetics*, January 21, 2015, https://doi.org/10.3389/fgene.2014.00462.

22. Tudor Parfitt and Yulia Egorova, *Genetics, Mass Media and Identity: A Case Study of the Genetic Research on the Bene Israel and the Lemba* (New York: Routledge, 2006), 43.

23. Neil Bradman and Mark Thomas, "Genetics: The Pursuit of Jewish History by Other Means," *Judaism Today* 10 (Autumn 1998): 4–6.

24. Several examples of mistaken or exaggerated conclusions based on a deterministic interpretation of the presence or absence of particular genetic markers can be seen in "Richard Henry Proves That the Paternal Haplogroup E1B1A Is the Real Israelite Lineage," PR Distribution, August 20, 2021, https://pressreleasejet.com/news/richard-henry-proves-that-the-paternal-haplogroup-e1b1a-is-the-real-israelite-lineage/1630504; "Do the Palestinians have Jewish Roots," *Shavei Israel* (blog), June 5, 2016, https://www.shavei.org/blog/2016/06/05/palestinians-jewish-roots/; and Dov Ivry, "Most Palestinians are Descendants of Jews," Times of Israel, August 21, 2016, https://blogs.timesofisrael.com/most-palestinians-are-descendants-of-jews/.

25. Marks, *98% Chimpanzee*, 110.

26. Marks, 248.

27. Cf. Raphael Patai and Jennifer Patai Wing, *The Myth of the Jewish Race* (New York: Scribner's Sons, 1975), 36–38.

28. Nadia Abu El-Haj, *The Genealogical Science: The Search for Jewish Origins and the Politics of Epistemology* (Chicago: University of Chicago Press, 2012), 25.

29. Abu El-Haj, 144.

30. Abu El-Haj, 222.

31. Abu El-Haj, 169.

32. Abu El-Haj, 30.

CHAPTER ELEVEN — LOST JEWISH TRIBES IN ETHIOPIA

1. Sidra DeKoven Ezrahi, *Booking Passage: Exile and Homecoming in the Modern Jewish Imagination* (Berkeley: University of California Press, 2000), 35.

2. Zvi Ben-Dor Benite, *The Ten Lost Tribes: A World History* (New York: Oxford University Press, 2009), 86–89.

3. Benite, 91.

4. Benite, 97.

5. Responsum of the Radbaz on the Falasha slave, pt. 7, no. 5, cited in Michael Corinaldi, *Jewish Identity: The Case of Ethiopian Jewry* (Jerusalem: Magnes, 1998), 196.

6. Tudor Parfitt, *Black Jews in Africa and the Americas* (Cambridge, Mass.: Harvard University Press, 2013), 23.

7. Parfitt, 35.

8. Parfitt, 51; Steven Kaplan, *The Beta Israel (Falasha) in Ethiopia: From Earliest Times to the Twentieth Century* (New York: New York University, 1992), 83.

9. Parfitt, *Black Jews*, 65.

10. Parfitt, 37.

11. David Kessler, *The Falashas: A Short History of the Ethiopian Jews* (London: Frank Cass, 1996), xii.

12. Kaplan, *Beta Israel*, 126–127.

13. Don Seeman, *One People, One Blood: Ethiopian-Israelis and the Return to Judaism* (New Brunswick, N.J.: Rutgers University Press, 2009), 53–56.

14. Kaplan, *Beta Israel*, 138.

15. David Ellenson, *Tradition in Transition: Orthodoxy, Halakhah, and the Boundaries of Modern Jewish Identity* (New York: University Press of America, 1989), 65.

16. Kaplan, *Beta Israel*, 140.

17. J. Abbink, "An Ethiopian Jewish 'Missionary' as Cultural Broker," in *Ethiopian Jews and Israel*, ed. M. Ashkenazi and A. Weingrod (New Brunswick, N.J.: Transaction, 1987), 21.

18. Kaplan, *Beta Israel*, 141.

19. Louis Rapoport, *Redemption Song: The Story of Operation Moses* (New York: Harcourt Brace Jovanovich, 1986), 39.

20. Steven Kaplan and Chaim Rosen, "Ethiopian Immigrants in Israel: Between Preservation of Culture and Invention of Tradition," *Jewish Journal of Sociology* 35, no. 1 (1993): 39.

21. Quoted in Kaplan, *Beta Israel*, 156.

22. Parfitt, *Black Jews*, 155.

23. Kaplan, *Beta Israel*, 148.

24. Kaplan, 123.

25. Kaplan, 110.

26. Don Seeman, "Ethnographers, Rabbis, and Jewish Epistemology: The Case of the Ethiopian Jews," *Tradition* 25, no. 4 (Summer 1991): 13.

27. Seeman, 22.

28. Corinaldi, *Jewish Identity*, 14–15.

29. Corinaldi, 140.

30. Corinaldi, 141–143.

31. Hagar Salamon, "In Search of Self and Other: A Few Remarks on Ethnicity, Race, and Ethiopian Jews," in *Jewish Locations: Traversing Racialized Landscapes*, ed. Lisa Tessman and Bat-Ami Bar On (New York: Rowman & Littlefield, 2001), 85.

32. Kaplan, *Beta Israel*, 158–163 (addendum).

33. Kaplan, 8.

34. Kaplan, 14–17.

35. Kaplan, 74.

36. Kaplan, 78.

37. Kaplan and Rosen, "Ethiopian Immigrants in Israel," 38.

38. Kaplan and Rosen, 42.

39. Tanya Schwarz, *Ethiopian Jewish Immigrants* (London: Curzon, 2001), 74.

40. Kaplan, *Beta Israel*, 10.

41. Kaplan, 10–11.

42. Kaplan and Rosen, "Ethiopian Immigrants in Israel," 36.

43. Kaplan and Rosen, 37.

44. Steven Kaplan and Hagar Salamon, "Ethiopian Jews in Israel: A Part of the People or Apart of the People," in *Jews in Israel: Contemporary Cultural and Social Patterns*, ed. Uzi Rebhun and Chaim I. Waxman (Waltham, Mass.: Brandeis University Press, 2004), 132.

45. Kaplan and Salamon, "Ethiopian Jews in Israel," 132–133.

46. Kaplan and Salamon, 143.

47. Schwarz, *Ethiopian Jewish Immigrants*, 202.

48. Schwarz, 229.

49. Schwarz, 230.

50. Hagar Salamon, *The Hyena People: Ethiopian Jews in Christian Ethiopia* (Berkeley: University of California Press, 1999).

51. Sholomo Ben Levy, "Beta Yisrael: A Historical Analysis," BlackJews.org, 2002, http://www.blackjews.org/Ethiopian%20Community/Ethiopian%20Chapter.htm.

52. Eric Maroney, *The Other Zions: The Lost Histories of Jewish Nations* (New York: Rowman & Littlefield, 2010), 51.

53. Ephraim Isaac, "The Question of Jewish Identity and Ethiopian Jewish Origins," *Midstream* 51, no. 5 (January 2005): 29.

54. Isaac, 31.

55. Isaac, 33–34.

56. Isaac, 29.

57. Isaac, 30.

CHAPTER TWELVE — RECOGNIZING BLACK JEWS IN THE UNITED STATES

1. There are, of course, individual African Americans who are members of mainstream synagogues and whose claims to being Jewish may be tied to family history, adoption, conversion and other reasons. This chapter is not dealing with that group of people but rather the Black Jews who were and are members of Black congregations that claim Jewish status without necessarily adhering to all the norms of mainstream American synagogues for determining Jewishness or for following traditional Jewish religious practices.

2. Michael T. Miller, "Black Judaism(s) and the Hebrew Israelites," *Religion Compass* 13, no. 11 (2019): 4, https://doi.org/10.1111/rec3.12346; Andre E. Key, "Toward a Typology of Black Hebrew Religious Thought and Practice," *Journal of Africana Religions* 2, no. 1 (2014): 32; Elias Fanayaye Jones, "Black Hebrews: The Quest for Authentic Identity," *Journal of Religious Thought* 44, no. 22 (1988): 35–49.

3. Howard Brotz, *The Black Jews of Harlem: Negro Nationalism and the Dilemmas of Negro Leadership* (New York: Schocken, 1970), 11.

4. Tudor Parfitt, *Black Jews in Africa and the Americas* (Cambridge, Mass.: Harvard University Press, 2013), 72.

5. Brotz, *Black Jews of Harlem*, 10.

6. For a useful typology of the different kinds of Black Judaism, see Key, "Black Hebrew Religious Thought," 31–66.

7. "The Israelite Academy," BlackJews.org, accessed August 7, 2021, http://www.blackjews.org/Israelite%20Academy%20Courses%20and%20History.htm.

8. Quoted in Brotz, *Black Jews of Harlem*, 6.

9. Yvonne Chireau, "Black Culture and Black Zion: African American Religious Encounters with Judaism, 1790–1930, an Overview," in Yvonne Chireau and Nathaniel Deutsch, *Black Zion: African American Religious Encounters with Judaism* (New York: Oxford University Press, 2000), 21.

10. Brotz, *Black Jews of Harlem*, 9.

11. Chireau, "Black Culture," 24.

12. Sholomo Ben Levy, "Who Are We?," BlackJews.org, accessed August 7, 2021, http://www.blackjews.org/Essays/WhoAreWe.html.

13. Janice W. Fernheimer, *Stepping into Zion: Hatzaad Harishon, Black Jews, and the Remaking of Jewish Identity* (Tuscaloosa: University of Alabama Press, 2014), 12, 31.

14. Fernheimer, 35.

15. James Baldwin, "From the American Scene: The Harlem Ghetto: Winter 1948," *Commentary* 6 (January 1948): 169, http://www.commentarymagazine.com/article/from-the-american-scene-the-harlem-ghetto-winter-1948/.

16. Baldwin, 169.

17. James Landing, *Black Judaism: Story of an American Movement* (Durham, N.C.: Carolina Academic, 2002), 123.

18. Landing, 189.

19. Walter Isaac, "Locating Afro-American Judaism: A Critique of White Normativity," in *A Companion to Afro-American Studies*, ed. Lewis R. Gordon and Jane Anna Gordon (Malden, Mass.: Blackwell), 531.

20. Mitchell B. Hart, *Social Science and the Politics of Modern Jewish Identity* (Stanford, Calif.: Stanford University Press, 2000), 88–89.

21. See Eric Goldstein, *The Price of Whiteness: Jews, Race, and American Identity* (Princeton, N.J.: Princeton University Press, 2006).

22. Goldstein, 186.

23. Landing, *Black Judaism*, 266.

24. Quoted in Landing, 207.

25. J. A. Rogers, "Harlem Black Jews Fakes Says Norman Salit," *Afro-American*, December 19, 1931, p. 8, https://news.google.com/newspapers?nid=2211&dat=19311219&id=hyYmAAAAIBAJ&sjid=6PoFAAAAIBAJ&pg=6555,6485495&hl=en.

26. Brotz, *Black Jews of Harlem*, 36–7.

27. Roberta S. Gold, "The Black Jews of Harlem: Representation, Identity, and Race, 1920–1939," *American Quarterly* 55, no. 2 (2003): 208.

28. Isaac, "Locating Afro-American Judaism," 513–515.

29. Isaac, 517.

30. It is true that not all Black Jews in America arrived at Judaism by way of Christianity. Blacks may have been introduced to Judaism from Jewish slave owners, through marriage to Jews, or through Jewish communities in the Caribbean and South America. Cf. Miller, "Black Judaism(s)," 5–6. Nonetheless, in the cases of most of the new groups of Black Jews that arose, especially that of Wentworth Matthew, the Christian background of the founders and many of the initial followers is fairly obvious.

31. Landing, *Black Judaism*, 10.

32. Landing, 276.

33. Landing, 276.

34. Tudor Parfitt, *The Lost Tribes of Israel: The History of a Myth* (London: Weidenfeld and Nicolson, 2002), 223–224.

35. Harold Goldfarb, "Blacks and Conversion to Judaism," in *A Coat of Many Colors: Jewish Subcommunities in the United States*, ed. Abraham Lavender (Westport, Conn.: Greenwood, 1977), 226.

36. Goldfarb, 227.

37. Goldfarb, 228.

38. Robert Coleman, "Black and Jewish—and Unaccepted," in Lavender, *Coat of Many Colors*, 229–232.

39. J. David Bleich, "Black Jews: A Halakhic Perspective," *Tradition* 15, nos. 1–2 (Summer–Spring 1975): 49.

40. Bleich, 50.

41. Bleich, 59.

42. Bleich, 59–60.

43. Bleich, 60.

44. Bleich, 65.

45. Levy, "Who Are We?"

46. Isaac, "Locating Afro-American Judaism," 531–532.

47. Isaac, 535.

48. Key, "Black Hebrew Religious Thought," 37.

49. Zev Chafets, "Obama's Rabbi," *New York Times Magazine*, April 2, 2009, https://www.nytimes.com/2009/04/05/magazine/05rabbi-t.html?action=click&module=RelatedCoverage&pgtype=Article&region=Footer.

50. Melanie Kaye/Kantrowitz, *Colors of Jews: Racial Politics and Radical Diasporism* (Bloomington: Indiana University Press, 2007), 157.

51. Kaye/Kantrowitz, 158.

52. For a thorough discussion of the academic debates about the ethnic identity of the ancient Israelites, see Kenton L. Sparks, *Ethnicity and Identity in Ancient Israel: Prolegomena to the Study of Ethnic Sentiments and Their Expression in the Hebrew Bible* (Winona Lake, Ind.: Eisenbrauns, 1998).

53. "Our History," Beth Shalom B'Nai Zaken Ethiopian Hebrew Congregation, accessed August 6, 2021, https://www.bethshalombz.org/history/.

54. Sarah Leiter, *True to Our God, True to Our Native Land: Establishing Communal Identity at a Black American Jewish Temple* (MA thesis, University of Chicago, 2015), 1.

55. Michel Martin and Capers C. Funnye, "Faith Matters: Black Rabbi Shares Story of Conversion, Unity," April 10, 2009, in *Tell Me More*, podcast, MP3 audio, 13:38, https://www.npr.org/transcripts/102953476.

56. For discussions of the meaning of "mixed multitude," see Gail Labovitz, "What It Means to Be 'Erev Rav,'" American Jewish University, February 4, 2017, https://www.aju.edu/ziegler-school-rabbinic-studies/our-torah/back-issues/what-it-means-be-erev-rav; and David J. Zucker, "Erev Rav: A Mixed Multitude of Meanings," TheTorah.com, accessed August 18, 2021, https://www.thetorah.com/article/erev-rav-a-mixed-multitude-of-meanings.

57. Kaye/Kantrowitz, *Colors of Jews*, 39.

58. Martin and Funnye, "Faith Matters."

59. Ken Koltun-Fromm, *Imagining Jewish Authenticity: Vision and Text in American Jewish Thought* (Bloomington: Indiana University Press, 2015), 183–184.

60. Koltun-Fromm, 183.

CHAPTER THIRTEEN — AUTHENTICATING CRYPTO-JEWISH IDENTITY

1. Marissa Newman, "Sharansky: Israel Must Ease Conversion of Crypto-Jews," *Times of Israel*, February 11, 2014, http://www.timesofisrael.com/sharansky-israel-must-ease-conversion-for-crypto-jews/.

2. Stephen Gomes, "My 50-Year Search for My Portuguese-Jewish Self," in *Under One Canopy: Readings in Jewish Diversity*, ed. Karen Primack (New York: Kulanu, 2003), 44–45.

3. Gomes, 46.

4. Gomes, 46.

5. Cary Herz, *New Mexico's Crypto-Jews: Image and Memory* (Albuquerque: University of New Mexico Press, 2007).

6. Ori Soltes, "Art, History, Memory, Identity, Truth: The Art and Craft of Cary Herz," in Herz, *New Mexico's Crypto-Jews*, 7.

7. Soltes, 7.

8. Jacobs, 109.

9. Garcia and Garcia.

10. Aviva Ben-Ur, review of *To the End of the Earth: A History of the Crypto-Jews of New Mexico*, by Stanley M. Hordes, *American Jewish History* 93, no. 2 (June 2007): 264–268.

11. Stanley M. Hordes, *To the End of the Earth: A History of the Crypto-Jews of New Mexico* (New York: Columbia University Press, 2005), 5.

12. David M. Gitlitz, *Secrecy and Deceit: The Religion of the Crypto-Jews* (Philadelphia: Jewish Publication Society, 1996), 84.

13. Gitlitz, 82–84.

14. Gitlitz, 45.

15. Gitlitz, 45.

16. Benzion Netanyahu, *The Origins of the Inquisition in Fifteenth-Century Spain* (New York: New York Review Books, 2001), 926–927.

17. Netanyahu, 928.

18. Netanyahu, 928–929.

19. Netanyahu, 932.

20. Netanyahu, 948.

21. Judith Neulander, "Folk Taxonomy, Prejudice and the Human Genome: Using Disease as a Jewish Ethnic Marker," *Patterns of Prejudice* 40, nos. 4–5 (September 2006): 386.

22. Judith Neulander, "Inventing Jewish History, Culture, and Genetic Identity in Modern New Mexico," in *Who Is a Jew? Reflections on History, Religion, and Culture*, ed. Leonard J. Greenspoon (West Lafayette, Ind.: Purdue University Press, 2014), 79.

23. Neulander, 83.

24. Neulander, 66; Gitlitz, *Secrecy and Deceit*, 47.

25. Judith Neulander, review of *To the End of the Earth: A History of the Crypto-Jews of New Mexico*, by Stanley M. Hordes, *Shofar: An Interdisciplinary Journal of Jewish Studies* 93, no. 1 (January 2007): 208–210.

26. Michael P. Carroll, "The Debate over Crypto-Jewish Presence in New Mexico," *Sociology of Religion* 63, no. 1 (2002): 12.

27. Seth Kunin, *Juggling Identities: Identity and Authenticity among the Crypto-Jews* (New York: Columbia University Press, 2009), 44.

28. Kunin, 57.

29. Jonathan Freedman, *Klezmer America: Jewishness, Ethnicity, Modernity* (New York: Columbia University Press, 2008), 215–216.

30. Jonathan Freedman, "Conversos, Marranos, and Crypto-Latinos," in *Boundaries of Jewish Identity*, ed. Susan A. Glenn and Naomi B. Sokoloff (Seattle: University of Washington Press), 194.

31. Freedman, 195.

32. Freedman, 195.

33. Jacobs, *Hidden Heritage*, chaps. 4–6.

34. Kunin, *Juggling Identities*, 37.

35. Kunin, 150.

36. Kunin, 147.

37. Kunin, 161.

38. Kunin, 172.

39. Kunin, 174.

40. Kunin, 178; Freedman makes the same point in "Conversos, Marranos, and Crypto-Latinos," 197.

41. Kunin, 205.

42. Seth Ward, "Converso Descendants in the American Southwest: A Report on Research, Resources, and the Changing Search for Identity," in *Jewish Studies at the Turn of the 20th Century*, ed. Judith Targarona and Angel Saez-Badillos (Leiden, Netherlands: E. J. Brill, 1999), 685.

43. Freedman, *Klezmer America*, 226.

44. Freedman, "Conversos, Marranos, and Crypto-Latinos," 199.

45. Kunin, *Juggling Identities*, 206.

46. Kunin, 212.

47. Kunin, 213.

48. Kunin, 215.

49. Kunin, 217.

50. Kunin, 222.

CHAPTER FOURTEEN — NEWLY FOUND JEWS AND THE REGIMES OF RECOGNITION

1. Israel Finkelstein and Neil Asher Silberman, *The Bible Unearthed: Archaeology's New Vision of Ancient Israel and the Origin of Its Sacred Texts* (New York: Free Press, 2001).

2. Tudor Parfitt, *The Lost Tribes of Israel: The History of a Myth* (London: Weidenfeld and Nicolson, 2002), 4.

3. Finkelstein and Silberman, *Bible Unearthed*.

4. Finkelstein and Silberman, 249.

5. Tudor Parfitt and Emanuela Trevisan Semi, eds., *Judaising Movements: Studies in the Margins of Judaism* (London: Routledge Curzon, 2002), 36.

6. Parfitt and Semi, 53.

7. Parfitt and Semi, 106.

8. "Our Goals," *Shavei Israel* (blog), accessed December 21, 2021, https://www.shavei.org/about-us/our-goals/.

9. "Our Goals."

10. "Our Goals."

11. Joan G. Roland, *Jews in British India: Identity in a Colonial Era* (Hanover, Conn.: University Press of New England, 1989), 13; Nathan Katz, *Who Are the Jews of India?* (Berkeley: University of California Press, 2000), 96.

12. H. Tinker, review of "The Children of Israel: The Bene Israel of Bombay," by Schifra Strizower, *Race* 14, no. 1 (1972): 98.

13. Katz, *Jews of India?*, 100.

14. Roland, *Jews in British India*, 11.

15. Joseph Hodes, *From India to Israel: Identity, Immigration, and the Struggle for Religious Equality* (Montreal: McGill-Queen's University Press, 2014), 8.

16. Katz, *Jews of India?*, iii–iv.

17. The earliest mention of the Bene Israel group is routinely reported as coming from the letter of a Danish missionary named Rev. Sartorius in 1738 who reports second or third-hand information about a group who call themselves Bene Israel, "sons of Israel." These reports have limited reliability and leave many unanswered questions.

18. Yulia Egorova, *Jews and India: Perceptions and India* (New York: Routledge, 2006), 84.

19. Roland, *Jews in British India*, 56–57, 65.

20. Roland, 66.

21. H. S. Kehimkar, *The History of the Bene Israel of India* (Tel Aviv: Dayag Press, 1937), 35.

22. Kehimkar, 37.

23. Kehimkar, 55, 59.

24. Benjamin J. Israel, *The Bene Israel of India: Some Studies* (New York: Apt Books, 1984), 51.

25. Hodes, *From India to Israel*, 124.

26. Joseph R. Hodes, "The Bene Israel and the 'Who Is a Jew' Controversy in Israel," in *Who Is a Jew? Reflections on History, Religion, and Culture*, ed. Leonard J. Greenspoon (West Lafayette, Ind.: Purdue University Press, 2014), 173–174.

27. Hodes, 187–189.

28. Israel, *Bene Israel of India*, 3.

29. Kelly A. Train, "Well, How Can You Be Jewish *and* European: Indian Jewish Experiences in the Toronto Jewish Community and the Creation of Congregation Bina," *American Jewish History* 100, no. 1 (January 2016): 7.

30. Train, 11.

31. Rivka Gonen, *The Quest for the Ten Lost Tribes of Israel: To the Ends of the Earth* (New York: Jason Aronson, 2002), 171.

32. Hillel Halkin, *Across the Sabbath River: In Search of a Lost Tribe of Israel* (New York: Houghton Mifflin, 2002), 134.

33. Halkin, 134.

34. Jack Zeller, "Welcome to Kulanu!," *Kulanu* 1, no. 1 (Spring 1994): 1, http://www.kulanu.org/wp-content/uploads/magazines/1994-spring.pdf.

35. Karen Primack, "Why Give? One Person's Reason," *Amishav USA* 1, no. 2 (Winter 1993–1994): 6, https://kulanu.org/wp-content/uploads/magazines/1993-winter.pdf.

36. Yulia Egorova and Shahid Perwez, *The Jews of Andhra Pradesh: Contesting Caste and Religion in South India* (New York: Oxford University Press, 2013), 108.

37. Egorova and Perwez, 112.

38. Karen Primack, "Visiting the Ugandan Miracle," *Kulanu* 2, no. 2 (Summer 1995): 4, http://www.kulanu.org/wp-content/uploads/magazines/1995-summer.pdf.

39. Jeffrey Summit, "Music and the Construction of Identity among the Abayudaya (Jewish People) of Uganda," in *Garland Handbook of African Music*, ed. Ruth M. Stone (New York: Routledge, 2008), 321.

40. Paul Wieder, "A Rave Review for Ugandan Music," *Kulanu* 5, no. 2 (Summer 1998): 1, http://www.kulanu.org/wp-content/uploads/magazines/1998-summer.pdf.

41. Summit, "Construction of Identity," 323.

42. "Abayudaya Safari Announced," *Kulanu* 10, no. 2 (Summer 2003): 2.

43. "Jewish Life in Uganda Mitzvah Tour & Wildlife Safari" (advertisement), *Kulanu* 11, no. 2 (Summer 2004): 3, http://www.kulanu.org/wp-content/uploads/magazines/2004-summer.pdf.

44. Laura Wexler, "Abayudaya Update," *Kulanu* 15, no. 2 (Summer 2008): 3, http://www.kulanu.org/wp-content/uploads/magazines/2008-summer.pdf.

45. The Be'chol Lashon mission statement can be found at "Be'chol Lashon / IJCR," Great Nonprofits, accessed December 16, 2021, https://greatnonprofits.org/org/bechol-lashon-ijcr.

46. This earlier version of the mission statement can be found here: "Be'chol Lashon," LinkedIn, accessed December 17, 2021, https://www.linkedin.com/company/bechollashon/.

47. Diane Tobin, Gary A. Tobin, and Scott Rubin, *In Every Tongue: The Racial and Ethnic Diversity of the Jewish People* (San Francisco: Institute for Jewish and Community Research, 2005), 67.

48. Tobin, Tobin, and Rubin, 67.

49. Tobin, Tobin, and Rubin, 13.

50. Tobin, Tobin, and Rubin, 25.

51. Tobin, Tobin, and Rubin, 98.

52. Tobin, Tobin, and Rubin, 171.

53. Tobin, Tobin, and Rubin, 172.

54. Tobin, Tobin, and Rubin, 175.

55. Stuart Hall, "Minimal Selves," in *Studying Culture: An Introductory Reader*, ed. Ann Gray and Jim McGuigan (London: Edward Arnold, 1993), 136–137.

56. Hall, 139.

57. Hall, 140.

CONCLUSION

1. Jean-Paul Sartre, *Antisemite and Jew: An Exploration of the Etiology of Hate* (New York: Schocken, 1995), 72.

2. See Phillip Vannini and J. Patrick Williams, *Authenticity in Culture, Self, and Society* (Farnham, U.K.: Ashgate, 2009), 2.

3. Jean-Paul Sartre, *Being and Nothingness: An Essay in Phenomenological Ontology* (New York: Washington Square, 1993), 136.

4. Daniel Boyarin and Jonathan Boyarin, "Diaspora: Generation and the Ground of Jewish Identity," *Critical Inquiry* 19, no. 4 (Summer 1993): 714.

5. Boyarin and Boyarin, 721.

6. Paul Gilroy, "Diaspora and the Detours of Identity," in *Identity and Difference*, ed. Kathryn Woodward (London: Sage, 1997), 335.

7. Paul Gilroy, "Routes and Roots: Black Identity as an Outernational Project," in *Racial and Ethnic Identity—Psychological Development and Creative Expression*, ed. H. W. Harris, H. C. Blue, and E. E. H. Griffin (London: Routledge, 1995), 26; Cf. Stuart Hall, "Forward," in *The Art of Being Black: The Creation of Black British Youth Identities*, ed. Claire Alexander (Oxford: Oxford University Press, 1996), 1–2.

8. Jonathan Freedman, *Klezmer America: Jewishness, Ethnicity, Modernity* (New York: Columbia University Press, 2008), 18, 35.

9. Freedman, 18, 38.

10. Adrienne Rich, "Split at the Root," in *Essential Essays: Culture, Politics, and the Art of Poetry*, ed. Sandra M. Gilbert (New York: W. W. Norton, 2018).

11. Adrienne Rich, "Jewish Days and Night," in *A Human Eye: Essays on Art in Society, 1997–2008* (New York: W. W. Norton, 2010), 32.

12. Cynthia Baker, *Jew* (New Brunswick, N.J.: Rutgers University Press, 2016), 127.

13. Baker, 98.

14. Baker, 129.

15. Staci Boris, *The New Authentics: Artists of the Post-Jewish Generation* (Chicago: Spertus, 2007).

16. Boris, 16.

17. Boris, 23.

18. Arnold Eisen, *Taking Hold of Torah: Jewish Commitment and Community in America* (Bloomington: Indiana University Press, 1997), 28.

19. Cf. Efraim Shmueli, *Seven Jewish Cultures* (Cambridge: Cambridge University Press, 1980).

20. Raymond Bach, "Identifying Jews: The Legacy of the 1941 Exhibition, 'Le Juif et la France,'" *Studies in 20th Century Literature* 23, no. 1 (1999): 1, https://doi.org/10.4148/2334-4415.1455.

21. Susan A. Glenn, "'Funny, You Don't Look Jewish': Visual Stereotypes and the Making of Modern Jewish Identity," in *Boundaries of Jewish Identity*, ed. Susan A. Glenn and Naomi B. Sokoloff (Seattle: University of Washington Press), 65–66.

22. Erik Erikson, *Insight and Responsibility* (New York: W. W. Norton, 1964), 90, 94, 102.

Bibliography

Abbink, J. "An Ethiopian Jewish 'Missionary' as Cultural Broker." In *Ethiopian Jews and Israel*, edited by M. Ashkenazi and A. Weingrod, 33–54. New Brunswick, N.J.: Transaction Books, 1987.

Abel, Lionel. "The Existence of Jews and Existentialism." *Politics* 6, no. 1 (Winter 1949): 37–40.

Abitbol, Michel, and Alan Astro. "The Integration of North African Jews in France." *Yale French Studies*, no. 85 (1994): 248–261. https://doi.org/10.2307/2930080.

Abrams, Elliot. *Faith or Fear: How Jews Can Survive in a Christian America*. New York: Free Press, 1997.

Abu El-Haj, Nadia. *The Genealogical Science: The Search for Jewish Origins and the Politics of Epistemology*. Chicago: University of Chicago Press, 2012.

Ahad Ha'am. *Selected Essays of Ahad Ha'am*. Translated by Leon Simon. New York: Atheneum, 1962.

Alexander, Claire E. *The Art of Being Black: The Creation of Black British Youth Identities*. Oxford: Clarendon, 1996.

Allport, G. W. *The Individual and His Religion*. New York: Macmillan, 1979.

———. *The Nature of Prejudice*. Reading, Mass.: Addison-Wesley, 1954.

Allport, G. W., and M. J. Ross. "Personal Religious Orientation and Prejudice." *Journal of Personality and Social Psychology* 5, no. 4 (1967): 432–443.

Almog, Oz. *The Sabra: The Creation of the New Jew*. Berkeley: University of California Press, 2000.

Alter, Gaby. "The Arts: A Musical Coat of Many Colors." *Hadassah Magazine*, October 2005. http://www.hadassahmagazine.org/2005/10/10/arts-musical-coat-many-colors/.

Appiah, Kwame Anthony. "The Case for Contamination." *New York Times*, January 1, 2006.

———. *The Ethics of Identity*. Princeton, N.J.: Princeton University Press, 2005.

Ascheim, Steven. *Brothers and Strangers: The East European Jew in German and German Jewish Consciousness, 1800–1923*. Madison: University of Wisconsin Press, 1982.

Ashkenazi, Michael, and Alex Weingrad, eds. *Ethiopian Jews and Israel*. New Brunswick, N.J.: Transaction Books, 1987.

Atzmon, Gil, Li Hao, Itsik Pe'er, Christopher Velez, Alexander Pearlman, Pier Francesco Palamara, Bernice Morrow et al. "Abraham's Children in the Genome Era: Major Jewish Diaspora Populations Comprise Distinct Genetic Clusters with Shared Middle Eastern Ancestry." *American Journal of Human Genetics* 86, no. 6 (June 2010): 850–859.

Baade, Christina. "Can This White Lutheran Play Klezmer? Reflections on Race, Ethnicity, and Revival." *Sonneck Society for American Music Bulletin* 24, no. 2 (Summer 1998): 37–38.

———. "Jewzak and Heavy Shtetl: Constructing Ethnic Identity and Asserting Authenticity in the New Klezmer Movement." *Monatshefte* 90, no. 2 (Summer 1998): 208–219.

Bach, Raymond. "Identifying Jews: The Legacy of the 1941 Exhibition, 'Le Juif et la France.'" *Studies in 20th Century Literature* 23, no. 1 (1999). https://doi.org/10.4148/2334-4415.1455.

Baker, Cynthia. *Jew*. New Brunswick, N.J.: Rutgers University Press, 2016.

Baldwin, James. "From the American Scene: The Harlem Ghetto: Winter 1948." *Commentary* 6 (January 1948): 165–170. http://www.commentarymagazine.com/article/from-the-american-scene-the-harlem-ghetto-winter-1948/.

Band, Arnold. "Ahad Ha'am and the Berdyczewski Polarity." In *At the Crossroads: Essays on Ahad Ha'am*, edited by Jacques Kornberg, 277–287. Albany: State University of New York Press, 1983.

"Bands and Performing Groups: Klezmer, Jewish, and Related or Derivative Musics." *Klezmer-Shack*. Accessed August 7, 2021. http://www.klezmershack.com/contacts/klezbands_d.html.

Banet-Weiser, Sarah. *Authentic™: The Politics of Ambivalence in a Brand Culture*. New York: New York University Press, 2012.

Batson, Daniel, Patricia Schoenrade, and W. Larry Ventis. *Religion and the Individual: A Social-Psychological Perspective*. New York: Oxford University Press, 1993.

Behar, Doron M., Bayazit Yunusbayev, Mait Metspalu, Ene Metspalu, Saharon Rosset, Jüri Parik, Siiri Rootsi et al. "The Genome-Wide Structure of the Jewish People." *Nature* 466 (2010): 238–242.

Beilin, Yossi. *His Brother's Keeper: Israel and Diaspora Jewry in the Twenty-First Century*. New York: Schocken, 2000.

Bendix, Regina. *In Search of Authenticity: The Formation of Folklore Studies*. Madison: University of Wisconsin Press, 1997.

Benite, Zvi Ben-Dor. *The Ten Lost Tribes: A World History*. New York: Oxford University Press, 2009.

Ben-Ur, Aviva. "To the End of the Earth: A History of the Crypto-Jews of New Mexico." *American Jewish History* 93, no. 2 (June 2007): 264–268.

Ben-Yehudah, Eliezer. *A Dream Come True*. Boulder, Colo.: Westview, 1993.

Berger, David. *The Rebbe, the Messiah and the Scandal of Orthodox Indifference*. London: Littman, 2001.

Berger, David, Walter S. Wurzburger, Marc D. Angel, Louis Bernstein, Reuven P. Bulka, Emanuel Feldman, Hillel Goldberg et al. "A Symposium: 'The State of Orthodoxy.'" *Tradition* 20, no. 1 (Spring 1982): 3–83.

Berk, Fred. *Ha-Rikud: The Jewish Dance*. New York: Union of American Hebrew Congregations, 1972.

Beyond the Pale. "*Bio.*" Accessed August 7, 2021. https://www.beyondthepale.net/about.

Biale, David, ed. *Cultures of the Jews: A New History*. New York: Schocken, 2002.

———. "Gershom Scholem and Anarchism as a Jewish Philosophy." *Judaism* 32, no. 1 (Winter 1983): 70–76.

Bleich, J. David. "The Prohibition against Intermarriage." *Journal of Halacha and Contemporary Society* 1, no. 1 (1981): 5–27.

———. "Black Jews: A Halachic Perspective." *Tradition* 15, nos. 1–2 (Spring–Summer 1975): 48–79.

Bloomfield, Diane. *Torah Yoga: Experiencing Jewish Wisdom through Classic Postures*. San Francisco: Jossey-Bass, 2004.

Borgen, Peter. "The Early Church and the Hellenistic Synagogue." In *Philo, John, and Paul: New Perspectives on Judaism and Early Christianity*, 55–78. Atlanta: Scholars, 1987.

Boris, Staci. *The New Authentics: Artists of the Post-Jewish Generation*. Chicago: Spertus, 2007.

Boyarin, Daniel, and Jonathan Boyarin. "Diaspora: Generation and the Ground of Jewish Identity." *Critical Inquiry* 19, no. 4 (Summer 1993): 693–725.

———. "Diaspora: Generation and the Ground of Jewish Identity." In *Identities*, edited by Kwame Anthony Appiah and Henry Louis Gates, 305–337. Chicago: University of Chicago Press, 1995.

Boyarin, Jonathan. "In Search of Authenticity: Issues of Identity and Belonging in the Twentieth Century." In *The Cambridge History of Judaism*, vol. 8, *The Modern World, 1815–2000*, edited by Mitchell Hart and Tony Michels, 942–964. Cambridge: Cambridge University Press, 2017.

Bradman, Neil, and Mark Thomas. "Genetics: The Pursuit of Jewish History by Other Means." *Judaism Today* 10 (Autumn 1998): 1–9.

Brantley, Ben. "A Cozy Little McShtetl." *New York Times*, February 27, 2004. https://www.nytimes.com/2004/02/27/movies/theater-review-a-cozy-little-mcshtetl.html.

Brickner, Balfour. "Orthodox Have No Lock on Authenticity." *Jewish Week* 209, no. 51 (April 1997): 31.

Brodesser-Akner, Taffy. "Is Yoga Kosher? How a Modern Orthodox Jew Struggled to Reconcile Her Yogic Practice with Her Judaism." *Tablet*, January 5, 2010. https://www.tabletmag.com/sections/community/articles/is-yoga-kosher.

Brotz, Howard. *The Black Jews of Harlem: Negro Nationalism and the Dilemmas of Negro Leadership*. New York: Schocken, 1970.

Bruder, Edith. *The Black Jews of Africa: History, Religion, Identity*. New York: Oxford University Press, 2008.

Bruner, Edward M. "Abraham Lincoln as Authentic Reproduction: A Critique of Postmodernism." *American Anthropologist* 96, no. 2 (1994): 397–415.

Butler, Judith. "Performative Acts and Gender Constitution: An Essay in Phenomenology and Feminist Theory." *Theatre Journal* 40, no. 4 (December 1988): 519–531.

Carette, Jeremy, and Richard King. *Selling Spirituality: The Silent Takeover of Religion.* Philadelphia: Taylor & Francis, 2004.

Carroll, Michael P. "The Debate over Crypto-Jewish Presence in New Mexico." *Sociology of Religion* 63, no. 1 (2002): 1–18.

Chabra, Deepak. "Authenticity of the Objectively Authentic." *Annals of Tourism Research* 39, no. 1 (2012): 499–502.

Chafets, Zev. "Obama's Rabbi." *New York Times Magazine*, April 2, 2009. https://www.nytimes.com/2009/04/05/magazine/05rabbi-t.html?action=click&module=RelatedCoverage&pgtype=Article&region=Footer.

Charmé, Stuart. "Heretics, Infidels, and Apostates: Menace, Problem, or Symptom." *Judaism* 36, no. 1 (Winter 1987): 17–33.

———. *Meaning and Myth in the Study of Lives: A Sartrean Approach.* Philadelphia: University of Pennsylvania Press, 1983.

———. "Varieties of Authenticity in Contemporary Jewish Identity." *Jewish Social Studies* 6, no. 2 (2000): 133–155.

———. *Vulgarity and Authenticity: Dimensions of Otherness in the World of Sartre.* Amherst: University of Massachusetts Press, 1991.

Charmé, Stuart, Jeffrey Kress, Tali Hyman, and Bethamie Horowitz. "Jewish Identities in Action: An Exploration of Models, Metaphors, and Methods." *Journal of Jewish Education* 74, no. 2 (2008): 115–143.

Chireau, Yvonne. "Black Culture and Black Zion: African American Religious Encounters with Judaism, 1790–1930, an Overview." In Chireau and Deutsch, *Black Zion*, 15–32.

Chireau, Yvonne, and Nathaniel Deutsch. *Black Zion: African American Religious Encounters with Judaism.* New York: Oxford University Press, 2000.

Christ, Carol P., and Judith Plaskow, eds. *Womanspirit Rising: A Feminist Reader in Religion.* New York: HarperCollins, 1992.

Cohen, Debra Nussbaum. "A Slice of America: Judaism among Non-Jews." *New York Times*, May 31, 2003.

Cohen, Erik. "Authenticity and Commoditization in Tourism." *Annals of Tourism Research* 15 (1988): 371–386.

Cohen, Erik H. *The Jews of France Today: Identity and Values.* Boston: Brill, 2011.

Cohen, Jonathan. "'If Rabbi Akiba Were Alive Today . . .' or the Authenticity Argument." *Judaism* 37, no. 2 (Spring 1988): 136–142.

Cohen, Shaye J. D. *The Beginnings of Jewishness: Boundaries, Varieties, Uncertainties.* Berkeley: University of California Press, 2001.

Cohen, Steven M. *American Modernity and Jewish Identity.* New York: Tavistock, 1983.

———. "Yes, Something Can Be Done: A 'Purple' Solution to Intermarriage." *Mosaic Magazine*, September 15, 2013. http://mosaicmagazine.com/supplemental/2013/09/yes-something-can-be-done/.

Cohen, Steven M., and Arnold M. Eisen. *The Jew Within: Self, Family, and Community in America*. Bloomington: Indiana University Press, 2000.

Cohen, Steven M., and Charles Liebman. *Two Worlds of Judaism: The Israeli and American Experiences*. New Haven, Conn.: Yale University Press, 1990.

Cohen, Steven M., and Kerry M. Olitzky. "Op-Ed: Conversion Shouldn't Be the Only Path to Joining the Jewish People." *JTA: Global Jewish News Source*, November 29, 2013. http://www.jta.org/2013/11/29/news-opinion/opinion/op-ed-conversion-shouldnt-be-the-only-path-to-joining-the-jewish-people.

Cohn-Sherbok, Dan. *Messianic Judaism*. London: Continuum, 2000.

Coleman, Robert. "Black and Jewish—and Unaccepted." In *A Coat of Many Colors: Jewish Subcommunities in the United States*, edited by Abraham Lavender, 229–232. Westport, Conn.: Greenwood, 1977.

Corinaldi, Michael. *Jewish Identity: The Case of Ethiopian Jewry*. Jerusalem: Magnes, 1998.

Cox, Harvey. *Turning East: Promise and the Peril of the New Orientalism*. New York: Simon & Schuster, 1977.

Cuddihy, John Murray. *The Ordeal of Civility: Freud, Marx, Levi-Strauss, and the Jewish Struggle with Modernity*. New York: Delta Books, 1974.

Damon, Maria. "Word-landslayt: Gertrude Stein, Allen Ginsberg, Lenny Bruce." In *People of the Book: Thirty Scholars Reflect on Their Jewish Identity*, edited by Jeffrey Rubin-Dorsky and Shelley Fisher Fishkin, 375–389. Madison: University of Wisconsin Press, 1996.

Dan, Joseph. *Kabbalah: A Very Short Introduction*. New York: Oxford University Press, 2007.

Dauermann, Stuart. "The Messianic Agenda: Varieties of Messianic Believers." *The Messianic Agenda*, July 1, 2011. http://www.messianicjudaism.me/agenda/2011/07/01/varieties-of-jewish-yeshua-believers-part-two/.

Davis, Avram, ed. *Meditation: From the Heart of Judaism*. Woodstock, Vt.: Jewish Lights, 1999.

Davis, Natalie Zemon. *The Return of Martin Guerre*. Cambridge, Mass.: Harvard University Press, 1984.

Dein, Simon. "Moshiach Is Here Now: Just Open Your Eyes and You Can See Him." *Anthropology and Medicine* 9, no. 1 (2002): 24–36.

De Lange, Nicholas. *Judaism*. New York: Oxford University Press, 1987.

Derrida, Jacques. "Abraham, the Other." In *Judeities: Questions for Jacques Derrida*, ed. Bettina Bergo, Joseph D. Cohen, and Raphael Zagury-Orly, 1–35. New York: Fordham University Press, 2007.

De Sola Pool, D. "Intermarriage." New York: Jewish Welfare Board, United States Army and Navy, ca. 1918. https://catalog.hathitrust.org/Record/007670418.

Diamond, Etan. "The Kosher Lifestyle: Religious Consumerism and Suburban Orthodox Jews." *Journal of Urban History* 28, no. 4 (May 2002): 488–505.

Di-Capua, Yoav. *No Exit: Arab Existentialism, Jean-Paul Sartre, and Decolonization*. Chicago: University of Chicago Press, 2018.

Dion, Shulamis. "The Klezmer Revival." *Humanistic Judaism* 20, no. 3 (Summer 1992): 52–55.

Divine, Donna Robinson. "Zionism and the Politics of Authenticity." Special issue, *Israel Studies* 19, no. 2 (Summer 2014): 94–110.

Dubov, Nissan Dovid. "What Is Wrong with Intermarriage?" Chabad.org, September 2005. https://www.chabad.org/library/article_cdo/aid/108396/jewish/Intermarriage.htm.

Dutton, Dennis. "Authenticity in Art." In *The Oxford Handbook of Aesthetics*, edited by Jerrold Levinson, 258–274. New York: Oxford University Press, 2003.

Egorova, Yulia. *Jews and India: Perceptions and India*. New York: Routledge, 2006.

Egorova, Yulia, and Shahid Perwez. *The Jews of Andhra Pradesh: Contesting Caste and Religion in South India*. New York: Oxford University Press, 2013.

Eisen, Arnold. *Taking Hold of Torah: Jewish Commitment and Community in America*. Bloomington: Indiana University Press, 1997.

———. "Wanted: Converts of Judaism." *Wall Street Journal*, July 24, 2014. http://online.wsj.com/articles/arnold-m-eisen-wanted-converts-to-judaism-1406244075.

Elazar, Daniel. *The Other Jews: The Sepharidim Today*. New York: Basic Books, 1989.

Eleff, Zev. *Authentically Orthodox: A Tradition-Bound Faith in American Life*. Detroit: Wayne State University Press, 2020.

El Harar, Daveed. "Q & A with Rabbi Daveed El Harar: An Interview." *Nefesh Haya* (blog). Accessed August 6, 2021. http://www.nefeshhaya.com/qa-with-rabbi-daveed-el-hara.html.

Elkins, J. E., E. N. Tinah, N. M. Myres, K. H. Ritchie, U. A. Perego, J. B. Ekins, L. A. D. Hutchison et al. "An Updated World-Wide Characterization of the Cohen Modal Haplotype." American Society of Human Genetics Annual Meeting, October 2005. http://www.smgf.org/resources/papers/ASHG2005_Jayne.pdf.

Ellenson, David. *Tradition in Transition: Orthodoxy, Halakha, and the Boundaries of Modern Jewish Identity*. New York: University Press of America, 1989.

Entine, Jon. *Abraham's Children: Race, Identity, and the DNA of the Chosen People*. New York: Grand Central, 2007.

Epstein, Jerome. "Congratulations to Mixed Marriage Families." *Rabbinical Assembly: Committee on Jewish Law and Standards* 16 (1989): 457–466. http://www.rabbinicalassembly.org/sites/default/files/public/halakhah/teshuvot/19861990/epstein_congratulations.pdf.

Erikson, Erik. *Insight and Responsibility*. New York: W. W. Norton, 1964.

Even-Zohar, Itamar. "The Emergence of a Native Hebrew Culture in Palestine, 1882–1948." *Poetics Today* 11, no. 1 (Spring 1990): 175–191.

Ezrahi, Sidra DeKoven. *Booking Passage: Exile and Homecoming in the Modern Jewish Imagination*. Berkeley: University of California Press, 2000.

Fackenheim, Emil. "The Dilemma of Liberal Judaism." In *Quest for Past and Future: Essays in Jewish Theology*, 130–147. Bloomington: Indiana University Press, 1968.

———. "The 614th Commandment." In *The Jewish Return into History: Reflections in the Age of Auschwitz and a New Jerusalem*, 19–24. New York: Schocken, 1978.

Falk, Jodi. "Rocking and Rolling through Judaism." 614: HBI eZine, 2010. http://614ezine.com/rocking-and-rolling-through-judaism/.

Falk, Raphael. "Genetic Markers Cannot Determine Jewish Descent." Frontiers in Genetics, January 21, 2015. https://www.frontiersin.org/articles/10.3389/fgene.2014.00462/full.

Fein, Leonard. *Where Are We? The Inner Life of America's Jews*. New York: Harper and Row, 1988.

Feldman, Ron. "My Mystical Encounter." *Moment Magazine* 22, no. 1 (February 1997).

Fernheimer, Janice W. *Stepping into Zion: Hatzaad Harishon, Black Jews, and the Remaking of Jewish Identity*. Tuscaloosa: University of Alabama Press, 2014.

FFOZ Staff Writer. "The Messianic Jewish Millennials." *First Fruits of Zion*. September 9, 2015. https://ffoz.org/discover/messianic-judaism/the-messianic-jewish-millennials.html.

Fink, Nan. "Stranger in the Midst: A Memoir of Spiritual Discovery." *Tikkun* 12, no. 1 (1997): 31–34, 76.

Finkelstein, Israel, and Neil Asher Silberman. *The Bible Unearthed*. New York: Free Press, 2001.

Finkielkraut, Alain. *The Imaginary Jew*. Translated by Kevin O'Neill and David Suchoff. Lincoln: University of Nebraska Press, 1997.

Fraser, Nancy. "From Redistribution to Recognition? Dilemmas of Justice in a Post-socialist Age." *Theory, Culture, & Society* 18, nos. 2–3 (2001): 21–42.

———. "Rethinking Recognition." In *The Philosophy of Recognition*, edited by Hans-Christoph Schmidt am Busch and Christopher Zurn, 211–222. New York: Rowman & Littlefield, 2010.

Fredriksen, Paula, and Oded Irshai. "Christian Anti-Judaism: Polemics and Policies." In *The Cambridge History of Judaism*, vol. 4, *The Late Roman Rabbinic Period*, edited by Steven T. Katz, 977–1034. Cambridge: Cambridge University Press, 2006.

Freedman, Jonathan. "Conversos, Marranos, and Crypto-Latinos." In *Boundaries of Jewish Identity*, edited by Susan A. Glenn and Naomi B. Sokoloff, 209–250. Seattle: University of Washington Press, 2010.

———. *Klezmer America: Jewishness, Ethnicity, Modernity*. New York: Columbia University Press, 2008.

Freund, Michael. "Fundamentally Freund: All in the Family." *Jerusalem Post*, June 18, 2010. https://www.jpost.com/opinion/columnists/fundamentally-freund-all-in-the-family.

Friedlander, Judith. "'Juif ou Israelite?' The Old Question in Contemporary France." *Judaism* 34, no. 2 (Spring 1985): 221–230.

———. *Vilna on the Seine: Jewish Intellectuals in France since 1968*. New Haven, Conn.: Yale University Press, 1990.

Friedman, Menachem. "Life Tradition and Book Tradition in the Development of Ultraorthodox Judaism." In *Judaism Viewed from Within and from Without: Anthropological Studies*, edited by Harvey Goldberg, 235–255. Albany: State University of New York Press, 1987.

Frish, Rabbi Robyn. "Converts Not Necessarily Wanted—an Open Letter to Arnold Eisen." *18Doors*, August 7, 2021. http://www.interfaithfamily.com/blog/iff/conversion/converts-not-necessarily-wanted-an-open-letter-to-arnold-eisen/.

Frith, Simon. "Music and Identity." In *Questions of Cultural Identity*, edited by Stuart Hall and Paul du Gay (London: SAGE, 1996), 108–127.

Fromm, Erich. *Escape from Freedom*. New York: Henry Holt, 1941.

———. *Psychoanalysis and Religion*. New Haven, Conn.: Yale University Press, 1950.

Funnye, Capers C., and Michel Martin. "Faith Matters: Black Rabbi Shares Story of Conversion, Unity." *Tell Me More*, April 10, 2009. Podcast, 13:38. https://www.npr.org/transcripts/102953476.

Garfinkle, Adam M. "On the Origin, Meaning, Use, and Abuse of a Phrase." *Middle Eastern Studies* 27, no. 4 (October 1991): 539–550.

Gauthier, François, and Tuomas Martikainen, eds. *Religion in Consumer Society: Brands, Consumers and Markets*. New York: Routledge, 2016.

Gewirth, Leonard. *The Authentic Jew and His Judaism*. New York: Bloch, 1961.

Gillman, Neil. *Sacred Fragments: Recovering Theology for the Modern Jew*. Philadelphia: Jewish Publication Society, 1990.

Gilroy, Paul. "Diaspora and the Details of Identity." In *Identity and Difference*, edited by Kathryn Woodward, 299–346. London: Sage, 1997.

———. "Roots and Routes: Black Identity as an Outernational Project." In *Racial and Ethnic Identity: Psychological Development and Creative Expression*, edited by Herbert Harris, Howard Blue, and Ezra Griffith, 15–30. New York: Routledge, 1995.

Gindin, Matthew. "Above the Sun: The Ancient (and New) Riches of Jewish Yoga." Jewish Yoga Network. https://vuvuzela-orchid-mfa9.squarespace.com/blog/above-the-sun-the-ancient-and-new-riches-of-jewish-yoga.

Gitlitz, David M. *Secrecy and Deceit: The Religion of the Crypto-Jews*. Philadelphia: Jewish Publication Society, 1996.

Glenn, Susan A. "'Funny, You Don't Look Jewish': Visual Stereotypes and the Making of Modern Jewish Identity." In *Boundaries of Jewish Identity*, edited by Susan A. Glenn and Naomi B. Sokoloff, 64–90. Seattle: University of Washington Press, 2010.

———. "The Vogue of Jewish Self-Hatred in Post–World War II America." *Jewish Social Studies* 12, no. 3 (Spring–Summer 2006): 95–136.

Glick, Ira O. "The Hebrew Christians: A Marginal Religious Group." In *The Jews: Social Patterns of an American Group*, edited by Marshall Sklare, 415–431. Glencoe, Ill.: Free Press, 1958.

Gold, Roberta S. "The Black Jews of Harlem: Representation, Identity, and Race, 1920–1939." *American Quarterly* 55, no. 2 (2003): 179–225.

Gold, Steven J. *Yoga and Judaism: Explorations of a Jewish Yogi*. Morrisville, N.C.: Lulu.com, 2007.

Goldfarb, Harold. "Blacks and Conversion to Judaism." In *A Coat of Many Colors: Jewish Subcommunities in the United States*, edited by Abraham Lavender, 226–228. Westport, Conn.: Greenwood, 1977.

Goldstein, Eric. *The Price of Whiteness: Jews, Race, and American Identity*. Princeton, N.J.: Princeton University Press, 2006.

Gomes, Stephen. "My 50-Year Search for My Portuguese-Jewish Self." In *Under One Canopy: Readings in Jewish Diversity*, edited by Karen Primack, 44–47. New York: Kulanu, 2003.

Gonen, Rivka. *The Quest for the Ten Lost Tribes of Israel: To the Ends of the Earth*. New York: Jason Aronson, 2002.

Gordon, Albert I. *Intermarriage: Interfaith, Interracial, Interethnic*. Boston: Beacon, 1964.

Gottschalk, Alfred. "Reform Judaism of the New Millennium." In Kaplan, *Contemporary Debates*, 235–243.

Gozlan, Audi. "Kabalah Yoga." Accessed August 6, 2021. http://www.kabalahyoga.com/kabalah-yoga.

Greenberg, Clement. "Self-Hatred and Jewish Chauvinism—Some Reflections of 'Positive Jewishness.'" *Commentary* 10 (1950): 426–433.

Greenberg, Irving. "Toward a Principled Pluralism." In *Towards the Twenty-First Century: Judaism and the Jewish People in Israel and America*, edited by Ronald Kronish, 183–205. Hoboken, N.J.: KTAV, 1988.

Greenberg, Rabbi Steve. "Between Intermarriage and Conversion: Finding a Middle Way." Spirit and Story. Accessed August 3, 2021. http://www.rabbiswithoutborders.net/ss43.html.

Greenspoon, Leonard J., ed. *Who Is a Jew? Reflections on History, Religion, and Culture*. West Lafayette, Ind.: Purdue University Press, 2014.

Gruber, Ruth Ellen. *Virtually Jewish: Reinventing Jewish Culture in Europe*. Berkeley: University of California Press, 2002.

Halkin, Hillel. *Across the Sabbath River: In Search of a Lost Tribe of Israel*. New York: Houghton Mifflin, 2002.

Hall, Stuart. "Cultural Identity and Diaspora." In Rutherford, *Identity, Community and Cultural Difference*, edited by Jonathan Rutherford, 222–237. London: Lawrence & Wishart, 1990.

———. "Cultural Identity in Diaspora." In *Cultural Discourse and Post-colonial Theory*, edited by Patrick Williams and Laura Chrisman, 392–403. New York: Columbia University Press, 1994.

———. "Minimal Selves." In *Studying Culture: An Introductory Reader*, edited by Ann Gray and Jim McGuigan, 134–138. London: Edward Arnold, 1993.

Hammer, M. F., A. J. Redd, E. T. Wood, M. R. Bonner, H. Jarjanazi, T. Karafet, S. Santachiara-Benerecetti et al. "Jewish and Middle Eastern Non-Jewish Populations Share a Common Pool of Y-Chromosome Biallelic Haplotypes." *PNAS* 97, no. 12 (2000): 6769–6774.

Handler, Richard, and Jocelyn Linnekin. "Tradition, Genuine or Spurious." *Journal of American Folklore* 97, no. 385 (1984): 273–290.

Hansen, David. *The Teacher and the World: A Study of Cosmopolitanism as Education*. New York: Routledge, 2011.

Harris, Lis. *Holy Days: The World of a Hasidic Family*. New York: Summit, 1985.

Harris-Shapiro, Carol *Messianic Judaism: A Rabbi's Journey through Religious Change in America*. Boston: Beacon, 1999.

Harshav, Benjamin. *Language in Time of Revolution*. Berkeley: University of California Press, 1993.

Hart, Mitchell B. *Social Science and the Politics of Modern Jewish Identity*. Stanford, Calif.: Stanford University Press, 2000.

Hashivenu. "A Vision for a Maturing Messianic Judaism." Accessed December 15, 2021, http://www.hashivenu.org/.

Haviv, Ayana Shira. "Next Year in Katmandu: Israeli Backpackers and the Formation of a New Israeli Identity." In *Israeli Backpackers: From Tourism to Rite of Passage*, edited by Chaim Noy and Erik Cohen, 45–88. Albany: State University of New York Press, 2005.

Heilman, Samuel. "Constructing Orthodoxy." *Transaction* 15, no. 4 (1978): 32–40.

Herman, Simon. *Israelis and Jews: The Continuity of an Identity*. Philadelphia: Jewish Publication Society, 1971.

Herz, Cary. *New Mexico's Crypto-Jews: Image and Memory*. Albuquerque: University of New Mexico Press, 2007.

Heschel, Susannah. "An Orange on Plate for Women—and Spit Out Seeds of Hate." March 19, 2013, https://forward.com/opinion/172959/an-orange-on-plate-for-women-and-spit-out-seeds/#.

Hess, Moses. "Rome in Jerusalem." In *The Zionist Idea: A Historical Analysis and Reader*, edited by Arthur Hertzberg, 119–139. New York: Atheneum, 1970.

Hodes, Joseph R. "The Bene Israel and the 'Who Is a Jew' Controversy in Israel." In *Who Is a Jew? Reflections on History, Religion, and Culture*, edited by Leonard J. Greenspoon, 169–192. West Lafayette, Ind.: Purdue University Press, 2014.

———. *From India to Israel: Identity, Immigration, and the Struggle for Religious Equality*. Montreal: McGill-Queen's University Press, 2014.

Hordes, Stanley. *To the End of the Earth: A History of the Crypto-Jews of New Mexico*. New York: Columbia University Press, 2005.

Horowitz, Bethamie. "Connections and Journeys: Shifting Identities among American Jews." *Contemporary Jewry* 19 (1998): 63–94.

———. "Reframing the Study of Contemporary American Jewish Identity." *Contemporary Jewry* 23, no. 1 (2002): 14–34.

Howe, Irving. "New Black Writers." *Harper's Magazine*, December 1969, 130–141.

———. "The Problem of Jewish Self-Definition." *Reconstructionist*, October 1983, 6–7.

———. "Tevye on Broadway." *Commentary* 38, no. 5 (November 1964): 73.

Huss, Boaz. "Kabbalah and the Politics of Inauthenticity: The Controversies over the Kabbalah Centre." *Numen* 62 (2015): 197–225.

Hymes, Dell. "Folklore's Nature and the Sun's Myth." *Journal of American Folklore* 88 (1975): 345–369.

Ingber, Judith Brin. "Shorashim: The Roots of Israeli Folk Dance." *Dance Perspectives* 7, no. 2 (1974): 35.

Isaac, Ephraim. "The Question of Jewish Identity and Ethiopian Jewish Origins." *Midstream* 51, no. 5 (January 2005): 29–34.

Isaac, Walter. "Locating Afro-American Judaism: A Critique of White Normativity." In *A Companion to African-American Studies*, edited by Lewis Gordon and Jane Gordon, 512–542. Malden, Mass.: Blackwell, 2006.

Israel, Benjamin. *The Bene Israel of India: Some Studies*. New York: Apt Books, 1984.

"The Israelite Academy." BlackJews.org. Accessed August 7, 2021, http://www.blackjews.org/Israelite%20Academy%20Courses%20and%20History.htm.

Jacobs, Janet Liebman. *Hidden Heritage: The Legacy of the Crypto-Jews*. Berkeley: University of California Press, 2002.

James, William. *The Varieties of Religious Experience: A Study in Human Nature*. London: Collier Books, 1969.

Joselit, Jenna Weissman. *New York's Jewish Jews*. Bloomington: Indiana University Press, 1990.

Judaken, Jonathan. *Jean-Paul Sartre and 'the Jewish Question': Anti-antisemitism and the Politics of the French Intellectual*. Lincoln: University of Nebraska Press, 2006.

Kabbalah Centre. "Frequently Asked Questions." Accessed June 2010. http://www.kabbalah.com.

Kadman, Gurit. "Folk Dance in Israel." In *Ha-Rikud: The Jewish Dance*, edited by Fred Berk, 26–27. New York: Union of American Hebrew Congregations, 1972.

———. "Yeminite Dances and Their Influence on the New Israeli Folk Dances." *Journal of the International Folk Music Council* 4 (1952): 27–30.

Kahn, Susan Martha. "Are Genes Jewish? Conceptual Ambiguities in the New Genetic Age." In *Boundaries of Jewish Identity*, edited by Susan A. Glenn and Naomi B. Sokoloff, 12–26. Seattle: University of Washington Press, 2011.

———. "Who Are the Jews? New Formulations of an Age-Old Question." *Human Biology* 85, no. 6 (2013): 919–924.

Kamenetz, Roger. *The Jew in the Lotus: A Poet's Rediscover of Jewish Identity in Buddhist India*. New York: HarperCollins, 1994.

Kanfer, Stefan. *Stardust Lost: The Triumph, Tragedy, and Mishugas of the Yiddish Theater in America*. New York: Vintage, 2007.

Kaplan, Aryeh. *Jewish Meditation: A Practical Guide*. New York: Schocken, 1998.

Kaplan, Dana Evan, ed. *Contemporary Debates in American Reform Judaism: Conflicting Visions*. New York: Routledge, 2001.

Kaplan, Lawrence. "Daas Torah: A Modern Conception of Rabbinic Authority." In *Rabbinic Authority and Personal Autonomy*, edited by Moshe Sokol, 1–60. Northvale, N.J.: Jason Aronson, 1992.

Kaplan, Mordechai. *Judaism as a Civilization: Toward a Reconstruction of American-Jewish Life*. New York: Schocken, 1967.

———. *Judaism without Supernaturalism: The Only Alternative to Orthodoxy and Secularism*. New York: Reconstructionist, 1967.

———. *The Religion of Ethical Nationhood*. New York: Macmillan, 1970.

Kaplan, Mordechai, and Arthur Cohen. *If Not Now, When? Toward a Reconstitution of the Jewish People*. New York: Schocken, 1973.

Kaplan, Steven. *The Beta Israel (Falasha) in Ethiopia: From Earliest Times to the Twentieth Century*. New York: New York University Press, 1992.

Kaplan, Steven, and Chaim Rosen. "Ethiopian Immigrants in Israel: Between Preservation of Culture and Invention of Tradition." *Jewish Journal of Sociology* 35, no. 1 (1993): 35–48.

Kaplan, Steven, and Hagar Salamon. "Ethiopian Jews in Israel: A Part of the People or Apart of the People." In *Jews in Israel: Contemporary Cultural and Social Patterns*, edited by Uzi Rebhun and Chaim I. Waxman, 118–148. Waltham, Mass.: Brandeis University Press, 2004.

Kaschl, Elke. *Dance and Authenticity in Israel and Palestine: Performing the Nation*. Boston: Brill, 2003.

Katz, Jacob. "Orthodoxy in Historical Perspective." *Studies in Contemporary Jewry* 2 (1986): 3–17.

Katz, Nathan. *Who Are the Jews of India?* Berkeley: University of California Press, 2000.

Kaufman, Ayalah. "Indigenous and Imported Elements in the New Folk Dance in Israel." *Journal of the International Folk Music Council* 3 (1951): 55–57.

Kaye/Kantrowitz, Melanie. *Colors of Jews: Racial Politics and Radical Diasporism*. Bloomington: Indiana University Press, 2007.

Kehimkar, H. S. *The History of the Bene Israel of India*. Tel Aviv: Dayag, 1937.

Kellner, Menachem. *Must a Jew Believe Anything?* London: Littman, 1999.

Kelman, Herbert C. "The Interdependence of Israeli and Palestinian National Identities: The Role of the Other in Existential Conflicts." *Journal of Social Issues* 55, no. 3 (1999): 581–600.

Kessler, David. *The Falashas: A Short History of the Ethiopian Jews*. London: Frank Cass, 1996.

Key, Andre E. "Toward a Typology of Black Hebrew Religious Thought and Practice." *Journal of Africana Religions* 2, no. 1 (2014): 31–66.

Kimmerling, Baruch. *The Invention and Decline of Israeliness: State, Society, and the Military*. Berkeley: University of California Press, 2001.

Kinzer, Mark. *The Nature of Messianic Judaism: Judaism as Genus, Messianism as Species*. West Hartford, Conn.: Hashivenu Archives, 2000. http://hashivenu.org/.

———. *Postmissionary Messianic Judaism: Redefining Christian Engagement with the Jewish People*. Grand Rapids, Mich.: Brazos, 2005.

Kohler, K. "David Einhorn: The Uncompromising Champion of Reform." In *Yearbook of the Central Conference of American Rabbis*, 10. New York: Central Conference of American Rabbis, 1910.

Koltun-Fromm, Ken. *Imagining Jewish Authenticity: Vision and Text in American Jewish Thought*. Bloomington: Indiana University Press, 2015.

Kunin, Seth. *Juggling Identities: Identity and Authenticity among the Crypto-Jews*. New York: Columbia University Press, 2009.

Kymlicka, Will. *Multicultural Odysseys*. Oxford: Clarendon, 1995.

———. *The Rights of Minority Cultures*. New York: Oxford University Press, 1995.

Labovitz, Gail. "What It Means to Be 'Erev Rav.'" American Jewish University. February 4, 2017. https://www.aju.edu/ziegler-school-rabbinic-studies/our-torah/back-issues/what-it-means-be-erev-rav.

Lamm, Norman. "Seventy Faces: Divided We Stand, but It's Time to Try an Idea That Might Help Us Stand Taller." *Moment* 2, no. 6 (June 1986): 23–28.

Landau, Jacob. "The Dönmes: Crypto-Jews under Turkish Rule." *Jewish Political Studies Review* 19, nos. 1–2 (Spring 2007): 109–118.

Landing, James. *Black Judaism: Story of an American Movement*. Durham, N.C.: Carolina Academic, 2002.

Leiter, Sarah. "True to Our God, True to Our Native Land: Establishing Communal Identity at a Black American Jewish Temple." MA thesis, University of Chicago, 2015.

Lerner, Michael. *Jewish Renewal: A Path to Healing and Transformation*. New York: G. P. Putnam's Sons, 1994.

Levine, Joel. "Why People in the Sunbelt Join a Synagogue." In Kaplan, *Contemporary Debates*, 58–63. London: Routledge, 2001.

Levi-Tanai, Sara. "Treasure out of Yemen." In *Ha-Rikud: The Jewish Dance*, edited by Fred Berk, 10–14. New York: UAHC, 1972.

Levy, S. B. "Beta Yisrael: A Historical Analysis." BlackJews.org, 2002. http://www.blackjews.org/Ethiopian%20Community/Ethiopian%20Chapter.htm.

———. "Who Are We?" Black Jews. Accessed August 3, 2021. http://www.blackjews.org/Essays/WhoAreWe.html.

Levy-Coffman, Ellen. "A Mosaic of People: The Jewish Story and a Reassessment of the DNA Evidence." *Journal of Genetic Genealogy* 1 (2005): 12–33.

Liebman, Charles. *Deceptive Images: Toward a Redefinition of American Judaism*. Piscataway, N.J.: Transaction, 1988.

———. "When Judaism Gets Personal." *Forward* 98, no. 31 (1999): 9.

Lindholm, Charles. *Culture and Authenticity*. Malden, Mass.: Blackwell, 2008.

———. "The Rise of Expressive Authenticity." *Anthropological Quarterly* 86, no. 2 (Spring 2013): 361–395.

Linnekin, Jocelyn. "Cultural Invention and the Dilemma of Authenticity." *American Anthropologist* 93, no. 2 (1991): 446–449.

———. "Defining Tradition: Variations on the Hawaiian Identity." *American Ethnologist* 10, no. 2 (1983): 241–252.

London, Frank. "An Insider's View: How We Traveled from Obscurity to the Klezmer Establishment in Twenty Years." In *American Klezmer: Its Roots and Offshoots*, edited by Mark Slobin, 206–219. Berkeley: University of California Press, 2002.

Luckmann, Thomas. *The Invisible Religion: The Problem of Religion in Modern Society*. New York: Macmillan, 1967.

Luz, Ehud. *Parallels Meet: Religion and Nationalism in the Early Zionist Movement*. Philadelphia: Jewish Publication Society, 1988.

Lyshaug, Brenda. "Authenticity and the Politics of Identity: A Critique of Charles Taylor's Politics of Recognition." *Contemporary Political Theory* 3, no. 3 (2004): 300–320.

Margolis, Joseph. "Talking to Myself." In *Jewish Identity*, edited by David Theo Goldberg and Michael Krausz, 322–336. Philadelphia: Temple University Press, 1993.

Markell, Patchen. *Bound by Recognition*. Princeton, N.J.: Princeton University Press, 2003.

Markowitz, Fran. "Plaiting the Strands of Jewish Identity." *Journal for the Comparative Study of Society and History* 32, no. 1 (1990): 182–187.

Marks, Jonathan. *What It Means to Be 98% Chimpanzee*. Berkeley: University of California Press, 2002.

Marks, Jonathan D. "Rousseau's Use of the Jewish Example." *Review of Politics* 72, no. 3 (Summer 2010): 463–481.

Maroney, Eric. *The Other Zions: The Lost Histories of Jewish Nations*. New York: Rowman & Littlefield, 2010.

Marty, Martin E., and R. Scott Appleby. *The Glory and the Power: The Fundamentalist Challenge to the Modern World*. Boston: Beacon, 1992.

Maslin, Simeon. "Who Are the Authentic Jews?" *Reform Judaism Magazine* 24, no. 4 (Summer 1996): 10–16.

Maslow, Abraham. *Religions, Values, and Peak-Experiences*. New York: Penguin, 1976.

Meir, Golda. "What We Want of the Diaspora." Quoted in Jeffrey Rubin-Dorsky, "Philip Roth and American Jewish Identity: The Question of Authenticity." *American Literary History* 1, 13 (2001): 79–107.

Memmi, Albert. *The Liberation of the Jew*. New York: Orion, 1966.

———. *Portrait of a Jew*. New York: Orion, 1962.

Mendes-Flohr, Paul. "Secular Forms of Jewishness." In *The Blackwell Companion to Judaism*, edited by Jacob Neusner and Alan Avery-Peck, 461–476. Malden, Mass.: Blackwell, 2003.

Merwin, Ted. "Jew-Face: Non-Jews Playing Jews on the American Stage." *Cultural and Social History* 4, no. 2 (June 2007): 215–233.

Michaelson, Jay. "The Myth of Authenticity." Forward, December 23, 2009. http://www.forward.com/articles/121663/.

Milgram, Goldie. "Introduction to Jewish Meditation." Reclaiming Judaism. Accessed August 6, 2021. http://www.reclaimingjudaism.org/teachings/introduction-jewish-meditation.

Miller, Michael T. "Black Judaism(s) and the Hebrew Israelites." *Religion Compass* 13, no. 11 (2019). https://doi.org/10.1111/rec3.12346.

Miterko, Joe. "Re(Jew)vinating Jazz Part II: Klezmer and Messianic Worship." Meuchad (blog). June 27, 2017. http://meuchad.org/blog?offset=1528322008761.

Morag, Shelomo. "The Emergence of Modern Hebrew: Some Sociolinguistic Perspectives." In *Hebrew in Ashkenaz: A Language in Exile*, edited by Lewis Glinert, 208–221. Oxford: Oxford University Press, 1993.

Moss, Aron. "Is New-Wave Kabbalah Authentic?" Chabad.org. Accessed December 13, 2021. https://www.chabad.org/library/article_cdo/aid/160990/jewish/Is-New-Wave-Kabbalah-Authentic.htm.

———. "What's This 'Jewish Soul' Thing? Aren't We All One?" Chabad.org. Accessed December 13, 2021. https://www.chabad.org/library/article_cdo/aid/166900/jewish/Whats-this-Jewish-soul-Thing-Arent-We-All-One.htm.

Mosse, George L. *The Crisis of German Ideology*. New York: Schocken, 1981.

Muršič, Rajko. "The Deceptive Tentacles of the Authenticating Mind: On Authenticity and Some Other Notions That Are Good for Absolutely Nothing." In *Debating Authenticity: Concepts of Modernity in Anthropological Perspective*, edited by Thomas Filitz and Jamie Saris, 46–60. New York: Berghahn, 2013.

Myers, Jody. *Kabbalah and the Spiritual Quest: The Kabbalah Centre in America*. Westport, Conn.: Praeger, 2007.

———. "The Kabbalah Centre and Contemporary Spirituality." *Religious Compass* 2, no. 3 (2008): 409–420.

Netanyahu, Benzion. *The Origins of the Inquisition in Fifteenth-Century Spain*. New York: New York Review Books, 2001.

Neulander, Judith. "Crypto-Jews of the Southwest: An Imagined Community." *Jewish Folklore and Ethnology Review* 16, no. 1 (1994): 64–68.

———. "Folk Taxonomy, Prejudice and the Human Genome: Using Disease as a Jewish Ethnic Marker." *Patterns of Prejudice* 40, nos. 4–5 (2006): 381–398.

———. "Inventing Jewish History, Culture, and Genetic Identity in Modern New Mexico." In Greenspoon, *Who Is a Jew?*, 70–103.

———. Review of *To the End of the Earth: A History of the Crypto-Jews of New Mexico*, by Stanley M. Hordes. *Shofar* 93, no. 1 (2007): 208–210.

Neusner, Jacob. *Death and Rebirth of Judaism*. New York: Basic Books, 1987.

Newman, Marissa. "Sharansky: Israel Must Ease Conversion of Crypto-Jews." *Times of Israel*, February 11, 2014. http://www.timesofisrael.com/sharansky-israel-must-ease-conversion-for-crypto-jews/.

Niculescu, Mira. "'Find Your Inner God and Breathe': Buddhism, Pop Culture, and Contemporary Metamorphoses in American Judaism." In *Religion in Consumer Society*, edited by Francois Gauthier, 91–108. New York: Routledge, 2013.

Noy, Chaim, and Erik Cohen, eds. *Israeli Backpackers: From Tourism to Rite of Passage*. Albany: State University of New York Press, 2005.

Odenheimer, Eleanor F., Rebecca Buchanan, and Tanya Prewitt. "Adaptations of Yoga: Jewish Interpretations." In *Muscling in on New Worlds: Jews, Sport, and the Making of the Americas*, edited by Raanan Rein and David Sheinin, 49–67. Leiden, Netherlands: Brill, 2014.

Ohana, David. "Zarathustra in Jerusalem: Nietzsche and the 'New Hebrews.'" *Israel Affairs* 1, no. 3 (Spring 1995): 38–60.

Ostrer, Harry. *Legacy: A Genetic History of the Jewish People*. New York: Oxford University Press, 2012.

"Our Goals." *Shavei Israel* (blog). Accessed December 21, 2021. https://www.shavei.org/about-us/our-goals/.

"Our History." Beth Shalom B'Nai Zaken Ethiopian Hebrew Congregation. Accessed August 6, 2021. https://www.bethshalombz.org/history/.

Parekh, Bhikhu. *Rethinking Multiculturalism: Cultural Diversity and Political Theory*. Cambridge, Mass.: Harvard University Press, 2000.

Parfitt, Tudor. *Black Jews in Africa and the Americas*. Cambridge, Mass.: Harvard University Press, 2013.

———. "The Construction of Jewish Identities in Africa." In Parfitt and Semi, *Jews of Ethiopia*, 1–42.

———. *The Lost Tribes of Israel: The History of a Myth*. London: Weidenfeld and Nicolson, 2002.

Parfitt, Tudor, and Yulia Egorova. *Genetics, Mass Media and Identity: A Case Study of the Genetic Research on the Bene Israel and the Lemba*. New York: Routledge, 2006.

Parfitt, Tudor, and Emanuela Trevisan Semi, eds. *Jews of Ethiopia: The Birth of an Elite*. New York: Routledge, 2005.

———, eds. *Judaising Movements: Studies in the Margins of Judaism*. London: Routledge Curzon, 2002.

Patai, Raphael. Review of *Life Is with People: The Jewish Little-Town of Eastern Europe*. *American Anthropologist* 54, no. 4 (October–December 1952): 543–545.

Patai, Raphael, and Jennifer Patai Wing. *The Myth of the Jewish Race*. New York: Scribner's Sons, 1975.

Perrin, Marius. *Avec Sartre au Stalag 12D*. Paris: Jean-Pierre Delarge, 1980.

Pew Research Center. "A Portrait of American Jews." October 1, 2013, http://www.pewforum.org/2013/10/01/jewish-american-beliefs-attitudes-culture-survey/.

Philo. *The Special Laws*. Vol. 7 of *Loeb Classical Library*, edited by Jefferey Henderson, translated by F. H. Colson (Cambridge, Mass.: Harvard University Press, 1937).

Plaskow, Judith. *Standing Again at Sinai: Judaism from a Feminist Perspective*. New York: HarperCollins, 1991.

Podhoretz, Norman, ed. "Jewishness and the Younger Intellectuals: A Symposium." *Commentary* 34, no. 1 (1961): 306–359.

Potter, Andrew. *The Authenticity Hoax: How We Get Lost Finding Ourselves*. New York: Harper, 2010.

Power, Patricia A. "Accounting for Judaism in the Study of American Messianic Judaism." PhD thesis, Arizona State University, 2015.

Primack, Karen. "Visiting the Ugandan Miracle." *Kulanu* 2, no. 2 (Summer 1995): 1, 4, 8, 10. http://www.kulanu.org/wp-content/uploads/magazines/1995-summer.pdf.

———. "Why Give? One Person's Reason," *Amishav USA* 1, no. 2 (Winter 1993–1994): 6. https://kulanu.org/wp-content/uploads/magazines/1993-winter.pdf.

Rapoport, Louis. *Redemption Song: The Story of Operation Moses.* New York: Harcourt Brace Jovanovich, 1986.

Raz-Krakotzkin, Ammon. "The Zionist Return to the West and the Mizrahi Jewish Perspective." In *Orientalism and the Jews,* edited by Ivan Davidson Kalmar and Derek J. Penslar, 163–181. Waltham, Mass.: Brandeis University Press, 2005.

Reason, Gabriela. "Competing Trends in Messianic Judaism: The Debate over Evangelicalism." *Kesher: A Journal of Messianic Judaism,* January 2, 2005. http://www.kesherjournal.com/index.php?option=com_content&view=article&id=51&Itemid=.

Reisinger, Yvette, and Carol J. Steiner. "Reconceptualizing Object Authenticity." *Annals of Tourism Research* 33, no. 1 (2006): 65–86.

Reuben, Steven Carr. *A Parent's Guilt-Free Guide to Raising Jewish Kids: Understanding Judaism in the Modern World.* Bloomington, Ind.: Xlibris, 2002.

Rich, Adrienne. "Jewish Days and Night." In *A Human Eye: Essays on Art in Society, 1997–2008,* 18–33. New York: W. W. Norton, 2010.

———. "Split at the Root." In *Essential Essays: Culture, Politics, and the Art of Poetry,* edited by Sandra M. Gilbert, 198–217. New York: W. W. Norton, 2018.

Rogers, J. A. "Harlem Black Jews Fakes Says Norman Salit." *Afro-American,* December 19, 1931. https://news.google.com/newspapers?nid=2211&dat=19311219&id=hyYmAAAAIBAJ&sjid=6PoFAAAAIBAJ&pg=6555,6485495&hl=en.

Rogovoy, Seth. *The Essential Klezmer.* Chapel Hill, N.C.: Algonquin, 2000.

———. "The Klezmer Revival: Old World Meets New." Berkshire Web. Accessed ca. May 2009. http://www.berkshireweb.com/rogovoy/interviews/klez.html (site discontinued).

Roland, Joan G. *Jews in British India: Identity in a Colonial Era.* Hanover, N.H.: University Press of New England, 1989.

Roof, Wade Clark. *Spiritual Marketplace: Baby Boomers and the Remaking of American Religion.* Princeton, N.J.: Princeton University Press, 1999.

Rosen, Jonathan. "A Dead Language, Yiddish Lives." *New York Times Magazine,* July 7, 1996, 26–27.

Roth, Jeff. *Jewish Meditation Practices for Everyday Life: Awakening Your Heart, Connecting with God.* Woodstock, N.Y.: Jewish Lights, 2009.

Rothenberg, Celia. "Jewish Yoga: Experiencing Flexible, Sacred, and Jewish Bodies." *Nova Religio: The Journal of Alternative and Emergent Religions* 10, no. 2 (2006): 57–74.

Ruah-Midbar, Marianna. "Current Jewish Spiritualities in Israel: A New Age." *Modern Judaism* 32, no. 1 (2012): 102–124.

Rubin-Dorsky, Jeffrey. "Philip Roth and American Jewish Identity: The Question of Authenticity." *American Literary History* 13, no. 1 (2001): 79–107.

Rudinow, Joel. "Race, Ethnicity, Expressive Authenticity: Can White People Sing the Blues?" *Journal of Aesthetics and Art Criticism* 52, no. 1 (Winter 1994): 127–137.

Sachar, Howard M. *A History of Jews in the Modern World.* New York: Vintage, 2006.

Sacks, Jonathan. *One People? Tradition, Modernity and Jewish Unity.* London: Littman, 1994.

———. *Will We Have Jewish Grandchildren: Jewish Continuity and How to Achieve It.* London: Vallentine Mitchell, 1995.

Sahagun, Louis. "At One with Dual Devotion." *Los Angeles Times*, May 2, 2006. https://www.latimes.com/archives/la-xpm-2006-may-02-me-jubus2-story.html.

Said, Edward. *The Question of Palestine.* New York: Vintage, 1992.

Salamon, Hagar. *The Hyena People: Ethiopian Jews in Christian Ethiopia.* Berkeley: University of California Press, 1999.

———. "In Search of Self and Other: A Few Remarks on Ethnicity, Race, and Ethiopian Jews." In *Jewish Locations: Traversing Racialized Landscapes*, edited by Lisa Tessman and Bat-Ami Bar On, 75–88. New York: Rowman & Littlefield, 2001.

Salkin, Jeffrey. "New Age Judaism." In *Blackwell Companion to Judaism*, edited by Jacob Neusner and Alan Avery, 354–370. Malden, Mass.: Blackwell, 2000.

Samet, Moshe. "The Beginnings of Orthodoxy." *Modern Judaism* 8, no. 3 (1988): 249–269.

Sapoznik, Henry. *Klezmer! Jewish Music from Old World to Our World.* New York: Shirmer Trade, 1999.

Sartre, Jean-Paul. *Antisemite and Jew: An Exploration of the Etiology of Hate.* New York: Schocken, 1995.

———. *Being and Nothingness: An Essay in Phenomenological Ontology.* New York: Washington Square, 1993.

———. *Existentialism Is a Humanism.* New Haven, Conn.: Yale University Press, 2007.

———. "Jean-Paul Sartre: A Candid Conversation with the Charismatic Fountainhead of Existentialism and Rejector of the Nobel Prize." *Playboy*, May 1965, 69–76.

———. *Quiet Moments in a War: The Letters of Jean-Paul Sartre to Simone de Beauvoir: 1940–1963.* New York: Scribner's Sons, 1993.

Satlow, Michael J. *Creating Judaism: History, Tradition, Practice.* New York: Columbia University Press, 2006.

Schoenberg, Eliot Sala. "Intermarriage and Conservative Judaism: An Approach for the 1990s." *Conservative Judaism* 43, no. 1 (Fall 1990): 13–17.

Scholem, Gershom. "Toward an Understanding of the Messianic Idea in Judaism." In *The Messianic Idea in Judaism: And Other Essays on Jewish Spirituality*, 1–36. New York: Schocken, 1995.

Schonfeld, Rabbi Julie, and Rabbi Jeffrey A. Wohlberg. "A Delicate Balance: The Rabbinical Assembly's Position on Outreach and Conversion." Leadership Council of Conservative Judaism (LCCJ), Keruv Commission, 2009.

Schwartz, Hillel. *The Culture of the Copy: Striking Likenesses, Unreasonable Facsimiles.* New York: Zone Books, 1996.

Schwarz, Tanya. *Ethiopian Jewish Immigrants.* London: Curzon, 2001.

Schweitzer, Ruth. "Beyond the Pale Creates Ruckus with New Album." *Canadian Jewish News*, June 19, 2017. http://www.cjnews.com/culture/beyond-the-pale-ruckus-new-album.

Seeman, Don. "Ethnographers, Rabbis, and Jewish Epistemology: The Case of the Ethiopian Jews." *Tradition* 25, no. 4 (Summer 1991): 13–29.

———. *One People, One Blood: Ethiopian-Israelis and the Return to Judaism*. New Brunswick, N.J.: Rutgers University Press, 2009.

Semino, Ornella, Chiara Magri, Giorgia Benuzzi, Alice A. Lin, Nadia Al-Zahery, Vincenza Battaglia, Liliana Maccioni et al. "Origin, Diffusion, and Differentiation of Y-Chromosome Haplogroups E and J: Inferences on the Neolithization of Europe and Later Migratory Events in the Mediterranean Area." *American Journal of Human Genetics* 74, no. 5 (2004): 1023–1034.

Shapiro, Rami M. "The Teaching and Practice of Reb Yerachmiel ben Yisrael." In *Meditation from the Heart of Judaism: Today's Teachers Share Their Practices, Techniques, and Faith*, edited by Avram Davis, 17–34. Woodstock, Vt.: Jewish Lights, 1999.

Shenhav, Yehouda. *The Arab Jews: A Postcolonial Reading of Nationalism, Religion, and Ethnicity*. Palo Alto, Calif.: Stanford University Press, 2006.

Shiloah, Amnon. *Jewish Musical Traditions*. Detroit, Mich.: Wayne State University Press, 1992.

Shmueli, Efraim. *Seven Jewish Cultures: A Reinterpretation of Jewish History and Culture*. Cambridge: Cambridge University Press, 1980.

Shohat, Ella. "Dislocated Identities: Reflections of an Arab Jew." *Movement Research* 5 (Fall 1991 / Winter 1992): 8. https://www.academia.edu/11961837/_Dislocated_Identities_Reflections_of_an_Arab_Jew_Published_simultaneously_in_Emergences_Movement_Research_5_Fall_1991_Winter_1992_p_8.

———. "The Invention of the Mizrahim." *Journal of Palestinian Studies* 29, no. 1 (1999): 5–20.

———. "Rupture and Return: Zionist Discourse and the Study of Arab Jews." *Social Text* 21, no. 2 (Summer 2003): 49–74.

Shoshana, Brenda. *Jewish Dharma: A Guide to the Practice of Judaism and Zen*. New York: Da Capo, 2008.

Silber, Michael. "The Emergence of Ultra-Orthodoxy: The Invention of a Tradition." In *The Uses of Tradition: Jewish Continuity in the Modern Era*, edited by Jack Wertheimer, 23–84. New York: Jewish Theological Seminary, 1992.

Slobin, Mark, ed. *American Klezmer: Its Roots and Offshoots*. Berkeley: University of California Press, 2002.

———. *Fiddler on the Move: Exploring the Klezmer World*. New York: Oxford University Press, 2000.

Smith, Anthony D. *Chosen Peoples: Sacred Sources of National Identity*. New York: Oxford University Press, 2003.

Sokol, Moshe, ed. *Rabbinic Authority and Personal Autonomy*. Northvale, N.J.: Jason Aronson, 1992.

Sokolow, Peter. "Mazel Tov! Klezmer Music and Simchas in Brooklyn, 1910 to Present." In *Jews of Brooklyn*, edited by Ilana Abramovitch and Sean Galvin, 179–185. Waltham, Mass.: Brandeis University Press, 2002.

Solomon, Alisa. "How *Fiddler* Became Folklore." *Forward*, September 1, 2006. https://forward.com/culture/1710/how-e2-80-98fiddler-e2-80-99-became-folklore/.

———. "On Jewishness, as the Fiddler Played." *New York Times*, October 17, 2013. https://www.nytimes.com/2013/10/20/theater/fiddler-on-the-roof-its-production-heritage.html.

———. "Tevye, Today, and Beyond." *Forward*, September 8, 2006. https://forward.com/culture/2422/tevye-today-and-beyond/.

———. "Tradition! The Indestructible *Fiddler on the Roof*." *New Yorker*, October 8, 2015.

———. *Wonder of Wonders: A Cultural History of Fiddler on the Roof*. New York: Metropolitan, 2013.

Soloveitchik, Haym. "Rupture and Reconstruction: The Transformation of Contemporary Orthodoxy." *Tradition* 28, no. 4 (Summer 1994): 64–130.

Soltes, Ori. "Art, History, Memory, Identity, Truth: The Art and Craft of Cary Herz." In *New Mexico's Crypto-Jews: Image and Memory*, edited by Cary Herz, 1–14. Albuquerque: University of New Mexico Press, 2007.

Södergren, Jonatan. "Brand Authenticity: 25 Years of Research." *International Journal of Consumer Studies* 45, no. 4 (2021): 645–663. https://doi.org/10.1111/ijcs.12651.

Sparks, Kenton L. *Ethnicity and Identity in Ancient Israel: Prolegomena to the Study of Ethnic Sentiments and Their Expression in the Hebrew Bible*. Winona Lake, Ind.: Eisenbrauns, 1998.

Spence, Rebecca. "Meditation Hits the Jewish Mainstream." *Jewish Forward*, August 11, 2006. http://www.forward.com/articles/623/.

Spiegel, Shalom. *Hebrew Reborn*. New York: Macmillan, 1930.

Strom, Yale. *The Book of Klezmer: The History, the Music, the Folklore*. Chicago: A Capella, 2001.

Suleiman, Susan. "The Jew in Jean-Paul Sartre's *Réflexions sur la question juive*: An Exercise in Historical Reading." In *The Jew in the Text*, edited by Linda Nochlin and Tamar Garb, 208–215. London: Thames and Hudson, 1995.

Summit, Jeffrey. "Music and the Construction of Identity among the Abayudaya (Jewish People) of Uganda." In *Garland Handbook of African Music*, edited by Ruth M. Stone, 312–324. New York: Routledge, 2008.

Susser, Bernard, and Charles Liebman. *Choosing Survival*. New York: Oxford University Press, 1999.

Sutton, Wesley K. "'Jewish Genes': Ancient Priests and Modern Jewish Identity." In Greenspoon, *Who Is a Jew?*, 105–116.

Svigals, Alicia. "Why Do We Do This Anyway: Klezmer as Jewish Youth Subculture." *Judaism* 47, no. 1 (Winter 1998): 43–49.

Tarlow, Rabbi Peter. "A Spring Break Mitzvah with the Huánuco Jewish Community." *Kulanu* 15, no. 2 (Summer 2008): 1, 12. http://www.kulanu.org/wp-content/uploads/magazines/2006-spring.pdf.

Taylor, Charles. *The Ethics of Authenticity*. Cambridge, Mass.: Harvard University Press, 1991.

———. "The Politics of Recognition," in *Multiculturalism: Examining the Politics of Recognition*. Edited by Amy Gutmann, 25–74. Princeton, N.J.: Princeton University Press, 1994.

———. *Sources of the Self: Making of Modern Identity*. Cambridge, Mass.: Harvard University Press, 1989.

Tenenbaum, Shelly, and Lynn Davidman. "It's in My Genes: Biological Discourse and Essentialist View of Identity among Contemporary American Jews." *Sociological Quarterly* 48, no. 3 (2007): 435–450.

Theodossopoulos, Dimitrios. "Laying Claim to Authenticity: Five Anthropological Dilemmas." *Anthropological Quarterly* 86, no. 2 (Spring 2013): 337–360.

Tinker, H. Review of *The Children of Israel: The Bene Israel of Bombay*, by Schifra Strizower. *Race* 14, no. 1 (1972): 98.

Tobin, Diane, Gary A. Tobin, and Scott Rubin. *In Every Tongue: The Racial and Ethnic Diversity of the Jewish People*. San Francisco: Institute for Jewish and Community Research, 2005.

Tobin, Gary A. *Opening the Gates: How Proactive Conversion Can Revitalize the Jewish Community*. San Francisco: Jossey-Bass, 1999.

Toft, Mark, Jay Sunny, and Rich Taylor. *Authenticity: Building a Brand in an Insincere Age*. Westport, Conn: Praeger, 2020.

Train, Kelly A. "Well, How Can You Be Jewish *and* European: Indian Jewish Experiences in the Toronto Jewish Community and the Creation of Congregation Bina." *American Jewish History* 100, no. 1 (2016): 1–23.

Trilling, Lionel. *Sincerity and Authenticity*. Cambridge, Mass.: Harvard University Press, 1973.

Turner, Terence. "Anthropology and Multiculturalism: What Is Anthropology That Multiculturalists Should Be Mindful of It?" In *Multiculturalism: A Critical Reader*, edited by David Theo Goldberg, 406–425. Malden, Mass.: Blackwell, 1994.

Umbach, Maiken, and Mathew Humphrey. *Authenticity: The Cultural History of a Political Concept*. London: Palgrave Macmillan, 2018.

Upton, Dell. "Ethnicity, Authenticity, and Invented Tradition." *Historical Archaeology* 30, no. 2 (1996): 4–5.

Vannini, Phillip, and J. Patrick Williams. *Authenticity in Culture, Self, and Society*. Farnham, U.K.: Ashgate, 2009.

Verman, Mark. *The History and Varieties of Jewish Meditation*. New York: Jason Aronson, 1977.

Waldron, Jeremy. "Minority Cultures and the Cosmopolitan Alternative." In Kymlicka, *Rights of Minority Cultures*, 93–119.

Wang, Nin. "Rethinking Authenticity in Tourism Experience." *Annals of Tourism Research* 26, no. 2 (1999): 349–370.

Ward, Seth. "Converso Descendants in the American Southwest: A Report on Research, Resources, and the Changing Search for Identity." In *Jewish Studies at the Turn of the 20th Century*, edited by Judith Targarona and Angel Saez-Badillos, 677–687. Leiden, Netherlands: Brill, 1999.

Webber, Jonathan. "Modern Jewish Identities: The Ethnographic Complexities." *Journal of Jewish Studies* 43, no. 2 (1992): 246–267.

Weinberg, David H. *Between Tradition and Modernity: Haim Zhitlowski, Simon Dubnow, Ahad Ha'am and the Shaping of Modern Jewish Identity.* New York: Holmes and Meier, 1996.

Werczberger, Rachel. *Jews in the Age of Authenticity: Jewish Spiritual Renewal in Israel.* New York: Peter Lang, 2017.

Werczberger, Rachel, and Boaz Huss, eds. "New Age Culture in Israel." Special issue, *Israel Studies Review* 29, no. 2 (Winter 2014): 1–16.

Wertheimer, Jack. "Judaism without Limits." *Commentary* 104, no. 1 (1997): 24–27.

———. "The Orthodox Moment." *Commentary* 107, no. 2 (1999): 18–24.

Wertheimer, Jack, Charles Liebman, and Steven M. Cohen. "How to Save American Jews." *Commentary*, January 1996, 47–51.

Wieder, Paul. "A Rave Review for Ugandan Music." *Kulanu* 5, no. 2 (Summer 1998): 1, 5. http://www.kulanu.org/wp-content/uploads/magazines/1998-summer.pdf.

Wolitz, Seth. "Imagining the Jew in France: From 1945 to the Present." *Yale French Studies* 85 (1994): 119–134.

Wuthnow, Robert. *After Heaven: Spirituality in America since the 1950s.* Berkeley: University of California Press, 1998.

Yoga Alliance. "2016 Yoga in America Study Conducted by Yoga Journal and Yoga Alliance Reveals Growth and Benefits of the Practice." 2016. https://www.yogaalliance.org/Get_Involved/Media_Inquiries/2016_Yoga_in_America_Study_Conducted_by_Yoga_Journal_and_Yoga_Alliance_Reveals_Growth_and_Benefits_of_the_Practice.

"Yoga and Judaism Center." *Torah-Veda* (blog). Accessed December 12, 2021. http://yajcenter.blogspot.com/.

Zavidowsky, Zvi. "Restoring the Meditative Side of Judaism: A Beginning." Nefesh Haya School. Accessed August 6, 2021. https://www.angelfire.com/pe/ophanim/Olam3.htm.

Zeller, Jack. "Welcome to Kulanu!" *Kulanu* 1, no. 1 (Spring 1994): 1. http://www.kulanu.org/wp-content/uploads/magazines/1994-spring.pdf.

Zemach, Benjamin. "The Beginning of Jewish Dancing." In *Ha-Rikud: The Jewish Dance*, edited by Fred Berk, 3–9. New York: UAHC, 1972.

Zoossmann-Diskin, Avshalom. "Are Today's Jewish Priests Descended from the Old Ones?" *HOMO: Journal of Comparative Human Biology* 51, nos. 2–3 (2000): 156–162.

Zucker, David J. "Erev Rav: A Mixed Multitude of Meanings." TheTorah.com. Accessed August 18, 2021. https://www.thetorah.com/article/erev-rav-a-mixed-multitude-of-meanings.

Index

Abayudaya Jews of Uganda, 219–221
Abbink, J., 260n17
Abel, Lionel, 28
Abitbol, Michel, 239n56
Abrams, Elliot, 50
Abravanel, Isaac, 196
Abu El-Haj, Nadia, 156–157
Ahad Ha'am: and collective authenticity, 107; on Hebrew, 115; on Jewish culture, 108; on Jewishness, 107–108; on nationalism, 107; on spiritual freedom, 108
Allport, Gordon, 63–64, 69
Almog, Oz, 110
Alter, Gaby, 254n40
American Jews: and *Fiddler on the Roof*, 125–127; and Israeli folk dance, 119; and Jewish survival, 28; and shtetl authenticity, 52, 124, 126; and Yiddish, 130
Amishav: and B'nei Menashe, 215–217; and Gush Emunim, 206; and Kulanu, 217; and "lost Jews," 207, 217, 221, 223
antisemitism, 6, 22–23, 27, 32, 43, 111
Appleby, Scott, 52
Arab Jews, 112–114, 118–119
Arabs, 119, 121; and Jewish genetics, 152; Zionist ambivalence toward, 113
Ascheim, Steven, 253n5
Ashkenazi Jews, 112–114, 116–118, 126, 214
Ashriel, Yoav, 120
Astro, Alan, 239n56
Atzmon, Gil, 258n14
authenticity: branding, 3–4; dialectical, 27, 39; essentialist, 5, 14, 18–19, 22, 46, 140; experiential, 17, 69–70, 75, 81, 132, 189; expressive, 12–14, 17, 47, 60; and genetic evidence, 157; and innovation, 16; invented, 19; in Israeli-Palestinian conflict, 111–112; and New Age spirituality, 122; as a process, 227; and recognition, 6, 26, 37, 40; and spirituality, 6. *See also* collective authenticity; existential authenticity; historical authenticity; Jewish authenticity; personal authenticity
authentic Jews, 127; Bene Israel as, 213; Beta Israel's claim to be, 163, 167–168; Blacks as, 180–182; conversion into, 139; lost Jews as, 219; Orthodox definition of, 43–44; and racial purity, 139; Reform Judaism's definition of, 62; Sartre on, 6, 28, 37

authentic Judaism: and essence of Judaism, 15; feminist approach to, 71; in Israel, 114; multiple forms of, 15, 86; Orthodox view of, 44, 48, 50, 56; position of Reform Judaism on, 61; redefined by ultra-Orthodoxy, 54–55
Avichail, Eliyahu, 206, 215–216

Baade, Christina, 135–136
Bach, Raymond, 270n20
bad faith, 19, 23, 32, 225
Baker, Cynthia, 229
Baldwin, James, 177
Band, Arnold, 249n13
Banet-Weiser, Sarah, 4
Batson, Daniel, 69
Beauvoir, Simone de, 236n4
Be'chol Lashon, 217, 221–224
Behar, Doron M., 257n2
Beilin, Yossi, 146
Bendix, Regina, 18
Bene Israel, 203; authenticity of, 213–214; Indianness of, 212; origin stories of, 208–209, 211
Benite, Zvi Ben-Dor, 259n2
Ben-Yehuda, Eliezer, 116
Berdichevski, Misha Josef, 109
Berg, Philip, 81–82
Berger, David, 56
Bernstein, Louis, 242n63
Beta Israel. *See* Ethiopian Jews
Biale, David, 85
Black Hebrews. *See* Black Jews
Black Jews, 183; Christian origins of, 180; origin stories of, 178; Orthodox attitude toward, 182; and racial dimension of Jewishness, 178, 180, 183; and relations with mainstream Jews, 177–179, 181; in the United States, 172, 174–176, 179. *See also* Ethiopian Jews
Black Judaism: as a distinct form of Judaism, 183–184; and Marcus Garvey, 174; as rooted in Black Christian sects, 180
Bleich, David, 137, 182
Bloomfield, Diane, 78–80
B'nei Menashe, 203, 215–217, 221
Borgen, Peder, 141
Boris, Staci, 269n15
Boyarin, Daniel, 227
Boyarin, Jonathan, 19, 124

Bradman, Neil, 258n23
Brantley, Ben, 125
Brickner, Balfour, 61
Brodesser-Akner, Taffy, 246n28
Brotz, Howard, 179
Bruner, Edward M., 235n41
Buchanan, Rebecca, 246n35
Buddhism, and Jewishness, 76, 79
Bulka, Reuven P., 242n64
Butler, Judith, 236n45

Carrette, Jeremy, 4
Carroll, Michael P., 198
Chabad, 100–101, 137
Chabra, Deepak, 233n2
Chafets, Zev, 263n49
Charmé, Stuart, 235n42, 237n7
Chireau, Yvonne, 262n9
Christ, Carol, 70
Christianity: and Beta Israel, 164; and B'nei Menashe, 215–216; early centuries of, 91; and Hebrew Christians, 89; and intermarriage, 94; Jewish attitudes about, 88, 90–91, 93–94; and Messianic Jews, 88–89, 91, 95–96; separation from Judaism, 90
Cohen, Debra Nussbaum, 257n27
Cohen, Erik, 235n41
Cohen, Jonathan, 241n40
Cohen, Shaye D., 15
Cohen, Steven M., 17, 46, 69, 146
Cohen Modal Haplotype, 151–154, 156
Cohn-Sherbok, Dan, 94
Coleman, Robert, 263n38
collective authenticity, 2–3, 11; essentialist approaches to, 14, 140; and "spirituality of dwelling," 68; and Zionism, 109, 122
Commandment Keepers, 175, 179, 184
Conservative Judaism, 60–61, 143
conversion, 143, 145; and authenticity, 140; forced, 90, 189, 193, 195, 198–199; nonreligious, 144
conversion to Judaism: and Black Jews, 182–183; in Conservative movement, 143; and intermarriage, 7, 137, 139–140, 145; and Jewish souls, 141; Orthodox model of, 207, 217; in Reform movement, 59
conversos. See crypto-Jews
Corinaldi, Michael, 168
crypto-Jews: and Christianity, 191–194, 196; and conversion to Judaism, 190–192, 202; cultural identity of, 198–199, 201–202; and essentialism, 189; historical authenticity of, 189, 191, 196, 198–201; and the Holocaust, 198; and Jewish authenticity, 192; and the Jewish people, 189, 195; and Jewish souls, 190–191; and Jewish survival, 198; and lost tribes of Israel, 195; origin stories of, 192, 197, 201; recognition of, 189, 191, 197–198, 202
Cuddihy, John Murray, 234n9, 253n5
cultural authenticity: of antisemites, 22; and Zionism, 105
cultural identity: diverse forms of, 49; dynamic quality of, 226; essentialist, 13, 29, 226; and forced conversion, 193; newly adopted, 215, 223; nonessentialist, 39, 201, 227; and recognition, 38; Zionist, 110, 120

Damon, Maria, 37
Dan, Joseph, 247n41
Dauermann, Stuart, 95
Davidman, Lynn, 256n7
Davis, Avram, 245n6
Davis, Natalie Zemon, 257n1
Dein, Simon, 249n27
De Lange, Nicholas, 256n15
Derrida, Jacques, 30, 36; on antisemitism, 36; on Jewish authenticity, 36; Jewishness of, 36; on Sartre, 36–37
De Sola Pool, David, 139
Diamond, Etan, 54
Di-Capua, Yoav, 250n21
Dion, Shulamis, 254n36
DNA, 149–150, 153–154, 156
Dubov, Nissan Dovid, 255n1
Dutton, Dennis, 234n3

Egorova, Yulia, 258n22, 267n18, 268n36
Eichmann, Adolph, 126
Einhorn, David, 142
Eisen, Arnold M.: and conversion to Judaism, 143; and the "Jew within," 69; on the limits of Jewish innovation, 229–230; and the "sovereign self," 46
Elazar, Daniel, 250n34
Eldad, 161–162, 167, 173
Eleff, Zev, 53
el Harar, Daveed, 74
Ellenson, David, 260n15
Epstein, Jerome, 142–143
Erikson, Erik, 38, 270n22
Eshkol, Levi, 213
essence of Jewishness, 11, 13, 15, 141, 227
essentialism: as bad faith, 18; cultural, 17, 22–23, 108; genetic, 7, 154, 156; racial, 142
Ethiopia: and ancient Israelites, 163, 176, 181; lost tribes in, 161, 166
Ethiopian Jews, 7, 164–175, 181; known as Beta Israel, 163–164, 166; recognized by Radbaz, 162
ethnic groups: and conversion, 141; and expressive authenticity, 13
European Jews, 230; emancipation of, 12, 16, 27, 112, 230; hybridity of, 213; in Israel, 113–114;

and rabbinic Judaism, 222, 224; racial status in the U.S., 178. *See also* Ashkenazi Jews
Even-Zohar, Itamar, 251n54
exile, and the land of Israel, 105–106, 110
existential authenticity, 17–21, 24, 109; and Jewish feminists, 70; and klezmer music, 134; and life in Israel, 105
Ezrahi, Sidra DeKoven, 259n1

Fackenheim, Emil: on God, 44; on the Holocaust, 45; on Jewish authenticity, 44; on liberal Jews, 45; and 614th commandment, 44
Faitlovitch, Jacques, 165–166, 169, 173
Falashas, 7, 165, 175, 179. *See also* Ethiopian Jews
Falk, Jody, 78
false messiahs, 88, 98
Fein, Leonard, 235n23
Feldman, Emanuel, 241n22
Feldman, Ron, 81
Fernheimer, Janice W., 177
Fiddler on the Roof, 7, 230; as Ashkenazi origin story, 126; authenticity of, 125–127; and non-Jewish actors, 125; portrayal of Eastern European Jewish life, 124, 126–127
Fierstein, Harvey, 125
Fink, Nan, 256n12
Finkelstein, Israel, 205
Finkielkraut, Alain, 30–37; on antisemitism, 32; on Jewish authenticity, 31, 33, 35; on Jewish culture, 33–34; on Jewish inauthenticity, 35; on Sartre, 33–34
Fishberg, Maurice, 178
Fraser, Nancy, 40
Freedman, Jonathan, 199–200, 228
French antisemites, 22, 24, 111
French Jews, 13, 28–29, 35–36
Freud, Sigmund, 64
Freund, Michael, 206, 216
Friedlander, Judith, 29
Friedman, Menachem, 242n55
Frish, Robyn, 144
Frith, Simon, 133
Fromm, Erich: on God, 65–68; and Hebrew prophets, 66; and humanistic religion, 64–65, 67, 75; on incestuous attachments, 40, 65–66; and the story of Rabbi Eliezer, 66
Funnye, Capers, 184, 186–187

Garfinkle, Adam M., 250n22
Garvey, Marcus, 174–175
Gauthier, Francois, 3
genetic markers, 151–152, 154, 156
genetics: and authenticity, 157. *See also* Jewish genetics
Gewirth, Leonard, 43, 46, 57
Gillman, Neil, 16, 20
Gilroy, Paul, 158, 227

Gindin, Matthew, 77
Gitlitz, David, 194
Glenn, Susan, 28, 270n21
Glick, Ira, 248n5
God: Maimonides on, 87; meditation and, 74, 76; and spiritual experience, 81; yoga and the experience of, 78
Gold, Roberta, 178–179
Gold, Steven J., 246n39
Goldberg, David Theo, 239n62
Goldfarb, Harold, 181–182
Goldstein, Eric, 139
Gomes, Stephen, 190
Gonen, Rivka, 267n31
Gordon, Albert, 256n10
Gordon, Judah Loeb, 238n27
Gordon, Lewis, 222
Goren, Shlomo, 167–168
Gottschalk, Alfred, 243n14
Gozlan, Audi, 247n42
Greenberg, Clement, 29, 32
Greenberg, Irving, 242n68
Greenberg, Steve, 144
Greenspoon, Leonard J., 258n12
Gruber, Ruth Ellen, 133
Gush Emunim, 206

halakha: as the foundation of authentic Judaism, 44, 49; intensified by ultra-Orthodox, 54–55; and Kabbalah, 82; and meditation, 73; and Messianic Jews, 95; and race, 181; rejected by non-Orthodox Jews, 61; rejected by Sabbateans, 99
Halevy, Joseph, 165, 169–170, 172
Halkin, Hillel, 267n32
Hall, Stuart, 20, 26, 158, 224
Handler, Richard, 14, 34
Hansen, David, 40
Harris, Lis, 51
Harris-Shapiro, Carol, 88
Harshav, Benjamin, 251n49
Hart, Mitchell, 178
Hart, Mitchell B., 262n20
Haviv, Ayana Shira, 252n79
Hebrew: authenticity of, 115–116, 122; authentic pronunciation of, 116–117; in Jewish meditation, 74, 80; revival of, 115–117, 121, 129–130. *See also* Ben-Yehuda, Eliezer
Hebrew Christians, 89, 96
Heilman, Samuel, 52
Herder, Johann Gottfried, 13, 32, 67, 107
heresy and heretics: followers of Jesus as, 90–91; later reclaimed as authentic, 16, 62, 83, 87, 90; liberal Judaism as, 48; messianic ideas about Lubavitcher Rebbe as, 100–101; and pluralism, 88; and suppression of alternative views, 15, 27, 86

heritage tourism, 4, 219–221
Herman, Simon, 121
Hertzog, Elizabeth, 124
Herz, Cary, 264n5
Herzl, Theodor, 112
Hess, Moses, 106
Hildesheimer, Esriel, 164–165
historical authenticity, 12–14, 51; of Hebrew language, 116; of Jewish meditation, 75
Hodes, Joseph, 267n15
Hollier, Denis, 236n4
Holocaust: and American Jews, 28, 124, 126–127, 130; and rise of ultra-Orthodoxy, 54
Hordes, Stanley, 194, 201
Horowitz, Bethamie, 243n15, 256n23, 257n26
Howe, Irving, 2, 68, 126
Huss, Boaz, 82–84
Hyman, Tali, 257n26
Hymes, Dell, 241n42

identity, 26; as a construction, 199–201; and consumerism, 3; and conversion, 139, 141; essentialist forms of, 22; and existential authenticity, 17–18, 25; as fluid, 29, 40, 229; and genetic evidence, 153, 156; as hybrid, 227–228; instability of, 35–36, 224, 226; and recognition by others, 6, 26, 38–39, 94, 231. *See also* Jewish identity
Indian Jews, 211–214. *See also* Bene Israel
Ingber, Judith Brin, 252n65
intermarriage: and Bene Israel, 212; and conversion, 139; and Jewish genetics, 153; and Jewish peoplehood, 148; and Jewish racial identity, 139; and Jewish survival, 147; non-Orthodox rabbinic responses to, 142; Orthodox positions on, 137–138, 145; and outreach to non-Jews, 142
Isaac, Ephraim, 172–173
Isaac, Walter, 178, 180
Israel: Arab Jews in, 114; authenticity of life in, 7, 31, 105–106, 129; hybrid culture of, 113, 120–121, 173; and Jewish-Palestinian conflict, 111; New Age groups in, 122; "New Jew" in, 110; racism in, 171; Zionist ideas about, 105, 110
Israel, Benjamin, 213
Israeli folk dance, 7, 117–121; authenticity of, 119–120; music for, 120, 122
Israeliness, 115, 120; and Ashkenazi Jews, 112; and Jewishness, 121; and Mizrahi Jews, 113
Israelis, and Palestinians, 112
Israelite priesthood, 151, 155–156, 186
Israelite religion, 155, 169, 204–205
Israelite tribes, 67, 211; as Africans, 173–174, 176, 178, 185; claimed as ancestors by African tribes, 162; and claims of the Beta Israel, 165, 173; conquest by the Assyrians and results on, 204; in Eldad's travelogue, 161; genetic history, 152; in India, 208–209, 215–216; and the myth of the lost tribes, 161–162, 165, 173, 204; and newly found Jews, 7, 162

Jacobs, Janet Liebman, 194
James, William, 70
Jesus: Jewish followers of, 15, 90–91, 99; Jewishness of, 91; Jewish rejection of messianic claims about, 88, 92–93, 98
Jewish authenticity: and Bene Israel, 208, 210, 212–214; of Beta Israel, 163–164, 170, 172; and Black Jews, 181; and Capers Funnye, 186; conflicting views of what is, 1, 127; contradictory nature of, 37; essentialist forms, 6, 127, 140–141; of Ethiopian Jews, 162; existentialist model of, 25, 109; expressive, 140; and *Fiddler on the Roof*, 125–126; and genetics, 7, 149, 158; and heresy, 86; and hybridity, 228; and Indian culture, 214; and individualism, 46–47; and intermarriage, 7, 139, 147; and Jewish spirituality, 72; and Kabbalah, 6; and klezmer music, 128, 131–132, 135; lack of essence, 15; and liberal Judaism, 6, 49, 56, 61–62; and Messianic Jews, 6, 89, 94–95, 98; new approaches, 228; of non-Orthodox Jews, 51, 58, 61; and Orthodox Judaism, 45, 47, 49, 53, 56, 61–62; and race, 178; and recognition, 5, 145, 147, 172, 219; Sartre's analysis of, 5, 23, 25; symbolized by the shtetl, 7, 52, 253; and Zionism, 7
Jewish Buddhists, 76
Jewish Cultural Affirmation, 147
Jewish culture: boundaries of, 38; diversity of, 15, 39, 56, 222; in France, 36; nonreligious, 146
Jewish feminism, 70, 78, 97
Jewish genetics, 7, 149–151; and genetic essentialism, 156–158; and Middle Eastern origins of Jews, 152–153; and mitochondrial DNA, 153–154. *See also* Cohen Modal Haplotype
Jewish identity: authentic, 4; boundaries of, 29; and consumerism, 3; inauthentic, 28; and positive Jewishness, 29; postmodern, 223; and recognition, 30
Jewish inauthenticity, 27, 32, 35, 43, 52; Sartre on, 27
Jewish law, 46, 49, 58; and Black Jews, 179–180; and conversion, 140, 191; and genetics, 154; and intermarriage, 142; and rabbinic authority, 66; stricter ultra-Orthodox approach, 55. *See also* halakha
Jewish meditation, 72–75, 79, 84, 122; Hindu roots, 72, 74
Jewish music. *See* klezmer music
Jewish mysticism, 4, 6, 72, 85, 87, 99, 122

Jewishness: and Arabness, 113–114; authentic, 28; boundaries, 27, 38, 60, 64, 181; branding, 4; definition of, 15–16; different species of, 20, 97; essence of, 17, 141, 198, 214, 223, 226–227; existential form of, 35; experiential, 69; flight from, 23, 44; fluid sense of, 28, 33, 36, 38, 109, 227–228; genealogical evidence, 182, 190, 201; genetic evidence, 150, 152, 154, 156; heretical, 87; and hybridity, 213, 227–229, 231; imaginary, 32; and Israeliness, 121; as a journey, 69, 143–144; and klezmer, 132; multidimensional, 46, 57; of newly found Jews, 215, 218–219; and race, 7, 89, 138, 178; recognition of, 39, 225, 230; of white Jews, 172

Jewish people: compared to Torah scroll, 138; creation of, 222; essence of, 107, 109; existentialist definition of, 39, 226; and genetics, 149–150, 153; hybridity of, 228; and Jewish soul, 141; joining without religious conversion, 146; as kinship, 46–47; as multicultural, 38, 48, 112, 172, 221–224; as nationality, 225; and race, 177–178, 213; and recognition, 39; Zionist agenda for the, 105–106, 111

Jewish peoplehood, 67, 138, 140, 148, 178

Jewish priests, 155, 258

Jewish social identity, 147

Jewish souls, 84, 141–142; Kabbalistic view of, 84; in lost Jews, 207; in non-Jews, 141

Jewish spirituality, 6, 72, 80–81, 85, 132

Jewish survival: and assimilation of American Jews, 28; intermarriage, 147; and "positive" Jewishness, 28; as standard for Jewish authenticity, 50

Jewish women, 70–71, 78; and authentic Judaism, 71; and genetics, 154; and practice of yoga, 77

Jewish yoga, 72, 75, 77–80, 82, 85, 122

Jews: and boundaries with non-Jews, 15, 58, 137, 140, 150, 228; cultural mixing with non-Jews, 14, 228; Eastern European, 114, 124–131; genetic makeup, 150–152, 154; inauthentic, 28, 32, 36, 43, 106, 218, 228; newly found, 203, 217, 223; self-hating, 28–29, 43

Jews by association, 145

Jews in France, 23, 31, 35

Jones, Elias Fanayaye, 261n2

Joselit, Jenna Weissman, 53–54

Judaism: ancient, 164, 174; and Buddhism, 76; essence of, 15, 24, 34, 76, 139; experiential dimension, 77; and feminism, 70–71, 78; and Kabbalah, 81–82, 84; multiple forms of, 1, 15, 46, 183–185, 222–223; non-Orthodox, 48–49, 51, 61; and yoga, 78

Judaken, Jonathan, 236n4

Kabbalah, 6, 80–85

Kadman, Gurit, 118

Kahn, Susan M., 258n9

Kakungulu, Semei, 219

Kamenetz, Rodger, 76

Kanfer, Stefan, 242n1

Kaplan, Aryeh, 73–74

Kaplan, Mordechai: on authentic Jewish wisdom, 68; on God, 68; on inauthenticity and immature wisdom, 68; on Jewish peoplehood, 67; on salvation, 68

Kaplan, Steven, 168, 181

Kaschl, Elke, 119

Katz, Nathan, 267n11

Kaufman, Ayalah, 251n64, 252n66

Kaufmann-Tobin, Dianne, 221

Kaye/Kantrowitz, Melanie, 264n50

Kehimkar, Haeem Samuel, 210

Kellner, Menachem, 50–51, 58

Kelman, Herbert C., 111–112

Kessler, David, 259n11

Key, Andre E., 261n2

Kimmerling, Baruch, 121

King, Richard, 4

Kinzer, Mark, 97

klezmer music: authenticity of, 127–128, 131–132, 134–135; hybridity of, 228; and Jewish assimilation, 132–133

kohanim, 151–152, 154–156. See also Israelite priesthood

Kohler, K., 256n19

Koltun-Fromm, Ken, 186

Kook, Rabbi Zvi Yehuda, 206

Kraft, Jessica Carew, 233n8

Krausz, Michael, 239n62

Kress, Jeffrey, 257n26

Kunin, Seth: on crypto-Jews, 198–200, 202; on cultural authenticity, 199, 201

Kwame Anthony Appiah, 158

Kymlicka, Will, 6, 26, 37

Labovitz, Gail, 264n56

Lamm, Norman, 49

Landau, Jacob M., 249n25

Landing, James, 180

Lavender, Abraham, 263n34

Leiter, Sarah, 264n54

Lerner, Michael, 235n25

Levi, Levy Ben, 184

Levine, Joel, 233n6

Levi-Tanai, Sara, 252n67

Levy-Coffman, Ellen, 152

Lewin, Kurt, 28

liberal Jews, 87, 106; insecurity of, 52; relations with Orthodox Jews, 39, 43, 46–47

liberal Judaism: defense against Orthodox Jews, 61; rejection by Orthodox Jews, 6, 47, 49, 56, 60

Lichtenstein, Aharon, 242n65

Liebman, Charles, 60, 94
Lindholm, Charles, 2, 12
Linnekin, Jocelyn, 14, 34
London, Frank, 134
lost Jews: and Christian missionaries, 162, 164–166, 205, 208, 216; and European colonialists, 111, 162–163, 206; and Jewish assimilation, 217, 219; and multiculturalism, 215, 217
lost tribes of Israel, 7, 205–206, 208, 217–218, 223; in Africa, 161–162, 164, 166–167, 173, 179; and African Americans, 174; and Christian missionaries, 162, 205, 215; and Jewish soul, 207; as myth, 204; recognition of, 203–205, 219; south Asia, 216
Luckmann, Thomas, 4
Luz, Ehud, 249n16
Lyshaug, Brenda, 38

Maimonides, 87, 114
Margolis, Joseph, 37
Markell, Patchen, 39–40
Markowitz, Fran, 239n53
Marks, Jonathan, 153
Maroney, Eric, 172
Martha, Susan, 281
Martikainen, Tuomas, 233n4
Marty, Martin, 52
Maslin, Simeon, 61–62
Maslow, Abraham, 70
meditation, 74–77; in Judaism, 72–74, 79
Meir, Golda, 106
Memmi, Albert: on authentic Jews, 30; on Jewish culture, 31–32; on Jewish inauthenticity, 31–32; on Sartre, 30–32
Mendes-Flohr, Paul, 20
Merwin, Ted, 253n8
messiah: Jesus as, 89, 91–93, 96; Jewish concept of, 93, 98; Lubavitcher Rebbe as, 100–101; Maimonides on, 87; Shabbatai Zevi as, 98–99
Messianic Jews: development as new movement, 89, 95–96; in Israel, 91–92; Jewish rejection of, 88–89, 93–96; and the original followers of Jesus, 89, 91; postmissionary, 95–97; in the United States, 92–93, 95
Michaelson, Jay, 24, 52
midrash, 20, 97, 184
Milgram, Goldie, 75
Miller, Michael T., 261n2
missionaries: and the Beta Israel in Ethiopia, 164; and lost Jews, 163, 215
Mizrahi Jews, 7; Arabness of, 113–114, 118–119; as embodiment of authenticity, 112. *See also* Sephardi Jews
Molina, Alfred, 125
Morag, Shelomo, 251n55

Moses: African roots, 65, 176, 179, 222; greatest prophet, 87; and Israelite priesthood, 151, 155; and Jewish idea of the messiah, 98; and Kabbalah, 83–84; and meditation, 73
Moss, Aron, 141, 247
Mosse, George L., 249n1
Mostel, Zero, 125
multiculturalism, 6, 27, 37–38; and Jews, 8, 215, 217, 221, 224
Muršič, Rajko, 235n36, 236n1, 285
music, 134; of the Abayudaya, 220; and Israeli folk dance, 120, 122; and Jewish authenticity, 132, 134–135. *See also* klezmer music
Myers, Jody, 247n46, 247n53

national identity: Israeli, 121–122; Jewish, 105, 107, 111, 115, 121; Palestinian, 111; Sartre's criticism of, 111
nationalism, 106, 107, 115; and Zionism, 7, 105, 122
Nazarenes, 90
Netanyahu, Benjamin, 61
Netanyahu, Benzion, 195–196
Neulander, Judith, 197, 200
Neusner, Jacob, 59
New Age Judaism, 72, 84, 122
Newman, Marissa, 264n1
Niculescu, Mira, 245n3
Nissim, Itzhak, 212
Noy, Chaim, 252n77

Odenheimer, Eleanor F., 246n35
Ohana, David, 249n14
Olsvanger, Immanuel, 210
orientalism: and Sephardi Jews, 180; in Zionism, 113
origin myths, 25; based on lost tribes of Israel, 204–205, 223; for Israelite priesthood, 155; for the Jewish people, 141, 155, 222; for Kabbalah, 84
origin narratives, 19, 204–205
origin stories: and authenticity, 11, 18, 173, 214; of the Bene Israel, 208–211, 213–214; of Black Jews, 168, 174, 176, 180–181; and *Fiddler on the Roof*, 126; of Israeli folk dance, 118
Orthodox Jews: and Kabbalah, 82, 84; modern, 54–56, 246; ultra-Orthodox, 54–56, 137, 230
Orthodox Judaism, 6, 15; authenticity of, 43–44, 49–50, 61–62, 69; and essentialism, 48; inauthenticity of, 57; "invention" of, 53; and other forms of Judaism, 46, 49, 51; rightward shift, 54–56; ways of interpreting the past, 52
Ostrer, Harry, 150

Palestinians: conflict with Jews, 111–112; and Jewish genetics, 152; and lost Jews, 208
Parekh, Bhikhu, 239n69

Parfitt, Tudor, 154, 181, 204
Patai, Raphael, 124
Perec, Georges, 238n52
Perrin, Marius, 237n6
personal authenticity, 2–3; emphasized by liberal Jews, 45, 47; and klezmer music, 135; and New Age Judaism, 72; and religion quest, 69
Pharisees, 15, 61, 90
Plaskow, Judith, 70
positive Jewishness, 28–29, 34, 65
Potter, Andrew, 4
Power, Patricia A., 95
Prewitt, Tanya, 246n35
Primack, Karen, 218

rabbinic Judaism, 46; and authentic Judaism, 70; and Beta Israel, 165, 167, 170; and Black Jews, 181; criticism by Reform Judaism's leaders, 61; critiqued by Mordechai Kaplan, 67; diversity of interpretations, 49, 55–56; and followers of Jesus, 90; ignored by Zionist nationalism, 110; and Jewish articles of faith, 87; and Jewish diversity, 224; and multiple Judaisms, 183; and newly found Jews, 223; and Shabbatai Zevi, 100; tension with Kabbalah, 83. *See also* halakha; Pharisees
Rabinow, Joel, 132
Radbaz, 162, 164, 167
Rapoport, Louis, 260n19
Rav Avraham Kook, 52, 122
Raz-Krakotzkin, Ammon, 113
"real Jews," 34, 52, 217; Beta Israel as, 167; Black Jews as, 178; converts as, 140; Eastern European Jews as, 125
Reason, Gabriela, 248n16
recognition: of the Abayudaya, 219–220; from antisemites, 23, 27, 37, 231; and authenticity, 6, 22, 26, 37, 215; based on genealogy, 182; and "being-for-others," 26; of Bene Israel, 209, 212–213; of Beta Israel, 165–171, 174; of Black Jews, 165, 174, 178, 184; of B'nei Menashe, 216–217; and boundaries of Jewishness, 27, 95, 137; of change and innovation, 26, 229; without conversion, 144–147; of converts, 140, 145; among different kinds of Jews, 30, 39–40, 101; and identity, 38; and intermarriage, 137, 143–144, 148; of Jewish authenticity, 6, 137, 173, 198, 230; and Jewish difference, 32–33; of Jewish women's experiences, 70; of Messianic Jews, 94–95; and multiculturalism, 6, 8, 37–38, 49, 221, 223–224; mutual, 37–38, 40, 56, 208, 231; of newly found Jews, 203–207, 219, 222, 224, 230; of non-Orthodox Jews, 6, 39, 47–50, 56; of non-white Jews, 222; normative, 8, 217; as open-ended process, 38–40, 224; and

political rights, 28, 30; positive, 30, 38; types of, 39, 49, 223, 229–230
Reconstructionism, 67, 94
Reform Judaism, 58–59, 62, 94; Orthodox critique of, 44, 60, 94
Reisinger, Yvette, 234n2
religion, 6, 63; authoritarian, 64–65; humanistic, 65, 67–68, 75; immature, 63, 68; mature, 63, 68; as quest, 6, 69. *See also* spirituality
religious experience, 70, 75
religious orientation, 63–64; extrinsic, 63, 69; intrinsic, 63–64; quest, 69
Reuben, Steven Carr, 145
Rich, Adrienne, 228
Rogers, J. A., 262n24
Rogovoy, Seth, 132–133
Roland, Joan G., 267n11
Roof, Wade Clark, 233n14
Rosen, Chaim, 260n20
Rosen, Jonathan, 130
Roth, Jeff, 76
Roth, Philip, 88
Rothenberg, Celia, 246n30
Rousseau, Jean Jacques, 12–13
Ruah-Midbar, Marianna, 252n80

Sabbatean movement, 86, 99–100
Sabra, 7, 110, 117
Sacks, Jonathan: on existential authenticity, 47; on Jewish authenticity, 46–47, 50–51, 65; on Jewish identity, 147; on Jewish tradition, 46; on non-Orthodox Judaism, 47–48; on Torah, 66
Sadducees, 61, 90
Sahagun, Louis, 246n24
Said, Edward, 111
Salamon, Hagar, 171
Samet, Moshe, 241n43
Sapoznik, Hank, 130
Sartre, Jean-Paul: on antisemitism, 6, 22–23, 27, 43, 111; on authenticity, 18–19, 24; on "being-for-others," 146; on construction of the self, 25; critique of essentialist authenticity, 22, 111, 225; on diaspora, 227; on identity, 35; and inauthentic Jews, 23–24, 106; on Jewish authenticity, 5, 13; and multiculturalism, 6, 22, 112, 236n6; and recognition, 30, 37
Satlow, Michael, 27
Schacter-Shalomi, Zalman, 81
Schneerson, Menachem, 100–101
Schoenberg, Eliot Sala, 256n20
Scholem, Gershom, 85, 99
Schonfeld, Julie, 256n22
Schwartz, Hillel, 238n40
Schwarz, Tanya, 171
Schweitzer, Ruth, 254n39
Seeman, Don, 260n13

self: and authenticity, 17, 47, 69; essentialist views of, 14; existentialist approach to, 25; lack of fixed essence, 227; modern view of, 12, 224; and origin stories, 192; premodern view of, 46; and recognition, 26
self-realization: and authenticity, 12, 60, 67; and consumerism, 3; and God, 68; Israeli quest for, 122; religious quest for, 6; and yoga, 79
Semi, Emanuela Trevisan, 266n5
Semino, Ornella, 258n11
Sephardi Jews, 116; and expulsion from Iberian peninsula, 188; in France, 29, 36; and Hebrew, 116–117; in Israel, 114, 116; and Zionism, 113. *See also* crypto-Jews
Shabbatai Zevi, 93, 98–99
Shapiro, Rami, 79
Sharansky, Natan, 189
Shavei Israel, 219, 221; and recognition of "lost Jews," 207–208, 216–217, 223; and religious Zionism, 206–207
Shenhav, Yehouda, 250n26
Shiloah, Amnon, 253n18
Shmueli, Efraim, 15, 56
Shohat, Ella, 114
Sholem Aleichem, 125–126
Shoshana, Brenda, 76
Silber, Michael, 241n43
Silberman, Neil, 204
Simon, Paul, 220
Skorecki, Karl, 151
Slobin, Mark, 130, 134
Smith, Anthony D., 14
Sokol, Moshe, 242n56
Sokoloff, Naomi B., 258n9
Sokolow, Peter, 254n28
Solomon, Alysa, 124, 126–127
Soloveitchik, Haym, 55
Soltes, Ori, 264n6
Södergren, Jonatan, 233n7
Sparks, Kenton L., 264n52
Spence, Rebecca, 246n25
Spiegel, Shalom, 115–116, 251
spirituality: and authenticity, 4, 60, 64, 67, 69; and Buddhism, 77; and Kabbalah, 82, 84; and Reform Judaism, 61; and religious quest, 69; and yoga, 78, 80
Staub, Jacob, 57
Stein, Eric, 131
Steiner, 234n2
Stern, Henry Aaron, 164
Strom, Yale, 254n21
Sturman, Rivka, 118
Suleiman, Susan, 236n4
Summit, Jeffrey, 268n39
Sunny, Jay, 233n13
Susser, Bernard, 243n8

Sutton, Wesley, 152
Svigals, Alicia, 134

Taylor, Charles: on authenticity, 12, 26; on recognition, 6, 37–38, 223
Taylor, Rich, 233n13
Tenenbaum, Shelly, 256n7
Theodossopoulos, Dimitrios, 235n40
Thomas, Mark, 258n23
Tinker, H., 267n12
Tobin, Gary A., 140, 221–222
Toft, Mark, 233n13
Topol, Haim, 125
Torah: and Jewish feminism, 97; and the Lubavitcher Rebbe, 101; and Maimonides, 87; and Messianic Judaism, 96–97; and Orthodox Judaism, 49, 66; and Reconstructionist Judaism, 67; and Shabbatai Zevi, 99; and ultra-Orthodox Judaism, 55, 138; and yoga, 79–80
Train, Kelly A., 267n29
Trilling, Lionel, 234n5
Turner, Terence, 239n67

Umbach, Maiken, 234n18
Union for Reform Judaism, 94–95
Union of Messianic Jewish Congregations, 95
Upton, Dell, 136

Vannini, Phillip, 269n2
Verman, Mark, 245n16

Wang, Nin, 233n2
Ward, Seth, 200
Webber, Jonathan, 234
Weinberg, David H., 254n33
Wentworth Matthew, 175, 181, 184
Werczberger, Rachel, 122
Wertheimer, Jack, 60
Wexler, Laura, 268n44
white Jews: authenticity of, 172, 180, 182; and Black Jews in the United States, 175–180, 183–184; and Ethiopian Jews, 165, 168, 172
Wing, Jennifer Patai, 259n27
Wohlberg, Jeffrey A., 256n22
Wolitz, Seth, 238
Wuthnow, Robert, 68

Yiddish: and American Jews, 126, 130; vs. Hebrew, 113, 115, 129; and klezmer music, 130
yoga: and existential authenticity, 19, 79; Jewish roots of, 73–74; and Jewish spirituality, 6, 60, 72, 77–80, 84; and Jewish women, 78; and Kabbalah, 80
Yosef, Ovadia, 167

Zavidowsky, Zvi, 75
Zborowski, Mark, 124
Zeller, Jack, 217
Zemach, Benjamin, 251n58
Zionism: and Arab Jews, 113–114; on Arabs in Israel, 113; and authenticity, 105–106, 112; and expressive authenticity, 12; and Hebrew, 115, 129–130; and Israeliness, 121; on its narrative of Jewish history, 110–111, 113; on Jewish life in diaspora, 17, 106, 117, 125; and lost Jews, 167; and the "New Jew," 111; and Palestinians, 111; and rabbinic Judaism, 110; and recent fractures in Israeli culture, 121; on traditional Judaism, 106
Zoossmann-Diskin, Avshalom, 258n11
Zucker, David J., 264n56

About the Author

STUART Z. CHARMÉ is a professor of religion at Rutgers University at Camden. He is the author of two books on Sartrean existentialism, *Meaning and Myth in the Study of Lives* (University of Pennsylvania Press, 1983) and *Vulgarity and Authenticity: A Sartrean Approach* (University of Massachusetts Press, 1991), as well as numerous articles on questions of Jewish identity and authenticity.